REGIONAL MINISTERS

Power and Influence in the Canadian Cabinet

A number of political scientists have in recent years argued that the era of strong regional ministers in Canadian government is passed. Herman Bakvis challenges this assumption in light of developments and experiences in cabinet and its supporting agencies over the past decade.

Bakvis argues that while in general the position of regional minister has been diminished, it has not disappeared. During the last Trudeau cabinet, 1980–4, the role actually revived and to a degree became institutionalized. After 1984 the Conservative government under Brian Mulroney felt impelled to implement its own version of the regional minister system, despite the prime minister's initial strong inclination not to do so.

Several federal undertakings reflect the role of regional ministers in recent years: programs in the fields of regional development, employment creation, and energy mega-projects. The activities of several recent cabinet ministers, both Liberal and Conservative, further illustrate Bakvis's thesis. The ministers include Lucien Bouchard, John Crosbie, Marc Lalonde, Romeo LeBlanc, Allan MacEachen, Donald Mazankowski, and especially one 'regional minister in a hurry,' Lloyd Axworthy, whose career suggests that mobilization of one's own portfolio is key to regional success.

Numerous other factors come into play: the role of the electoral system in contributing to the parochial behaviour of certain ministers and in making all ministers highly sensitive to local influences; the capacity of provincial governments to influence federal policy through regional ministers; and the long-term implications for intra-state federalism.

HERMAN BAKVIS is Professor of Political Science and Public Administration at Dalhousie University. He is co-editor, with William M. Chandler, of *Federalism and the Role of the State*.

REGIONAL MINISTERS
Power and Influence in the Canadian Cabinet

HERMAN BAKVIS

UNIVERSITY OF TORONTO PRESS

Toronto Buffalo London

© University of Toronto Press 1991
Toronto Buffalo London
Printed in Canada

ISBN 0-8020-2622-2 (cloth)
ISBN 0-8020-6698-4 (paper)

∞

Printed on acid-free paper

Canadian Cataloguing in Publication Data

Bakvis, Herman, 1948–
Regional ministers

Includes bibliographical references and index.
ISBN 0-8020-2622-2 (bound)
ISBN 0-8020-6698-4 (pbk.)

1. Cabinet ministers – Canada – History.*
2. Cabinet system – Canada – History.
3. Regionalism – Canada – History.
4. Representative government and representation – Canada – History.
5. Canada – Politics and government.
I. Title.

JL97.B34 1991   354.7104   C91-093223-9

For David and Julia

I have to ask the honorable gentlemen opposite how they are going to organize their Cabinet, for these provinces, according to this so called Federal scheme? I think I may defy them [the government] to shew that the Cabinet can be formed on any other principle than that of a representation of the several provinces in that Cabinet ... The Cabinet here must discharge all that kind of function, which in the United States is performed, in the Federal sense, by the Senate.

Christopher Dunkin
Confederation Debates,
Quebec City, 1865

Contents

Tables and Figures

Tables

Figure

Preface

This study has its origins in a number of sources and events. One incident, however, more than others, served to focus my thoughts on the overall significance of regional ministers for Canadian cabinet government. It happened during the course of an interview one cold February morning in 1984 with a senior federal government official, the 'federal economic development co-ordinator' for one of the western provinces. The subject for discussion was regional economic development policy. The official began by asking, 'I suppose you want to know all about my regional minister?' I was slightly taken aback, for I had long been schooled in a literature which argues that the regional minister phenomenon was a fixture of the distant past. Nonetheless, I quickly allowed that, yes, I would be interested in hearing more about the regional minister. What followed was a detailed account of how the minister, with the assistance of the co-ordinator, played an all-important role not only in the area of regional development expenditures but in other areas as well. Later, accounts from other officials in other provinces and in Ottawa made clear that this minister was not alone or unusual in pressing local and regional concerns within cabinet and within the executive-administrative branch generally.

By the summer of 1984 I had decided that regional ministers very likely represented an unheralded aspect of Canadian politics, worthy of close examination. In pursuing this project over the next six years I have incurred a great many obligations. Let me try and spell out some of them.

Much of the book is based on interviews with government officials, politicians, and assistants to politicians at the federal, provincial, and municipal level. I am grateful to them for giving me much of their valuable time – in some instances several hours spread over a number of separate interviews – their insights into the Canadian political process, and access to numerous documents and studies. Without their help this book would not have been possible.

The study began in earnest in 1985–6. The political science department at the University of Toronto kindly agreed to accept me as a sabbatical visitor for that year. I am grateful to Marsha Chandler, J. Stefan Dupré, A.W. (Al) Johnson, Carolyn Tuohy, Peter Russell, Robert Vipond, and others in the department for helping to sharpen some of my intellectual thinking on the topic and setting the study off in the right direction.

Several individuals at institutions elsewhere were helpful in offering timely advice, important suggestions for avenues of inquiry, or critical pieces of information to resolve long-standing puzzles. In this respect I would like to single out Peter Bakvis of the Confederation of National Trade Unions in Montreal, Ken Carty at the University of British Columbia, Richard Lochead at the National Archives, Paul Thomas at the University of Manitoba, and Steven Wolinetz at Memorial University for help beyond what can normally be expected, even from friends and relatives. People less directly involved in the project but to whom I owe debts for moral support and intellectual stimulation over the years (though I suspect some will disagree with the arguments presented here that their writings and discussions stimulated) include: Ed Black, Donald Blake, Alan Cairns, William Chandler, John Courtney, David Elkins, William Irvine, Neil Nevitte, Joan Pond, Mildred Schwartz, Richard Simeon, Grace Skogstad, the late Donald Smiley, David Smith, Richard Stubbs, Ronald Watts, and Robert Young.

My colleagues at Dalhousie University were of assistance, primarily by allowing me to pester them with questions on a variety of topics in their fields of expertise. I would in particular like to thank J. Murray Beck, Paul Brown, David M. Cameron, James Eayrs, Andrew Heard, Dale Poel, Paul Pross, Tim Shaw, Jennifer Smith, and Peter Waite for their careful and gracious responses to my often imperious queries. To Robert Boardman and Gil Winham, chairpersons of the political science department at Dalhousie, I am indebted for their support of the project, which manifested itself in part by their not unduly burdening me with administrative duties. Christine Nielsen, at the time director of research services at Dalhousie, supplied not only valuable assistance when it came to submitting research grant applications but also detailed comments on the completed manuscript four years later. In the realm of research support services there is little more one could reasonably ask for. Beryl Davis, Jill Dudar, and Anne Emery worked as research assistants. I thank them for their good judgment and initiative as well as their labours.

Financial support from a number of sources helped fund research assistance, travel to conduct interviews, and, most important of all, time to write. A sabbatical leave fellowship for the year 1985–6 and research grants for the period 1987–9 from the Social Science and Humanities Research Council of Canada supported the research phase. A Senior Killam Research Fellowship from Dalhousie University for the year 1988–9 provided a welcome opportunity to compose a complete draft of the book. The book itself has been published with the help of a grant from the Social Science Federation of Canada, using funds provided by the Social Sciences and Humanities Research Council of Canada.

Some of the themes and findings in this book were first presented in two articles: 'Regional Ministers, National Policies and the Administrative State in Canada' was published in the *Canadian Journal of Political Science* 21 (September 1988); and 'Regional Politics and Policy in the Mulroney Cabinet, 1984–88' appeared in *Canadian Public Policy* 15 (June 1989). I am also obliged to the Office of the Auditor General of Canada for permission to reproduce the diagram that appears as Figure 1.

For his encouragement of the enterprise well before it showed signs of completion and, later, his expert help in expediting the manuscript through the process of editorial approval and revision, I am most grateful to Virgil Duff of the University of Toronto Press. The manuscript benefited from helpful comments made by readers for the Press and the Social Science Federation. Diane Mew exercised her considerable skills as copy editor to bring order and polish to my unruly prose and to entrap more than a few inconsistencies in style and facts. Not least, she gently convinced me of the wisdom of decreasing the length and increasing the number of chapters. The book is the better for her excellent work.

My colleague at Dalhousie, Peter Aucoin, contributed in many ways. Initially, he persuaded me to become involved in a study we conducted in 1983–4 for the Royal Commission on the Economic Union and Development Prospects for Canada on regional development and government organization. It was during the course of this study that my interest in the regional minister phenomenon was first kindled. Subsequent work with Peter in related areas allowed me to gather further information directly on the topic of regional ministers. He helped in selecting an appropriate focus for the book. Later he provided detailed comments on the entire first draft and did the same on several of the revised chapters. Among friends and colleagues, he more so than any other has helped shape the substance and contours of this book. I am deeply appreciative of the help and advice he has given me.

Finally, I wish to thank all my family for their support and forbearance, particularly during those times when completion of the project seemed a rather distant prospect. They include my wife and son, my mother, Wilhelmina Nieboer, and my in-laws, Harry and Sheila Eastman.

Notwithstanding all of the above, I acknowledge my full responsibility for all errors of fact and interpretation.

Regional Ministers

CHAPTER 1

Introduction

In the literature on Canadian political parties and cabinet government it is commonplace to view regional ministers as a phenomenon of the past. Alan Cairns writes: 'Early Cabinets were collections of regional notables with independent bases of their own who powerfully asserted the needs of their provinces at the highest political level in the land ... Now, however, regional spokesmen of such power and authenticity are only memories. Although the regional basis of Cabinet appointment continues, the regional power brokers are gone.'[1] Donald Smiley, writing in 1980, argued that the federal cabinet minister's role in 'aggregating and articulating the interests specific to their provinces and regions ... has been vastly diminished.'[2] In chronicling the increasing importance of the 'special-interest state,' Paul Pross writes: 'It seems clear that cabinet "prima donnas" are defunct. Perhaps occasionally a Romeo LeBlanc can run his department in the old style, but in general the Jimmy Gardiners and the C.D. Howes are out of place in today's cabinets.'[3] J.R. Mallory, echoing sentiments appearing frequently in the press, states: 'What remains of it [the regional ministers system] is chiefly demonstrated in the heavily partisan distribution of benefits, grants, contracts, and the like.'[4]

These statements concerning the present-day role of regional ministers, and the factors that have shaped it, are accepted as valid by most Canadian political scientists. In turn these presumptions have played an important role in forming the views of many decision-makers and the public at large, especially outside of Ontario and Quebec. The present quest for Senate reform, for example, arising in part out of the Meech Lake imbroglio, has nonetheless occurred in a climate which academics have helped to create.[5] Common knowledge has it that central government institutions have failed to represent adequately regional interests and aspirations.

The aim of this book is to assess these assumptions about the present-day cabinet. Certainly, compared to the days of the 1930s and 1940s when figures such as long-time minister of agriculture J.G. Gardiner loomed large, regional ministers likely have become less important.[6] Yet the received wisdom that regional ministers are no longer influential may fail to capture important nuances and variations or, for that matter, changes since Smiley and others reached their conclusions in the early 1980s. Smiley himself in 1985, with his co-author Ronald Watts, began questioning the importance of barriers ostensibly limiting regional influence in cabinet, noting that certain ministers in the Trudeau government 'were able to advance the interests of their respective regions and provinces demonstrat[ing] that those obstacles were not completely insuperable.'[7]

What are the reasons given for the alleged decline of regional ministers? There are several. Both Richard Simeon and Smiley have argued that the advent of executive federalism and federal-provincial diplomacy has meant a change in the locus of decision-making and the representation of regional interests.[8] Since the early 1960s the truly important decisions have, more often than not, been the product of federal-provincial bargaining. The dramatic increase in the relative importance of policy areas under provincial jurisdiction, such as natural resources and health and welfare, and the intertwining of federal and provincial responsibilities in most fields, means that provincial governments are invariably involved in national decisions of any significance. Further, as Roger Gibbins contends, provincial governments have come to see themselves, and to be seen by many, as *the* legitimate articulators of regional interests.[9]

It has been suggested as well by Frederick Fletcher that changes in the election campaigns conducted by the national parties, changes in good part induced by the 'imperatives of television,' have served to focus attention almost exclusively on the party leaders. 'The long-established pattern of cabinet government ...,' Fletcher writes, 'in which strong regional ministers represented their locales in Ottawa and campaigned with the party leader in their regions, has been replaced by an increasingly presidential style of campaigning – and of governing.'[10] In this vein, and following Mallory, the role of regional ministers has come to be seen as restricted to the less public one of dispensing patronage, that somewhat unsavoury but still necessary function in modern party politics to help maintain local party machinery.

Finally, changes in the organization and management of cabinet decision-making have been cited as factors. According to J.S. Dupré, the 'departmentalized' cabinet has been displaced by the 'institutionalized' cabinet with its emphasis on shared knowledge and collegial decision-making and dependence on advice from central agencies, such as the Privy Council Office, rather than line departments.[11] Beginning in the late 1960s, individual ministers, and their departments, found themselves with reduced autonomy. Simply put, it is argued that federal ministers no longer have either the time or the opportunity to act as brokers of regional interests within the confines of cabinet or to act as interlocutors between federal and provincial governments.

As with all worthwhile theories, these explanations of alleged regional ministerial decline deserve scrutiny. This study thus seeks to understand both those features of the regional minister system that have been neglected and the dynamics of the changes that have occurred. In doing so, the following themes are stressed: that while the position of regional minister has been diminished, it has not disappeared; that indeed during the last Trudeau cabinet, from 1980 to 1984, the role actually revived and to a degree became institutionalized; and that after 1984 the Conservative government under Brian Mulroney also felt impelled to implement its version of the regional minister system, despite the initial strong inclination of the prime minister not to do so. This study will also demonstrate that, for most ministers, the administrative state has displaced the traditional political party as the basis of regional influence. The re-emergence of the regional minister phenomenon can be attributed in good measure to the discovery by politicians of how to circumvent the awkward government machinery created during the Trudeau era and how to use to advantage the resources within their own departmental portfolios. Finally, it will be argued that the regional minister system still represents a significant means through which provincial governments can make their influence felt within the federal cabinet. By establishing links with the senior minister in their province, these governments have been able to sway discussion of, and decisions on, a wide range of federal issues of importance to them.

The book will examine, first, the origins and development of regional representation in the Canadian cabinet up to the middle Trudeau period. A reinterpretation of the past is presented to suggest that the halcyon days of strong regional figures were not always what they appeared to be; that there was in fact considerable unevenness within and across cabinets in the strength of such representation.

Chapters six through eleven will then focus on a number of case studies highlighting the involvement of regional ministers in programs implemented by the last Trudeau government and by the post-1984 government under Mulroney. The first three cases involve structural change, or, more precisely, a series of structural changes and innovations in cabinet organization and the machinery of government in the early 1980s that enhanced or offered advantage to ministers acting in their regional capacity. These organizational changes were associated with, though certainly not restricted to, three national programs: 1) economic and regional development delivered through the so-called Economic and Regional Development Agreements, signed with the provinces; 2) the Special Employment Initiative, a $300 million employment creation program implemented in 1982 and delivered through a special secretariat within the Department of Employment and Immigration; and 3) the Special Recovery Capital Projects, a $2.4 billion program intended to stimulate economic activity during the height of the recession by advancing approval of major capital projects already in the planning stage. A further case study focuses on a single individual in the Trudeau cabinet, the Honourable Lloyd Axworthy, minister of employment and immigration (1980–3) and minister of transport (1983–4), who might best be described as a 'regional minister in a hurry.' Member of Parliament for Winnipeg–Fort Garry and the only elected cabinet minister west of Ontario, Axworthy exploited and tested to the limit the structural innovations noted above and used his portfolios to construct a political machine based primarily in Winnipeg but extending in influence to the rest of the province and to other areas in western Canada. It was a machine that relied primarily on the resources of his portfolios rather than on those of the Liberal party, either federally or provincially.

It can be argued that the circumstances of the 1980–4 period were unusual and thereby constituted an extreme case. There was a major recession, it was Trudeau's last term as prime minister, and there were only two Liberals elected from western Canada, leading to the most pronounced regional imbalance in the government caucus ever. Yet it is often the extreme or deviant cases that are most useful in bringing to light factors that might otherwise remain hidden. Lloyd Axworthy may not necessarily have been the most effective regional minister, but his forceful, brusque personality, combined with his wish to do things quickly, made his activities much more transparent and hence more amenable to study. Furthermore, the techniques and practices introduced by ministers such as Axworthy have altered for ever the relations between the politicians and the administrative state. Subsequent ministers, for good or ill, are unwilling to discard these lessons of what can be achieved by the adroit use of one's portfolio.

In part as a test of this thesis – that the enhanced stature of regional ministers under Trudeau survived that era – chapters ten and eleven will examine the effect of those changes on the subsequent Conservative government. These chapters will note how the Conservatives' initial disavowal of the regional minister system was soon altered by a series of events, one of the more notable being the controversy over the awarding of the CF-18 maintenance contract, which impressed upon the government the significance of the regional dimension. Within three years the Conservatives had in place their own version of the regional minister system, including two special ministerial committees mandated to supervise regional development programs in specific regions, and three separate geographically based agencies to deliver these programs. The means used to bring the regional dimension to the cabinet table, and the role that regional ministers have played, differed under the Liberals and the Conservatives, as did the problems associated with the disbursement of public funds for partisan purposes. Yet the constants that remain – the felt need by ministers to become directly involved in local and regional issues in their province and the recognition by the prime minister of the need to develop institutional support for managing regional tensions within cabinet – can be demonstrated by developments during the Mulroney period. Furthermore, this period, punctuated by some of the more critical events in Canadian political history relating to the failure to ratify the Meech Lake Accord, also highlighted the perennial problem bedevilling the Conservative party: finding a suitable representative from Quebec to act as the prime minister's 'Quebec lieutenant' in cabinet.

The Role of Regional Ministers

In examining the activities of regional ministers we will need to discuss the environment in which they operate and the figures – federal, provincial, and municipal – with whom they interact. Before turning to a historical overview of the Canadian cabinet, and then to the case studies, let us review the basic framework and assumptions used in the book.[12]

In contemporary parlance the term regional minister refers to those individuals designated as the 'lead' or 'political' minister for a particular province by the prime minister.[13] Their status and power have evolved in a number of ways in recent years and the norms governing their position tend to be informal. Regional ministers have at varying times been responsible for many of the following functions: being accountable for the party organization in their province or subregion within a province; dispensing patronage; influencing expenditures affecting their region made by their own as well as by other departments; and injecting a regional dimension into the delivery of departmental programs. One particular figure, the Quebec lieutenant, is often given special recognition because of the unique problems and culture of the province he represents in cabinet. Under recent Liberal and Conservative governments, regional ministers have had control over the dispensation of federal patronage and are the dominant figures within the provincial caucuses, the formalized *in camera* meetings of government MPs from that province. Aside from pressing the concerns of regions on departments and within cabinet, regional ministers are also seen as responsible for the converse: communicating the decisions and views of the centre to the regions, explaining the less palatable outcomes of Ottawa's deliberations to provincial or local constituents, and helping ensure that local supporters remain within the fold.

The term region itself must necessarily remain ambiguous, if only because of the enormous variation in the size of the provinces.[14] A region within a province such as Ontario can be substantially larger than the entire province of Prince Edward Island. At the same time, in the past, region has often implied an expanse greater than a single province – the prairies or the maritimes, for example – and ministers such as J.G. Gardiner in the 1930s and 1940s were clearly in control of such broad areas. More frequently, however, and particularly in the present era, region for purposes of ministerial representation tends to be defined as a province or, in the case of Ontario and Quebec, subsections within a province.

As will become evident, the world of the regional minister is populated by a rich array of individuals. It includes other regional ministers, MPs, departmental deputies and other public servants, heads of crown corporations, elected provincial and municipal leaders, interest group leaders, individual constituents, and not least the prime minister. The prime minister is not only the single most powerful figure within cabinet and responsible for all ministerial appointments; he is also accountable for the basic design of the machinery of government in operation during his term in office. The relationships ministers have with all these individuals are not necessarily conflictual, though frequently there is a fair degree of tension associated with the interplay and bargaining among them. It should never be assumed that a regional minister has a natural ascendency over others. Under certain circumstances, however, individual regional ministers, in alliance with a provincial premier for example, can easily stymie the efforts of other ministers or senior civil servants.

What motivates regional ministers? It is frequently accepted that politicians seek to reap maximum advantage from the implementation and delivery of programs for which they are responsible, mainly with the view to being re-elected.[15] This advantage obtains primarily when benefits can be concentrated on a limited constituency and the costs in turn externalized to a much broader population. The present study does not contradict this position. Yet while virtually all ministers recognize the need to at least appear to respond favourably to requests from local or regional constituents, some are content to try and satisfy basic demands while others will want to do all they can. Some eschew the role; others cultivate it wholeheartedly. As well, variability in emotional commitment to the province or a particular locale of the province may determine the extent to which ministers feel the need to act as regional champion. Furthermore, not all regional ministers are created equal. Some are much more adept at using their portfolios, in targeting programs, or in engaging in battle around the cabinet table. Others, not for want of trying, may not be up to the task. The role of regional minister may also be at odds with the needs of his or her riding and not infrequently with those of other government MPs in the province. At times the regional minister may feel compelled to play the role of regional statesman rather than chief of the regional pork-barrel. It is probably wise, therefore, not to assume too much about the constants underpinning the behaviour of regional ministers.

The Institutional Context

The institutional context is important primarily for the manner in which it structures conflict and negotiation and either restricts or enhances the representation of any given interest. It embraces Parliament and the constitutional framework, including the federal-provincial distribution of powers and the interstices between formal institutions. It provides the background and frequently the specific settings for the settling of disputes or forging of alliances. Eric Nordlinger has argued persuasively that the sites and arenas in which negotiations are conducted, and hence the choice of such sites, can have an important bearing on the outcome of these negotiations.[16] Certainly in Canada Simeon has found that the nature of the sites used for the conduct of federal-provincial diplomacy has had an impact on decisions in a number of policy areas.[17]

For regional ministers the important sites are not federal-provincial conferences but cabinet and, especially, cabinet committees such as those for Priorities and Planning, and Economic and Regional Development during the later Trudeau period, and the Operations Committee in the Mulroney cabinet. Given the informal nature of regional ministerial influence, much of the interaction between ministers or with others takes place in the fissures between formal institutional settings, literally the hallways and byways found between cabinet committee meeting rooms and departmental offices. Attention should also be paid to the departments themselves, central agencies such as the Privy Council Office, and interdepartmental committees, populated mainly by civil servants but which can be penetrated by members of ministers' political staff.

The behaviour of ministers in dealing within cabinet committees and with other ministers is shaped in part by the rules governing the budgetary process. From 1979 until circa 1986 the federal government employed the Program Expenditure Management System (PEMS), more colloquially known as the envelope system, which joins together policy and expenditure decisions. Efforts to expand the size of departmental budgetary envelopes or to escape the discipline of the envelopes were a major preoccupation for many ministers in both their sectoral and regional capacities.[18] In the Mulroney cabinet the Expenditure Review Committee became a major arena in which ministers sought to protect their budgetary resources. Treasury Board, the longest-standing cabinet committee, is responsible for approving detailed expenditure plans initially outlined and approved in broad form in the Estimates, and ministers can expend considerable effort to test the limits of their expenditure authorizations and to circumvent Treasury Board rules and guidelines.[19]

The political party and its different components, especially the parliamentary wing of the party, generally referred to as the government caucus and in turn divided into regional or provincial caucuses, also constitute important arenas.[20] The need to run in elections can also play a pivotal role by forcing ministers to pay close heed to their ridings. In his classic article on electoral competition in Canada, J.A.A. Lovink notes that the turnover of MPs in individual ridings is much higher, and the number of safe seats far fewer, than in other countries.[21] According to C.E.S. Franks, this high turnover results in a high proportion of politically inexperienced MPs and, as a consequence, both a weakening of Parliament and the limiting of the pool of experienced candidates for cabinet positions.[22] Equally important, most ministers are aware of their vulnerability and will often use their portfolios to ensure an above-average number of projects for their riding, quite possibly at the expense of other parts of their province. As will become evident, this aspect of the electoral system has a definite effect on the manner in which ministers acquit themselves in their regional role.

It has generally been contended that Canada's particular form of 'interstate' federalism affords relatively little opportunity for the representation of regional or provincial government interests in central institutions. Further, the interstate model, based on the premise of a national government serving national constituencies and ten provincial governments responsible for provincial and local matters, reinforces the notion that the main concern of the federal government is, or should be, those programs and policies that are national in scope.[23] In both formal and informal senses this limits the opportunities for federal politicians to interact with local or provincial constituencies, particularly in regard to those areas under provincial jurisdiction. When there is interaction, it frequently takes place in conjunction with, or with the approval of, the provincial government. When the stakes involved in a particular issue are seen to be very high – such as in the area of energy or the constitution – it becomes a matter of high politics to be handled by the prime minister directly or one or two senior ministers, leaving little room for specific ministers from the affected provinces to interject their views.[24] The arenas in which individual ministers may become involved, and thus be more influential, are meetings of federal and provincial ministers in specific areas, where programs are more easily divisible, such as transport and economic development. Meetings between the federal minister and his or her counterpart from a specific province usually take place on a bilateral basis, where there is more room for negotiation and opportunity for ministers to act on their own preferences.[25] As well, most federal line departments are responsible for a number of federal-provincial agreements.[26] Beyond these agreements, a number of federal programs, though national in scope, are nonetheless frequently tailored to fit regional or local conditions.[27] Thus there are still numerous opportunities for regional ministers to exercise a regional prerogative.

Strategies and Tactics

The strategies and tactics deployed by ministers can be as varied as the goals and personalities of the ministers themselves and the resources available. It is generally thought, however, that ministers seeking to achieve certain policy objectives, whether sectoral or regional, need the co-operation of their senior officials. Andrew Johnson notes that a relationship of mutual dependence between cabinet ministers and senior public servants tends to prevail during the process of policy innovation or reform.[28] Ministers promote and legitimize the new policy in cabinet and before the public, while the senior officials overcome obstacles within the department, draft the actual legislation, and subsequently implement it. Johnson also notes that a minister may well need to play a role in the selection or disengagement of senior officials, promoting those officials favourable to the new scheme and shifting those opposed to other units or departments. As will be shown later, especially in chapter eight, ministers may need to go even further. They may choose to act in the face of almost universal opposition from senior officials in their department. They may undercut or bypass lines of communication to lower levels of the department or centralize decision-making within their own office. Especially in the case of regional objectives, it may become difficult to find support among public servants; indeed, the pursuit of such objectives is often likely to be actively resisted by the bureaucracy. Thus less formal and often more political means may have to be used in achieving those goals that favour the minister's region.

A basic rule of thumb remains, however, that one's own portfolio is the key element in attaining regional ambitions, even when desired projects are in the purview of other ministers' portfolios. The traditional techniques of log-rolling and horse-trading, otherwise described as mutual back-scratching, have been and will continue to be very important; and in order to engage in these practices one needs to have discretion over a range of program items attractive to cabinet colleagues. In short, the desire of most ministers is to be in control of their department and not just to fulfil regional goals. In practice, however, the notion of control is problematic, if not misleading. It implies a degree of mastery over an array of portfolio responsibilities that almost no contemporary minister can hope to achieve. 'Ministerial influence' is a more appropriate term, denoting the ability to influence the overall direction of the department and, at various times, the instigation or outcome of a limited selection of programs or activities.

In seeking to influence the direction or shape of programs or the behaviour of civil servants, both within and outside the department, the tactics used by ministers and their political staff are akin to those used by any well-organized political entity. Ministers will collect detailed information on agencies and programs, make approaches to line managers responsible for specific programs, and mobilize outside constituencies.

Resources

The minister's department constitutes the single most important resource. Typically a department includes responsibility not only for a number of line functions but also for various regulatory agencies and crown corporations. Programs administered by a department can number in the hundreds, specific projects in the thousands, and expenditures in the millions of dollars. These assets can only be mobilized, and then only in limited ways, when more specific resources are available. Perhaps the most valuable commodity is staff, primarily the political or 'exempt' staff over which the minister has considerable control. Staff may also include, however, sympathetic public servants who can be persuaded to work directly in the minister's office. In the United States, senators and congressmen have come to depend on huge staffs for help in dealing with the executive branch and its agencies, 'skilled professionals who can play the bureaucracy like an organ – pushing the right pedals to produce the desired effects.'[29] In Canada such staffs are smaller and regarded as less competent.[30] As the case studies in this book will demonstrate, however, the recruitment and use of staffs can be crucial to a minister's success.

The second critical resource lies within the minister himself or herself. A faculty for persuading colleagues in a collegial setting and a capacity for 'surveillance,' the ability to grasp the essential issues, 'to criticize, scrutinize and refine,' and 'to infuse one's values ... into a policy' are highly desirable qualities.[31] The other quality attached to a minister is status and political authority. In earlier times control over a province's or region's party machinery, or status derived from an individual's standing as former provincial premier, translated into political leverage in the federal cabinet. Currently, this appears to be much less the case, primarily because there has been much less movement of prominent provincial figures to the federal arena, figures who in earlier years might have brought with them actual or potential bases of electoral support.[32] In more recent times, support given to the incumbent prime minister during a leadership race can be used later to obtain cabinet positions and favours from the prime minister.

An additional factor that carries influence is the size of the provincial caucus. There is weight in numbers. Regional ministers with the backing of their caucus can exert enormous pressure on a whole range of issues, particularly if the provincial caucus dominates the government caucus as a whole, as was the case with the Quebec caucus in the last Trudeau government and to a lesser extent in the 1988 Mulroney government. The key, however, may well be how the regional minister is able to mobilize this asset. Individual MPs are independent actors in their own right, and in pursuing their own interests they can hamper the efforts of regional ministers. In this sense a sizeable caucus can be a liability and a minister lacking a caucus of any size may well find advantage in the freedom of movement and in not having to share valued projects with others. Other political resources lie well outside the parameters of the federal government proper, such as provincial governments and ministers, municipalities, and local interest groups. Alliances with these actors can prove to be unstable and difficult, but the mobilization of those outside one's party and government can be valuable, indeed crucial, if there is no caucus of any size to help in bringing pressure to bear on cabinet and line departments, and ultimately on the prime minister.

The framework sketched above captures only part of the broader world inhabited by regional ministers. Their beliefs and activities are part of the broader social and economic foundation of the Canadian nation state, and indeed of the political economy of North America as a whole. The wider backdrop includes the existence of the two main linguistic groups, an economy heavily dependent on the export of primary commodities, mainly to the United States, a limited manufacturing base, much of it foreign-owned, and pronounced regional disparities in economic well-being, combined with a strong sense of alienation from the centre on the part of the peripheries.[33] These factors have conditioned federal-provincial relations and, on a daily basis, affect a variety of issues ranging from social programs to regional development schemes that are of interest to regional ministers. Finally, all western nations have experienced to varying degrees what has been referred to as the 'political economy of fragmentation.'[34] The decline of basic industries, the growth of the service sector, and the changes in economies of scale in the production of newer products have led to a reconfiguration of economic interests and changes in political alliances. The perceived inability of national governments to sustain high levels of economic growth in combination with the advent of the 'embedded state' – namely, the mutual interpenetration of state and societal interests – may also contribute to the increased salience of regionally based coalitions.[35]

The regional minister system in its current form is a relatively little-understood phenomenon. Thus Donald Savoie notes: 'The place of regionalism and the role of regional ministers in federal government spending has not received the attention it deserves in the public policy literature in Canada.'[36] Nor is much known about the activities of regional ministers in shaping the federal-provincial agenda or in acting as a conduit for provinces seeking to pressure Ottawa. Particularly in the post Meech Lake era, with a variety of broad-ranging constitutional options before us, it is of manifest importance to have a full understanding of present-day central institutions, how they operate, and how they would mesh with, or could be successfully replaced by, new institutional arrangements.

More has been written about earlier periods, but here, particularly in light of the alleged failings of current political practices, there is danger in attributing qualities to previous cabinets they may never have had. On several grounds, therefore, it is desirable that more attention be paid to the regional dimension in cabinet decision-making, both past and present. In this way we can comprehend not only the ways in which regional ministers have declined, but also the ways in which they remain important and, indeed, have become more influential. Let us begin, therefore, by turning first to an examination of the cabinets in the era of John A. Macdonald and Wilfrid Laurier.

CHAPTER 2

Cabinet as Chamber of Regional Compensation under Macdonald and Laurier

It is commonly understood, and frequently lamented, that federal government institutions lack means for the adequate representation of regional interests. Unlike the United States, where Congress, and especially the Senate, has been seen as the primary arena for the mediation of state and broader regional interests, Canada is regarded as an excellent example of an interstate federation: regional interests are represented primarily through or by provincial governments *to* the federal government in Ottawa as opposed to having these interests represented directly *within* central institutions.[1]

In 1867 it was the intention that the Canadian Senate would in part serve the purpose of representing and protecting provincial interests: the smaller provinces were given representation greater than their size warranted while in the Commons representation was allied more closely with population. Realistically, expectations regarding this provincial overrepresentation were not high. As Peter Waite observes: 'It is impossible to believe that Macdonald, and perhaps others, were not shrewd enough to see the gist of this point: that a responsible cabinet would suck in, with silent, inexorable, vertiginous force, the whole regional character of the Senate and with it all the strength that lay in the Senate's regional identities.'[2]

The question arises whether cabinet government, in depleting the Senate of its regional character and responsibilities, ended up destroying these characteristics in the process of assimilating them. The hope of Macdonald and others was likely for their destruction. In the event, entry to the first cabinet in 1867 was based mainly on regional considerations. This first ministry essentially reflected a bargain struck by the prime minister and the three provincial premiers. In that initial formative period it came to constitute 'a chamber of political compensation, where the provincial spokesmen traded their support for national policies in return for concessions to their region.'³ The expectation was that each of the premiers would have the opportunity to serve in the new government. Within the strictly determined limit of no more than thirteen ministers, including the prime minister, Macdonald was also expected to heed what have come to be regarded as the canons guiding Canadian cabinet construction: the three 'Rs' – race, religion, and region. Both the absolute limit of thirteen and the regional breakdown – five from Ontario, four from Quebec, and two each from New Brunswick and Nova Scotia – were agreed upon by the delegates to the Westminster Conference in 1867. The overlay of personal, religious, and communal interests, however, made the actual cabinet formation process a rather more complicated affair.⁴

The appointments in part represented reward for those who had helped bring confederation about. They also constituted a means to ensure that the practical and symbolic interests of the affected provinces were looked after. Practical considerations included the completion of railway links such as the Intercolonial linking Nova Scotia and New Brunswick with central Canada, although the practical and symbolic were in a sense intertwined. Railways were a commodity in which politicians such as Leonard Tilley of New Brunswick and Joseph Howe of Nova Scotia had invested a great deal of emotional energy. The completion of these transportation links attained, therefore, a value that easily exceeded direct economic benefits.⁵ By the same token, arguments for appointing to cabinet representatives of communal groups, such as English-speaking Catholics, were made in terms of symbolic significance. These claims, however, also served well the personal ambitions of individuals seeking to fill those particular positions. And despite the sometimes acrimonious struggle over cabinet positions, there was also evidence of self-sacrifice in the name of the greater good. Charles Tupper, on his own initiative, persuaded Thomas D'Arcy McGee to give up his strong claim to a cabinet post by declining his own in favour of an Irish Roman Catholic from Nova Scotia, thereby ensuring the representation of at least one English-speaking Catholic in cabinet. This self-abnegation on the part of both Tupper and McGee broke a deadlock that threatened to scuttle the whole enterprise and represented an example of what in modern parlance has been called élite accommodation or 'consociationalism.'⁶

The subtleties of making appointments, the high value several aspirants set on gaining entry, and the high value someone like Tupper placed in not seeing the cabinet formation process fail, are all indicative of the standing of the cabinet in the newly born federation. To the extent that the first cabinet represented a careful balance of regional interests, in which the gains for some were coupled with little or no perceived loss for any single province, the equation worked out rather well. 'The cabinet of 1867, with great difficulty, worked out a rough justice in terms of Canadian convention. Those who suffered, suffered only slightly. They were the English Conservatives of Ontario, and the French of Quebec. Those who benefited, if anyone did, were the Maritimers, but this was a necessity of Confederation.'[7]

The intricacies of the first cabinet formation have been conscientiously examined.[8] The consideration remains, however, to what extent this carefully structured arrangement of regional and communal interests came to be transformed into something more permanent, into well-understood conventions that would be applied in the formation of subsequent cabinets. This first cabinet was after all a Liberal-Conservative coalition, although to speak of a bipartisan coalition would be misleading given the very limited meaning that party labels had in the era of 'loose fish' and 'waiters for providence.'[9] Party lines and attachments became much firmer in the late nineteenth century, and with the changing composition of the Canadian population, increasing urbanization, and the relative decline of the maritimes (both in numbers and in wealth), the subtleties of the rules governing cabinet formation would presumably also change.

From the vantage point of the present, the religious criterion has definitely become less obvious, and the terms 'language' and 'ethnicity' have replaced the appellation 'race.' At the same time 'region,' or more frequently 'province,' as a criterion has remained important, and has probably increased in relevance. Virtually all provinces, even Prince Edward Island, can expect at least one representative in cabinet, and the larger ones significantly more, subject only to the availability of government members in the House from that province. Even that contingency can be overcome through means of senatorial appointments. Yet if the reasons for regional *appointment* on the basis of convention appear straightforward, the meaning attached to regional *representation* in cabinet is not. Furthermore, the path to present-day conventions was, in fact, very uneven. In most textbooks, regional balance in cabinet is treated largely in symbolic terms. It is something that prime ministers must do. Flouting the rules will result in difficulties not only within the party, but also with the regional press, quite possibly with provincial governments, and with disaffected groups. Nonetheless, what ministers in cabinet are expected to do for their regions, or whether their mere presence in cabinet is sufficient, is not always made explicit.

In this chapter and the next the evolution of regional representation, and its variability over time, will be traced up to the beginning of the St Laurent government in 1948. Changes in the expectations and responsibilities of ministers acting in their regional capacities will be discussed, as will the expansion of departmental activities and changes in the operation of the administrative state, including those resulting from the introduction of the merit system in 1921. In the view of many, the present bureaucratic apparatus and 'institutionalized' form of cabinet differs considerably from that prevailing in the era of patronage-based politics and limited administrative responsibilities in the nineteenth century. The nature of party politics and electioneering has also changed. As students of Canadian parties have noted, the party system has metamorphosed through three distinctive stages: from the epoch of patronage and caucus parties prior to the First World War, through the period of strong ministers and brokerage politics until 1957, to the current era, which began with the pan-Canadianism of John Diefenbaker and his stress on personalized national leadership.[10] It will be argued, however, that there is likely more continuity with the past than many would concede. The practices in question are not the same; in fact many of them are now illegal. The motivation, intent, and outcome are similar, however, as are the forces that drive them.

Nation-building, Patronage, and Limited Administration

It was in this period, from 1867 until the defeat of Laurier in the election of 1911, that many of the conventions concerning regional representation in cabinet hardened. They included understandings on the status of the Quebec lieutenant, the prerogative of ministers to intervene in the affairs of other portfolios when regional issues were at stake, and, especially, the disbursement of patronage. This last item was of overwhelming importance. In the eyes of most historians the entire system – government operations, regional representation, federal-provincial relations, and party politics – was driven by patronage. In several ways patronage was an end in itself, and the disbursement of cabinet positions and senatorships was seen as rewards for hard work in the past, and control over government departments as opportunity for dispensing patronage to others. But patronage also constituted a means to an end. In the early post-confederation period and beyond, it was this 'natural currency of public life' that made a minister's portfolio viable, giving 'his office meaning and substance.' He was, after all, 'primarily a politician, and only to a minor degree an administrator.'[11] Above all, it could be used for nation-building purposes.

The preoccupation with patronage was central to Canadian politics in this period, a centrality that was in some ways puzzling, for in Britain and the United States during this same era patronage lacked the legitimacy it appeared to enjoy in Canada and was in actual decline.[12] In Britain the extension of the franchise in 1832 made political power less dependent upon the exercise of patronage, and after the civil service reforms of 1854 such appointments became increasingly rare. In contrast, in Canada the patronage system gained strength and remained in place until the reforms of the Borden ministry beginning in 1911. Given its importance to understanding the regional character of the Canadian cabinet and the role played by ministers, the origins of the patronage system and the uses to which it was put should be made clear.

The roots of the system go back to 1791, with the establishment of the two Canadas under a constitution that provided for exceptionally strong executives in the two colonies. While representative assemblies were created, under the arrangements of 1791 virtually all power remained in the hands of the governor and his council. No provisions for co-operation between the executive and the assembly were made, and the executive could proceed to collect revenues and disburse patronage without reference to the assembly. Much of the controversy and instability that followed could be attributed to the intransigence of the Family Compact in Upper Canada and the Chateau Clique in Lower Canada, an obstinacy that pushed a small minority of reformers in both Canadas to revolt in 1837. The intransigent élites consisted largely of a small group of Anglican-Compact-tory office-holders and they maintained their exclusivity through the selective disbursement of patronage, entrenching their position of power by making appointments and allocating salaries 'for every post from customs officer to judge in a conscious effort to create an anglicized ruling class.'[13]

Nonetheless, excepting radicals such as William Lyon Mackenzie, the main body of reformers remained committed to both monarchy and strong executive government. Their interest was not in weakening government but in broadening its base, and specifically in allowing the assembly to have access to, and control over, the distribution of patronage. In a sense these claims were moderate. But precisely because of the lack of power of the assemblies and the intransigence of the governors and their executive councils, and the absence of any links between them, the language employed by both sides was bitter and abusive in the extreme. As well, reformers such as Robert Baldwin realized that under Canadian conditions, particularly after 1815, when social and economic relations were rapidly developing and in flux, access to patronage was crucial in order to build networks of power in the broader community. When Baldwin, LaFontaine, and their fellow reformers did achieve power after 1848, they set about doing precisely that with a vengeance, using patronage to cultivate political loyalties in a variety of social and economic groups.

It was in this setting that John A. Macdonald came to be schooled in the ways and mores of Canadian politics. Macdonald lived and breathed patronage.[14] He came to know intimately the names of lawyers and their political qualities in Toronto and elsewhere in Ontario, and would spend hours vetting recommendations for patronage positions received from constituency organizations. Like Baldwin before him, he used patronage to engender loyalty among party supporters. But he did far more: patronage was used to create not just loyalty but also organization. Appointments to judgeships, for example, could occasionally be made to non-tories for strategic purposes, to take a competitor out of the running. In the main, Macdonald tried to impress on MPs and constituency associations the importance of appointing only 'cold water' men, those with a demonstrated willingness to work under all conditions.[15]

The end result was that by the 1880s Macdonald had an effective national party based on local networks of committed supporters. When Wilfrid Laurier came to power he slavishly followed Macdonald by using the same techniques, with the same degree of personal attention, to build the Liberal party. Historians would also write of the Laurier period that 'the distribution of patronage was the most important single function of the government.'[16] Patronage and the two main parties built on this practice cut across all classes and occupations. To be an engineer or a lawyer and not be involved in one of the two parties meant lack of standing in the community, to say nothing of a very restricted livelihood. This was in evidence at the provincial as well as federal level. Oliver Mowat, Liberal premier of Ontario from 1872 to 1896, was a formidable competitor of Macdonald's in the patronage battle, using it to bolster Reform/Liberal influence at the local level. The jurisdictional battles between the federal and Ontario governments over things like waterways and liquor licensing in many ways represented battles over patronage resources. Without access to those resources Macdonald felt he could well lose closely fought constituency contests and, more generally, destroy the vitality of local Conservative party organizations.[17] And in the long run it would also sap the strength of the federal government in controlling Canada's destiny.

Such was the political context in the nineteenth century. It should be stressed that the demand for patronage was not something pressed on an unwilling or blasé populace by political élites. In filling positions a 'minister did not need to make too many enquiries, for a cloud of applications would descend upon him the moment the post was known to be open. Indeed, the body of the newly deceased incumbent of the office would still be warm when the letters would be off to Ottawa. With judges, the letters would often arrive before the judge was dead.'[18] Nor did all ministers share Macdonald's taste for the practice. Joseph Howe of Nova Scotia, an important convert to the confederation cause who became secretary of state for the provinces in 1869, was apparently a reluctant practitioner, regarding it 'as the least pleasant of his official duties.'[19] Sir John Thompson, also from Nova Scotia and Conservative prime minister from 1892 to 1894, as MP from Antigonish was often shocked and offended by the imperious claims for office made by many of his constituents. 'I revolt against Antigonish the more I think of it,' he told his wife one day in 1887.[20]

The significance of Macdonald's behaviour resided not so much in his fostering of patronage, though he did nothing to discourage it, but in his control and channelling of it to achieve particular political ends: building the Conservative party and, conjointly, the Canadian nation. The impression of Macdonald as almost totally preoccupied with the distribution of patronage – an image partially the product of recent historiography – is somewhat at odds with Macdonald as visionary politician, as nation-builder and architect of the National Policy. There is no necessary contradiction between these two images, however. In fact one can discern considerable convenience in the marriage between visionary politics and patronage. The construction of the Canadian Pacific Railway and the Intercolonial provided ample opportunity to reward friends of the party both large and small. The introduction of the National Policy, based on high tariff barriers against imports primarily from the United States and intended to foster horizontal trade links between the provinces, would, it was hoped, result in the increased usage of the railways. At a minimum, it would lead to expansion of the customs service and the availability of positions such as clerks and 'tide-waiters' to be allocated to supporters of the party. The justification for appointing partisan workers ('workers,' not simply 'friends') was not mere expediency but nurtured by Macdonald's beliefs, acquired during his early political life, that his opponents were at base disloyal to both crown and country. Many of the reformers in Upper Canada, and some in Lower Canada, had publicly entertained annexationist thoughts prior to confederation. Afterwards Grit leaders such as George Brown opposed the first coalition cabinet at a time, Macdonald thought, when there really was no need to uphold party distinctions. The use of patronage, Macdonald felt, was fully legitimate.[21]

The nature of economic development in nineteenth-century Canada made the activities of government, and hence patronage, loom much larger. Business enterprises in Canada, ranging from railway consortiums to small manufacturing enterprises looking for hydroelectric power at reasonable cost and markets for their goods, were highly dependent on government for assistance. These burgeoning state or state-supported enterprises generated patronage slots to be filled. The public, and in particular the still developing professional middle classes seeking remuneration for their skills, frequently saw in government work the only opportunity to exercise their chosen professions. By the early 1880s the National Policy still had not taken hold and the economic future was uncertain, so the role of government as provider of jobs became even more important. What made a position in the dominion civil service, or with the government-owned Intercolonial, attractive was the respectability and, above all, the security accorded to the occupants. While political considerations would play a role in obtaining a government position, once in place the incumbent had reasonable prospects for tenure. There was no wholesale turnover of positions so characteristic of Jacksonian democracy in the United States.

There was, it can be argued, unity of purpose in Macdonald's vision of railway links from east to west, the opening up of the west, the fostering of indigenous enterprises, the establishment and strengthening of the Conservative party, and the extensive use of patronage. Some contradictory images remain, however, between that of Macdonald as the great centralizer and that of the cabinet as a 'chamber of sectional compensation.' Macdonald clearly had hopes that regional representation was but a temporary necessity. 'Eventually, when the provinces had become more intimately united, ... the only question would be to choose the best man to come into the Government.'[22] This temporary necessity turned into something more permanent, however, and Macdonald himself played a role in entrenching sectional norms.

Initially a number of the ministers, George-Etienne Cartier in particular, brought with them their own sources of political power, based in good part on control over patronage, but also deriving from their role in helping to bring confederation about.[23] In addition, Macdonald's capacity in the French language was singularly limited. If only for that reason, he had to depend on a Quebec minister for advice on patronage matters within the French-Canadian community. In the case of Charles Tupper, Macdonald had come to depend on him as his chief lieutenant on a variety of matters, feeling obliged to him for his help and support, first during the Quebec and Charlottetown conferences, and later during the dark period following the Pacific Scandal and electoral defeat in 1874. In return, Tupper became undisputed chieftan for the maritimes, eclipsing Leonard Tilley, even though in 1876 Tupper had essentially left Nova Scotia, having taken up residence in Toronto.[24]

Anointing ministers as regional representatives also meant sharing control over patronage. The negotiations with Joseph Howe, for example, led not only to better terms for Nova Scotia and a seat at the cabinet table for Howe, but also to Howe being given significant influence over patronage for that province. This influence, however, was not simply reward for pro-confederation support but more important became an instrument to be used by Howe to placate the 'Antis.' For example, 'In January [1870] he gave Alexander Campbell, the postmaster general, the names of ten Nova Scotian MPs whose advice on appointments he might take without reference to himself. By the year's end, apart from Isaac Vesconte of Richmond, who was drunk more often than not and hence unreliable, all but three were giving the government "fair support".'[25]

The lesson to be inferred, and one that would have been evident to Macdonald, was that the prime minister needed to turn to, and become dependent on, the power and support of provincially based figures, both to garner support for the party and to placate those opposed to confederation. This was true not only in the early years but also during the later period of Macdonald's tenure. Thus in 1888 efforts to entice Newfoundland to enter confederation were in part delegated to John Thompson who, in outlining the benefits to a Halifax MP, T.E. Kenny, stressed the fact 'that the smaller provinces have obtained a far larger share of consideration (including expenditure) than the larger [provinces], and have more influence than could be claimed on account either of territorial extent or population. The fact that they have always been more troublesome than the larger ones is perhaps one of the reasons.'[26] It could well have been New Brunswick's 'troublesome' nature that accounted for Tilley's success in obtaining two cabinet posts for that province in the 1878 government (albeit one without portfolio), despite having delivered only five of the sixteen seats to the Conservatives in the election of that year. The smaller provinces did rather well in terms of cabinet representation in the initial decades after confederation, a fact which may have been overlooked in the attention usually focused on Quebec.

Of all regional ministers, however, the position of Quebec lieutenant is usually seen as being by far the most significant. The more successful prime ministers such as Macdonald and William Lyon Mackenzie King, it is said, enjoyed the support and wise counsel of the senior minister from that province, while ones such as Robert Borden and John Diefenbaker ran into difficulties in part because they were unable, or unwilling, to cultivate such a figure.[27] The origins of the Quebec lieutenant role under Macdonald are worth noting. Cartier had accepted, as part of the confederation package, a minority position for Quebec within cabinet, a departure from the principle of dualism operative during the United Canadas period. The number of ministers agreed upon was three plus a fourth English-speaking representative. During the actual cabinet formation process there was some pressure for a fourth French Canadian to be appointed, but this request was denied. Cartier, however, was given the right to designate the three French-Canadian members (he chose himself, Hector-Louis Langevin, and Jean-Charles Chapais) and recognition as the second man in cabinet. This concession was not based on any formal recognition of the senior Quebec minister as principal lieutenant; it related more to Cartier's general weight and influence stemming from his past relations with Macdonald in various cabinets of the Province of Canada. Significantly Cartier had no control, or at least no power of veto, over the appointment of the one English-speaking cabinet member from Quebec.[28]

Cartier died in 1873. In forming his second ministry in 1878, Macdonald attempted to follow some of the same practices, involving the senior Quebec representative in the process of selecting the three French-Canadian ministers. Significantly, these efforts were made in the face of some difficult circumstances, including the apparent absence of a senior Quebec leader willing to play that role. No one, it seems, was willing, or able, to pick up Cartier's mantle. Langevin still suffered from his involvement in the Pacific Scandal and, as well, had been defeated in his constituency of Rimouski in the election of 1878. One heir apparent was Louis-François-Rodrigue Masson, recognized leader of Montreal-area MPs, member of the Macdonald-Cartier 'old guard,' an eloquent and frequent speaker in the House of Commons. Macdonald leaned in his direction, but Masson made things difficult. With an election imminent he nonetheless decided in June to depart for France, and did not return until the middle of October, a full month after the election. Despite his absence, he was safely re-elected in his own constituency. Macdonald proceeded to put together most of his cabinet, excepting the three positions being held for the French-Canadian contingent. When Masson finally arrived, he and Macdonald were able to decide fairly quickly on the three names, which included Masson himself. Creighton refers to Masson's influence on the process as mainly 'confirmatory' in character. Yet the willingness of Macdonald to stretch the length of the proceedings to its limits in order to accommodate Masson does signify that the position of Quebec *chef* was recognized to a degree.[29]

Masson, largely through lack of interest and will, faded into obscurity. Macdonald failed in his efforts to persuade Chapais to return to cabinet, so the role of Quebec lieutenant fell upon Langevin. The style of the man, and his being from Quebec City rather than Montreal, made him less useful than Cartier; but he was an effective and hard-working administrator who remained as *chef* for Quebec until Macdonald's death in 1891. Yet as much as he valued the role played by Langevin, Macdonald was unwilling to concede to Quebec ministers a role in formulating and deciding national issues. They were discouraged from making forays into subjects of national import and, instead, told to occupy themselves with patronage.[30] Quebec, largely because of its unique socio-economic structure, provided fertile ground for patronage to flourish.[31] Macdonald's treatment of Quebec ministers, particularly in encouraging their preoccupation with patronage aspirations, was thus doubly unfortunate and likely helped lead to a restricted view of the role of the Quebec lieutenant, and Quebec ministers generally. This view notwithstanding, the importance of sectional criteria in determining the composition of cabinet was firmly established by the 1890s. In 1893 Prime Minister Thompson stated in the House: '[We] must remember that in this country we have still the system of provincial representation in the Cabinet. That system was founded in 1867 ... I doubt very much, indeed, if any of the provinces will be willing to give up the share of representation which it had at the time of the union.'[32]

Wilfrid Laurier, in forming his government in 1896, continued the practices established by Macdonald with respect to cabinet construction and the use of patronage. The cabinet formation process was, as always, a delicate balancing act, taking into account the three 'Rs' but with predominant weight given to regional considerations. This was a period of decentralization, and Laurier's victory could be attributed in part to the support given by the provincial premiers, who had been unreservedly hostile to Macdonald's centralized vision of Canada. As a reflection of this, Laurier was anxious to bring into cabinet men such as Oliver Mowat, premier of Ontario, and W.S. Fielding, premier of Nova Scotia, and succeeded in doing so. Two years later Laurier returned to the provinces control over the voters' lists used in federal elections, control over which Macdonald had fought so hard to keep.[33]

The public role assigned to Mowat was almost a mirror image of earlier practices. He was depicted in the press as being to Laurier what Cartier had been to Macdonald, and there was talk of a Laurier-Mowat administration.[34] His subsequent impact was much more limited, however. Initially it appears he may have had power of veto over the Ontario appointments to cabinet, but beyond this there is little evidence he had much influence over cabinet affairs. After little more than a year he left his portfolio, and his seat in the Senate, to become lieutenant-governor of Ontario. Laurier himself assumed the mantle of *chef* of Quebec, although he did bring into cabinet his chief Quebec party organizer, J. Israel Tarte, a former Conservative and ultramontanist. Laurier's sense that he himself would be able to represent Quebec interests could well account for the overall weak representation of French Canadians in cabinet, both in numbers (only four, including Laurier, in a seventeen-man cabinet) and in terms of portfolios, despite the high number of Liberal MPs from Quebec (forty-nine of sixty-five seats) and majority electoral support among French Canadians.[35] There was little overt complaint within the Liberal party, either in Quebec or elsewhere, but there was considerable consternation on the part of the Conservative press in Quebec. *Le Temps* described the consequences for Quebec as 'the deepest national humiliation'; and the congratulations offered by the Toronto *Globe* on Quebec's apparent moderation in demands for cabinet positions was widely reprinted.[36] What could be seen as limited Quebec representation, however, probably had more to do with the complexity of Quebec politics than any sense of inferiority. For Laurier it was not so much a matter of who to bring into cabinet as who to keep out. To create a more solid basis in that province required developing links with, or at least neutralizing, the church hierarchy, and this could not be accomplished by appointing traditional *Rouges* with their anticlerical baggage. The nitty-gritty of political organization at the constituency level was left to Tarte, who became minister of public works. This was the same department headed by Langevin, whose career had been cut short by a corruption scandal over government contracts, involving, among other items, the construction of the Langevin block in Ottawa.[37]

The pattern of patronage itself continued with the new government. Indeed, it continued right down to the eve of the First World War.[38] Like Macdonald, Laurier used the tools of patronage to develop a well-knit political party that penetrated all groups and strata in Canada, and which extended into newspapers, legal firms, and a variety of social institutions. One of Laurier's differences with Macdonald, however, was his willingness to decentralize patronage to his ministers. According to Laurier, they were in the best position to judge what was right for the party at the local and regional level. In turn, the rights of ministers in relation to their regions were codified. Thus in 1904 the cabinet issued an order-in-council specifying that: 'In the case of members of the Cabinet, while all have an equal degree of responsibility in a constitutional sense, yet in the practical working out of responsible government in a country of such vast extent as Canada, it is found necessary to attach a special responsibility to each minister for the public affairs of the province or district with which he has close political connections.'[39]

Under Laurier all patronage was channelled through and controlled by the regional ministers: Fielding for Nova Scotia, Andrew Blair for New Brunswick, Clifford Sifton for the west, and first Mowat, then William Mullock, followed by Allan Aylesworth for Ontario.[40] Illustrative of how the principles and spirit of the 1904 order-in-council affected decisions, Laurier himself was scolded by Richard Cartwright from Ontario for being 'highly impolitic' in daring to suggest a name for a senatorial position for that province. Laurier in turn exercised his own regional prerogative when he prevented the postmaster general, Mullock, from dismissing on the basis of incompetence Arthur 'Boss' Dansereau as postmaster of Montreal. Laurier's intuition in rescuing Dansereau yielded handsome dividends when the latter, on becoming editor of *La Presse*, switched the allegiance of the paper from Conservative to Liberal.[41]

In 1888 Macdonald had appointed to cabinet, for the first time, someone directly from the west,[42] Edgar Dewdney, as minister of the interior and superintendent general of Indian affairs. Previously lieutenant-governor of the North-West Territories, Dewdney's tenure lasted until 1892 when he returned to his home province of British Columbia as lieutenant-governor. He was seen as a sensible administrator with a reputation for having a 'cool head with Indians,' which in the aftermath of the Riel rebellions was of no small importance. While unspectacular, he apparently served Macdonald well.[43] In Macdonald's era the west as a whole constituted only a small proportion of the total Canadian population. By 1896, however, the west came into its own. The National Policy and the completion of the Canadian Pacific Railway were finally beginning to bear fruit, and as a consequence the population began expanding rapidly. It was in this setting that Laurier's policy of devolving substantial authority to his regional ministers had spectacular results. While Dewdney had a reputation as a careful and reasonable humane administrator, albeit apt to be brusque and not adverse to making money, he apparently entertained no grandiose schemes; and in the history books he remains a relatively obscure figure.[44] The same cannot be said for Clifford Sifton, former attorney general in the Manitoba government, who became Laurier's minister of the interior and left his imprint permanently and in numerous ways. According to Jeffrey Simpson, 'Nowhere was the decentralization of patronage authority under Laurier clearer than in Clifford Sifton's empire.'[45] And further, 'As minister of the interior and Liberal party organizer for the entire Canadian West, Sifton held sway over a territory stretching from the Ontario border to the Pacific Ocean ... His ministry's regulation of the North-West Territory and the Yukon included homesteading and settlement, immigration, schools, forestry, mineral rights, grazing, railways and national parks. No Canadian politician, before or since, ever ruled such a vast geographic territory.'[46]

It was in the settlement of this vast and largely empty space that Sifton had the greatest impact. He set out to populate the west by seeking immigrants not only from the United States and Britain but also from central and eastern Europe. It was these non-English settlers who proved to be physically and mentally the best equipped to deal with the rigours of the prairies. In the United States during the same period most non-English immigrants settled in large urban areas. In the Canadian west, in contrast, the same immigrants passed through eastern and central Canada on closed trains, settling directly in small communities on the lonely prairie.[47] Their isolation readily lent itself to the organizing efforts of the Liberals. Sifton's policies also had other consequences, in particular the enhancement of localism. Combined with what David Smith refers to as Canada's linear development and 'longitudinal' mentality, Sifton's strategy for settling the west had, over the long term, the effect of reinforcing a deep sense of sectional alienation and the region's insularity in national politics.[48]

Sifton was ruthless and uncompromising in pursuing Liberal hegemony over the west. He was equally uncompromising in dealing with what Laurier and others considered basic principles. Thus in 1905, with the creation of the new provinces of Alberta and Saskatchewan, Sifton resigned over the inclusion of separate school rights in the initial autonomy legislation. The basic pattern had, nevertheless, been set. The population of the prairie west had expanded more than threefold since Sifton's taking office in 1896, and it was now much less Anglo-Saxon or French in character than either the maritimes or the central Canadian provinces. Sifton's successor as minister of interior, Frank Oliver, essentially continued his immigration policies.[49]

Thus under Laurier the basic model of patronage and party organization as developed by Macdonald was affirmed, but decentralized to provide regional ministers with greater control. The effects of the Macdonald-Laurier approach on the nature of cabinet government and the administrative apparatus were profound, and in light of the extensive evidence on the pervasiveness of patronage and corruption it would be easy to conclude that these effects have been almost entirely negative. But such a conclusion would be unwise. First, patronage was important in helping to create stable, all-encompassing political parties in an era when issues over race and religion were potentially deeply divisive. Secondly, preoccupation, or perhaps fascination, with the patronage issue by modern scholars can detract from a proper analysis of the extent to which certain areas of the Canadian public service were protected from its ravages, as well as the extent to which the politicians themselves recognized a need to balance partisan needs with broader goals.

Limited Administration and 'Political Nomination'

Turning first to the administrative apparatus, the federal civil service inherited by the newly minted nation was essentially that of the United Provinces.[50] Operating in an era when the predominant public philosophy was one of limited government, the new civil service remained relatively small up to the eve of the First World War, despite extensive support for railway construction and related economic development activities. In 1900 federal government spending was approximately $55 million, representing only 5 per cent of the gross national product (GNP), which contrasts sharply with the over 25 per cent of GNP in the 1990s. Of that $55 million, $24 million was for spending on railways, an area in good part in the hands of private companies.[51]

Limited government would suggest that ministers had ample time to concern themselves with broad issues. This was not necessarily the case, however. In a telling 1912 report on administrative practices, ministers were chided for being preoccupied with departmental detail, and it bluntly recommended that 'the business of a Minister is not to administer, but to direct policy.'[52] But it was in the actual administration of policy that ministers could involve themselves in local affairs and tend to patronage needs, and it was in this connection that ministers would make contact with the 'outside service.'

From early on a distinction was made between the 'inside service,' based in Ottawa, and the 'outside service,' those public servants based outside of Ottawa where the majority of government operations were to be found. Significantly, in 1867 there was practically no representation from the maritimes within the inside or 'senior' branch of the service, a sore point among Joseph Howe and others. No accurate data exist but estimates suggest that at the turn of the century the total number of civil servants was approximately ten thousand, with the inside service constituting roughly four thousand.[53] Certainly the size of some departments was very small. John Thompson, upon becoming minister of justice (which included responsibility for the penitentiary service) in 1885, found an Ottawa-based department of fifteen men plus three or four messengers.[54] Other units, particularly the nation-building or 'barometer' departments such as the Department of the Interior and Department of Public Works, were larger. Most of the staffing was done on the basis of 'political nomination'; in other words, appointments were made on the basis of party credentials. The nomination would, more often than not, originate with the local MP (or defeated government candidate) or constituency association, particularly if the position were in the outside service. It would then be approved by the minister for the province or region. Under the provisions of the Civil Service Act of 1868, candidates were examined by the Civil Service Board; but typically this examination did not occur until *after* the appointment had been made.[55] Should the candidate be unlucky enough to fail, he would have at least two additional opportunities to make up the deficiency. Furthermore, the examination system, and the limited control exercised by the Civil Service Board, applied mainly to the inside service. Thus, in 1876 it was found that in the Department of Marine (outside service) a total of 1350 employees out of 1596 were appointed on the basis of political nomination and very few of them were actually subjected to the examination procedure.

The prevalence of patronage in the nineteenth century was much discussed; several parliamentary committees and commissions lamented the problem and made recommendations for dealing with the evil. One MP, George Elliott Casey, made a career out of promoting civil service reform. Macdonald, no doubt simply reflecting the dominant views of the time, labelled these efforts as trying to put Canada back to the 'age of Adam and Eve before the apple.'[56] Nevertheless, figures on the size of individual departments appear elusive and the actual proportions of appointments subject to patronage even more so. Hodgetts et al. have expressed a certain amount of scepticism over some of the figures bandied about, especially those on dismissals, and sensibly recommend a degree of caution in interpreting opposition charges on the extent of patronage.[57] Some generalizations can be made, however. First, although no part of the public service was immune, the lowest levels were most prone to outright partisan considerations. Second, the efforts at reform resulting from royal commissions in 1868–9, 1880–1, 1891–2, and 1907–8, to the extent they had much effect, were targeted mainly at the inside service.[58] The outside service remained largely a partisan preserve subject to political nomination, a situation that was not really tackled until the reforms of 1918.

This state of affairs was important in two ways. Within the public service it sharpened the distinction that already existed between those at headquarters and those out in the field; and among ministers it increased the resentment of those in the maritimes who felt aggrieved at the lack of maritime representation at the senior levels of the bureaucracy. It also reinforced their sense of wishing to control the appointments made in their regions. For most, this influence represented a patronage resource to help local party organizations and, in many instances, to help out family and friends. The ability to use the outside service, however, could also be taken advantage of for broader purposes. In the case of Clifford Sifton, Simpson writes: 'Within a year of assuming office, he had placed his own men in positions of authority within the immigration section of the ministry. When the Klondike gold rush opened up the Yukon, most of the officials sent to bring a semblance of order to the unruly territory were Liberals. The homestead agents who fanned out across the prairies – spear carriers in "Sifton's army" – were often the first personal contact immigrants experienced with Canadians.'[59] More so than other ministers, Sifton, in actively using his department to pursue his vision of the Canadian west, was a harbinger of the ministerial entrepreneurship that would arrive later under Mackenzie King.

Thus the political nomination process, especially with regard to the outside service, gave regional ministers considerable influence over the operations of departments in their regions, both their own departments and those of others. A minister's own portfolio offered the greatest opportunity for using the resources of the government to advantage, and portfolios tended to be allocated on the basis of regional considerations. Marine and fisheries was of interest to, and generally held by, maritime ministers, not only because of the subject matter but because the construction of wharves, breakwaters, and the like was an obvious patronage staple in the region. Quebec ministers were frequently given public works since that department, more so than others, lent itself to patronage and pork-barrelling. It was not that the Quebec contingent in cabinet was unusually venal.[60] Rather Macdonald and most of his successors were reluctant to give financial portfolios to French-Canadian ministers and the lucrative public works portfolio could be used as a trade-off. In Macdonald's first cabinet, for example, public works was given to Langevin in 1869, in part to compensate for the demotion of another Quebec minister and for the general underrepresentation of French Canadians in cabinet.[61]

Influencing the affairs of one's own department on patronage or local issues was reasonably straightforward. The affairs of other departments were subject to negotiation with the minister concerned, some ministers such as Thompson from Nova Scotia being more strait-laced than others. An additional and striking feature was that such negotiations more often than not took place directly in cabinet – for example, over such picuyane matters as tender calls for a pump in a particular constituency – with the consequence that a number of conventions developed that remain unique to the Canadian cabinet. The 1904 order-in-council of the Laurier cabinet concerning the prerogatives of regional ministers has already been noted. The order-in-council instrument itself, however, is reflective of the conventions and practices that evolved during the Macdonald-Laurier period. Much more so than the cabinet in the United Kingdom, the Canadian cabinet operates on the basis of collegiality, with a concomitant reduction in the power of individual ministers. This point was noted in 1912 by Sir

George Murray, who had experience of both systems, in his inquiry into civil service practices in Canada.[62] Thus in Canada ministers in some crucial respects have limits on their authority: delegated power is conferred on the 'governor-in-council' rather than on individual ministers. According to J.R. Mallory, 'Ministers [do not have] untrammelled authority over the policy of their departments. Each minister tends to have a sort of veto of executive actions affecting the part of the country which he is known to "represent" in the Cabinet, and Ministers in the exercise of their powers thus prefer to have the authority of the Governor in council for almost any power which they exercise.'[63] Ministers, therefore, in explaining or accounting for their decisions to the House, will typically refer to a cabinet decision rather than one of their own. It makes life more comfortable for ministers and can be used to disguise regional log-rolling. But, as complaints dating back to the 1880s and 1890s testify, the preoccupation of ministers and cabinet with minutiae associated with local matters and the time spent in dealing with several ministers can detract from broader policy issues; and, within departments, under certain circumstances it can increase the influence of civil servants vis-à-vis their ministers in so far as broader policy issues are frequently left to them by default.[64] Thus the stress on cabinet collegiality and collective decision-making, often seen as the product of the modern 'institutionalized cabinet,' is in fact rooted in part in the sectional nature of the nineteenth-century cabinet.

Local Politics and the National Good

The recent literature on patronage, fuelled in part by present-day problems of conflict of interest and various forms of pork-barrelling, as well as patronage as traditionally understood (namely, benefits conferred directly on specific individuals as opposed to benefits on groups or communities), has made undue partisan influence over public expenditures the best-known political inheritance from the Macdonald-Laurier period. Certainly the regional minister phenomenon cannot be understood without reference to the patronage aspect and its origins. Yet it is important to realize that Macdonald and Laurier retained some semblance of the larger public good to be served by government activities and also some limits on what could be done with the resources of the state. Ministers themselves, although frequently eager to help their constituency, were often less magnanimous outside of their own particular bailiwick. For example, at one point Macdonald, in his capacity as minister of railways, successfully defended his deputy minister, Collingwood Schrieber, against the predatory efforts of the minister of marine and fisheries, Charles Hibbert Tupper (son of Sir Charles Tupper) who wished 'a little better treatment at the hands of your Chief Engineer regarding matters in my county,'[65] to wit coal contracts for constituents in Pictou County. Macdonald resisted, informing Tupper that 'we must find you a seat where there are no coal mines, or we shall have annual trouble.'[66]

The senior Tupper, as minister of canals and railways in Macdonald's cabinet from 1879 to 1884, played a rather curious role with respect to his native province. As former premier of Nova Scotia and as senior minister representing the maritimes it could be thought that he would use his portfolio to the benefit of his province, particularly if Conservative interests were at stake. Yet, though willing in 1882 to promote the interests of the railway running through his own constituency of Cumberland County (the Oxford and Pictou line), he did little to help the Conservative provincial government, a government facing a difficult election in the same year, in its efforts to consolidate its railway mess through the new Nova Scotia Railway Company. Indeed, Tupper's support of the Oxford and Pictou line probably helped undermine the provincial scheme. The Nova Scotia Conservatives lost a close election.[67] The merits (or demerits) of the provincial scheme notwithstanding, Tupper's lack of support, no doubt on the advice of Macdonald, does indicate that neither individual ministers nor cabinet as a whole were always or necessarily susceptible to provincial interests.

John Thompson, as minister of justice in the Macdonald cabinet, while often impelled to respond to the imperious requests for patronage in his own constituency, could be highly resistant to demands from other quarters; to the parachuting, for example, of a politically nominated penitentiary warden.[68] Later, as prime minister, he opposed government financial support for the construction of the Chignecto Ship Railway in New Brunswick, a project supported by Charles Tupper. George Foster, Thompson's minister of finance, was also opposed to the project on the reasonable grounds of fiscal prudence, even though he was the minister from New Brunswick.[69] To be sure, this kind of defence of the public good was more easily accomplished in jurisdictions outside of one's own constituency. Yet these examples are telling all the same.

Under Laurier, regional ministers were given freer rein. Yet here, too, one can find examples of instances, such as the issue of separate schools, and the creation of the two new western provinces in 1905, where western interests, as articulated by Sifton, in opposing separate schools were to a degree compromised by broader concerns. This issue led to Sifton's resignation from cabinet; and in accepting his resignation Laurier was very likely also indicating an increasing unwillingness to tolerate the major figure that Sifton had come to represent, a minister in complete control of the western region.[70]

Overall, the two major figures, Macdonald and Laurier, were willing to strike a balance of sorts between national and regional interests; and individual cabinet ministers at various times could assert what they conceived of as the public good, conceptions that could be at odds with local or provincial interests. Equally important, regional ministers were expected to, and in fact did, mobilize support for the government at times of stress or crisis, within the Commons or out on the hustings. Hector Langevin, for example, not noted for striking oratorical performances in the House, gave one of his stronger speeches in 1886 in the aftermath of the Riel crisis and, by various means, helped ensure that the majority of Quebec Conservative MPs voted against the motion to censure the government for the Riel hanging.[71]

The Persistence of Localism

One further legacy of the Macdonald-Laurier period is worth noting. It is a legacy that helps to account for the sectional character of cabinet and continuing pressures on the bureaucracy – the persistence of localism. Writers such as Gordon Stewart and Reg Whitaker have pointed to one of the great ironies of Canadian political development: in drawing on localistic traditions to build national parties, nineteenth-century political leaders at the same time succeeded in permanently entrenching these traditions.[72] The practice of appealing to local sentiments and interests was made possible, indeed made necessary, by the largely agricultural conditions prevailing throughout the nineteenth century. In the census of 1881, 81 per cent of the population was classified as rural and half of the labour force was engaged in 'agricultural pursuits.'[73] From then on began a continual flow of labour from rural to urban occupations so that by 1901, 40 per cent of the labour force was in agriculture and by 1941 only 25 per cent was so engaged.[74] The rural and small-town legacy remained, however, and while localism is most clearly identified with the original four provinces, the settlement patterns of the west, with enclaves of non-English-speaking settlers on the raw open prairie, produced their own variant of localistic norms.

To capture the essential character of these traditions, a number of political scientists have described social and political conditions at the local level in terms of 'patron-client' relations, linkages in which patronage obviously plays an important role.[75] Patron-client models are used extensively in anthropological studies and have been used to good effect in the political development literature. Yet there are dangers in using these models in the Canadian setting. While applicable in certain circumstances, they can give a misleading impression. The patron-client linkage implies stability, predictability, control, and a high level of trust among participants.[76] Yet nineteenth-century party politics at the local level in Canada was anything but stable and controlled. Electoral contests were frequently very close, with individual electors easily switching from one candidate to the other. Peter Waite has described the Nova Scotia constituencies held by the two Tuppers and Thompson as 'difficult,' and his graphic descriptions of relations between these men and their constituents suggest that, if anything, the clients tended to control the patron. The links between the different elements − electors, MPs, ministers, and the national party − held together through patronage, were capable of producing reasonably stable results at the national level; but locally things could shift radically from one election to the next.

Precisely because there were two well-organized parties, electoral politics was a highly competitive business. Canadian political parties were never able to generate at the local level all-encompassing political machines of the sort found in the United States, where any semblance of competition was excluded through control over voters and the voting process.[77] Rather, it has been the *lack* of control over local matters, over the importuning demands of local citizens and groups, that made MPs and ministers so sensitive to local pressures and issues. Ministers, in turn, were doubly sensitive to these pressures. Until the practice was ended in 1931, MPs, upon being invited to join the cabinet, had to resign their seats in the Commons and stand once more in their constituency in a confirming election![78] While patronage was actively promoted by parties and politicians, resistance to changing the practice tended to be lodged within the clientele rather than the leadership.[79]

Overall, one primary theme needs to be reiterated: regional ministers of the period tended to be lukewarm in pressing provincial or broader regional interests. Instead, their focus tended to be a combination of local and national issues. The behaviour of Tupper and Thompson has been noted. As well, W.S. Fielding, the Nova Scotia premier who pledged in 1886 to take the province out of confederation, walked the straight and narrow after 1896 when he entered the Laurier cabinet as minister of finance. Due consideration was given to constituency and Nova Scotia demands, but his reputation was that of nation-builder rather than as representative of Nova Scotia interests.[80] Quebec ministers defended (rather than promoted) the interests of their province, as well as those of their race and religion, when these were under attack or endangered; but they rarely sought to increase their number in cabinet, certainly not with any vigour. They were usually more concerned with local matters – Montreal in the case of J.A. Chapleau, who had entered the cabinet in 1882, Quebec City in the case of Langevin – and they feuded frequently with each other. Chapleau questioned only the quality, not the number of the portfolios assigned to French Canadians.[81] Sifton is perhaps the figure who came closest to being a regional overlord and an advocate of specifically western interests. But even here his role is generally seen in the broader context of national economic development, the opening up of the west harmonizing with the expansion of Canadian industry both in central Canada and in the maritimes.

The arrival of regional ministers with broad bases of support in, and explicitly promoting the interests of, whole regions extending beyond specific provinces, and having the prime minister depend upon them both for advice and for electoral support, did not come until at least a decade later. In the interval there was a period when the capacity of regional ministers to influence government policy was questioned – in fact, in the case of Quebec ministers, almost eliminated.

CHAPTER 3

From Borden to King: The Decline and Rise of Regional Ministers

In a number of ways Robert Borden's victory in the election of 1911 marked a break with the past. The subsequent decade saw, under the pressures of the Great War, significant reforms of the civil service, a major rift in the Liberal party of Laurier, and the failure of both cabinet and the prime minister to bridge French-English differences. The regional minister system was turned into shambles, effectively destroyed by the creation of the Unionist government in 1916. The Conservative party was almost destroyed as well. By 1921 the Conservatives were in third place in the Commons, displaced by the Liberals and a new third party movement, the Progressives, which had its primary roots in western Canada. The Liberals fell under the leadership of a slightly rotund, humourless individual with specialist training in industrial relations, William Lyon Mackenzie King. He in turn ushered in an era which eventually saw the regional minister system reach its apotheosis.

Borden began well intentioned enough. In 1907, in keeping with reform sentiments that were wending their way northward from the United States, he had gone publicly on record as opposing patronage, promising to curtail its abuses if elected. At the same time, in keeping with past practices, Borden realized the need to build alliances with Conservative provincial premiers. Electoral failure in 1904 had effectively demonstrated the limitations of running campaigns solely on the basis of an ill-organized national Conservative association. Conservative premiers Whitney (Ontario), Roblin (Manitoba), and McBride (British Columbia) obliged, lending Borden skilled personnel to create organizations that would serve both federally and provincially. Already in 1900, acting on the basis of past tradition, Borden had moved quickly to appoint a French-Canadian lieutenant; too quickly, as it transpired, for his chosen lieutenant, Frederick Monk, spent most of his time 'brooding over imagined conspiracies' and, just before the 1904 election, abruptly resigned his post.[1] Borden was sufficiently soured by the experience that he vowed never again to formally designate a Quebec lieutenant. Monk, however, did regain the position in 1909 and joined the cabinet in 1911.[2]

In winning the 1911 election, Borden was helped both by the reciprocity issue and by his colleagues in the four Conservative-run provincial governments.[3] Borden, once more following tradition, turned to the four premiers and invited them to join the cabinet, acting in part out of appreciation but also because he needed their skills and authority in cabinet. The candidates available from among elected Conservatives were, to Borden's mind, far from adequate. Unfortunately, unlike 1896 when Laurier had been able to entice Mowat and Fielding to Ottawa, only one of the four premiers accepted Borden's invitation, John D. Hazen from New Brunswick, considered the weakest of the lot.[4] Two of the others, Roblin and Whitney, nominated instead individuals from their own cabinets: Robert Rogers from Manitoba, political fixer and party strategist who became minister of the interior; and Frank Cochrane, the vigorous minister of lands, forests and mines of Ontario and skilled party organizer who was named minister of railways. These two appointments were unfortunate. While the two men were both specialists in machine politics, this was all they knew. Rogers in particular revelled in, and was later reviled for, his love of patronage. The premiers themselves were not only absent from the government in Ottawa, but remained in their provincial capitals to make life difficult for Borden. Whitney, for example, wrote to Borden that he expected the latter's firm support in Ontario's dispute with Manitoba over boundaries.[5] The practice of appointing strong provincial figures to bring the provinces into the centre was notable by its absence in the Borden cabinet of 1911.

The appointment of French Canadians to cabinet was handled with more finesse, or at least done as well as possible under difficult circumstances.[6] Borden had played a wily, albeit dangerous, game in developing links with the Nationalistes under Henri Bourassa. The majority of Conservatives elected in Quebec owed their success to their affiliation with them, and by this stage Monk had also gravitated to the Nationalistes. Borden felt bound to invite both him and Bourassa into the cabinet. Monk accepted while Bourassa declined, but the latter did suggest the names of other Nationalistes. Two of them, L.P. Pelletier and W.B. Nantel, were appointed postmaster general and minister of inland revenue respectively. In doing so, Borden deliberately passed over an older generation of Quebec Conservatives from the *Bleu* era. The crisis over the Naval Bill, which soon followed, led to the condemnation of the government by Bourassa and, in 1912, to the resignation of Monk. Pelletier and Nantel remained in place until 1914, when they retired to restful sinecures in the judiciary and the Railways Commission respectively. Five more French Canadians were recruited to cabinet, this time mainly traditional *Bleus*, but all had either resigned by, or were defeated in, the election of 1917. Conscription and the creation of the Unionist government in 1916 essentially put paid to any notion of the cabinet as a regionally and ethnically representative body.

The specific events that undermined the overall credibility of the government were the scandals arising out of patronage practices. The single most disastrous appointment Borden had made was that of Sam Hughes. Descriptions of this strong-willed, rambunctious individual are staple items in accounts dealing with this period of Canadian history.[7] The mistake was not only to have appointed Hughes to the cabinet but to have made him minister of militia and defence, a position rivalling that of postmaster general and minister of public works for patronage opportunities.[8] In this respect, with the outbreak of the Great War the Department of Militia came into its own as the primary agency for purchasing war matériel. With the help of Rogers, nicknamed 'Minister of Elections,' Hughes ran the department to the advantage of Conservative cronies and ne'er-do-wells who profited enormously from open-ended contracts for everything from footwear to rifles. It was when the footwear began to leak and the rifles to misfire that the troubles for Hughes, and for the Borden government, began in earnest. 'Of patronage much had always been forgiven and forgotten; in war, nothing was forgiven and everything was remembered.'[9] By 1916, with the scandals growing and the war bogged down in the muddy plains of western Europe, public opinion as well as Borden himself realized that the mobilization effort could not continue on the same basis. Certainly in English Canada sentiment favoured conscription. As well, patronage as a whole, and not just relating to the Department of Militia and Defence, came to be identified with inefficiency.[10] Like nothing else, the episodes arising out of Hughes's administration of his department steeled Borden's innate revulsion of patronage practices. His experience gave rise to two initiatives: the formation of a Unionist government (and shortly thereafter the calling of a general election in 1917), and significant reform of the civil service through the Civil Service Act of 1918.

Under this act most of the civil service, and specifically the outside service, was placed under the jurisdiction of the Civil Service Commission (CSC). Temporary employment was curtailed, the right of departments to recommend appointments was eliminated, and the certification of all personnel became the sole prerogative of the CSC. Several of the provisions in the new act had, in fact, been given effect earlier by orders-in-council under the authority of the War Measures Act. It was the product of unusual circumstances, which allowed died-in-the-wool reformers free rein. As a result, the emphasis was heavily on control mechanisms, providing little scope for freedom to either bureaucrats or politicians. Its chief feature was the definition and implementation of the merit principle: special preferences were to be accorded only to veterans, local residents, and those already holding government jobs. Language skills were not considered meritable qualities, though candidates did have the option of taking the examinations in either French or English.[11]

The act of 1918 played a major role in altering the nature of patronage and in sharply reducing the number of French Canadians in the civil service. The Unionist government of 1916 did not, however, survive long enough to see the full-scale impact of the act. Initially it appeared that the Liberals would suffer the graver consequences from the creation of the Unionist government. The party had been rent into two halves: the Laurier Liberals who, under the former prime minister, refused either to endorse conscription or to join with Borden's Conservatives in forming an all-party government; and the Liberal-Unionists, led primarily by Fielding, who accepted both. The latter, however, had no support in Quebec (the same was true of the Conservatives) and furthermore ran into difficulties in western Canada. There, many of the settlers and their offspring, large numbers of them of East European origin, suffered the inequities of internment and loss of, or restrictions on, their rights of citizenship. Conscription also directly affected the well-being of farmers who depended on their sons for help, particularly at harvest time.[12] While the vast majority of MPs and voters in the west supported conscription and coalition, underneath there was suspicion of both parties – indeed of party government per se – particularly within the various farm organizations; and these suspicions were in turn based on a sense of unfair exploitation by eastern interests.

In the post-war period these non-party sentiments would explode electorally at both the federal and provincial level. For the remainder of the war Borden was able to maintain an awkward coalition of provinces (excepting Quebec) and interest groups. By 1919, however, the

Unionist government was visibly and quickly disintegrating as its more prominent members, such as T.A. Crerar, a Manitoba agricultural reformer and minister of agriculture in the cabinet, resigned. Borden himself resigned as prime minister in 1920, and with his leaving the Unionist party, such as it existed, disappeared, leaving Arthur Meighen to lead a rump of Ontario-based Conservatives into the election of 1921. By 1920 there were three leaders facing the electorate: Meighen, the young Montreal lawyer, headed the Conservatives; T.A. Crerar, led ten former Unionist MPs who titled themselves the National Progressive Party, supported by a number of the provincially based agrarian movements such as the United Farmers of Ontario; and Mackenzie King headed the Liberal party, being one of only two Ontario Liberal MPs who had remained loyal to Laurier, a fact which stood him in good stead in gaining the support of Quebec Liberals at the leadership convention in 1919.

The Canada of 1921 was vastly different from Canada in 1896 or even 1911. The war had expanded considerably the industrial base of the country.[13] In western Canada sizeable cities now stood where previously none existed. For example, in 1901 Saskatoon was a small settlement of 113 souls; by 1921 it had become a city of over 25,000. Winnipeg over the same period had grown more than fourfold, becoming a major metropolitan centre of 176,000 people, the Chicago of Canada.[14] It was also where the vast influx of newcomers had arrived and growth in the industrial labour force had taken place. Unorganized and unsocialized by the kind of political machine so typical of American cities, the arrival of new immigrants helped fuel class-based tensions, culminating in the Winnipeg strike of 1919.[15]

Agriculture, suffering from the serious depletion of manpower as young men were drawn to the cities, had at the same time become more mechanized, more export-oriented, and was conducted on a much larger scale. This was particularly true in western Canada. Many of the traditional techniques of political organization were no longer viable. In the west patronage and corruption came to be identified with eastern establishment interests and linked to issues such as the tariff. Demands for less expensive farm machinery, better facilities for grain handling, and the like were not easily deflected by the distribution of small-scale patronage to selected individuals. In all three prairie provinces, power had shifted to farmers' organizations such as the Saskatchewan and Manitoba Grain Growers' Associations and the United Farmers of Alberta. Both were organized on a province-wide basis and enjoyed strong interprovincial links. The state had also extended its reach into economic life, though more by happenstance than design. The bankruptcy of the Canadian Northern and Grand Trunk railways, among others, led the Borden government to run them as public undertakings in the form of a crown agency, which became the Canadian National Railways Corporation. At the provincial level, state enterprises and government regulatory activities were becoming increasingly important. By 1920 both Ontario and Manitoba had created government-owned electrical utilities, primarily at the urging of manufacturers.[16]

In the results of the 1921 election one thing was clear: the traditional two-party system was on weak ground, and it was in the prairies that the ground was weakest. The non-party tradition there had become an established fact. For the first time there was no majority government: of the 235 seats in the House the Liberals had 117, the Progressives 64, and the Conservatives 50. In addition there were three Labour members and one independent. Of the forty-three prairie seats, none went to the Conservatives, only three to the Liberals, and thirty-seven to the Progressives. Conservative strength was in Ontario (thirty-seven versus twenty-four and twenty-one for the Progressives and Liberals respectively) while the Liberals took all sixty-five seats in Quebec. The Liberals also did well in the maritimes, taking twenty-five of thirty-one seats. More so than ever before, the elected Commons was based on regional differences, and this sectionalism was closely tied to differences in economic interests: protectionism in industrialized central Canada, and anti-tariff sentiment among agrarians everywhere but particularly in the west.[17]

Constructing the King Cabinets

It was amidst this wreckage of the traditional two-party system that Mackenzie King set about constructing his cabinet. Well before the election King had approached leaders of the Progressive movement with the view to developing some kind of coalition. King's propositions were rejected by Crerar and his colleagues; but after the election King remained convinced of the need to bring the Progressive movement into the Liberal fold, and invited Progressives to join the cabinet. This was a tricky manoeuvre, for neither Ontario nor Quebec Liberals had much sympathy for the Progressives – the Ontario Liberals because they had been bested by them in the provincial election of 1919, the Quebec Liberals both because of the Unionist Liberal taint of many Progressives and because the Progressive anti-tariff stance ran counter to Quebec Liberal protectionism, primarily in the Montreal area.

King's fine sense for strategy, however, detected possibilities in the divisions within the sixty-five member Quebec contingent. Dating from the time of Langevin and Chapleau in the Macdonald period, there were still tensions between the group centred around Quebec City and the one based in Montreal. The latter had connections with manufacturing, financial, and railway interests, at least indirectly; hence their protectionist leanings. The Quebec City group was based more on traditional farming and professional interests. While not avowedly anti-tariff, they were at least flexible; there were no direct economic interests at stake. It was in King's juggling of this constellation of geographically based interests that the acknowledged leader of the Quebec City group, Ernest Lapointe, an unassuming lawyer of rural background, came to the fore. He superseded Lomer Gouin, a former Quebec premier and up to that point the individual considered preeminent among French-Canadian leaders. Lapointe was the first candidate summoned to Ottawa. The second call went out to Crerar. With Lapointe King reviewed his choices for the different portfolios. By and large Lapointe concurred with King's proposed cabinet and particularly on the point of including Crerar. In keeping with past practice, King had in mind three French-Canadian ministers. Lapointe pressed for four members plus the solicitor general. King readily acquiesced. Most important of all, they were of one mind on the need to have strong representation from both Quebec and the west and on the importance of a representative cabinet generally in rebuilding the Liberal party.

In the end Crerar and the Progressives chose to remain outside the cabinet; and Lapointe was persuaded to relinquish his claim to the justice portfolio to Gouin in order to satisfy strong pressures from the Montreal area. The size of the French-Canadian contingent was, however, increased to five (plus one English Canadian from Quebec). Within little more than two years, Lapointe had become minister of justice, taking over from the retiring Gouin not only the portfolio but also the position at the cabinet table directly on King's left. From this point on Lapointe was confirmed as King's closest confidant and adviser, both on Quebec and Canada as a whole.

King remained highly sensitive to the need to broaden the base of his cabinet and the Liberal party, and to do so primarily by re-establishing a presence in the west. In 1925 he persuaded the Liberal premier of Saskatchewan, Charles A. Dunning (the only prairie province incidentally where the Liberal party was in power), to join the cabinet as minister of finance. In 1926 Robert Forke, leader of the Progressive members of Parliament, had been enticed into the cabinet as minister of immigration and colonization, though he proved to be an ineffectual administrator. King continued to woo Crerar, who finally agreed in 1929 to become minister of railways and canals. The area which remained relatively neglected was the maritimes, despite obvious signs of economic and political discontent in the form of the Maritime Rights Movement and weak support for the party in the 1925 and 1926 elections.[18] For King, however, Quebec and the west were the key to Liberal survival and long-term success. In order to assure it he was willing to give considerable leeway to, and depend for advice on, the principal political lieutenants from those regions: Lapointe from Quebec, Dunning and later Crerar from the west.

Providence in the form of the King-Byng constitutional crisis had helped King to a bare majority in 1926; and providence in the form of the precipitous decline in economic fortunes after 1929 helped him to defeat in 1930, allowing the Conservatives under R.B. Bennett to bear the brunt of the ravages of the depression in the following half-decade. The Liberal defeat in 1930 was due, aside from the decline in the economy and the overall appeal of protectionist sentiment, to increased Conservative support in Manitoba and Quebec.[19] Bennett, in constructing his cabinet, paid due regard to regional considerations. He did not, however, designate a Quebec lieutenant; at the swearing-in ceremony he was unable even to recall the name of Alfred Duranleau, one of the two French Canadians in his cabinet.[20] But then Bennett appeared to have little use for lieutenants of any kind. He held few cabinet meetings, took little advice, and depended on his own judgment on all issues large and small. Defections from Bennett's cabinet were but a prelude to general defeat in 1935.

For King, victory in 1935 allowed him the opportunity to construct a cabinet that was truly representative of the major regions of the country, and to bring into the fold those individuals, and the interests they represented, who had eluded him earlier. The result, which lasted well into the post-war period, can be considered the high point of the regional minister system. Lapointe was solidly entrenched as *chef* of the Quebec contingent, a position from which he exercised considerable influence over Quebec representation in cabinet, though King still retained ultimate authority over appointments. J.L. Ilsley from Nova Scotia became minister of national revenue, to be followed five years later by the Nova Scotia premier, Angus L. Macdonald, who became minister of national defence for naval services. Crerar, representing Manitoba, became minister of the interior. The newly elected businessman-engineer from northwestern Ontario, C.D. Howe, accepted the portfolio of railways and canals, which now embraced responsibility for marine affairs.

The 1935 cabinet also included the individual whose name, more than any other, has come to be associated with the term regional minister, James (Jimmy) G. Gardiner. Both the manner of his recruitment and his subsequent career are illustrative of, indeed exemplify, the nature of regional representation in the King cabinet. As incumbent Liberal premier of Saskatchewan, he was for King someone who had to be recruited at almost any cost. Gardiner, taking over as premier from Dunning in 1925, had in place one of the most potent provincial political machines in the country and was recognized for his superb organizing abilities. King's hold on his own seat in Prince Albert, Saskatchewan (1926 to 1945), to which he moved after his personal defeat in Ontario in 1925, would not have been possible without Gardiner's help.[21] The Saskatchewan Liberals had been defeated in 1929, thus enjoying the benefit of being in opposition during the worst of the depression, and easily swept the Conservatives from office in 1934, putting Gardiner in a good position to move to Ottawa.

Gardiner in turn harboured strong ambitions. He had designs not only on a major cabinet position but, at times, thought of himself as a potential prime minister.[22] During the 1935 cabinet formation Gardiner proved a hard bargainer. King had already promised him a position before the election. What Gardiner wanted, however, was not only a major financial portfolio but a guarantee that Saskatchewan would be his sole preserve. The problem here was his rivalry with the former premier of the province, Dunning, whom King wanted back in cabinet as minister of finance. On this point, according to King, 'Both Lapointe and I assured Gardiner that he would have the say, and we would back his issues on western matters; that we would both let Dunning fully understand this.' Part of this understanding was that Dunning would 'come in by an eastern door,' for all intents and purposes as the English-speaking minister from Montreal.[23] The other component was Gardiner's portfolio. King wanted him in Agriculture, a department which in those days was not highly regarded. Gardiner countered with a proposal to transfer the Board of Grain Commissioners to Agriculture. The final compromise saw part of the Wheat Board, created by the Bennett government, placed under the supervision of a cabinet committee to be chaired by Gardiner.[24]

Gardiner held the Agriculture portfolio for twenty-two years, and used it to establish himself both in the west and in Ottawa. He was, first and foremost, a forceful proponent of western interests at the cabinet table. Yet there was much more to his role than this. He succeeded in transforming regional concerns into national concerns. Through his efforts in cabinet and the effective use of his own department, the well-being of all farmers (not just western farmers) was elevated to the status of a national goal.[25] Furthermore, his pursuit of regional and agrarian goals did not in any sense conflict with his own deeply felt partisan identity as a Liberal. For him modern-day Liberalism, with its respect for minority rights and emphasis on national conciliation, fitted well with his loyalty to both region and country. Finally, he had a strong belief in the viability of the parliamentary form of government. In particular his distrust of bureaucrats and various interests outside the realm of agriculture led him to see the cabinet as the best single forum for waging his arguments, for cajoling his colleagues into supporting his policies, and ultimately for reconciling opposing views. If his views were adopted by cabinet, he knew he could count on complete support. In turn, he would defend totally those decisions of cabinet to which he might originally have been opposed. It was this energizing quality of cabinet which led him to concentrate most of his efforts there, bringing with him letters, petitions, and other forms of ammunition and evidence.[26]

Within this system, King played the role of conciliator. At times he found the unflagging energies of Gardiner and his recitations of agricultural facts tiresome. But he recognized Gardiner's exceptional organizational skills and his loyalty to the national party. In the same way, he deeply appreciated and trusted Lapointe, not only for his advice on Quebec but also for his ability to see things in national terms. In fact, to the extent that he thought Lapointe had faults, they related to what he felt was Lapointe's inability to be sufficiently tough on some of his less competent Quebec colleagues. These misgivings notwithstanding, one of King's operating rules was to defer to his ministers on issues that were essentially of a regional or local nature, even if they sometimes had national or even international import. For example, King concurred with the refusal of the director of the Immigration Branch to permit even limited immigration of Jewish refugees during the war, largely because of the opposition expressed in cabinet by Lapointe and despite the willingness of the minister in charge of the branch, Crerar, to permit the entry of Jews.[27] King also refrained from appointing Max Factor, a Toronto Jewish MP, to cabinet for much the same reason. The internment of Japanese Canadians and later the deportation of several of them was a policy vigorously, and successfully, pursued in cabinet and the House by the British Columbia minister, Ian Mackenzie, who at one point argued that denying British Columbia 'the right to adequate internal security ... would be striking a blow against Confederation.'[28] Long after American authorities had permitted the return of Japanese Americans to their west coast in 1944, Japanese Canadians were still being forcibly resettled in areas east of Alberta, or repatriated or deported to Japan. Not until 1949 were the relevant order-in-council regulations, authorized under the War Measures Act, rescinded.[29] To some extent these internment and immigration policies may have coincided with King's own inclinations, but only to a degree. It is known, for example, that he was keen to have Factor in the cabinet, and by 1946 he had concluded that continued restrictions of the liberties of Japanese Canadians was a mistake.[30] He deferred, however, to the arguments of the ministers and the regional opinions that these men represented, in good part because he accepted the notion that regional ministers had a right to make claims on behalf of their provinces.

'Regional Barons' and the Limitations of Regional Representation

It was the influence of men such as Lapointe and Gardiner that led many contemporary scholars to recall King's sixteenth ministry (October 1935 to November 1948) as the heyday of cabinets, composed 'of regional notables with independent bases of their own who powerfully assert the needs of the provinces at the highest political level.'[31] In examining this untroubled period, and in using it as a standard with which to assess the performance of subsequent cabinets, it is important both to emphasize some of the salient features and to dispel some myths.

First, cabinet size, and the number of provinces represented, were limited. In 1935 King was determined to streamline the cabinet by collapsing a number of the portfolios, thereby reducing its size from eighteen to fourteen. For King two things were important: representation from Quebec and the west; and individuals who were capable of handling the more difficult portfolios. The maritimes do not appear to have figured prominently in King's deliberations. Nova Scotia received a representative because in J.L. Ilsley King found a capable successor to J.L. Ralston, the respected finance minister from 1926 to 1930. Ilsley in a sense continued a tradition established earlier by men such as Tupper, Thompson, and Fielding: upon taking federal office they became known for their strong national orientation and for their proclivity to downplay their own province's interests in cabinet discussions. These Nova Scotians became known for their probity, good judgment (albeit rather narrowly based), and a willingness to play the role of honest broker, all of which made them ideal candidates for portfolios such as finance.[32] While enjoying the support of their provincial party organizations, as regional representatives they were certainly not in the mould of either Gardiner or Lapointe. Prince Edward Island, which had gone solidly Liberal in 1935, received no cabinet posts, largely because none of the four MPs were up to standard.[33] J.-E. Michaud from New Brunswick received Fisheries, in good part because of his demonstrated organizational talents in local politics. It was also an appointment which risked controversy in that Michaud succeeded another Acadian and, it was felt, the English and Protestant community in that province might have protested this fact; but it was a risk that King was willing to take. In the west Gardiner and Crerar were assiduously courted, but Alberta, which failed to return a single Liberal, was deliberately excluded from the cabinet. 'It is the only way,' King stated, 'to teach that province a lesson.'[34] The genial Mackenzie from British Columbia was reappointed. During the period in opposition he had made an impression as being loyal and proficient though not brilliant. With the onset of the war in 1939 he was demoted from the defence portfolio, where he was thought to be beyond his capabilities. Dunning was recruited, not because of his western background but for his financial acumen and his standing in eastern business circles.

In short, the reputation of the later King cabinet as a body dominated by regional interests rests almost entirely on the shoulders of two key individuals, Gardiner and Lapointe. The other name that should be added to the list is C.D. Howe. Though generally regarded first and foremost as a national figure, by all accounts he assiduously cultivated and promoted the interests of northwestern Ontario, playing a key role, for example, in revitalizing the Algoma Steel mill in Sault Ste Marie and in dominating the federal wing of the Liberal party in Ontario. Because not all provinces were represented, and not all ministers took it upon themselves to act as provincial spokesmen, the influence of Gardiner, Lapointe, and Howe arose in part through default. Gardiner was able to become a regional spokesman, as opposed to simply a provincial one, in good part because there was no cabinet representation from Alberta and the representation from Manitoba was weak, Crerar at that stage being well past his prime. Furthermore, this regional influence, and the results that stemmed from it, frequently were at the expense of other regions. Thus J.L. Ilsley and Angus L. Macdonald (who left the Nova Scotia premiership to join the cabinet for the duration of the war) were disconcerted to discover that wartime contracts for shipbuilding and repair were being directed primarily to Ontario, and that the Dominion Coal and Steel Company (DOSCO) in Cape Breton was being deliberately starved of capital in favour of Algoma Steel, all through the influence of C.D. Howe.[35]

These disparities in regional influence are not unexpected. While region was the most important consideration, it was not all-pervasive or the only consideration. Loyalty, experience, and the intricacies of federal-provincial relations could affect the representation of provincial interests in the cabinet. Particularly with the onset of war, King placed a high priority on finding capable individuals to run difficult and demanding portfolios. To give weight to the west and Quebec was, for King, sufficient. These were the key anchors in his schema for national unity. The maritimes, it should be noted, had since 1917 seen the number of its cabinet representatives reduced from the previous four to sometimes no more than two, largely in order to provide increased representation in the west. As Norman Rogers wrote in 1933: 'It is evident ... that the line of least resistance lay in the Maritime Provinces, the policy of reduction ... being recommended also by the diminution of the parliamentary representation of these provinces with each succeeding redistribution after 1891.'[36] By the same token, despite the imbalance in regional advocacy, links with provincial governments or provincial parties were maintained through the regional ministers, to some extent limiting the possibility of the government being out-flanked by the provincial premiers. Significantly, the three provinces that rejected the recommendations of the Rowell-Sirois Commission report at a special meeting of first ministers on federal-provincial financial relations were also the provinces with which the King government had weak links at the time: Ontario, Alberta, and British Columbia.

In assessing the role of regional ministers under King and their links with party organizations, changes should be noted both in the realm of party finance and with respect to the administrative state. The Civil Service Act of 1918 had, as its intended consequence, the wholesale reallocation of the appointing power from the realm of patronage to an independent board using the instrument of the competitive examination. Almost immediately some exceptions were made, in part in response to complaints from deputy ministers who resented the loss of control over staffing in their departments. But overall, the direct effect of the changes can be seen in the dramatic decline in the participation rate of French Canadians: in 1918 it was estimated that they made up 22 per cent of all federal employees; by 1946 the proportion had dropped to less than 13 per cent.[37] The preference given to veterans, most of whom were English-speaking, accounts for part of the drop. The major cause, however, was likely the emphasis placed on technical qualifications, where French Canadians were at a disadvantage. Previously the 'political appointment' process had allowed this obstacle to be circumvented.

This decline of patronage at the federal level was not, however, matched by a similar decline at the provincial level. Indeed, as the responsibilities of provincial governments increased in the realm of road construction, social services, education, and the like, so did opportunities for patronage.[38] In Quebec the Liberal government under Taschereau lived and breathed patronage.[39] Lapointe, and particularly his junior colleague from Quebec City, C.G. (Chubby) Power, provided the crucial links between the federal and provincial organizations and the conduit along which cash from provincial party coffers flowed to the federal party.[40] Thus during the 1920s the national Liberal party began to depend more on provincial-level party organizations, both for personnel at election time and for cash. This decentralization had already taken place to a large degree under Laurier. It was refined further, and to an extent encouraged, by King's own proclivities. It made the brokerage function he exercised so well all that much more important. To successfully tap the resources of the provincial organizations meant putting a premium on reconciling conflicting provincial or broader regional interests as expressed through the regional ministers. At the same time, the trend towards giving provincial organizations a greater role allowed King to distance himself from the process of patronage distribution and fund-raising, which he found distasteful.

Yet the dependence on provincial organizations disturbed King, and from 1930 on a series of specific events led to the creation of a national party organization and the development of new and separate fund-raising techniques. Both developments to some extent undermined the authority of ministers in the realm of organization and patronage. The first, the creation of the National Liberal Federation (NLF), was largely a response to the defeat of the Liberals in the 1930 election and King's realization that the party was deficient in its electoral machinery, in its fund-raising capabilities, and perhaps overly dependent on provincial associations for help. For example, it was felt that somewhat strained relations between Taschereau and Lapointe had led to a loss of at least twenty seats in Quebec in 1930.[41] Secondly, as the subsequent unfolding of the Beauharnois scandal demonstrated, the party had at best used unwise and amateurish means to obtain campaign funds, at worst quite possibly fallen prey to corruption at the highest level. King himself was personally tainted by the scandal, in his own words putting him and his party into 'the valley of humiliation.'[42] To King's mind, this aspect of party organization had to be put on a more professional basis, a view which led him to recruit Vincent Massey, who in turn recruited Norman Lambert as secretary of the National Liberal Federation in 1932.

The third development, which for King underscored his apprehensions about the role of the provincial Liberal organizations, was the 1934 election in Ontario of a Liberal government under the mischievous Mitchell F. Hepburn. At first glance, the election of a government of the same partisan stripe was providential, a useful adjunct for the forthcoming federal election. But King was profoundly distrustful of Hepburn, seeing him as an unreliable drunkard with potentially embarrasing connections (with mining promoters in the main) and one who, in seeking to exercise his provincial clout at the national level, would have an unhealthy influence on the NLF. King accepted Hepburn's initial offers of help in Ontario by-elections in the form of cash and personnel, but only with considerable reluctance. His suspicions about Hepburn were soon borne out. King began receiving calls and visits from Hepburn's cronies, primarily in relation to demands for changes in mining tax laws. All of King's worst fears were confirmed when Hepburn later launched an all-out battle against the federal government, including court challenges and, by threats against potential helpers of the federal party, undermining the efforts of Lambert in raising money in Ontario.[43]

More so than any other development, King's experiences with Hepburn reinforced his desire to strengthen the financial well-being of the NLF, a task that Lambert performed with considerable skill.[44] Lambert honed and refined the technique of soliciting contractors, government suppliers, and the like for funds *after* they had received government contracts, the implied understanding being that future contracts were contingent on donations. This technique, otherwise known as 'toll-gating' and still used to some extent at the provincial

level, though now illegal, had the benefit of reducing the party's dependence on provincial organizations and also on large corporations.
Toll-gating provided a steady stream of funds from several sources
with only limited obligations. This new role for the national-level organization meant that more power came to be lodged in party headquarters in Ottawa, something that was resented particularly by the
Quebec Liberals. Chubby Power was convinced that Quebec Liberals
could handle party finances very well on their own, and the Quebec
wing never formally participated in the NLF. Quebec's cause for complaint was limited, however, for in 1935 the Liberals there were defeated by Maurice Duplessis and his Union Nationale. Thereafter the
Quebec party became dependent on Ottawa for support. Gardiner,
on the other hand, was an active supporter; indeed, he had his own
connections in eastern financial circles that he was willing to use for
the benefit of the national party. And well he should, because the
Saskatchewan machine, effective as it was in delivering the vote, became heavily dependent on the central party for funds. British Columbia was also deeply indebted to Ottawa for the infusion of funds
to maintain the party organization. The province that was self-sus-
taining, and indeed a net provider, was Ontario, where Lambert and
Howe were able to work their magic despite the contrary efforts of
Hepburn.[45]

The 1935 election for the first time saw the Liberals use radio advertisements developed by the advertising agency of Cockfield, Brown.
The electronic medium was to become much more important later,
but the use of this technique, in combination with the national office
in the form of the NLF and the centralization of fund-raising, marked
the beginnings of a transition. It was a shift in which the dependence
on patronage, party-controlled newspapers, and, of course, strong regional ministers would come to be displaced by an emphasis on party
professionals, polling techniques, and national leaders communicating
directly with electors through the medium of television. During the
thirties, however, these developments appeared to hinder only in a
limited way the activities of Gardiner and Howe. If anything, these
men thrived in this environment.

There were other developments, however, in the realm of administrative practices and departmental organization, which had the potential to limit the endeavours of ministers in servicing their regions.
The cabinet over the years had grown but slowly, and indeed King in
1935 reduced its size to the same level as Macdonald's first cabinet.
The responsibilities, however, had grown. To reduce cabinet size King

had resorted to collapsing a number of portfolios. For example, the portfolio of mines now included responsibility for Indian affairs, immigration and colonization, interior and resources (it became the Department of Mines and Resources in 1936). The principles of hierarchy and scientific management began to penetrate the public service, manifesting themselves in schemes for the classification of personnel. Of particular importance was the fact that the outside service had been brought under effective control. Lines of authority now flowed down to the units and operations of departments in a much more defined fashion.

A related development was the professionalization of the public service at the highest levels. By the late 1920s King had begun recruiting academics from Queen's, McGill, and the University of Toronto as deputy ministers. This group included figures such as O.D. Skelton, who in 1925 became undersecretary for external affairs, Clifford Clark, who became finance deputy in 1932, and W.A. Mackintosh, who worked for the Rowell-Sirois Commission and drafted many of the more important research studies accompanying the report. They in turn recruited promising young graduates such as Lester Pearson, J.J. Deutsch, and R.B. Bryce – men who would make their mark at a later stage. By the late thirties there was a well-established cadre of highly competent individuals staffing key positions.[46]

At the same time, there had been some backtracking on the civil service reforms of 1918 through the so-called Spinney amendments of 1921 and 1922.[47] These exempted certain classes of employees, such as rural postmasters earning below a certain amount, casual labourers, and a range of technical and scientific employees, from the purview of the Civil Service Commission. The 1918 act itself contained the proviso that the commission could decide, 'with the approval of the Governor in Council,' when the act's provisions need not apply.[48] In the 1930s the authority of the commission in staffing matters began to be undermined by the ascendency of the Treasury Board. The Board represented both bureaucratic control and more direct political influence, and tended to benefit both ministers and deputy ministers, particularly if they were able to persuade Treasury Board, as a committee of cabinet, to increase their departmental allocation.

These developments at the administrative level affected the nature of regional representation within the cabinet. First, the ability of individual ministers to influence the operations of departments other than their own was to a degree diminished. The latter part of King's regime saw the advent of what is called the 'departmentalized cabinet.'[49] Ministers and their deputies tended to be in control of their departments. While formidable operations in their own right, these departments could nonetheless be effectively managed by a small group of skilled individuals. In this environment two ministers in particular were able to attain almost complete mastery over their portfolios: Jimmy Gardiner and C.D. Howe. They were able to use their departments to good effect in their regions, using all the resources available and exploiting opportunities for patronage. Thus Gardiner, under the authority of the Prairie Farm Rehabilitation Act, passed by the Bennett government in 1935, created and used the Prairie Farm Rehabilitation Agency in a fashion that recalled the days of Clifford Sifton.[50] Howe used his various portfolios, which over the years included transport, munitions, and reconstruction, in similar fashion. J.L. Ilsley, while highly proficient and regarded as someone who was able to manage effectively his portfolios, was 'rather impatient, or even intolerant, of political and organizational matters.'[51] As for other ministers, it appears many had difficulty providing direction. King wrote in his diary: 'It is perfectly appalling how little many Ministers will exercise authority themselves and how completely they get into the hands of members of the permanent service.'[52]

Those few ministers who had the skills and the gumption, such as Howe and Gardiner, were able to deploy their departments to good effect. But at the same time, these individuals were much less willing to brook the requests or efforts of other ministers, even where specific regional or communal interests were involved. As related in his correspondence, Lapointe was completely frustrated in his efforts to increase the proportion of French Canadians in Howe's Department of Munitions and Supply. Lapointe's poignant missive to Howe – 'you have done such tremendously splendid work in the carrying out of the war effort that it is a tragedy that this virtual exclusion of French-speaking Canada from the activities of your Department may cause a dangerous disruption of [our] unity'[53] – was unavailing. Howe would refer to the difficulties in finding French Canadians 'with the right qualifications'; apparently there were none, for up to November 1940 there was not a single French-speaking official in his department, not even in the field service in Quebec.[54] Lapointe's behaviour in the face of Howe's intransigence nonetheless illustrates the other side to the role of regional ministers – a commitment to ensuring unity even in difficult circumstances. Lapointe refused to resort to ultimate threats. In his disputes with Howe he never called up the full resources of the Quebec caucus and he never threatened to resign if his minimum demands were not met. Up to his death in November 1941, Lapointe did his best to ensure the loyalty of the Quebec representatives in cabinet and the House to the King government.

Howe's stubbornness was not restricted to limiting French-Canadian representation in the bureaucracy. Ministers from the maritimes such as Ilsley, Macdonald, and Ralston also expressed considerable frustration with Howe, in this instance relating to his disinterest in the well-being of the maritimes. For example, Macdonald, as minister of national defence for naval services, found his efforts in promoting endeavours such as constructing graving docks in Halifax harbour, or reopening the idle ship's plate mill in Sydney, continually stymied by Howe. All told, the maritimes had four representatives in cabinet during the war, three of whom (Macdonald, Ilsley, and Ralston) were on the all-powerful nine-member War Committee of cabinet, the committee that for all intents and purposes had displaced the full cabinet for most important decisions. Yet even here they were unable to make much headway in protecting the interests of the maritimes. According to E.R. Forbes, 'That they were unable to do so may be explained in part ... by the extraordinary power of the Department of Munitions and Supply under the leadership of C.D. Howe.'[55] In addition, in almost all such disputes involving Howe and the maritime ministers, King invariably backed his minister of munitions. Despite, or very likely because of, strong protests from the three Liberal maritime premiers as well as the press, ministers such as Macdonald publicly defended the actions of the government in its allocation of wartime production. Much like Lapointe, the maritime ministers played out their role as loyal statesmen and did their best to reconcile their local populations and interest groups to the fate that the exigencies of wartime had apparently dealt to the region.[56]

In summary, in recalling the glory days of the King cabinet it is useful to keep in mind the constraints as well as the benefits of regional representation. While practically all ministers played the role of national conciliators, helping the cause of national unity, only three ministers were able to maximize benefits for their regions. Gardiner, to be sure, represented a region that spanned at least three provinces; but other regions, the maritimes for example, did much less well. In the case of Quebec, the primary legacy of Lapointe's efforts was some headway in obtaining better treatment of the French language in the civil service, protection of some of Quebec's key industries during wartime, and, ultimately, King's achievement in staving off for as long as possible the introduction of conscription. The region that did best,

Ontario, is the one usually not thought of in regional terms. Under Howe's direction, the wartime mobilization effort put Ontario, including Howe's own northwestern corner of the province, in the best possible position to benefit from the post-war creation of a more centralized and integrated North American market for manufactured goods.

CHAPTER 4

From the Departmentalized to the Institutionalized Cabinet

Ministerialism under 'Uncle Louis'

The caveats in the previous chapter notwithstanding, it is generally agreed that the regional minister system under King did reach a pinnacle of sorts, and that after his departure in 1948 it went into decline. From Mackenzie King, Louis St Laurent, the new prime minister, inherited a cabinet that was well tested by wartime experience, containing stalwarts such as Gardiner, Howe, and Brooke Claxton, and which also contained a good balance of the three Rs. The year 1948, however, also represented an altogether different era, and St Laurent himself had his own distinct criteria for what constituted appropriate ministerial timber. The post-war era saw the full flowering of the departmentalized cabinet, operating in an environment in which concerns for economic well-being and development were visualized in national terms under the direction of a prime minister who, compared to his predecessor, was somewhat less concerned with partisan interests and the spoils of power. The civil service had grown threefold since 1940, largely through the impetus of the war, but even after 1945 it continued to expand. The Ottawa mandarinate of senior-level civil servants truly came into its own.

Given the increasing size and complexity of the burgeoning administrative state, deputy ministers and other senior officials such as Jack Pickersgill, A.F.W. Plumptre, Norman Robertson, Robert Bryce, Louis Rasminsky, Mitchell Sharp, and J.J. Deutsch came to occupy unique positions of power. They were not technical specialists but generalists in the best sense of the word, enjoying broad understanding of the world and a capacity to master difficult issues in several areas. Recruited through competitive examinations, they were schooled and promoted under the tutelage of the first generation of mandarins –

Skelton, Clark, and Mackintosh. They all enjoyed intimate knowledge of the issues and the workings of departments.[1] As a consequence, it was to their deputy ministers rather than their cabinet colleagues that many ministers turned for advice and to whom they entrusted their problems. Some, such as Howe, were much less cowed by their deputies but still came to value their ideas and competence. Overall, the special relationships that prevailed between ministers and their deputies reinforced the departmentalized nature of the cabinet throughout this period. Furthermore, the collective direction and co-ordination required of a government operating in a complex environment tended to be provided less through cabinet collegiality and discussion and more through the links that existed among the mandarins themselves. Specific arrangements were made daily and informally by this closely linked group over lunch in the cafeteria of the Chateau Laurier Hotel.[2]

'The Ottawa Men,' as Jack Granatstein has called them, possessed one further characteristic: they tended to be strongly national and international in outlook. For them Ottawa and the world were their main foci. Though many came from modest backgrounds, there is little evidence that they had much in the way of direct contact with ordinary people and their problems, especially in the peripheries, or that those problems weighed heavily in their deliberations. To their minds, problems relating to regional disparities, for example, were best treated in the context of broad economic management strategies, direct transfers to individuals in the form of the newly instituted mothers' allowance, and through tax-sharing and fiscal transfer arrangements with the provinces.

As was the case in most western nations, the motif underpinning the policies of post-war Liberal governments was Keynesianism. But more so than in other countries, the tenets of this economic philosophy had a much more pronounced effect in Canada.[3] Mandarins such as Mackintosh, Clark, Bryce, and Plumptre fully understood Keynes's ideas – indeed, Bryce and Plumptre had studied under Keynes at Cambridge in the thirties – and in light of wartime experiences they reversed their earlier opposition to the Keynesian doctrines on countercyclical fiscal measures and full employment. Given their close ties and the positions they occupied, the adoption of a Keynesian framework had an immediate effect. The organizational consequence was to concentrate many of the levers of power directly in the Department of Finance, since it was this department, along with the Bank of Canada, that had primary responsibility for deploying the new techniques of macro-economic management. The other departments that became crucial, all three of which were held by C.D. Howe between 1948 and 1956, were the departments of Reconstruction and Supply, Defence Production (the exigencies of the Second World War now being replaced by the exigencies of the Korean War), and Trade and Commerce. These, along with Finance, became the leading departments.

As an indicator of the change in orientation on the part of the new prime minister and Ottawa generally, St Laurent arranged for the promotion of Lester Pearson from the civil service to the cabinet as minister of external affairs. Pearson had neither ties with nor partisan inclinations towards the Liberal party but did have the credentials as Canada's foremost diplomat. Another top-level civil servant, Jack Pickersgill, joined the cabinet in 1953. In urging French Canadians to take on a broader, national outlook, St Laurent placed them in non-traditional portfolios. Hugues Lapointe (son of Ernest) was made minister of veterans' affairs, Jean Lesage minister of northern affairs and national resources. In turn, portfolios generally regarded as the preserve of French Canadians such as justice and public works were given to English Canadians.[4]

The concern with national economic management and the preoccupation with questions of national identity, as exemplified by the 1953 Royal Commission on the Arts and Letters in Canada, served to push issues of a regional character into the background. When a minister such as the former premier of Manitoba, Stuart Garson, did press issues, such as improved financial support for the poorer provinces, he did so by calling for 'greater "centralization" in fiscal matters,'[5] a tack which at the time meant greater control by the Department of Finance.

The most telling development was the waning of Gardiner's influence. Increasingly his demands for support for agriculture and for the west struck a discordant note within cabinet. And ultimately he failed to realize his single most important project, the building of the South Saskatchewan Dam, a project, Gardiner felt, that would have been undertaken 'if King had survived three years longer.'[6] Gardiner's failure to have his way in constructing the dam 'signalled,' according to David Smith, 'a readjustment in the balance of region and nation that had last been deliberately set in the thirties.'[7] Yet regional ministerial influence was not absent. C.D. Howe, best known as 'minister of everything,' was also St Laurent's de facto English-Canadian lieutenant and came to exercise a predominant influence in vetting new cabinet appointments and in steering protégés into particular portfolios. In Ontario, Howe had complete authority over all party matters, other

Ontario ministers having at best only local influence. He also functioned as an 'auxiliary regional minister' for western Canada, and there is every indication that he continued to promote the particular interests of northwestern Ontario.[8] Being in charge of what was by far the largest 'expenditure' department, Trade and Commerce, allowed him ample leeway to direct projects to specific locations.

St Laurent continued the tradition of relying on the senior minister from each province for advice on cabinet appointments and patronage questions. In turn these ministers were expected to help maintain the party machinery and to keep abreast of political developments in their province. Robert Winters was responsible for Nova Scotia. Representing the south shore constituency of Lunenberg, Winters boasted in the 1953 election campaign that he was responsible for new provisions under the Unemployment Insurance Act, making special benefits available to fishermen in recognition of the seasonal nature of the industry.[9] In British Columbia the election of the provincial Social Credit government in 1952 was considered an embarrassment to the federal government. Blame for it fell in part on Ralph Mayhew, minister of fisheries, who was henceforth dropped from the cabinet to be replaced by Jimmy Sinclair, considered to be a much better organizer.[10]

Thus a minister's performance in his regional capacity could easily affect his overall standing. The converse was also true, as illustrated by the case of Stuart Garson, former Manitoba premier. His alleged mishandling of the justice portfolio in 1948, which involved his failure to table in the House the Combine Commissioners' report in timely fashion, led to an unfortunate denouement. Bothwell and Kilbourn write: 'Garson was, government supporters concluded, tragically out of his depth in the national arena. Even his performance as a prairie minister suffered; he often seemed to be overshadowed by the powerful ministers who represented the regions on either side of Manitoba – Gardiner in Saskatchewan and Howe in northwestern Ontario. Now more than ever the western Liberals would have to depend on Howe's leadership.'[11]

The St Laurent cabinet, in being dominated by only a few individuals and regions, was thus far from a cartel of provincial premiers. In addition, the federal government faced non-Liberal governments in many of the provinces: Quebec for example, which was firmly in the grip of Maurice Duplessis, and Saskatchewan, which had been under CCF rule since 1944. There were still links, however. In an interesting combination of the old and the new, Jack Pickersgill, the ex-mandarin, took a seat in Newfoundland at the urging of the Liberal premier of that province, Joey Smallwood, who thought that Pickersgill would be a useful pipeline into Ottawa. Pickersgill in turn, quite unlike Pearson, demonstrated a flair for political organization that belied his bureaucratic background.[12] The other links between the federal government and the provinces that were at least as important, if not more so, were those provided by civil servants. Working under the rubric of 'co-operative federalism,'[13] the implementation of various cost-shared programs in education or the construction of the Trans-Canada highway, for example, also led to the sharing of expertise and professional values. In the event, with the exception of Quebec, which remained aloof from the co-operative process and engaged the federal government only in order to argue over constitutional issues, major rifts with the provinces were still on the horizon.

Despite these links, and despite the continuation of the regional minister role in cabinet, there were problems. The dominance and political control that ministers thought they had in their regions was taken too much for granted. By the early fifties the Liberal party was essentially a cadre party in which the parliamentary wing dominated the extra-parliamentary wing, using it primarily for electoral purposes.[14] Patronage still played a role, but not nearly to the same extent as in the heyday of Macdonald and Laurier. There was little in place at the local level that gave presence to the party or that could cater to local needs and sentiments. Certainly the regional activities of ministers were not terribly visible. Howe was known primarily for his presence on the national stage, and his considerable prominence in the St Laurent cabinet (sometimes referred to as the St Laurent–Howe government), in combination with his proclivity for using hard-nosed means to get what he wanted, contributed to the downfall of both Howe and the Liberal government. Despite his ostensible role in placating prairie farmers, Howe proved remarkably insensitive on such issues as advance payments for wheat intended for export.[15] This point was not lost on the new leader of the opposition, John Diefenbaker, who during the 1957 election campaign promised prompt help for western farmers and agriculture generally.

With the easy movement of some senior civil servants into the ranks of the Liberal party, the close, at times almost personal, links between ministers and their deputies, and Howe's peremptory behaviour within and outside the House, the actions of the St Laurent cabinet came to be perceived as increasingly high-handed. This 'ministerialism' provided a basis for Diefenbaker's call for a change, a cry which struck a responsive chord in the electorate and which helped the Conservatives to a narrow victory in the 1957 election, a victory which was then consolidated in the Diefenbaker landslide of 1958. Liberal defeats in 1957 and 1958 marked the end of an era both for party politics and for the nature of regional representation in cabinet. It did not mean the end of regional ministers but it did foreshadow a more circumscribed role for them. It also meant the beginning of a new era, one where regional ministers had to find different ways to respond to the demands of local and regional constituents and alternative means of dealing with a rapidly evolving administrative apparatus.

Diefenbaker and 'Pan-Canadianism'

Mackenzie King, and to a lesser extent St Laurent, had exercised leadership primarily by serving the ends of accommodation. They presided over a system in which the major interests, largely though not exclusively regionally based, were reconciled under the guidance of the prime minister. Electoral success was based as much on the ability of regional ministers to deliver the vote as on the aura of competence projected by King and the avuncular St Laurent. For students of the Canadian party system, John Diefenbaker's elevation to the prime ministership in 1957 marked a sharp transition to a new kind of politics, one in which image and the oratorical skills of national leaders became more important and in which regional concerns and linguistic divisions were subsumed under a rubric of slogans emphasizing 'pan-Canadian' themes.[16] Through the new medium of television, the connection between individual voters and the party leader was now more immediate and direct. Regional chieftains were being bypassed. Eleven years later, Pierre Elliott Trudeau, although different in many ways from Diefenbaker, was also master of the new medium and proponent of pan-Canadian motifs, using them to circumvent traditional elements within the Liberal party.

The 1957 election marked, as well, a more gradual but equally significant transition in the nature of the Canadian administrative state – a transition that had been under way since the mid-fifties, and one that was to culminate in the 1970s with a phalanx of central agencies set up to provide information to ministers with the intent of counterbalancing the influence of line departments. The traditional mandarinate was losing its grip. There was increasing demand for more specifically technical skills, and the ever-increasing size of the Ottawa bureaucracy meant that the cohesion so characteristic of the earlier mandarinate was becoming more difficult to maintain. Most important, the basis of 'ministerialism' under St Laurent and Howe, the close links between ministers and their deputies, was no longer tenable now that the previous critics of the system were the political masters. Senior civil servants did not necessarily lose power vis-à-vis their superiors, at least not immediately, for they still retained the all-important knowledge of how to run their departments. But there was now a marked hostility between many of the deputies and their new ministers.[17]

Diefenbaker's meteoric rise in 1957 and 1958, his decline in 1962 and 1963, and his ouster from the Conservative leadership in 1967 have been well chronicled.[18] His handling of the question of Quebec representation was at least as inept as Bennett's in the thirties and considerably worse than the efforts of Borden.[19] He refused to appoint a French-Canadian lieutenant, and not until 1960, when Leon Balcer became minister of transport, did any French Canadian hold a major portfolio. He also refused permission for the Quebec caucus to meet together on its own.[20] His failure in dealing with Quebec ministers and MPs, and Quebec as a whole, was demonstrated in 1962 when the Conservatives lost all but fourteen of the fifty seats they had won in 1958. This failure can be attributed to Diefenbaker's deeply felt commitment to unhyphenated Canadianism, his inability to delegate, and his distrust of anyone who was not associated with him from his early days in politics. Yet the Diefenbaker cabinet did see continuation of certain traditions, and at the same time it broke new ground in incorporating the regional dimension in the design and delivery of government programs.

Tradition and Innovation

In many ways Diefenbaker's cabinet was relatively orthodox. Excepting the weak Quebec representation, there was good regional and ethnic balance; and despite his populist image, key ministries such as Finance and Justice were put in the hands of individuals who enjoyed the confidence of the business and legal communities respectively. In 1960 H.J. Flemming, premier of New Brunswick, entered the cabinet as minister of forestry. George Nowlan from Nova Scotia, in the tradition of Ralston and Ilsley, occupied, first, the revenue portfolio and later finance, and provided links with the Nova Scotia government through his close friend Robert Stanfield, premier since 1956. Nowlan also inherited the role of minister for the Atlantic region, a position that soon exposed him to the constant and unceasing flood of requests for patronage – requests that were scripted, almost word for word, from the same timeless prose familiar to ministers in Macdonald and Laurier's day, expressing indignation at being passed over or pleas for special consideration. For Nowlan it proved to be a difficult and time-consuming preoccupation. It was a task that had been rendered even more difficult by changing conditions, for as Margaret Conrad notes: 'The bureaucratization of government services in the twentieth century did not eliminate patronage headaches for federal politicians. It merely altered the process. Instead of having jobs and contracts directly at their disposal, ministers were increasingly required to exercise their influence with various government structures to secure their objectives.'[21]

Like the good regional minister he was, Nowlan began lobbying almost immediately for subventions for the transportation of coal within the maritime provinces, and over subsequent years succeeded through various manoeuvres in keeping the coal-mines in Cape Breton alive. In other respects, serving 'as an intermediary between provincial and federal jurisdictions, he invariably favoured Nova Scotia over other Atlantic provinces.'[22] As in all cabinets, success of this sort came at the expense of other provinces and their ministers, and in this case it happened to be Newfoundland. William Browne, Newfoundland's representative in cabinet, first as minister without portfolio, later as solicitor general, had the misfortune to be caught in the war of wills prevailing between Premier Smallwood and Diefenbaker. Browne failed to obtain support for virtually every proposal he raised in cabinet, such as for assistance for hydro development.[23]

The Diefenbaker government also introduced some non-traditional means for responding to special needs from the regions. Given Diefenbaker's western background and the broad support that the party had elicited from the peripheries, both east and west, his party was well positioned to shift government priorities and policies towards the needs of the regions. In some respects it began doing so almost immediately by sharply increasing expenditures on agriculture and by transferring more funds to Atlantic provincial governments.[24] In other respects, innovations were seriously delayed, ironically because that same western background contributed towards Diefenbaker's profound distrust of both the bureaucracy and the Liberals. In 1955 the St Laurent government had struck the Royal Commission on Canada's Economic Prospects chaired by Walter Gordon. Its report, delivered after the coming to power of the Conservatives in 1957, was received with considerable suspicion by Diefenbaker, despite the fact that the report was critical of the narrow policies pursued by the previous Liberal regime. It pointed to the shallow nature of the post-war economic boom and to basic structural inequalities in the economy, especially where regional inequalities were concerned, and recommended more direct and specific targeted policies as remedies.

The changes wrought by Diefenbaker, when they finally did arrive, were nonetheless significant innovations. Alvin Hamilton, who was made minister of agriculture in 1960, and Diefenbaker himself were willing to embark on new policies and structures to help a constituency with which they felt considerable empathy, the 'disadvantaged.' In their eyes these were primarily residents of the prairies and the maritimes, who frequently had little choice but to move to urban areas in central Canada. At the core of Hamilton's belief was that the population base and the way of life in the peripheries were worth preserving, and that it was quite legitimate to bring jobs to people rather than having people leave their home communities for work elsewhere. Out of this belief and Hamilton's fondness for experimentation (already evident as minister of northern development and natural resources), emerged the Agriculture and Rural Development Act (ARDA) in 1961, followed by a special ARDA secretariat based within the Department of Agriculture.[25]

In creating this institution Hamilton ran solidly against the grain of thinking in the department. The deputy minister, S.C. Barry, was opposed to its creation; later he and other civil servants wanted little to do with it, seeing it as a political boondogle.[26] Previous experience with the highly independent Prairie Farm Rehabilitation Agency under Gardiner undoubtedly contributed to opposition to innovations of this kind. What prevented ARDA from fulfilling the dire predictions of Barry and others was its staffing by Hamilton with young economists, mostly with non-agricultural backgrounds, the use of outside consultants, and the holding of open conferences with the provinces. It is quite possible that over time Hamilton would have used it for more direct partisan purposes. In 1962, however, he fell ill, and by 1963 the life of the Diefenbaker government was finished. The immediate legacy included a number of federal-provincial cost-shared agreements on agricultural rehabilitation. ARDA itself survived the government, was expanded under Pearson, and became one of the major program entities incorporated into the new Department of Regional Economic Expansion (DREE) in 1969.

ARDA was not the only innovation. Diefenbaker himself in 1958 extended the federal government's equalization program, intended to help the have-not provincial governments in the delivery of basic services, by introducing the Atlantic Provinces Adjustment Grants scheme. H.J. Flemming, drawing on his earlier exposure to regional economic studies done for the New Brunswick government, was sympathetic to many of the recommendations made by the Gordon Commission – a sympathy that was communicated directly to the cabinet and which resulted in the creation of the Atlantic Development Board (ADB) in the closing days of the Diefenbaker era.[27] The ADB, at the behest of the civil servants in the Department of Finance, was stripped of any financial clout, despite active support by Nowlan for a board with expenditure authority.[28] It became simply an advisory board with a planning function. Later under the Liberals it did obtain funding.

These innovations were not part of any systematic plan. Nor were these innovations in programming matched by more sophistication in government machinery. During the Second World War, in addition to the War Committee of cabinet, and the Treasury Board, which had been in existence since 1869, more specialized standing committees dealing with defence production, food production, and the like were struck. The practice of delegating a number of more mundane cabinet tasks to standing committees of cabinet continued under St Laurent. Diefenbaker, however, reflecting his populist bias, decided that cabinet as a whole, not committees, should make all decisions.[29] Consequently, the number of cabinet meetings almost doubled. As well, the size of the cabinet increased from the about twenty under St Laurent to nearly thirty by the time Diefenbaker left office in 1963. Diefenbaker did establish a special committee on Atlantic Canada, in addition to ones dealing with coal and energy. But on the whole, the limited successes Nowlan and others enjoyed were due more to behind-the-scenes negotiation and control over their own portfolio than to any influence over decisions reached directly in the chaotic conditions of Diefenbaker's cabinet room.

Diefenbaker's contribution to the practice of Canadian government thus did not lie in the field of organizing cabinet business. Among his more enduring legacies, and those of supporters such as Hamilton and Gordon Churchill, was making the west a solid bulwark of Conservative support, something that had eluded the party since Borden. Secondly, the Diefenbaker government had made regionalism and regional economic disparities a legitimate criterion for the design of government policies, whether in the realm of federal-provincial finance or special programs targeted at remedying economic conditions in specific regions. In implementing such programs one minister in particular, Alvin Hamilton, demonstrated that often unusual means had to be used in dealing with recalcitrant civil servants: techniques such as using outside consultants and willingness to break rules, if the desired policies were to become a reality. This also marked a watershed of sorts in the efforts of politicians to come to grips with the growing size of the administrative state. As Nowlan discovered, old-fashioned patronage was either no longer available or insufficient in quantity to respond to broader political demands from the region. Furthermore, many of the provincial governments were becoming more sophisticated, both in their thinking and in framing their demands to Ottawa. For ministers like Nowlan, to respond effectively required a capacity to become involved in policy-making at an earlier stage, a process that more likely than not took place at the subministerial level within departments.

The bitter conflicts over economic management and nuclear weapons, culminating in the Coyne affair of 1961 and the Bomarc missile crisis in 1962, as well as Diefenbaker's capacity for indecision, tended both to obscure and to limit the achievements of Hamilton, Flemming, and Nowlan. The full decline, however, of the regional minister system from the pinnacle under King came not with Diefenbaker, but with his two Liberal successors, Lester Pearson and Pierre Elliott Trudeau.

Pearson: The Changing Dimensions of Inter- and Intra-governmental Relations

The nature of regional ministerial decline, it should be stressed, was twofold. In part it represented a genuine decline in influence as the locus of decision-making shifted to other arenas, specifically to the federal-provincial first ministers' conference. In part it was simply a decline in visibility, a process that was already evident in the election campaigns of 1957 and 1958.

The largest single development was the Quiet Revolution. The transformation of Quebec's social and political institutions and attitudes, the abandonment of its insularity with respect to economic life, and above all, its wholesale embracement of the concept of the positive state had major ramifications. By 1963, having Liberals in office in both Ottawa and Quebec City offered no advantage in terms of improved communication and co-operation. There was certainly more interaction between the two governments, and Lester Pearson, compared to his predecessor, was more fully aware of, and sympathetic to, the goals of the Lesage government. Yet there was still a major gap between the demands that the Quebec government were making of Ottawa and what Ottawa was able to deliver; and within the federal cabinet there was, at least initially, an absence of notable individuals from Quebec, figures who could both represent the interests of Quebec in cabinet deliberations and act as intermediaries with the Quebec government. It was a sign of the times that the premier of Quebec was a former federal minister rather than vice versa.[30] Furthermore, Lesage indicated that in communicating with the federal government he would deal only with Pearson himself or Pearson's two most trusted advisors, Gordon Robertson, clerk of the Privy Council, and Tom Kent, chief policy co-ordinator for the cabinet and Pearson's right-hand man.[31]

At the administrative level, the cumulative effect of merit-based civil service recruiting had resulted in a dramatic decline in the size of the French-Canadian component of the Canadian public service, and this underrepresentation was most pronounced at the highest levels.[32] This further reduced the capacity of the federal government both to comprehend and to respond to the changes in Quebec's challenge to the constitutional status quo. This paucity of French-Canadian expertise within the federal government was unlikely to change quickly. Ottawa was unattractive both culturally and politically for politicians and members of Quebec's new young middle-class professionals, who instead were gravitating towards the opportunities offered by Quebec's rapidly expanding bureaucracies.

Although well intentioned, Pearson contributed to the overall inadequacy of Quebec representation in cabinet. It was this failing which turned into crisis by 1965 and which threatened his efforts to forge a new consensus between English and French Canada. He had selected Guy Favreau, former associate deputy minister of justice, as his Quebec lieutenant, and then failed utterly to back him up.[33] By 1964 Favreau, as minister of justice, had become embroiled in the Rivard bribery scandal and the alleged failure of the Department of Justice to prosecute the wrongdoers. The subsequent judicial inquiry cleared Favreau of wrongdoing; but Pearson had already distanced himself from his minister when the scandal first broke and declined to defend him in the House, even when he had a clear opportunity to do so. Pearson's reluctance to defend him and Favreau's subsequent resignation did little to reinforce morale among other Quebec ministers and MPs.

In 1965 Quebec representation was bolstered by the arrival of the 'three wise men' – Trudeau, Gerard Pelletier, and Jean Marchand. Marchand, the senior of the three, entered the cabinet in 1965 as secretary of state, but declined the mantle of the Quebec lieutenancy, seeing it as an outmoded concept. Furthermore, the position of the three on Quebec's role in confederation was at odds, in many ways sharply so, with the views of those in the Lesage government and, after 1966, with those in the newly elected Union Nationale government under Daniel Johnson. At a fundamental level the ideas and beliefs of Trudeau did not differ greatly from those inherent in Diefenbaker's pan-Canadianism. As a direct consequence, the triumvirate did little to mediate issues involving Ottawa and Quebec. Differences were worked out primarily through direct negotiations between the two governments.

Quebec's new-found strength of purpose affected federal-provincial relations as a whole. The issue of constitutional reform, although arising out of demands put by Quebec, directly engaged the interests of all the provinces. Other issues relating to the Canada pension scheme and the future of federal-provincial fiscal relations, where Quebec had major demands or alternative propositions on the table, were beyond being resolved through quiet diplomacy by either civil servants or individual ministers. Attention was now firmly fixed on the federal-provincial first ministers' conference, where most of the tough bargaining was perceived to take place.[34] The more aggressive stance taken by Quebec affected the role taken up by the other provinces: at a minimum there was now the sense that they had to participate; that they could not afford to abstain from the intergovernmental process. Equally important, Quebec acted as a role model. The Ontario government, for example, was struck by the manner in which the Quebec government was able to marshal its resources and prepare its arguments, and decided that it too would create a co-ordinating agency to handle intergovernmental issues and strategies.[35] A number of the other provinces, over time, put into place similar internal co-ordinating mechanisms. All the provinces had become more attuned to the changing environment, and particularly to the politicization of the intergovernmental process, even prior to the Quebec renaissance.

The term province-building is often used to describe the growth of provincial governments in their capacity for administration and governance. The concept has come under critical scrutiny, but certainly by the mid-1960s it was clear that provincial expenditures were growing at a greater rate than those of the federal government. This development was hardly unexpected given provincial responsibilities for the major fixtures of the welfare state, such as education and health care.[36] Secondly, provincial governments, even the less well-off ones, were becoming more sophisticated in planning and in their willingness to adopt technocratic methods to foster local economies. Both Nova Scotia under Stanfield and New Brunswick under Flemming, and even, to a more limited extent, Newfoundland under Smallwood, were already in the 1950s and early 1960s employing consultants and economists such as Merril Menzies and W.Y. Smith, men who were strongly opposed to Ottawa's preoccupation with national economic growth and who favoured planning and co-operation at the regional level.[37] In short, even the smaller provinces were reasonably well prepared to participate and press their claims in direct negotiations with the federal government.

The cabinet came to be overshadowed by these developments. In putting his cabinet together Pearson paid due attention to regional balance, but only Pickersgill, representing Newfoundland and one of the few holdovers from the St Laurent period, carried any real weight as a regional representative. Mitchell Sharp, a former minister as well as mandarin, was clearly identified with the business interests of central Canada instead of any specific region. Paul Martin, minister of external affairs, while dominating the immediate area surrounding the city of Windsor, was not considered to be the minister for Ontario. Other ministers, including finance minister Walter Gordon, as well as many MPs, during their stint in opposition had had ample opportunity to reflect on the last years of C.D. Howe and Jimmy Gardiner. They were convinced that the Liberal party's dependence on regional ministers and provincial organizations had been the cause of its defeat in 1957 and 1958.

The momentum for reform, for a 'new politics' emphasizing broad participation by ordinary citizens, centred around the national organizer for the party, Keith Davey, and a small group based primarily in Toronto. Their enthusiasm was reinforced by events such as the 1961 Kingston Thinkers' Conference, which drew on the academic community and stressed policy innovations in such areas as pensions. Pearson himself favoured reform and the elimination of the traditional regional kingpins, calling for 'a direct link between federal electoral districts ... and the national office of the party.'[38] To this concern for a new national organization which would bypass provincial party structures was added a fascination with television advertising, the use of public opinion polls, and heavy dependence on the expertise of the MacLaren advertising agency. Significantly, among the first items arising out of the reorganization was the creation in 1961 of the Leader's Advisory Committee. Comprised of senior party officials and former Liberal ministers still in the caucus, its significance resided in part in the fact that, 'except for J.W. Pickersgill, it included no one with ties outside the St. Lawrence Valley, and even from that region the Quebec contingent was weak.'[39] A further innovation introduced after the 1963 election was the federal campaign committees, which were to act as intermediaries between federal and provincial organizations. They were intended to supplant MPs, and to a degree even ministers, in the patronage process, all with the view to eliciting more grass-roots participation.

These changes at the level of the party organization were paralleled by innovations elsewhere. Pearson, in a direct reversal of Diefenbaker's practice, systematized and expanded the use of cabinet committees and allocated to these committees responsibilities for broad areas of government activity, such as external policy and defence, economic policy, and social policy. These broad areas represented issues and concerns spanning more than one, and in many instances several, departments. There were now ten standing cabinet committees, including Treasury Board, and cabinet procedures specified that all matters brought to cabinet must first go to the relevant committee, a reversal of previous procedure.[40] Further, the deliberations of the committees were supported, and to an extent promoted, by staff in the Privy Council Office (PCO) and a growing network of interdepartmental task forces. The 'departmentalized' cabinet, in which the interests of departments were represented directly by the relevant minister, was being challenged by the 'institutionalized' cabinet, in which departmental activities were increasingly subject to scrutiny by cabinet committees, interdepartmental committees of civil servants, and central agencies such as the PCO.[41] The long-standing prerogative of ministers to affect the programs of other departments, under the rubric of regional or local concerns, meant that collegial influence over one's department was not an entirely new development. What was new, however, was that the rationale was now based on much broader concerns: international trade, social welfare, to give examples. And the criteria employed were now more technocratic in nature, involving the use of quantitative data on large classes of individuals or subjects, be they fishermen or measures of economic performance.

The emergence of central agencies as significant actors was thus an important feature of the Pearson era, and this development arose in good part as a response to what were seen to be major problems in the management of the public service. In 1960 the Diefenbaker government had struck the Royal Commission on Government Organization (the Glassco Commission), and the tenor of its recommendations is best captured by a popular slogan of the period: 'Let the managers manage.'[42] Ministers, so the commission recommended, should be concerned with overall policies and objectives, while the implementation and details of program management should be left to officials. The overall thrust was to introduce a strong element of administrative decentralization into the system, primarily by delegating to departments a good deal of authority for financial and personnel management. In helping ministers and cabinet as a whole to establish overall goals and monitor performance, the commission recommended strengthening central agencies, and specifically the removal from the Department of Finance responsibility for what was the oldest committee of cabinet, Treasury Board, shifting it to a separate support unit.

It fell to the Pearson government to implement these recommendations. By 1966 there was in place a separate Treasury Board Secretariat (TBS) under a new ministerial portfolio, president of the Treasury Board. It represented the coming into play of a new agency, and a concommitant loss of influence by the Department of Finance, primarily in the area of budgetary allocations among departments. The proposed measures for giving departments increased authority over personnel and financial administration proved much more difficult to implement. As developments subsequently demonstrated, guidelines accompanying delegation of authority in personnel matters were very restrictive; and in the field of financial controls, line managers often lacked both the skills and the time to develop and implement appropriate systems at the departmental level.[43] The net result was centralization of power at the centre, specifically within central agencies such as the PCO, TBS, and the Public Service Commission.

The Liberal party's fascination with American technology in the realm of polling and advertising was paralleled by the TBS's love affair with the budgeting and monitoring systems created in the United States. Based on cost-benefit analysis models used in the private sector, the planning, programming, budgeting system (PPBS) of resource allocation came to be the best known and most widely used of the new techniques. It promised not only more rigorous assessment of various alternatives for attaining any given objective but also continual monitoring of progress achieved. To be effective, or at least for it to be useable, PPBS required the quantification of data on inputs and outputs. Assessment and performance monitoring were done centrally by TBS technicians and as a consequence 'the formation of the budget became a distributive rather than aggregative process.'[44] Several programs came under the purview of the new systems people and were subjected to the rigours of PPBS. The full implementation of these systems, however, did not come until later, and some of the programs begun under Diefenbaker were spared full-scale rationalization. The Hamilton legacy, ARDA, was successfully protected by its strong-willed director, A.T. Davidson, who resisted both political forces that would have made it a patronage tool and more stringent controls from Finance and the TBS that would have robbed the agency of its capacity to innovate. In 1964 ARDA was moved from the Department of Agriculture into the newly created Department of Forestry (later Forestry and Rural Development) where it received sympathetic treatment under the minister, Maurice Sauvé. Under his regime ARDA was expanded with the addition of the Fund for Rural Economic Development (FRED).

Sauvé, as did Davidson, placed more emphasis on planning and adjustment than on economic development as such; but, like Hamilton, he favoured striking deals with provincial governments for both the initiation and delivery of programs. Thus have-not provinces were invited to designate special areas as focal points for FRED-funded projects, and out of this process developed reasonably good relations between ARDA staff and provincial governments. Reflecting Sauvé's wish to maintain harmonious relations with the Quebec government, FRED initiatives from that province received less severe scrutiny from ARDA officials than did proposals from the other provinces.[45]

While ARDA broke new ground in developing linkages within the federal-provincial relations arena and allowed officials a fairly free hand, other agencies were handled in more traditional fashion. Pickersgill, well schooled in the partisan traditions of C.D. Howe and Jimmy Gardiner as well as a close confidant of Pearson, became the minister in charge of the Atlantic Development Board and promptly put the ADB under his direct control, endowing it at the same time with a $100 million expenditure fund. When Pickersgill moved from secretary of state to transport he simply had the agency relocated to his new portfolio.[46] As to be expected, the province represented by Pickersgill, Newfoundland, did rather well in obtaining ADB funding. Other instances of traditional behaviour could be found in the Pearson era. Sauvé, for example, although a relatively junior minister, did act as an intermediary between Ottawa and the Quebec government during a crucial phase of the Canada and Quebec pension plan negotiations.[47] But the fact that it was a junior minister, not one of the more senior ministers, who played this role was indicative of changed circumstances. As well, with the possible exception of Mitchell Sharp, Pickersgill represented the last remnant of an era that had ended with the defeat of the St Laurent government. His departure from cabinet in 1967 permanently closed that era and heralded further changes that were to come a year later.

CHAPTER 5

Trudeau and the New Rationality: Stifling Regional Representation

While the seeds were planted beforehand, the new administrative technology and emphasis on 'rational' decision-making truly came into their own with the arrival of the government in 1968 under Pierre Trudeau. Systematic efforts were made to structure and streamline further the flow of cabinet business. The number of cabinet committees was reduced from ten to nine, regular meeting times were set, and the Priorities and Planning Committee (P&P), created in January 1968, became the senior committee, responsible for overall goal-setting and for channelling specific tasks to the other committees.[1] Efforts were also made to link cabinet committee decision-making to the new central agency monitoring systems. The cabinet committee system now included committees on government operations, federal-provincial relations, legislation and house planning, and four policy areas (economic, social, external and defence, and culture and native affairs) in addition to the Treasury Board and P&P. The Privy Council Office (PCO) was expanded in order to service the enhanced responsibilities of cabinet committees, and this servicing was now to include not just the packaging and routing of materials (a task important enough in itself) but also the preparation of briefing notes assessing departmental proposals. The other central agencies were also revamped and expanded. The Treasury Board Secretariat (TBS) acquired a planning branch and the Prime Minister's Office (PMO), which under Pearson had a staff of about twenty, more than quadrupled in size to ninety-two.

The changes in cabinet organization, and in the machinery of government more generally, were premised on a highly developed paradigm of 'rational management.' It was a model of politics and administration arising directly out of Trudeau's Cartesian intellect, his belief in a system of checks and balances, and his personal experiences as a minister in the unruly atmosphere of the Pearson cabinet.

Trudeau was persuaded that knowledge would increasingly become the source of all political power, and that its management would require the development of finely honed political instruments based not on 'mere emotionalism' but 'designed and appraised by more rational standards than anything we are currently using in Canada today.'[2]

Trudeau's application of these new instruments, and his overall philosophy, had a distinct effect on the operations of cabinet in three respects. First, his approach was premised on collegial decision-making. Collegiality has always been a feature of Canadian cabinets, but in Trudeau's scheme of things decisions would be based not so much on consensus or mutual considerations as on rational debate wherein some ideas would prevail and others would not. Secondly, the ideas or propositions to be debated would not be based solely on those put forward by departments. Rather, bureaucratic counterweights in the form of central agencies would provide ministers with extensive briefing material on the pros and cons of departmental proposals. Though much less suspicious of the bureaucracy than Diefenbaker – indeed he strongly favoured a specialized and professional bureaucracy – Trudeau was nonetheless fully aware of the inordinate power of mandarins to shape policy outcomes. In his view this influence was best countered by ministers operating collectively rather than individually and by having available to them alternative sources of information and advice.[3] Furthermore, this alternative advice would flow not only from the central agencies already in place – the PCO, PMO and TBS – but also from newly created 'co-ordinating portfolios' or 'ministries of state,' portfolios that were not 'departments in any traditional sense, but rather ministries whose initiatives would inevitably and consistently involve the responsibilities of other ministers.'[4] Two agencies created immediately were the Ministry of State for Science and Technology and the Ministry of State for Urban Affairs. All told, this matrix arrangement of multiple committees and co-ordinating agencies 'was meant to ensure that individual ministerial autonomy was countered by the collective authority of cabinet committees.'[5]

The effect of the full flowering of the institutionalized cabinet was in one sense immediate. Mitchell Sharp, comparing the new regime with the one under St Laurent, was struck by the 'numerous and voluminous cabinet papers we are presented with from week to week.'[6] Gordon Robertson noted that both cabinet committee meetings and the number of cabinet documents considered more than doubled from 1967 to 1971.[7] The implications for those ministers expecting or seeking to represent regional interests were clear: they simply had much less time available to exercise their own ministerial, let alone regional, responsibilities. Beyond this, Trudeau's views limited ministerial autonomy in other respects. In his own words: 'I don't think I could operate in the kind of government system ... where each minister brings his own power base.'[8] The contrast with Mackenzie King, or even Lester Pearson, could not be clearer.

To ensure that links with the regions and with the rank and file were maintained a number of innovations were introduced. First, the agency responsible for tendering purely political advice, the PMO, was now endowed with a system of 'regional desks' – four to be precise – for the gathering of political intelligence, for the west, Ontario, Quebec, and the Atlantic. These regional desks, staffed by junior people, did not replace regional ministers, but they did contribute to other, broader efforts to submerge their influence. A cumbersome structure was devised that saw the creation of provincial advisory groups, consisting of the senior minister from the province, a federal MP, a representative from the provincial Liberal party, and a representative from party headquarters in Ottawa to act as secretary. These groups were to pass on information to the national advisory group, composed of representatives from caucus, the PMO, and the National Liberal Federation, and were responsible for the day-to-day welfare of the party. In addition, there was the 'political cabinet' – essentially the cabinet in its partisan capacity meeting with representatives from caucus and the federation to discuss election financing, regional discontent, and the like. To add to the complexity, the currency of 'participatory democracy' gained momentum with the election in 1968 of Richard Stanbury as party president. Constituency organizations were expected to debate, over a one-year period, a series of policy proposals developed by ten task forces, with the whole process culminating in the National Policy Convention in November 1970.[9]

On several grounds the role of the provincial advisory groups and participatory democracy generally was found wanting, not least because of the unfulfilled expectations of the rank and file. Ministers and MPs for their parts were frustrated in having the party organization forced upon them. As Stanbury noted in explaining why one of the provincial advisory groups was not functioning: 'there is a blockage in B.C. ... It seems to be because neither Arthur Laing [the senior minister] nor the Caucus want the Party Organization to have a voice.'[10] The politicians were still able, therefore, to resist the imposition of the non-elected party organization. Yet the mere presence of the cumbersome party apparatus and the energies expended in having to fight it made life more difficult for ministers. Furthermore, fund-raising and the conduct of election campaigns were now firmly in the hands of the national party organization in Ottawa. Finally, in a number of provinces the rupture between federal and provincial party organizations, already evident under Pearson, was now complete, and in provinces such as Saskatchewan this rupture was transformed into something approaching open warfare. In many ways the conflict in that province was inevitable given the presence of two strong personalities in the form of the Liberal premier, Ross Thatcher, and the senior minister from 1968 onwards, Otto Lang. But the decision to 'establish a Federal Affairs Committee' to handle federal patronage that would 'be influenced more by the federal constituency Presidents and the defeated candidates rather than by the Premier'[11] was a blatant affront to Thatcher. It was also a natural outcome of the party reforms promoted by Davey and Stanbury.

In other respects it is useful to recognize how the Trudeau government responded to the regional dimension. Under Diefenbaker and then Pearson a number of regional development initiatives were launched that frequently bore the stamp of strong regional figures such as Hamilton and Pickersgill. Under Trudeau the various regional development programs and agencies, ARDA, ADB, and FRED among others, were brought together in a single portfolio and department, the Department of Regional Economic Expansion (DREE). Launched in 1969, it combined the characteristics of a standard line department with the features of the new ministries of state concept: it had expenditure authority for programs of its own and was responsible for co-ordinating the regional development efforts of all government departments.

As an organizational innovation DREE had considerable merit. It integrated the widely scattered regional programs into a single unit and, in keeping with the spirit of the times, allowed the application of systematic and sophisticated techniques to the problem at hand: the alleviation of regional disparities. Under the direction of its first minister, Jean Marchand, and his deputy, Tom Kent, a staff of economists was recruited and an appropriate theoretical focus selected. Many of the joint federal-provincial programs launched under ARDA were terminated or the agreements allowed to lapse. The programs that replaced them were premised on the growth pole model: under the special areas program, 'growth' areas were selected – for example, Halifax-Dartmouth, Moncton, Quebec City, and Trois Rivières – which then became focal points for infrastructure improvements such as water and sewage systems, schools, roads, and industrial parks. An additional incentives program under the Regional Development Incentives Act (RDIA) of 1969 was used to persuade industrial enterprises to locate in these growth centres. It was thought that the accelerated industrial surge in these core areas would then filter into the surrounding tertiary regions, eventually spawning growth there as well.[12]

Beyond integrating a policy area that hitherto had been highly fragmented, DREE stood out for other reasons. First, its staff collectively embraced the new PPBS technology, a technology that most regular line departments strongly resisted. In return DREE received the blessing and support of the Department of Finance and, particularly, of the Treasury Board Secretariat. Thus, in the 1968–71 period, a time when there was a general retrenchment in government expenditures, DREE's budgetary situation improved.[13] But the adoption of the new technology also reflected DREE's penchant for central control. Marchand and Kent ran the department in a secretive, centralized, albeit innovative fashion.[14] The majority of staff was based in Ottawa and most decisions were made there. This approach entailed limiting the influence not only of provincial governments but also of federal ministers and MPs. Marchand, as senior minister for Quebec, still paid close attention to what he considered to be the important needs there; and the discretionary ministerial powers under the special areas and RDIA programs allowed plenty of scope for channelling funds to specific regions in that province.[15] Kent, however, was left to handle all matters outside Quebec. His penchant for secrecy and his position as a civil servant made it very difficult for the regional ministers, or anyone else, to influence the DREE allocation process.

In summary, changes in the conduct of cabinet business, the new administrative technology associated with these changes, party reforms, and, not least, Trudeau's rational approach to the operation of government and the selection of cabinet ministers all served to suppress the role that regional ministers had played in the past. To be sure the 1968–72 cabinet paid due regard to regional balance; and while Jean Marchand refused to label himself as Quebec lieutenant, it was generally conceded that as senior minister and one of Trudeau's closest confidants, and later as co-chairman of the Liberal National Campaign Committee, he had considerable influence over most decisions affecting that province. As well, in cabinet committee assignments, effort was made to ensure fairly even regional apportionment.[16]

Overall, in the early years of the Trudeau era it was difficult to point to ministers whose activities or reputation identified them as strong regional figures. James Richardson from Manitoba vigorously pursued projects for his province, successfully as evidenced by the Air Canada overhaul facility for Boeing 727s and the new Royal Canadian Mint, both of which arrived in Winnipeg in the early 1970s. But apparently this did not compensate for his inability to control the Manitoba 'federal affairs committee' or generally to provide leadership to Manitoba Liberals. According to Joseph Wearing, Richardson's performance as Manitoba minister 'was little short of disastrous.'[17] Otto Lang, minister from Saskatchewan and responsible primarily for the Wheat Board during his first two years in cabinet, made his reputation for introducing the highly unpopular (certainly among western farmers) Lower Inventories for Tomorrow (LIFT) program and for his public feud with Saskatchewan premier Ross Thatcher. It was only on the east coast that Allan MacEachen from Nova Scotia and Donald Jamieson from Newfoundland operated in traditional fashion, quietly funnelling largesse in the form of patronage and projects to their riding or particular region. Even MacEachen, however, found himself with reduced influence after 1968. In Ontario, home base for 'Cell 13,' the notion of having a distinct regional presence in cabinet, never strong to begin with, seemed to have disappeared altogether.

The Limits of Rationality

The diminished role of regional ministers, the technocratic approach to regional development, and overall changes in the machinery of government can all be linked to the rational management paradigm. But the model also contained distinct limitations. Peter Aucoin writes: 'The fundamental flaw in this design was that it was too optimistic about the collegiality of ministers: that is, about their willingness, in the absence of a strong prime ministerial presence, to compromise their personal objectives and departmental ambitions in pursuit of coherent corporate policies.'[18] These limits of collegiality and rationality on policy-making might not have been fully evident to Trudeau and his immediate advisers in the early 1970s. What did have immediate impact, however, were the 1972 election results. Trudeau's aversion to 'emotionalism' in politics was evident in the austere election slogan used that year, 'The Land Is Strong.' The voters responded by electing a minority Liberal government of 109 members, a distinct drop from the 155 in 1968. Virtually all the losses occurred west of Quebec: Alberta lost all four Liberal seats, British Columbia was reduced from sixteen to only four, and Saskatchewan and Manitoba reduced to one and two members respectively where previously they had two and five.[19]

The government responded, not by altering the thrust of the basic paradigm – in the area of machinery of government the reforms continued unabated – but by placing more direct control over patronage and political matters back in the hands of ministers and by seeking to cultivate better relations with the provinces, particulary in western Canada. In party matters, authority over the provincial advisory groups fell under the complete control of designated 'political' or regional ministers, and the groups themselves were now called federal affairs committees, a title already common in many of the provinces. The PMO still played a role in allocating patronage, but now it was more a matter of compiling lists of upcoming order-in-council appointments to be made available to the regional ministers and their federal affairs committees. As well, the PMO regional desks, which had evoked the ire of ministers and MPs alike, were abolished. The cumbersome apparatus created to link the extra-parliamentary party with the caucus and cabinet was whittled down, some elements falling into disuse, others being revamped. For example, the 'political cabinet,' which had consisted of the entire cabinet meeting with party officials to discuss 'political issues,' was abandoned and replaced by the much smaller, and more effective, Political Planning Committee, which consisted solely of the ten regional ministers plus the party president, the prime minister's principal secretary, the chairman of caucus, and the co-chairmen of the national campaign committee.[20]

In party and patronage matters, therefore, the regional ministers had regained much of what they had lost during the 1960s. At the same time, the connections between the federal and provincial parties remained relatively weak, either because the provincial parties themselves were weak, as in Alberta and Manitoba, or because the regional ministers had little to do with the provincial parties, as in Saskatchewan and Quebec. Furthermore, control over patronage appointments did not translate into a heightened ministerial profile. If anything it likely had the opposite effect, for patronage distribution in an era of technocratic politics, while perhaps still necessary to reward the core of party faithful, was not something to be touted publicly, at least not in the more urbanized provinces such as Ontario and British Columbia.

As well, the expanded influence of regional ministers did not necessarily enhance their position vis-à-vis provincial premiers, for the other initiative arising out of the Liberal government's response to their near defeat was a more conciliatory approach to federal-provincial relations. This was evident in two areas: efforts to respond to the long-standing western economic grievances as voiced by the provincial governments, and reorientation of DREE programs in order to give provinces much more say in policy development and delivery. In both cases it elevated the status of provincial governments and by implication reduced that of regional ministers.

In early 1973 the federal government announced that a Western Economic Opportunities Conference (WEOC), would take place later that summer, out of which would come new programs in agriculture, transportation, finance, and industry. The four western provinces were asked to make submissions in these four areas. Depicted by Otto Lang and others as an epochal event, likely to 'alter the course of history,' the promotional fanfare leading up to the WEOC generated all sorts of expectations.[21] The provinces, in a rare display of interprovincial co-operation, drafted detailed joint submissions, outlining specific complaints – several hundred all told – and what should be done to rectify them.[22] The sheer volume of the recommendations, and the fact that many were inherently contradictory, made it impossible for the federal government to respond in other than very general terms. But the result of the WEOC was to promote the legitimacy of the four provinces in voicing concerns over policies under federal jurisdiction and to list in detail, for all to see, the nature of the complaints over ostensibly misguided federal policies. It also, incidentally, helped create a permanent forum – the annual Western Premiers Conference – in which these concerns could be voiced on a regular basis, much to the subsequent discomfort of the Liberal government. For regional ministers, and the Liberal party in western Canada as a whole, it meant being pushed even further to the margins.[23]

Complaints made at the WEOC over regional policy, or lack thereof for western Canada, coincided with developments taking place on the other side of the continent. The highly centralized, top-down approach of DREE, under the guidance of Marchand and Kent, had succeeded in promoting changes in the growth regions identified in 1969; it had also, however, succeeded in generating considerable ill will with the provinces. Kent and his staff had frequently bypassed provincial governments and their development agencies and dealt directly with municipalities. While the provinces eventually acquiesced in the spending of federal dollars in the designated locations, they were still resentful over the lack of consultation. They particularly resented seeing expenditures restricted to the so-called growth poles, preferring instead more widespread distribution of monies throughout the province.[24] In response to provincial complaints, as well as misgivings over the efficacy of the growth pole approach and the industrial incentive programs, Marchand initiated a comprehensive review of all DREE programs, DREE's internal organization, and its relations with provincial governments. Under the guidance of the new deputy minister, J.D. Love, the review gained momentum with the 1972 election results and the appointment of a new minister, Donald Jamieson, the senior minister from Newfoundland.[25]

The results of the review were fourfold. It was recommended: 1) that the geographical reach of DREE's responsibilities be extended beyond the Atlantic and Quebec regions to Ontario and the west; 2) that in the 'identification and pursuit of development opportunities' such efforts should not be restricted to specific urban areas but made in all slow-growth parts of any given province; 3) that programs be undertaken only with the agreement and support of the province involved; and 4) that DREE itself be decentralized with respect not only to operations but also to actual decision-making regarding project design and approval. These recommendations, backed up by detailed 'yellow books,' received the approval of full cabinet.[26] Jamieson, in making his presentations to cabinet and the House Committee on Regional Development, tended to stress the expansion of DREE's horizons, both within provinces and across the country, and the wish to elicit co-operation with the provinces. Little effort was made to brief MPs and cabinet ministers on the mechanisms to be used to structure federal-provincial co-operation or what was entailed by the DREE decentralization. Rather, the interest of the politicians was quickly captured by the promise of a more wide-ranging distribution of expenditures and the promise of DREE offices physically relocated to their regions under the decentralization scheme.[27] As well, the eligibility of the western provinces for DREE funding fitted easily with the promises made at the WEOC to promote development opportunities in that region. It was the proposed mechanisms for implementing the promised expenditures, however, that would in fact restrict the role and leverage of minister and MPs in significant fashion.

The tool selected to implement the new regional development strategy was labelled the General Development Agreement (GDA) approach. The aim was to obtain the agreement of each province in the form of a GDA that would outline the priorities, goals, and the manner in which joint decisions would be made to pursue development opportunities over a ten-year period. There were no expenditure commitments in the GDA itself, other than the relative proportions of funding to be provided by the two levels of government for projects to be decided on later. These proportions were quite generous by any standard: up to 90 per cent federal funding for Newfoundland, 80 per cent for Nova Scotia and New Brunswick, 60 per cent for Quebec, Manitoba, and Saskatchewan, and 50 per cent for Ontario, Alberta, and British Columbia.[28]

The GDA, however, was only a broad template or enabling document. It was given effect primarily through subsidiary agreements that covered specific proposals outlining who was going to do what over a certain time frame for a given sum of money. In theory DREE could implement projects on its own. In practice the agencies responsible for the actual delivery of programs were either other federal departments or agencies, or provincial departments; over the long term the agencies doing the lion's share of program delivery were provincial ones. This was not surprising, for the expectation from the beginning was that the provincial governments would initiate and propose most of the development projects. DREE officials, in turn, were involved primarily in vetting and approving proposals brought forward by the provincial governments, ensuring that they were consistent with the goals of the GDA. It was here that the new decentralized format of DREE came to play a special role. The authority that had been devolved to the regions – in the shape of the four regional and nine provincial offices – was primarily expenditure authority, that is, decisions on proposals which could be made without reference to Ottawa: up to $500,000 for DREE officials based in the provincial branches and $1.5 million for DREE regional officials. The DREE officials themselves were of senior rank: assistant deputy ministers (ADMs) headed the four regional offices in Moncton, Montreal, Toronto, and Saskatoon, and directors general (DGs) headed the provincial offices.

Provincial government politicians and civil servants were doubly pleased by these arrangements, especially in Atlantic Canada. The province would be primarily responsible both for initiating and implementing specific projects yet the bulk of the funding would come from the federal government. These arrangements, however, generated over time a special set of relationships involving mainly DREE and provincial government officials, relationships that worked to the disadvantage of federal ministers and MPs, or at least it was so perceived. At a certain point some provincial politicians also began to express a degree of unhappiness. Provincial officials and DREE field officers created between them a relatively closed community of interests.[29] In the Atlantic region DREE monies were used to expand the administrative and policy capacities of provincial departments dealing with development, mines and resources, and agriculture as well as to support the programs delivered by those departments. DREE officials, being close at hand, were able to shape or alter proposals, applying their expertise through interactions with provincial officials. Decisions, especially on smaller projects, could be made much more quickly than if they had been channelled through Treasury Board in Ottawa.

The new DREE thus proved to be highly responsive, at least to the needs as defined by provincial officials and politicians. But this responsiveness was felt to be at the expense of MPs and ministers. While they were frequently consulted and kept aware of progress on particular development projects unfolding in their riding – a bridge or tourism project for example – MPs had little sense of being able to either initiate or control any given proposal. Furthermore, any control they might normally be able to exercise, through a federal line department for instance, was vitiated by the fact of provincial delivery; so, too, was political credit that would normally accrue from direct federal expenditures and direct contact with grateful recipients. As S.J.R. Noel put it in 1976, with only slight exaggeration:

> ... the most important dispenser of public goods to private interests and individuals is not a local party man or even a sitting member of the governing party in Ottawa or the provincial capital. It is the man from DREE, or his counterpart in some similarly named ... provincial department ... He is usually less well liked than his predecessors, for he appears arrogant or obtuse and speaks a bewildering jargon ... Still, though his purposes may be as inscrutable as his criteria for the selection of recipients, his patronage is highly visible, much of it being in the traditional form of jobs, fees, contracts, real estate purchases, commissions, and other lucrative benefits.[30]

For politicians the power to distribute, or even simply to be seen to participate in the distribution of valued benefits, was an important means to help ensure future electoral success and to help shape programs to fit their notion of what was good or proper. Their role was now much more limited. Even provincial politicians found their influence restricted. Public servants, in turn, typically saw their goal as meeting established standards of good planning and efficient use of public resources. Savoie, in his detailed examination of the New Brunswick GDA, provides the telling example of a 'visitor orientation centre' funded under the tourism subsidiary agreement. The MLA from Edmundston, who also happened to be minister in charge of the provincial Treasury Board, insisted on a particular location for the centre slated for the Edmundston area. Provincial officials, relying on their cost-benefit calculations, had a different location in mind. After some months of dispute, provincial officials, with the backing of DREE officials, won. According to Savoie, 'Provincial government officials unreservedly accept that had the centre not been a GDA-sponsored project, then without doubt the minister's position would have prevailed.'[31]

Similar instances of federal ministers and departments being ignored or bypassed can also be found. In the case of a proposed Ottawa–New Brunswick fisheries agreement, the federal minister of fisheries and minister for New Brunswick, Romeo LeBlanc, was thoroughly miffed that DREE and the New Brunswick government had struck a tentative agreement bearing on fisheries issues. Aside from not having been consulted on the full scope of the agreement, LeBlanc felt that the monies in question should have been channelled through his department. In the end both DREE and LeBlanc refused to bend and the agreement was never consummated.[32]

The exact conditions of GDA decision-making and implementation varied from province to province and the lack of influence by politicians, both federal and provincial, may have been more a matter of perception than actual fact.[33] Nonetheless, in politics perceptions frequently are all that matter. Along with DREE success in cultivating federal-provincial collaboration at the field level came growing resentment among politicians and senior federal officials in line departments. At a minimum they were envious of what appeared to be much less stringent financial controls over DREE expenditures and increases in budgetary resources during a time of restraint. This resentment was later to contribute to DREE's demise as a department. But this event did not come about until 1982, and during the 1970's an unresponsive DREE was not the only obstacle that ministers faced.

Bureaucratic Pluralism and Ministerial Influence

DREE, in both its centralized mode under Marchand and its decentralized mode under Jamieson, provided illustrations of how the influence of MLAs, MPs, and ministers would be limited. DREE was not the only obstacle to influence, however. The central agency machinery grew apace. In 1975, stimulated in part by the heightened tension with the western provinces over energy and the continuing dilemma of constitutional reform, the Federal-Provincial Relations Office (FPRO) was created in order to improve intragovernmental co-ordination and support for the relevant cabinet committee. In the same year Trudeau's close friend and adviser, Michael Pitfield, took over the most senior position in the bureaucracy, clerk of the PCO and secretary of cabinet, which effectively placed him in charge of all major organizational and process issues. The subsequent impact of his appointment can be measured in part by his beliefs as stated shortly after he stepped down in 1983: 'My own view is that dealing with the governmental problems of which so many Canadians complain is a matter of process and machinery more than it is a matter of personalities and philosophies.'[34]

Definitions of what constituted 'governmental problems' of course varied widely. To the extent, however, that they related to matters of co-ordination and therefore were amenable to solution through improved organizational design, the solutions imposed by Pitfield and his predecessors proved to have limited effect. Equally important, they generated problems of their own. Among central agencies an overlapping of responsibilities led to conflicts. For example, TBS, in the hope of improving its assessment of proposed departmental expenditures, wanted access to these proposals at an earlier stage, a request to which PCO refused to accede for several years. An agreement between the two agencies was finally struck in 1976.[35] At the same time, in its annual reports to Parliament, the Office of the Auditor General continued to present what it claimed were woeful examples of government neglect in safeguarding the integrity of the expenditure process. The solution was the creation of yet another central agency in the form of the Office of the Comptroller General (OCG). Ostensibly it operated in tandem with TBS, but lines of authority between the two agencies soon crossed, serving to disperse further central agency management capacity rather than strengthening it.[36]

In a number of respects the central agencies, rather than improving co-ordination and the capacity for exerting central direction, appeared to have the opposite effect; this was evident not only in relations among departments and agencies but also in management problems within departments. A highly publicized conflagration in the form of the air traffic controllers' strike in 1976 revealed the difficulties senior officials in the air administration branch in the Department of Transport had in controlling their own personnel at headquarters in Ottawa.[37] The strike by air traffic controllers and pilots was clear evidence in the eyes of French Canadians that francophobia was still alive and well in English Canada and still entrenched in sectors of the Ottawa-based civil service. It triggered the resignation of Jean Marchand, the most senior minister from Quebec, from cabinet and played no small role in helping to set the stage for the Parti Québécois (PQ) victory that November. It was also evidence of serious management problems at the departmental level. At the initial stages neither the deputy minister nor the chief administrator of the air administration branch played much of a role in attempting to resolve the issue.[38]

These problems were not restricted to the Department of Transport. In almost all departments many senior officials lacked the knowledge of, or control over, the day-to-day operations of their departments enjoyed by their counterparts twenty years earlier. Expansion in the size of departments and the new administrative technologies meant that actual power tended to devolve to lower levels. Added to this was the mandatory participation of most senior civil servants in numerous interdepartmental committees that sapped them of both time and energy. In the view of many, the deputy had become the weak link. A close and comfortable relationship between the minister and his deputy was no longer sufficient to secure control over any given department.

Thus, in the 1970s the obstacles facing a minister, whether seeking to respond to the needs of a functional interest group or a regionally defined constituency, were formidable indeed. But while the task was difficult, it was not impossible, and for many ministers the pressures to do something for their regions were still there. Furthermore, amidst the chaos of conflicting agencies, recalcitrant middle-level managers, and seemingly impenetrable federal-provincial policy communities, there were also opportunities. Some of these opportunities resided in programs emanating from the PMO designed to ensure partisan advantage to MPs and ministers; others could be found through the application of a little ingenuity in bypassing, or even undermining, established procedures. In both instances it was necessary to be schooled in the vagaries and foibles of the Ottawa system. Above all, it required a recognition that power derived mainly from being able to use the resources of the administrative state.

Restricted Horizons:
The Provincialization of Regional Ministers

Before discussing the means that evolved during the 1970s for tapping administrative resources, we should focus briefly on the personalities and motives of the crop of regional ministers who became prominent during the 1970s. These figures had little in the way of independent power bases or strong connections with provincial party organizations. Indeed, two of them, Romeo LeBlanc and Marc Lalonde, were in a sense direct protégés of the prime minister, working in the PMO respectively as press secretary and principal secretary during the 1968–72 period. The factors stimulating this new crop of ministers varied considerably, but two types of motives can be identified. Some – for example, Allan J. MacEachen and Donald Jamieson – by their own admission placed themselves in the left wing of the party and openly identified with the culture and problems of their region.[39] They were also committed to doing something to help people overcome these problems, difficulties that related to the wide gap in income and employment prospects between the have-not provinces and central Canada.

The second set of motives can be put simply under the heading of self-preservation. As John Thompson, Charles Tupper, and John Macdonald well knew, getting elected and staying elected in one's own constituency was the all-important first step, and the pressures resulting from tight constituency races had by no means receded with the onset of nationally oriented election campaigns. While ministers no longer faced the odious double-election procedure (this requirement being eliminated after the 1930 election), the possibility of defeat still remained very high, certainly much higher than in the United Kingdom or the United States.[40] Even when governments are returned with an overall majority – in itself no mean feat, having occurred only twice in the post-war period – the turnover in seats among government members can still be significant. In 1988, for example, six incumbent ministers lost their seats. In short, there are relatively few constituencies in Canada that can be deemed to be truly safe.

The importance of national leadership and its effect on the overall vote limits what an MP or minister can do in his or her constituency to sway voters. But in a competitive three-way race a shift of a few hundred or even a few dozen votes can make all the difference. This acts as a powerful incentive for ministers to find means to sway or buttress what they perceive to be the crucial votes on the margin. If the minister were responsible for a whole province with several seats at stake, as was Jean Marchand for Quebec, these electoral considerations loom even larger. Marchand was thus responsible for the Quebec campaign strategy, the goals of which included capturing the seats held by the Ralliement Créditiste under Réal Caouette. At the same time Marchand faced stiff competition in his own Quebec City riding of Langelier. In the 1972 election, for example, the Conservatives nominated a complete unknown to face Marchand in the hope that this would allow the Créditiste candidate to squeeze through and defeat the province's lead minister in cabinet.[41] However, Marchand succeeded in winning his seat by a reasonable margin.

The 'Laird' of Cape Breton

Limited power bases and the danger of electoral failure served to restrict the horizons of ministers. Allan J. MacEachen is a useful case in point. Throughout his career as MP and minister his primary preoccupation was not Nova Scotia as much as Cape Breton and that part of the Nova Scotia mainland encompassed by his constituency of Cape Breton Highlands–Canso. This preoccupation can be attributed in part to his Cape Breton roots; but it was also conditioned by his experiences, beginning with his first foray into the political arena in 1949. At that time he lost the Liberal nomination for Inverness-Richmond to the seventy-two year-old but still precocious former Nova Scotia supreme court justice William Carroll, described as a 'veteran of the days of the "brass knuckle" politics.'[42] In 1953 Carroll retired and the nomination, and the seat, became MacEachen's. While re-elected in 1957, he was defeated by sixteen votes in the Diefenbaker landslide of 1958.

During his subsequent four-year stint as Pearson's special assistant, MacEachen gained both insight into parliamentary procedure and a special place in the heart of Mike Pearson. Regaining Inverness-Richmond in the 1962 election, he never lost again, though at times his margin did slip below one thousand. In 1963 he joined the Pearson cabinet as minister of labour, at the same time becoming a member of the special cabinet committee on economic growth and employment.[43] As minister of labour MacEachen ended the long-running saga of Hal Banks and the Seafarers International Union (SIU) by placing the SIU and four other unions under trusteeship. Later, as minister of health and welfare, he oversaw the implementation of universal medicare, and in 1967 added to his duties the chores of House leader. As well, with Jack Pickersgill's retirement in 1967, MacEachen was confirmed as senior Atlantic minister and given responsibility for the Atlantic Development Board. His success in Ottawa notwithstanding, MacEachen's defeat in 1958 and slim 909-vote majority in 1962 made him acutely aware of the vagaries of local political pressures. He tended to these needs with extreme care, capitalizing on announcements from Ottawa at every opportunity and promoting the cause of Cape Breton in cabinet.[44] In short order the 1960s saw the arrival of heavy water plants in Glace Bay and Port Hawkesbury and an oil refinery on the Strait of Canso, as well as the creation of the Cape Breton Development Corporation (DEVCO).

The arrival of the Deuterium of Canada Limited (DCL) heavy water plant in Glace Bay had its origins in the efforts made by the previous federal Conservative government and the Nova Scotia provincial government. In the final decision made by the federal cabinet, however, which saw the DCL proposal pitted against one from the Western Deuterium Company, the combined will of Pearson and MacEachen prevailed.[45] The timing of the decision (2 December 1963), the lengthy construction period during which upwards of two thousand men were employed on the site, and the official opening in 1967 gave MacEachen opportunity to participate in making announcements and cutting ribbons at every stage.[46] In 1965 the government announced that a second heavy water plant would be constructed in Port Hawkesbury by Canadian General Electric on the basis of a government-guaranteed contract. At the same time, since the province was primarily responsible for the DCL plant, in fact becoming the sole owner in 1969, the serious delays, labour strife, and cost overruns could be blamed by MacEachen on the provincial government.[47]

The rescue of the Sydney steel plant and the Cape Breton coalfields was supported not only by MacEachen but also by the provincial government under Robert Stanfield, local business interests, and the federal government as a whole. Yet the shaping of the final outcome – namely, the creation of federally owned DEVCO to manage the coalmines and to create new industrial enterprises, provincial ownership of the steel mill itself in 1968, and the subsequent takeover of the coke ovens by DEVCO – can be attributed largely to MacEachen. Stanfield, for example, favoured continued government support for private enterprise rather than public ownership.[48] As well, with its mandate to generate alternative employment opportunities, DEVCO became the single most important agency for regional development in the area, providing grants in support of a variety of projects, ranging from a chip- and sawmill at Inverness to the BA oil refinery at Point Tupper. The latter likely would not have been built without the support of $15 million in federal grants and loans, $4.5 million of which came from DEVCO.[49]

Yet for all his success, MacEachen's role and influence remained circumscribed, a fact that became obvious in 1968 when MacEachen was decisively defeated during the Liberal leadership race. His poor showing of only 165 votes on the first ballot demonstrated a lack of national support and a failure on the part of Nova Scotia delegates to come through.[50] While MacEachen was able to deliver his delegates to Trudeau on the second ballot, the provincial Liberal leader and later premier, Gerald Regan, marched his supporters over to the Robert Winters camp. In the June 1968 election, running in the newly created constituency of Cape Breton Highlands–Canso, MacEachen won by the less than comfortable margin of 578 votes, and furthermore was the only Liberal elected from Nova Scotia, the native son vote having gone mainly to the Conservative leader, Robert Stanfield. The senior minister from the Atlantic region was shown to have little influence outside of his own constituency.

In the new Trudeau cabinet he was given the portfolio of Manpower and Immigration but he lost his position as House leader. Within a few years, however, he regained the power he had lost in the 1968 débâcle and did so using the same means that had commended him to Pearson: his complete mastery of House rules, tactics, and strategies. Becoming House leader once more in 1970, he came truly into his own when the 1972 election put the government into a minority position. His task was to find ways to keep Parliament preoccupied with issues that would not lead to an early defeat and to negotiate deals with the opposition parties, primarily the NDP. With time, it was hoped, government credibility would improve and so would its chances in an election. MacEachen succeeded admirably: the government was kept alive for more than two years and regained its majority in the 1974 election. By June 1973 he had risen to number two in the cabinet pecking order, becoming deputy prime minister and outranking the minister of finance.[51] Once more MacEachen was in a favoured position. His reward was twofold: the external affairs portfolio beginning in 1974 and the protection of Cape Breton interests. The latter involved primarily the salvaging of the two heavy water plants. The DCL plant never did (nor ever would) function properly and by 1971 had all but been abandoned by the Nova Scotia government; the General Electric plant, while functional, had been rendered uneconomic by the sharp increase in oil prices over the 1973–4 period. The DCL plant was purchased by the federal government for $66 million in 1973, after expenditures of $225 million to make it operational, and the GE plant for $93 million in 1975. The plants were kept operating until 1985 at an annual cost of $120 million.[52]

MacEachen's influence during most of the 1970s derived almost solely from his adroit handling of the House. He administered neither a department nor programs. As House leader his administrative support consisted of a personal staff of a half-dozen tucked away in an office on the fourth floor of the Centre Block.[53] For other ministers, however, control over a major expenditure department with activities relating directly to their province was the main route to political power. The career of Romeo LeBlanc, Trudeau's former aid, presents a near perfect illustration of how a single department could be utilized to this end.

'The Fishermen's Friend'

Entering Parliament in 1972 LeBlanc had, by his own admission, no influence, 'no coat-tails,' of his own.[54] In 1974 he became minister of state for fisheries at a time when fisheries was part of the Department of Environment and considered a relatively minor portfolio.[55] By 1975 he gained responsibility for the environment portfolio as a whole and, as an indication of his own interests and priorities, obtained the title of minister of fisheries and the environment. He was to remain in charge of fisheries until 1982. Over that eight-year period he presided over major transformations in the east coast fisheries, changes that witnessed an enormous expansion in the size of the inshore fishing fleet, populated mainly by small independent fishermen, and a decrease in the power of the major fish processors. Significantly, a good portion of the impoverished inshore fishery was located along the shores of northeastern New Brunswick.

In 1974 major companies such as National Sea dominated the industry and the federal Department of Fisheries, essentially dividing allowable fish catches among themselves at annual meetings of the Fisheries Council of Canada.[56] In becoming minister LeBlanc took up the cause of fishermen: 'I told this to the prime minister. I wanted to do for fishermen what Eugene Whelan was doing for the farmers.'[57] He was willing to accept the need for a commercially viable fishery, 'but not at the expense of outlying fishing communities ... Fish is the property of the state and should be used to generate the widest possible benefits.'[58] LeBlanc began carrying out his self-ordained mandate by getting the fishermen themselves to organize, 'to make sure their voice is heard ... Make it possible for us to listen, and we will do our part,' he informed them.[59] For his part LeBlanc announced measures to assist the herring fishery, based on an under-utilized fish species.[60] Herring fishermen, principally those in the Bay of Fundy, received income supplements; a newly organized herring seiner co-operative, concentrating on the higher-value human rather than pet food markets, was given special quotas. Somewhat akin to the field officers employed by Sifton's Department of the Interior at the turn of the century and Gardiner's PFRA in the thirties and forties, LeBlanc introduced a new level of field officials, community service officers, to help fishermen in the organization of co-operatives and generally to adapt to the new regulatory regime.[61]

Both the fisheries and LeBlanc truly came into their own with the declaration of the two-hundred-mile offshore limit in 1977. LeBlanc ensured that the benefits would flow primarily to inshore fishermen by allocating to them more favourable quotas. Increased demand for fish and the decline of foreign fishing vessels resulting from the new limit resulted in substantial economic windfalls and made it easier to implement the new fish allocations. The increase in the value of the fisheries and the huge expansion in the number of participants also made the fisheries portfolio a much more important actor, both in the region and in Ottawa. When the inshore fisheries did come under pressure in the late 1970s, LeBlanc readily acquiesced in restricting access to fish stocks in certain areas to smaller vessels only, in the Northumberland Strait area, for example.[62]

These actions, in addition to a myriad of other programs, ranging from fishing vessel construction subsidies to special aid to compensate for storm damage, tended to benefit inshore fishermen in all provinces, especially Newfoundland but also in Nova Scotia and Quebec. Yet this fishery was of particular importance to the northeastern shore of New Brunswick, the core of LeBlanc's political constituency and the people with whom he identified most closely. Those who tended to benefit least from the LeBlanc regime, the large fish processors such as National Sea and Nickerson and offshore fishermen, were based primarily in Nova Scotia.[63] LeBlanc's support for New Brunswick culminated in September 1980 in the creation of a new administrative region specially for the Gulf of St Lawrence fishery, 'one of my best decisions,' according to LeBlanc.[64] Creation of the new region, with its new quarters and support staff in Moncton, came at the expense of the Newfoundland region, which had traditionally administered the Gulf fisheries. The decision was made at a time, coincidentally, when Newfoundland had only weak representation in cabinet.

Like MacEachen in Nova Scotia, LeBlanc became adept at exploiting news of any new federal initiatives or expenditures affecting the province of New Brunswick, whether they concerned expansion of port facilities, housing projects, or studies examining the feasibility of peat-fired generating plants. It was rare when LeBlanc failed to speak on behalf of a fellow cabinet minister in announcing a new project or participating in a ribbon-cutting ceremony.[65] It went further, however. In pursuing projects that he considered crucial for New Brunswick – highways, for example, and especially Route 11 in the northeast – he would cultivate links not only with ministers from the relevant departments but also directly with officials in those departments, getting 'to know the highway projects office at MOT almost as well as my own staff.'[66] These were officials not at the deputy or assistant deputy minister level but much lower, at the director (middle-management) level, for example.

LeBlanc had at best only limited faith in Ottawa-based officials, both within and outside his department, and depended in the main on his 'field generals,' the directors general in charge of the regional offices, for 'when it [a problem] hits question period you need to talk to these people, not some abstract policy analyst in Ottawa.' Many of his initiatives were taken after only limited consultation with senior officials in his department. The decision to create a separate Gulf fisheries region, for example, was presented essentially as a fait accompli. Leonard Cowley, the regional director for Newfoundland, was appointed 'to create the structure for the new region immediately, not to study it.'[67] To have asked for advice beforehand would have given the bureaucracy a chance to argue and delay, LeBlanc felt, which in turn would have led to paralysis. His propensity to bypass Ottawa-based officials also applied to interdepartmental matters. A safety problem with the overloading of herring seiners on the west coast, which required the co-operation of the RCMP, Transport, and National Defence, was resolved only, LeBlanc claims, when he was able to bring together the relevant officials out in the field, thereby avoiding Ottawa-based interdepartmental disputes over costs and compensation.[68]

For LeBlanc the battle waged on behalf of New Brunswick had to be fought in a number of arenas; and it involved not only deployment of departmental resources, pressuring other departments, or log-rolling with other ministers, but also 'changing the mindset' of officials and ministers. In arguing before Treasury Board, LeBlanc noted, 'if you can convince them of the validity of your case and you win, then you can also win the next three.' Unlike MacEachen, LeBlanc tended towards a broader province-wide view, promoting the Saint John shipyard as well as northeastern development. He also had a much larger caucus – six or seven of the ten New Brunswick seats in the 1974–84 period – which he was able to mobilize in support of his positions, such as that on the need to complete construction of Highway 11. MacEachen, in contrast, was at times a caucus of one (1968–74). When it grew to a caucus of two in 1974, his relations with Coline Campbell, elected in the riding of South West Nova, were lukewarm at best. While willing to respond to pleas from mainland Nova Scotia constituencies, he saw his primary obligations, and the focus of his initiatives, as lying in Cape Breton. In other respects MacEachen and LeBlanc were closer. Neither had strong links with the provincial party. In New Brunswick this was primarily because the Liberals were never in power provincially during LeBlanc's tenure as minister. As well, LeBlanc felt no obligations towards, nor had links with, the older generation of New Brunswick Liberals dating from the Louis Robichaud period. His success was essentially self-made and his aim was to preserve his independence, to constitute an autonomous voice for New Brunswick. He did not want to follow the course of his predecessor, J.-E. Dubé, who LeBlanc felt had been no more than an intermediary between Robichaud and the prime minister.[69]

In Nova Scotia, in the aftermath of the 1968 leadership débâcle, there was little love lost between MacEachen and Regan, the Liberal premier from 1971 through 1978. Nonetheless, there was co-operation between the two, involving the federal purchase of the two heavy water plants on MacEachen's side, thereby relieving the provincial government of a considerable financial burden, and smaller projects such as the province extending the runway at the Port Hawkesbury municipal airport for MacEachen's benefit. Federal and provincial financial support for the provincially owned Sysco steel mill in Sydney was to everyone's benefit. But this co-operation and set of reciprocal obligations differed little from what had prevailed when Stanfield, for example, had been in power.[70] Nor did the links between MacEachen and the provincial government noticeably change when the provincial Conservatives under John Buchanan took office again in 1978. In short, both LeBlanc and MacEachen, for differing reasons perhaps, stood aloof from provincial Liberal affairs.

Patronage versus the Pork-barrel

LeBlanc and MacEachen were alike in one further respect. The means they used to engender popular support in their provinces, support they hoped would translate into votes at election time, were only loosely related to traditional patronage techniques. Unlike the workers in Clifford Sifton's Department of the Interior or the field officers of Jimmy Gardiner's PFRA, fisheries officers working in New Brunswick were *not* at the same time acting on behalf of the Liberal party. Nor were the employees of DEVCO in Cape Breton. For LeBlanc it was the hope that members of the new fishermen's organizations and co-operatives he had helped spawn and supported with grants and quota allocations would remember that fact on election day.

Equally, MacEachen no doubt had the hope that constituents would make the connection – indeed, he would remind them of it – between his position as minister and some local project funded by DEVCO. He was not, however, in the position to ensure that any given project would be supported or that only Liberal supporters would receive the benefits in the form of either jobs or services. As MacEachen noted in explaining delays in the approval of a proposed chip- and sawmill in the Cape Breton town of Inverness: 'I cannot prejudge Devco's decision, but certainly there is no question about my support of this project.'[71] Some forms of traditional patronage still played a role, but it was the pork-barrel, expenditures by federal agencies aimed at collectivities rather than individuals, that had become increasingly important. For politicians it became the task to try and shape these expenditures to ensure maximum political advantage. This was the case not only in New Brunswick and Nova Scotia but throughout Canada.

Ironically, the ethos of participatory democracy during the 1960s and 1970s and the expansion of government services did result in more patronage opportunities becoming available: appointments to the large variety of boards, commissions, and agencies created to administer or adjudicate the myriad of regulations concerning parole and immigration appeals, for example, or to advise or direct museums, granting agencies, and the like. These appointments were, and still are, very much small potatoes, carrying at best honoraria of only a few thousand dollars. These order-in-council appointments, numbering in the thousands, would be compiled in the PMO and then sent to the federal affairs committees in thick black binders. Under the supervision of the regional minister, the positions would be allocated to MPs and defeated candidates for distribution to the faithful. Yet while numerous, their scale, both in number and in remuneration, was nothing like what had been available under Macdonald and Laurier. And while important for party stalwarts who kept the local machinery ticking over between elections, this kind of patronage was at best only of indirect help in capturing the loyalties of actual voters. In fact, given the opprobrium that came to attach itself to patronage practices, particularly in urban areas, it could easily have the opposite effect by feeding public cynicism.[72]

Given these limits, ministers needed to turn to other sources to build political support. The decade of the 1970s saw the rise of a number of programs that were designed in part to meet partisan considerations. There were also certain programs that over time proved to be susceptible to influence exercised by particular ministers. These programs would be used to help buttress support among marginal voters but, it should be stressed, they had limitations. They depended on bloc expenditures which provided mainly universal or indivisible public goods such as public parks or a new federal office building, and such expenditures cannot be directed to, or away from, any specific individual.

Like patronage, the pork-barrel has a long tradition in Canadian politics. Most kinds of public policy, ranging from tariff protection for specific products to breakwaters and post offices, can be used to curry favour with the local citizenry.[73] Precisely because the line between legitimate and quasi-legitimate public expenditures is often so difficult to discern, pork-barrelling as a technique is easier to deploy than direct patronage. It is, of course, possible to couple together patronage and pork-barrelling – for example letting without tender a construction contract for an office building to a favoured firm – and it has been done. But in the present era this can be a highly explosive combination, pregnant with the possibility of abuse and scandal, and it is something that the wise politician avoids.[74] At the same time, in so far as it is both difficult and unwise to direct pork-barrel benefits to individuals, it makes such expenditures less efficient in ensuring that benefits reach marginal voters, which adds pressure to increase expenditures in order to overcome these limitations.

From Local Initiatives to New Fighter Aircraft

Some of these limitations, and the partisan purposes to which pork-barrel expenditures may be put, can be illustrated with brief reference to four programs: the Local Initiatives Program (LIP) of the early 1970s, the RDIA program administered by DREE, the administrative decentralization program implemented by Treasury Board in the mid-1970s, and defence expenditures in the latter part of the 1970s.

Since coming into existence in 1966, the Department of Manpower and Immigration (becoming Employment and Immigration in 1977) has had responsibility for a variety of programs designed to provide short-term employment in high unemployment areas, particularly during the winter months, and also seasonal employment for categories such as university students. Consistent with the 'participationist' thrust of the Trudeau government and the increasing importance of younger voters – the voting age was lowered from twenty-one to eighteen in 1971 – the various make-work projects were updated and repackaged, resulting in innovative programs such as Opportunities For Youth (OFY) announced in 1970 and the LIP program in 1971.[75] In both cases applications for projects of short duration, from local youth groups in the case of OFY and community groups in the case of LIP, were submitted to local manpower offices. In the case of LIP, the program on which most information exists, a provincially based LIP co-ordinator made recommendations on individual applications to Ottawa where final decisions were made. According to a study by Donald Blake, in the first year of the program the LIP co-ordinator did consult the MPs but on a rather unsystematic basis. In subsequent years, in light of criticisms, this consultation was formalized and based in part on input from constituency advisory groups, appointed primarily on the nomination of the local MP.[76] The MPs, it should be noted, included opposition as well as government MPs, though the extent to which opposition MPs were involved in the first year of the program is not clear.

What was clear, however, was that in that first year (1972–3), excepting Alberta and Manitoba, Liberal ridings on average did better. The initial allocation of funds was ostensibly based on considerations such as average winter unemployment in Canada Manpower Centre districts. Using three separate measures of need at the constituency level – percentage unemployed in 1971, percentage of natives, and percentage of the population over age fifteen with a primary education or less – Blake discovered that even when controlling for these three need factors, partisan factors such as competitiveness of the seat, Liberal incumbency, and cabinet minister incumbency were positively associated with LIP allocations. Furthermore, in examining those seats held by cabinet ministers, Blake discovered that eleven of the fourteen seats deemed to be marginal or competitive received more than would be expected, even taking into account the three partisan factors. 'For example, Donald Macdonald's constituency of Rosedale ... would have been "entitled" to less than one dollar per capita according to the model.'[77] The riding received several times that. Two other ministers,

Allan MacEachen and Ronald Basford (Vancouver Centre), also did very well; and even safe seats held by ministers such as Jamieson, Dubé, Marchand, Lalonde, and Drury received much larger LIP allocations than would be expected, although some, such as that of Jack Davis, minister of fisheries in the competitive riding of North Vancouver, received less than would have been warranted under the model. Thus, while Liberal MPs (especially in Quebec), ministers in particular, fared much better in the allocation process, there was variation, suggesting that some ministers, for example, were either less adept or perhaps had difficulties with their colleagues. Blake cautiously suggests that the results of the LIP allocation process were not necessarily due to any comprehensive or conscious policy. Rather, separate and discrete decisions were made concerning a program that was distributive and open-ended in character and hence those with superior access to ultimate decision-makers fared much better.

In the two subsequent years of the program, the criteria were tightened and the effects of partisan advantage reduced. There was also much less money available: in 1974–5 only $79 million was allocated, down from the $235 million available in 1972–3. At the same time Blake may have underestimated the possibility of more systematic efforts made to bias LIP expenditures in a partisan direction, for later evidence in a different policy area – regional development – but also collected on a constituency basis shows some of the same patterns, at least for Quebec. DREE programs for the 1969–73 period, it will be recalled, were centrally controlled and specifically designated for special growth areas, much to the regret of provincial governments and some MPs and ministers, mainly in the Atlantic region. For Quebec, however, while there was the same emphasis on federal delivery, the program criteria for what constituted special areas were defined more loosely.[78] The DREE minister, Jean Marchand, was also the political minister for Quebec. The regions defined as special areas could be so designated by a cabinet order-in-council, which provided considerable flexibility, and there were suggestions prior to the 1972 election that this flexibility was being used to designate marginal or competitive ridings as special areas.[79] Certainly evidence of the various infrastructure projects funded by DREE was prominently displayed in Liberal campaign advertising, including the new 'Jean Marchand dam' in the city of Lachute.

In the case of the RDIA incentives program – a program administered by DREE in tandem with the special areas program – manufacturing firms would be subsidized for investing in designated regions. The act was both broad – authorizing the minister to use 'special measures to facilitate economic expansion and social adjustment' – and so vague in its criteria 'that its provisions are almost meaningless.'[80] Although there were rules defining maximum support for firms as well as the designated regions, the minister had almost complete discretion on the granting of subsidies and size of the award. Similar to Blake in his analysis of LIP, Macnaughton and Winn analysed RDIA expenditures and electoral results at the riding level, using indicators of economic need such as unemployment, labour force participation, and mean family incomes as controls. They found that the mere presence of a Liberal member or cabinet minister had little effect. They did, however, uncover one link that closely resembled one found by Blake: a much higher level of expenditures in Quebec ridings held by Créditistes. These ridings clearly were targeted by Liberal party strategists for Quebec, including the chief strategist, Jean Marchand. The Créditistes, who at one point held twenty-six seats during the 1960s, had effectively denied the Liberals a majority government in 1963 and 1965. In 1968 and 1972 they still held fourteen and sixteen seats respectively; and at a time of growing separatist agitation it became all that much more important to demonstrate Liberal hegemony over Quebec. That it was Marchand's aim to single out Créditiste ridings, or ridings where they threatened, is corroborated by newspaper accounts. In ridings that were considered safe, such as in the Lac Saint-Jean area, Marchand would tell audiences that DREE grants would be pumped into the area only if it could be proved they made economic sense. He would then launch into 'a discourse on the problem of underdeveloped regions in France, the southern United States and China,' effectively ignoring local issues. In contrast, in long-time Créditiste ridings such as Roberval in eastern Quebec, Marchand bluntly stated that a Liberal MP would be able to put the case for incentive grants much more forcefully.[81]

The RDIA was altered in other ways to accommodate political pressures. In late 1970, in the aftermath of the FLQ crisis and declining economic prospects, the city of Montreal was made a 'temporary' designated region for a two-year period beginning in 1971, along with Hull and the easternmost counties in Ontario. As well, Marchand created a special sixty-person DREE office based in Montreal to handle all applications for subventions from the new southwestern Quebec special region. At the end of the two-year period 360 incentive grants had been accepted by firms in the new region, leading, it was claimed, to capital commitments of $225 million and the creation of fourteen thousand jobs.[82]

It seems reasonably clear that in the case of RDIA, and possibly LIP as well, Marchand was able to use these programs to help effect a broad strategy for attaining Liberal hegemony over Quebec, identifying possible weak ridings, including his own, and in particular targeting the Créditiste strongholds for a long-term assault. That the strategy was successful was evident in the 1980 election, when the last of the Créditistes was eliminated from the electoral map and the Liberals obtained all but one of the seventy-five Quebec seats.

After the 1972 election Marchand left the DREE portfolio, and the decentralized GDA approach replaced the centralized design and implementation mode of the Marchand-Kent regime. The GDA approach, premised on close federal-provincial co-operation, made it more difficult for regional ministers to influence developments, as LeBlanc discovered in New Brunswick. At the same time, the new DREE minister, Donald Jamieson, was able to do well for his own province. The federal share of DREE-Newfoundland sponsored joint projects under the GDA was 90 per cent of project costs, compared to 80 per cent in Nova Scotia and New Brunswick. The Burin peninsula, encompassing most of Jamieson's constituency of Burin-Burgeo, received special attention. As minister of transport, Jamieson had already seen to the construction of a 165-mile highway linking the towns of Marystown and Swift Current.[83] Under the Newfoundland GDA, highway construction became the largest single component, more than $137 million of the $651 million GDA total.[84] One senior Newfoundland official recalls participating in meetings with Jamieson, Frank Moores (Newfoundland premier at the time), and other officials from DREE and the provincial government 'on a weekend over a case of beer' to decide on 'which roads were going to be built where.'[85] As it turned out, most of the money was spent in the Burin peninsula and northern peninsula sections of the province. At one point, when there was $500,000 left over, Jamieson had a bridge constructed over the Black River in his riding, noting that 'If you build a bridge, you can be damned sure somebody will build a road to it.'[86]

In September 1975 Jamieson was replaced by Marcel Lessard who, according to Savoie, 'was not a regional minister, as were the first two, and he was new in the cabinet, and thus a "junior minister."'[87] This may explain why officials within DREE became more influential, as well as more adept in limiting political influence. It may also explain why DREE lost ground within cabinet, possibly contributing to its later demise. Lessard did prove susceptible, however, to influence from the seven Montreal-region ministers who wanted their area to become eligible once more for RDIA incentive grants, a demand that Jamieson had been able to resist and to which Marchand had acceded only on a temporary basis from 1971 to 1973. In 1977 the wishes of André Ouellet, Jean-Pierre Goyer, Warren Allmand, and Bryce Mackasey, among others, prevailed and the Montreal area was designated eligible for discretionary grants targeting certain high-growth manufacturing industries. The arguments made in cabinet by Montreal-area ministers were buttressed by the PQ victory the previous year, the departure of investments from Montreal, and the fact that east-end Montreal in particular was a PQ stronghold. As a quid pro quo, the rest of the cabinet extracted promises that the RDIA program would be extended to other low-growth areas of Canada, such as eastern Ontario and Northern British Columbia.

The extension of the RDIA program also signalled that the promise made initially by Marchand in 1969, namely that 80 per cent of DREE spending would take place east of Trois-Rivières, would never be consummated.[88] In the year 1980–1 the ratio between east and west was almost the reverse: only 36 per cent was being spent in the Atlantic region broadly defined.[89] Furthermore, by that year 50 per cent of the population and 93 per cent of Canada's land mass were eligible for DREE support. A set of programs that originally enjoyed nearly 2 per cent of the annual federal budget and was targeted towards a specific undeveloped area of the nation had become primarily distributional in character, accessible to any minister with some claim to having an economically lagging region within his or her province.

While unhappy with the changes resulting from the adoption of the GDA approach in 1974, cabinet ministers did find attractive one feature of the DREE reorganization: the decentralization of the department. Prior to 1974 more than 80 per cent of DREE staff were based in Ottawa; afterwards this figure fell to less than 40 per cent.[90] Ministers such as Otto Lang and Romeo LeBlanc were able to welcome the physical presence of the regional headquarters for western Canada and Atlantic Canada into their respective communities of Saskatoon and Moncton. When certain departments such as Revenue Canada indicated a need for new facilities and increased data-processing capacity, cabinet began expressing interest in having this expansion take place outside of Ottawa. It was in this light that the president of the Treasury Board, Jean Chrétien, announced in May 1975 that other departments would be examined with a view to relocating some or all of their operations outside of the National Capital Region and other major metropolitan centres. The ostensible aim of the new deconcentration program was to bring the administration of certain programs into closer proximity to people affected by them; to heighten the federal presence in certain areas; and to promote growth and reduce unemployment in economically weak areas of the country.[91]

A special task force within the Treasury Board Secretariat was created to examine issues such as the type of operations and critical size of units that could most easily be shifted, to draft guidelines, and ultimately to identify actual units for relocation. Fairly quickly it was able to identify a number of units as suitable. Equally quickly, ministers became involved in the allocation process. Once the initial test had been met – that the unit in question could be moved from Ottawa and operate reasonably well in smaller communities – the other criteria, such as the 'economic need' of target communities and the need for 'federal visibility,' came into play. These criteria were open-ended and flexible. The other criterion of bringing units closer to affected client groups soon became irrelevant as only one or two relocations at the most could be justified on those grounds. It was a setting that provided ample opportunity for making good on earlier promises and the exercise of ministerial clout. As one member of the task force described it, the prevailing practice was essentially one of log-rolling with fellow ministers: 'Trade-offs were made, outfits were moved and shuffled so that everyone was happy.'[92]

By the end of 1976 the relocation of nine units had been announced, including the headquarters of Veterans' Affairs to Charlottetown; the cheque redemption centre of Supply and Services to Matane, Quebec; the superannuation unit of Supply and Services, responsible for administering public service pensions, to Moncton; the annuities and central index unit of the Unemployment Insurance Commission to Bathurst, New Brunswick; and new National Revenue Taxation data centres to St John's Newfoundland, Jonquière and Shawinigan, Quebec, Winnipeg, and Surrey, British Columbia. In October 1977 the government announced a further fifteen units as candidates for relocation, including the Canada Post philatelic centre to Antigonish, Nova Scotia, the Telecommunications Regulatory Service of the Department of Communications to Quebec City, and the headquarters of the Farm Credit Corporation to Camrose, Alberta. All told, the twenty-four units represented approximately 4500 full-time and 5600 temporary jobs.

In many cases the political connection was clear cut: the minister of veterans' affairs, Daniel MacDonald, was also the senior (and only) minister from Prince Edward Island; Camrose was home to Jack Horner, the new minister of industry, trade and commerce and recent defector from the Conservative party. Of the twenty-four units, sixteen were slated for Liberal ridings and eight of these ridings were held by cabinet ministers.[93] The initial announcement, however, represented only the first, and in some respects the easiest, stage for ministers in bringing a much-needed economic boast to communities in their province or region. There still remained significant hurdles to leap before overcoming the resistance both from public sector unions and from Ottawa-based departments. A high proportion of employees in affected units were unwilling to move – only one-third were willing to do so in the case of the first ten units, for example – which meant an increase in costs as special guidelines concerning employee rights were developed and implemented in consultation with affected unions. Despite the consultation, the Public Service Alliance continued to question publicly the costs and the political motives of cabinet.

Resistance from senior executives was no less strong, albeit much less public. A senior official in Supply and Services, while accepting the legitimacy of cabinet's right to make such decisions, nevertheless saw decentralization 'as a motherhood issue – anti-Ottawa, anti-bureaucratic.'[94] Canada Post officials did everything possible to delay planning for the new philatelic centre, and with the defeat of the Liberals in 1979 it appeared that they would succeed in keeping the unit in Ottawa.[95] Re-election of the Liberals in 1980, however, meant that pressure was applied once again, this time buttressed by directives from Treasury Board that departments would need to include in their annual strategic overviews and operational plans accounts of their efforts to relocate units.[96] By mid-1982 the new philatelic centre in downtown Antigonish was open for business.

In other instances ministers had to make special efforts to ensure that the unit in question would end up in a particular location within their region. Thus the superannuation centre, originally slated for Moncton, was eventually constructed twenty miles away in Shediac, just inside Romeo LeBlanc's constituency.[97] For LeBlanc the end result was still less than satisfactory. The $10 million contract to construct the new facility was let to an Ottawa firm. According to LeBlanc, between the bids from a local firm and the Ottawa firm was a 'difference of only a couple of hundred thousand; no such contract should be let nationally.'[98] LeBlanc's arguments to Treasury Board that the original contract be overturned was rejected.

For LeBlanc letting the contract locally would have generated even greater benefits for the region. Two years later and one hundred miles away, another contract was let, this time for the construction of the Canada Post philatelic centre in Antigonish, in Allan MacEachen's riding. In this instance the construction contract did go to a local firm but, much to the chagrin of local Liberals, it happened to be a firm with strong Tory connections. Wisely MacEachen resisted demands from the Liberal faithful that something be done about this, just as he had earlier declined to act on behalf of some of the same individuals who happened to have choice pieces of Antigonish real estate to sell, appropriate, they felt, to the needs of the philatelic centre.[99] MacEachen knew fully the dangers of mixing direct patronage with the pork-barrel. For him it was enough to bring into Antigonish a substantial infusion of economic activity in the form of several permanent jobs. To do more was to have courted danger in skirting if not actually violating the criminal code and, equally important, in opening a Pandora's box of demands, ranging from the improbable to the impossible, from eager constituents, many without doubt direct descendants of those who had plagued poor John Thompson nearly a century before.

The Treasury Board decentralization program was illustrative of one of the more direct ways in which programs were designed, and implemented, to suit the partisan needs of cabinet ministers. But it was also indicative of some of the more fundamental problems facing ministers and civil servants in responding to the obvious need to be seen doing something for the regions. To officials, especially those in line departments, the program represented an unfortunate and costly distortion of departmental operations. The decisions and directives had to be acted upon since they were after all made by cabinet; but they felt them to be unfortunate decisions nonetheless. Ministers and many MPs for their part saw the behaviour of officials largely as expressions of self-interest and an insular Ottawa mentality. These differences in views were reconciled only to a limited extent by the actual implementation experience, for the results of the program provided evidence for both views.

The most controversial relocation was that of the Department of Veterans' Affairs to Prince Edward Island. The costs of the move itself, $44 million including costs for retraining as well as $21 million for land and the new building in Charlottetown, have drawn criticism. The most telling drawback, however, has been the continuing need to shuttle the senior staff, including the deputy minister, back and forth between Charlottetown and Ottawa. Senior officials and the minister found it necessary to interact on a frequent basis both with each other and with officials from other departments.[100] However, further moves, such as those of the cheque redemption centre to Matane and the superannuation centre to Shediac, proved surprisingly successful. Largely because these are stand-alone operations, requiring only limited communication and interaction with Supply and Services headquarters in Ottawa, the need for the continual travel by senior staff to Ottawa does not exist. The existence of stable populations in the Gaspé and eastern New Brunswick has led to low turnover in staff, which in turn has meant lowered training costs and increased productivity. In short, these two units, in addition to providing more than six hundred jobs in the two communities, also proved less costly to operate. Other technically oriented but still labour-intensive operational units, such as the five regional data taxation centres of the Department of National Revenue, also continue to function in efficient fashion.

The lessons of the pros and cons of the decentralization program may have been lost, however. In 1981 the Treasury Board president, Donald Johnston, disbanded the special decentralization task force and with it went the pool of expertise that could help judge the feasibility of any proposed move. For ministers such as Romeo LeBlanc the positive experiences of the Shediac and Bathurst units were proof that Ottawa bureaucrats were prone to over-react and that, if anything, more units could be moved. Unfortunately, it is probable that by 1980 most of the likely candidates for relocation had already been identified and as a result the pool of suitable units more or less depleted. Kenneth Kernaghan claims that subsequent decisions on relocations came to be based increasingly on political criteria rather than on rational operational grounds.[101] The one lesson that Romeo LeBlanc had learned, and in fact one he already knew, was the long lead time required before a project became a concrete entity set firmly in native soil. It was a matter of first 'getting it into the estimates' and then continuing to apply pressure on the officials and ministers responsible.[102]

The fourth area of expenditure of interest by ministers and MPs concerns those programs relating to national defence. No area of government operations or expenditure is entirely free from ministerial consideration as to possible effects, beneficial or otherwise, on their region, and those of the Department of National Defence are no exception. It has been suggested, for example, that in the early 1950s Jimmy Gardiner supported the acquisition of the pride of Canada's navy, the aircraft carrier HMSC *Bonaventure*, in the expectation that it would result in increased sales of tinned meat and other agricultural products to Great Britain. Certainly shipbuilding contracts throughout the 1950s and 1960s for frigates and destroyers, including the four Tribal class destroyers laid down in 1969, were regionally disbursed.[103]

In the early 1970s there were two problems facing cabinet and the military. First, Canada was spending less and less of its budget on national defence and hence there were fewer military purchases. In this connection it was becoming increasingly evident that much of Canada's aging military equipment, such as the Argus maritime patrol aircraft, was in imminent need of replacement. Secondly, given the increasing complexity and sophistication of weapons systems and military equipment generally, it had become more difficult to purchase military matériel domestically. At the same time there was a growing sense within Ottawa of the need for, and acceptance of, what has been called 'military Keynesianism,' the use of military expenditures to promote broadly defined social welfare goals such as the generation of employment.[104] As defence minister in the 1960s, Paul Hellyer had promoted the notion of industrial offsets and used it to bring substantial work to Canadair when the armed forces acquired the CF-5 fighter aircraft. At the time the military were far from enthusiastic about the concept, feeling that with the CF-5 they had been pressured into accepting an inferior and unsuitable aircraft.[105] By the early 1970s, however, when military expenditures had reached rock-bottom, they came to the realization that this was the only means to obtain increased funding. The acceptance by both the cabinet and the bureaucracy of the need for a military replacement program resulted in a strategy that saw military orders being placed abroad on condition that they would provide offsetting benefits for domestic manufacturers and suppliers, both military and non-military.

For ministers and others who carried the hope that this would provide opportunities for regionally based suppliers there were some distinct limitations, despite the fact that procurement requests from 1975 onward would now ask suppliers 'to assist in meeting the Government's objectives for less economically developed regions.' First, ministers collectively were struck by the magnitude of the overall costs. Thus they gave instructions, both in the case of the new long-range patrol aircraft (LRPA) and the new fighter aircraft (NFA) programs, that costs not exceed certain limits. In the case of the NFA, cabinet directives were particulary explicit, emphasizing Canada's existing defence priorities, delivery schedules, and 'off-the-shelf procurement.' The only category left open-ended was in the area of industrial offsets.[106] In order to meet the three basic objectives – military needs, cost containment, and industrial offsets – special teams drawing experts from the departments of National Defence, Supply and Services, and Industry, Trade and Commerce were set up to evaluate competing bids. These initial cabinet directives and the nature of the task facing the evaluation teams had two immediate effects: they narrowed considerably the available hardware choices and limited the opportunity for bureaucratic politics.

In the case of the detailed evaluation procedures for the LRPA, it soon became evident that an updated version of the Lockheed Orion aircraft was the front-runner, ahead of two other proposals: the military version of the Boeing 707 and the retro-fitting of the Argus by Canadair. The 707 would have been significantly more expensive, both to purchase and to operate; the retro-fitted Argus was judged inferior as a modern aircraft and, interestingly, would have provided only limited industrial offsets. They were, however, the two options favoured by two regional ministers. James Richardson, defence minister at the time, had a strong preference for the 707 since a good portion of the offset work would fall to the Boeing components plant in Winnipeg. Jean-Pierre Goyer, supply minister, had cast himself as the protector and promoter of Montreal-based Canadair and therefore argued on behalf of the Argus. In the end the contract went to Lockheed, though not without a certain amount of delay due to a shortfall in start-up financing. Furthermore, neither Richardson nor Goyer could be termed losers. Sperry Univac, a Lockheed subcontractor, opened a Winnipeg plant to manufacture digital magnetic tape units and, as part of the offset agreement, a large portion of the Orion contract was directed to Canadair.[107]

In part because of the start-up delays experienced with the LRPA contract, cost considerations loomed even more important when the bidding for the NFA began. Again, in light of the cabinet's directives and the availability of relatively few 'off-the-shelve suppliers,' the options were limited. The short list consisted of the General Dynamics F-16, a single-engined fighter aircraft already purchased by a number of NATO countries, and the McDonnell Douglas F-18A, an existing twin-engined aircraft flown by the US navy. The military had already decided that it needed a two-engined aircraft, which favoured the F-18A, and the evaluation team had judged the McDonnell Douglas industrial offset package to be superior. At the same time the F-16 was considerably cheaper, which meant more aircraft for the same amount of money. As well, National Defence felt that a short list of only one would be unwise for both diplomatic and strategic reasons; at a minimum it would reduce the government's ability to negotiate the best possible deal with McDonnell Douglas.[108]

More so than in the case of the LPRA, controversy over the NFA came to be dominated by regional overtones. Canadair and Pratt and Whitney, both located in Montreal, were extensively involved in the F-16 bid. The Quebec premier, René Lévesque, and federal Liberal MPs from Quebec, mainly in the Montreal area, made it clear that in their view Quebec deserved the contract to counterbalance the fact that the automobile industry was located predominantly in Ontario. The final decision by cabinet favoured the F-18A. By this time, the spring of 1980, Goyer was no longer in cabinet, and none of the three ministers, Gray, Lamontagne, and Blais of Industry, Trade and Commerce, National Defence, and Supply respectively, were willing to support the F-16. Only one of the three ministers was from Quebec – Gilles Lamontagne, minister of national defence – and he represented a riding near Quebec City and was thus less affected by pressure from the Montreal area. The key Quebec minister at that stage, Marc Lalonde, who had succeeded Marchand as political minister for the province, declined to use his influence to force a decision favouring the F-16. He did, however, arrange meetings between Lamontagne and Montreal-area ministers and MPs. In the end a number of offsetting trade-offs were made, including promises of subcontract work for Canadair.[109]

For both the LRPA and NFA it can be said that the overall integrity of the evaluation process was maintained and that the cabinet displayed reasonably strong discipline in the face of considerable pressure, including publicly stated opposition from its own backbenchers. But it is important to stress that this discipline was buttressed by the *absence* of bureaucratic conflict. Atkinson and Nossal point out that the bureaucracy, specifically the interdepartmental evaluation team, fully aware of the stakes involved, presented a united front.[110] Differences between departments were worked out beforehand at the bureaucratic level, and the evidence carefully prepared and presented. Ministers who sought alternative sources of advice or support from within the bureaucracy for their positions favouring one of the other bids were simply out of luck. Both programs were still bent to a degree to accommodate the interests of certain ministers, such as André Ouellet, but many of the trade-offs made were outside of the procurement programs themselves. The $100 million Complexe Guy Favreau in east-end Montreal was one such item; an actual reduction in a commitment made to Ontario was another.[111] Yet most of the substance and, most important, the overall public appearance of the integrity of the process, especially outside of Quebec, remained intact.

Beyond the LRPA and NFA programs there were some bitter conflicts among ministers over the distribution of lesser defence contracts. For example, Richardson, as defence minister, had promised to CAE Electronics in 1974 that its Winnipeg facility would receive an overhaul contract for military Boeing 707s. After Richardson left the cabinet in 1976, Goyer succeeded in reversing the decision in favour of Canadair. When CAE threatened legal action it gained the impression that at least two forthcoming contracts would be endangered if they proceeded with their suit.[112] CAE did proceed and eventually took the case to the Federal Court of Canada in 1980, successfully arguing that it had been caught, as an innocent party, in the cross-fire between two warring ministers.[113]

The LRPA and NFA decisions, and the processes leading up to them, did illustrate the limits of regional ministerial influence. On truly large items, where the bureaucracy was both united and acting in a manner consistent with explicit directives received from cabinet, it became very difficult for either individual ministers or cabinet as a whole to reverse the overall thrust of the advice tendered by officials. Opportunities were to be found more at the margins of such programs. Ministers, in seeking opportunities, were more likely to target smaller programs, still sizeable expenditures but ones they had a realistic chance of obtaining through trade-offs with other ministers. In a smaller province, moderate-sized expenditures can go a long way. In Prince Edward Island, for example, the Department of Veterans' Affairs has become the third-largest, and best-paying, employer in the province.[114]

The range of programs influenced by ministers for regional purposes was not limited to the four areas discussed above. Crown corporations, for example, are favourite targets. Although the relationship between individual corporations and cabinet ministers is often supposed to be arm's length, crown corporations are susceptible to informal approaches from ministers, particulary those ministers responsible for their well-being in cabinet. Crown corporations in turn try to adapt by giving way on those issues they feel will maximize political support for their activities while at the same time preserving the integrity of what they perceive to be their core operations.

In these respects Air Canada is an excellent example. Until its privatization in 1988 and 1989 it was directly dependent on cabinet for major decisions on capitalization for expansion or the acquisition of new aircraft, and on the minister of transport for making its case in cabinet. It was also expected to cross-subsidize marginal or unprofitable routes deemed important for social or economic reasons. Over the years Air Canada had bowed to ministerial requests to fly certain routes. Jet service to a smaller community represents more than direct economic advantage; it can be seen as a powerful symbol of a minister's influence. The corporation had typically been unwilling to tolerate undue interference in what it deemed a key operational area: the selection of new aircraft types. Thus, shortly after Jean Marchand became minister of transport in 1972, Air Canada began service to the city of Trois-Rivières, largely in support of a young up-and-coming minister from the area, Jean Chrétien. In turn, in the latter part of the 1970s Air Canada successfully resisted efforts by cabinet to steer it towards the purchase of the Airbus A310, opting instead for the Boeing 767. In other instances cabinet did issue explicit instructions and Air Canada was forced to comply. Thus in 1974, just prior to the election, Air Canada was told to re-establish a maintenance base in Winnipeg employing eight hundred workers. James Richardson, seen as the hand behind the decision, retained his seat – by just eight hundred votes.[115]

Summary

By May 1979, on the eve of the Liberal defeat and temporary removal from office, the regional minister system was intact. To be sure it had been recast, and no single minister had near the power enjoyed by the likes of C.D. Howe or Jimmy Gardiner. But compared to a decade earlier the system had been revived to a degree. By extending their traditional responsibilities for patronage into broader and newer areas of government expenditure, as in community development and certain types of regional incentive programs, ministers acting in their regional capacities had acquired considerable clout in the distribution of federal expenditures. As well, ministers such as Romeo LeBlanc and Donald Jamieson were able to evade the obstacles inherent in the institutionalized cabinet and to use both their own portfolios, and the resources of others, to improve conditions and build political support in their provinces. In Quebec, while eschewing the formal title of Quebec lieutenant, Jean Marchand became instrumental in forging a potent electoral machine that by 1980 had succeeded in dominating completely the electoral map of Quebec on the federal level. He was also responsible for helping to recruit younger talent, for example André

Ouellet and Pierre De Bané, who later as cabinet ministers would help demonstrate that French power in Ottawa could have some beneficial results, certainly as measured by federal expenditures.

A number of characteristics stand out, however. Regional ministers had essentially become provincialized, in the sense that their influence rarely extended beyond the borders of their own provinces. Admittedly, the Quebec lieutenant has rarely attempted to exercise direct influence outside of Quebec. Looking after Quebec, a sizcable province in its own right, has usually been a sufficient task in itself. The largest province, Ontario, rarely has had a minister who possesses the stature and authority of his Quebec counterpart. The notion of regional minister has much more meaning for the smaller provinces. But in the case of Allan MacEachen, the focus was even narrower than the province and restricted in the main to one particular corner of Nova Scotia.

Secondly, the political support they were able to generate or bring to Ottawa had little to do with connections they enjoyed or did not enjoy with their provincial counterparts in the party. Even where the same party was in power for at least some of the time, as in Quebec, relations between federal and provincial wings were lukewarm at best. Instead, influence was largely self-created and, as best illustrated by Romeo LeBlanc, usually within the confines of their own portfolios. It was the resources of the administrative state that enabled them to develop an autonomous power base.

Thirdly, the regional minister system essentially stopped at the Ontario-Manitoba border. By 1979 the only minister of significance in western Canada (there were only two) was Otto Lang, whose interests and vision were much more national than regional in scope. Finally, the pork-barrelling and the intense concern with electoral considerations had once again put local politics front and centre in a manner that had not been seen since the heyday of Macdonald and Laurier. Regional barons Gardiner and Howe may have been, but near the end of their era they had effectively lost touch with developments at the local level. Yet while Macdonald and Laurier were able to link together local practices with national appeals, local politics in the context of the 1970s was different. In the nineteenth century patronage was a highly effective instrument for creating strong party organization at the constituency level. At the end of the 1970s, after nearly two decades of Liberal party reform, party organization at the local level was weak. Local politics remained important, however, in the sense that competitive ridings made support from marginal voters pivotal. It was in the hope of capturing this support that ministers came to depend on the pork-barrel as an alternative technique. Yet these hopes were to some extent misplaced. Pork-barrelling as such provided at best only fleeting loyalty and little direct leverage over voters. Party support remained unstable, as demonstrated by the fact that the Trudeau government was never able to win back-to-back victories and lost most of its support outside of Quebec in 1979. This also points to a further characteristic of the regional minister system of the 1970s: aside from the paucity of western representatives, ministers lacked the profile, the clout, and the means to mobilize their provincial citizenry in support of broader goals adopted by the centre. As far as the issue of national unity was concerned, attention tended to be focused on the prime minister and the ten provincial premiers.

The question of national unity took on even greater prominence with the return of the Liberals in March 1980, after their victory in the February election, and it threw in even sharper relief the roles of the two main protagonists, Pierre Trudeau and René Lévesque. At the same time, the strategies that came to be pursued by the federal government in doing battle with Quebec in particular and the provinces in general had the effect, ironically, of strengthening the hand of regional ministers. Interestingly, they also gave provincial governments greater opportunity to influence federal decisions. It is to these developments in the last Trudeau cabinet which we now turn.

Formalizing the Role of Regional Minister: Regional Development and Organizational Change

The Liberals saw in their February 1980 election victory, and in the 'No' vote in the Quebec referendum later that year, a mandate to provide strong leadership in shaping Canada's economic future and the authority to counter directly Quebec's proposal for sovereignty-association. The former goal was premised on a program of energy self-sufficiency and, perforce, effective control by the federal government over natural gas and oil, resources primarily under provincial jurisdiction. The latter entailed constitutional change, through pre-emptive and unilateral action if necessary in the face of perceived provincial obstinacy.

The aggressive thrust of the federal government in the areas of constitutional reform, energy policy, and economic development policy was rooted in the federal-provincial conflicts of the 1970s. In the main the battle appeared to be centred over winning the hearts and minds of Quebeckers, pitting the strongly federalist Trudeau government against the equally strongly anti-federalist Parti Québécois (PQ) provincial government under René Lévesque. The PQ was only somewhat chastened by its defeat in the 1980 referendum and was bolstered by its re-election in the spring of 1981. But the battle was not restricted to Quebec. Overall, Ottawa sought to re-establish what it saw as a loss of presence in the minds of all Canadian citizens. As Bruce Doern wrote: 'Federal ministers were increasingly tired of ... being perceived as a mismanaged, debt-ridden and remote government, while the provincial governments basked for most of the 1970s in the political glory of balanced budgets, perceived competence, and sensitivity and closeness to "their" people.'[1]

The resulting political and economic repercussions have been extensively documented.[2] The Liberal government engaged the provinces on two fronts: the energy issue involving mainly Alberta but also drawing in the other western provinces and Newfoundland; and the issue of constitutional patriation, stimulated largely by Quebec's unique position but of major concern to all provinces. As the federal government became increasingly embittered by what it perceived as provincial intransigence, it began skirmishing with the provinces over other issues as well: the fiscal equalization program and the Established Programs Financing (EPF) arrangements for medicare and post-secondary school financing, to name but two examples. Throughout, the federal government's overriding complaint was the lack of credit given by the provinces for the federal transfer payments they received. The federal government also had two subsidiary concerns: its relative lack of House of Commons representation in western Canada (only two members, both from Manitoba), even though Liberals had obtained close to 25 per cent of the vote there; and the lack of regional intelligence. What it sought above all was a more direct link to citizens and to regions.

This heightening of conflict between the federal government and the provinces across a wide array of issues is typically seen as an expression of the highly competitive nature of Canadian-style interstate federalism. It gives pride of place to provincial premiers, the prime minister, and a few other principals, such as the federal and Alberta ministers of energy, and enhances the role of central agencies such as the Federal-Provincial Relations Office (FPRO) in Ottawa and the intergovernmental affairs agencies in the provincial capitals.[3] Within this context, it would appear there was little room for an expanded role for regional ministers. Yet 1980–4 was also the period when ministers, acting in their regional capacity, gained in influence and saw their role formalized. The explanation of how this contradiction came about – increased centralization within federal and provincial governments yet enhancement of the regional ministerial role – lies in part in the initiatives launched by the federal government in doing battle with the provinces. Simply put, the emphasis on 'visibility' and 'direct delivery' provided opportunities to regional ministers to help shape the outcome of programs designed to help recapture the hearts and minds of the Canadian populace. And despite the accent on direct delivery, many provincial governments, working through regional ministers, were still able to benefit from these new programs.

These opportunities cropped up in a number of areas. This chapter examines one major program, in the field of regional development policy, that illustrates the changes and the overall trends. The chapter immediately following focuses on two related 'special' expenditure programs, ostensibly created to generate employment during the time of the recession. The changes in question involved not only new programs but, significantly, alterations in government organization. These innovations in the machinery of government provided institutional support for those regional activities that many ministers had previously undertaken with relatively little direct help from public servants or even their own political staff.

The Quest for Federal Visibility

The Liberal ministers sworn in on 3 March 1980 were a tough-minded lot, ready to play hard-ball with the provinces, a frame of mind that was easily supported by a feisty Liberal caucus. The seventy-four member Quebec contingent in particular, comprising slightly over half of all Liberal MPs, was fully committed to demonstrating the efficacy of 'French power' in Ottawa to their compatriots. They were also pledged to an alternative vision of Quebec's role in confederation, a vision sharply at odds with that put forward by the PQ. On the whole, the objective of the federal government was to steal away from provincial governments some of their prestige and authority, especially that which was based on expenditures made possible through the generosity of Ottawa. The federal Department of Finance, for example, pointed out that not only did provincial governments increase their share of overall revenue from 42 per cent in 1960 to 53 per cent in 1980 (before transfers), but also federal government transfers to the provinces had increased as well: in 1960 slightly over 13 per cent of provincial expenditures originated out of federal transfers, by 1980 it was close to 20 per cent.[4]

Unfortunately, despite the strong sense of grievance on the part of ministers, the opportunities for regaining the federal government's lost visibility and political credit were distinctly limited. The areas in which the greatest expansion had taken place with federal financial help were also those areas most clearly under provincial jurisdiction, for example, health care and education. In its October 1980 budget the federal government stated its intention to begin reducing the rate of growth in transfers to the provinces, and in February 1981 it struck a special committee of Parliament to act as a Parliamentary Task Force on Federal-Provincial Fiscal Arrangements. The task force was expected to hold public hearings across the country, thereby inviting citizens to air their concerns on the manner in which the provinces were disbursing federal funds. The task force proceeded to do precisely that, and it succeeded in eliciting the views of a wide assortment of individuals and community groups. But the results, in the form of the task force's report submitted seven months later, were not necessarily that helpful to the government's cause. While emphasizing that there should be both stricter accountability and greater visibility in the way monies on Established Programs Financing (EPF), for example, were spent, the report also recommended that the federal government spend more rather than less money in these areas.[5]

The primary tool in the government's economic development strategy was the National Energy Program (NEP), also announced in the October 1980 budget. Coupled with it was the 'mega-project strategy' announced a year later in the MacEachen budget of November 1981.[6] While linked together in the 1981 budget statement, the NEP and the mega-project strategy had rather different origins. The NEP, designed to ensure the security of future oil supplies and to promote Canadian ownership and participation in energy development, was initially forged in the heat of the February 1980 election campaign, where security of energy supplies and the future of Petro-Canada were major issues. Its architects were a small group of Liberal party campaign strategists centred around the new energy minister, Marc Lalonde, and senior officials in Energy, Mines and Resources (EMR) who had long been frustrated in their dealings with Alberta, not only during the earlier Liberal period but also under the brief Clark government.[7] The mega-project strategy had a longer and more honourable pedigree, originating in the early 1970s when debates over new industrial strategies were in vogue, and given shape by the 'Major Projects Task Force on Major Capital Projects in Canada to the Year 2000,' which reported in 1981. Struck by the Department of Industry, Trade, and Commerce (IT&C) in 1978 and headed by the president of Nova Corporation, Robert Blair, and the executive vice-president of the Canadian Labour Congress, Shirley Carr, this task force identified $440 billion worth of actual projects covering all regions, most of them in the energy and resources field.[8]

Other elements dating from the industrial policy debates of the 1970s, such as the proposals developed by Herb Gray calling for a strengthened Foreign Investment Review Agency (FIRA) and more explicitly interventionist industrial policies, were entered into the policy hopper as well. The end result – an emphasis on mega-projects to be linked to the benefits generated through the NEP – was outlined in the November 1981 *Statement on Economic Development for Canada in the 1980s* that accompanied the budget. The interventionist policies favoured earlier by Gray and other ministers, aimed at the manufacturing sector, were not in evidence. Projected industrial benefits were mainly in the form of spin-offs from the mega-projects, such as demand for steel and heavy machinery for new pipelines and heavy-oil processing plants. The interventionist aura of that period derived largely from the takeovers of Belgian-owned Petrofina by Petro-Canada and of French-owned Elf Aquitane by the Canada Development Corporation, by the 'back-in' provision allowing Petro-Canada to purchase retroactively up to 25 per cent of newly discovered oilfields, and by the Petroleum Incentive Payments (PIP) program that allowed Ottawa to channel funds to Canadian-owned energy companies. Beyond these instruments there was little in the way of direct interventionist measures envisioned in the government's overall strategy.[9] As well, there was no specifically regional dimension. In a sense none was needed, since projects were planned across the country: coal-mining in northeastern British Columbia and offshore oil in Newfoundland and Nova Scotia, in addition to heavy-oil processing in Alberta and Saskatchewan. Beyond this, it was simply hoped that the benefits from the massive expenditures in these projects would percolate down into the nooks and crannies of Canada's peripheral economies.

There was one specifically regional component, however, that rounded out the government's development strategy for the 1980s, the Western Development Fund. It was designed to help win back the west for the Liberals and was promoted primarily by the one elected minister from western Canada, Lloyd Axworthy, his brother Tom in the Prime Minister's Office (PMO) who was to become principal secretary to the prime minister in 1981, and senators Bud Olson and Hazen Argue from Alberta and Saskatchewan respectively. The aim of this fund, announced in the October 1980 budget, was to ensure that up to $4 billion of NEP-generated downstream revenues would be spent on projects in the west that promoted economic diversification. Prior to the announcement of the fund, the special Cabinet Committee on Western Affairs was created, chaired by Lloyd Axworthy, the only cabinet committee charged with looking after the affairs of a single region. At the same time, it was advisory only, having no authority over the new fund.[10]

If the federal government's efforts to enhance its public profile in the area of fiscal transfers and EPF could be deemed at best a limited victory, the outcome of the NEP and the mega-project strategy can be labelled a failure by almost any standard. The various expenditure components of the NEP, such as PIP, became a major drain on the federal treasury, and Alberta proved intractable on energy pricing, that issue not being resolved until 1983. Furthermore, contrary to the basic assumptions underpinning the whole strategy, the price of oil plummeted and along with it the economies of most industrialized nations. Thus the mega-project strategy, largely dependent on increasing oil prices, was rendered useless.

The failure of the federal government's economic development strategy can be blamed largely on the unfortunate effects of the recession that began taking hold in late 1981. But even without the recession or the drop in energy prices, the federal government still faced enormous difficulties in implementing its desired policies, as illustrated by the Ottawa-Alberta energy wars. Two mega-projects – the proposed oil tar sands plants at Cold Lake and Allsands – were halted by Alberta premier Peter Lougheed as a retaliatory move against the NEP.[11] On the east coast Ottawa's success in signing an offshore agreement with Nova Scotia was counterbalanced by the lack of an agreement with Newfoundland. Finally, what should have been the Trudeau government's crowning achievement – the patriation of the constitution and the new charter of rights and freedoms – was accomplished without Quebec's participation or consent and only after bitter argument with most of the remaining provinces. The title of the book by Banting and Simeon, *And No One Cheered*, accurately captured prevailing public and private sentiment that accompanied the official patriation ceremonies held that rainy Ottawa afternoon, 17 April 1982.

In pressing its initiatives on the provinces, the federal government had come face to face with the reality confronting most modern federal nations: the interdependence of functions of both levels of government in practically all areas, leaving little room for independent central government initiatives, or at least not ones that could be undertaken without considerable opposition from the constituent units.[12] There was, however, one area where jurisdictional authority seemed reasonably clear and where the federal government felt it could alter the status quo without too much difficulty: the field of regional development policy.

From DREE to DRIE, from MSED to MSERD

A number of studies have noted the frequent and often abrupt shifts in the federal government's dealings with the provinces. Harmonious and co-operative relations cultivated over a number of years in an area such as occupational training can suddenly be broken off by a unilateral demand from Ottawa that new philosophies and funding principles be implemented.[13] This action is likely to be followed a few years later by a much more conciliatory approach. Probably nowhere is this pendulum effect more obvious than in the regional economic development field. The unilateral 'growth-pole' approach, first adopted by the Department of Regional Economic Expansion (DREE) in 1969, displaced the co-operative arrangements that had prevailed under the Agricultural Rural Development Act (ARDA). The growth-pole strategy in turn was superseded a few years later by the General Development Agreement (GDA) approach featuring a predominance of federal funding for provincially delivered programs. Each swing of the pendulum typically left in its wake a swirl of old and new acronyms. The shift back towards a more Ottawa-centred delivery of programs in the early 1980s was no exception. In this case, however, the amplitude of the swing was magnified by the poor state of federal-provincial relations in the early 1980s.

The GDAs, most of them struck in 1974 for ten-year periods, and the various subsidiary agreements for specific projects that gave concrete effect to the GDAs, were set to expire no later than 1984, and some of the subsidiary agreements in fact expired earlier. GDA expenditures represented 80 per cent of DREE's total budget. For the federal government this presented a golden opportunity to wrest back control in an area which typified the problem of lack of federal visibility. In some provinces the federal government was funding up to 90 per cent of programs that were delivered almost entirely by the provinces, arrangements supported by relatively closed policy communities consisting of DREE officials in the field and provincial officials. These arrangements, and DREE itself, had already come under public fire by regional ministers such as Romeo LeBlanc in New Brunswick. In Ottawa officials in many of the line departments were also resentful of DREE, both for interfering in departmental jurisdictions and out of jealousy for the apparent ease with which the department was able to obtain funding and to make decisions on sizeable expenditures without having to go through Treasury Board. Even at the provincial level, politicians were somewhat unhappy in not having greater influence over the decisions made by DREE and provincial officials. In short, by the early 1980s DREE and its programs were in a highly vulnerable position.

To complete the circle, in 1980 Trudeau appointed, as the new minister of DREE, Pierre De Bané, an individual with a keen interest in regional development policy who had studied the workings of DREE while in opposition in 1979–80, and who had specifically asked for the portfolio upon the Liberal return to power. While a firm proponent of regional development, De Bané was frustrated not only with the GDA arrangements but with Canadian federalism as a whole and its effects on central institutions and administration. 'If Canada were a unitary state,' he notes, 'then it would easily have found ways to build in the regional dimension [into government programs and institutions].'[14] He indicated to DREE officials that the status quo represented by the GDA approach was no longer acceptable to him; that he was aware of the opposition to DREE prevailing among his cabinet colleagues; and that he was not prepared to spend all his time defending present DREE policies.[15]

Evidence of changes to come was soon in the offing. In August 1981 De Bané refused to renew a subsidiary agreement with the Manitoba government because Ottawa 'was not getting sufficient political credit for its expenditure.'[16] 'Up till now the federal government discharged its responsibility by giving money to the provinces. That will no longer suffice,' he announced.[17] In October of the same year he refused to proceed with the third phase of the Prince Edward Island Development Plan, calling instead for the direct delivery by the federal government of programs in sectors such as fisheries and agriculture.[18] In the end, approximately half of the money that had previously been spent through the Prince Edward Island government now became the responsibility of federal departments.[19] Shortly thereafter a similar redirection of funds occurred for New Brunswick and in late October 1981 Romeo LeBlanc was able to announce a special DREE five-year development plan for southeastern New Brunswick, again with all $10 million to be spent by federal departments.[20]

Not all subsidiary agreements suffered the same fate. In fact throughout 1980–1, and even in 1982, after DREE officially ceased to exist, some twenty-one such agreements were renewed in the traditional GDA format, including forestry agreements with New Brunswick and Newfoundland, and a large-scale northern development agreement with the province of Manitoba.[21] De Bané continued to express unhappiness with the GDA approach however, and in late 1981 he actually wrote the prime minister recommending that DREE be disbanded.[22] At the same time he succeeded in allaying criticisms from his cabinet colleagues, very likely because of his stated intention to do away with the GDA format. He also obtained an increase in the DREE budget because, as Savoie suggests, fellow ministers, especially those on the Cabinet Committee on Economic Development, anticipated having the opportunity to spend money earmarked for DREE through their own departments.[23]

The axe fell on 12 January 1982 when the prime minister announced the end of DREE and a major reorganization of all the portfolios and central agencies in the economic development field.[24] To understand the nature of this organizational redesign and its consequences for regional policy, as well as for the role of regional ministers, requires a brief digression into developments in the machinery of government and budgeting practices.

Turning first to the machinery of government, in August 1978 the prime minister, upon returning from the Bonn economic summit, decided to effect major budget cuts while at the same time giving priority to new initiatives in the area of economic development. Under these conditions all ministers and their departments realized that any new money for their programs could likely only be justified in terms of contributing to the newly elevated goal of economic development. At the same time the prime minister, as well as the PMO and PCO, felt that the existing machinery would not be up to the task of handling the competition between departments in the scramble for economic development funds. Hence the machinery of government directorate of the PCO was given the task of devising new mechanisms to ensure the requisite degree of co-ordination and integration among departmental activities. The PCO considered at least three options: a new super department, integrating IT&C, DREE, and Science and Technology; a strengthened interdepartmental committee for the three departments in question; and a 'board' of ministers. The third option was recommended to the prime minister, and in November the new Board of Economic Development (BED) was struck.[25] It was composed of the deputy prime minister, the minister of finance, and the president of the Treasury Board as ex-officio members, and the ministers of EMR, Science and Technology, Labour, DREE, IT&C, Canada Employment and Immigration Commission (CEIC), National Revenue, and Small Business. BED subsumed the existing cabinet committee on economic policy and in this sense it could be seen as a strengthened and revitalized version of the latter with a special mandate to formulate policies with respect to: 'appropriate means by which the government ... may ... have a beneficial influence on the development of industries and regional economies in Canada'; 'the integration of programs and activities providing direct support to industry'; and 'the fostering of cooperative relationships ... with the provinces, [and] with business and labour.'[26]

The innovations, however, did not stop with the new mandate. The new committee was headed by a president, Robert Andras, and supported by its own support staff in the form of a new Ministry of State for Economic Development (MSED). Finally, in what was likely the most important innovation of all, the new structure brought together policy *and* expenditure decision-making in one ministerial body. Hitherto decisions taken by cabinet or cabinet committees on new policies or programs were then discussed in a different context as to their budgetary implications, in Treasury Board or, equally likely, in informal lobbying sessions with the minister of finance or the Treasury Board president. In BED, however, ministers for the first time were being forced to deal directly with the costs of new programs by virtue of having an assigned budgetary 'envelope' out of which all program decisions were to be funded.[27] In effect BED assumed some of the powers of Treasury Board, an arrangement that was expected to lead to greater discipline among ministers, and MSED, in providing support to BED, took over some of the functions performed by the programs branch of the Treasury Board Secretariat (TBS).

Whether greater discipline was in fact exercised or decision-making became more effective is difficult to assess. Under Andras, BED did have one success during its brief life before the defeat of the government in May 1979, namely the realization of a federal-provincial agreement on pulp and paper modernization involving federal expenditures of $250 million. It represented the culmination of more than two years of negotiations by DREE and reinforced the half billion dollars already spent on forestry assistance programs. It also represented the sole example of a national integrated sectoral strategy that helped put a beleaguered industry on a competitive footing with its counterpart in the United States.[28] In the event, the integration of policy and expenditure decision-making proved to be a precursor of things to come for all policy sectors. Under the Clark government, BED became the Cabinet Committee for Economic Development (CCED) and the principle of super-ministries to co-ordinate broad policy sectors was extended to the social policy field with the creation of the Ministry of State for Social Development (MSSD). Thus both CCED and the Cabinet Committee on Social and Native Affairs now enjoyed the support of their own central agencies. The remaining committees, other than Treasury Board, continued to be supported by the PCO. There was one additional new element underpinning the activities and deliberations of cabinet committees, the so-called mirror committees composed of deputy ministers of departments represented on each cabinet committee. The deputies would meet prior to the meeting of the cabinet committee in question to inform themselves of the agenda and to deal with any problems related to administration or procedural matters. This also served to help them advise their ministers on what to expect in committee discussions.

Finally, the Clark regime introduced the most significant change in budgeting practice since PPBS, the Program Expenditure Management System (PEMS). PEMS extended the envelope system employed by BED/CCED to all policy sectors and to each department within those sectors. There were nine budgetary envelopes all told, and allocations within each envelope were the responsibility of the relevant cabinet committee. The economic development envelope encompassed departments and programs ranging from transport to agriculture to labour, and was handled by CCED. Some committees were responsible for more than one envelope; the Cabinet Committee on Social Development, for example, handled both the social and native affairs envelope and the justice and legal envelope. Certain envelopes, such as those for fiscal arrangements and the public debt, were handled directly by the inner cabinet, another Clark government innovation.[29] Allocations between envelopes (made essentially by the inner cabinet), and within envelopes between departments, were based on two considerations. The first, for continuing programs and obligations (statutory transfers to the provinces, for example), was referred to as the A budget; the second, for new items, was called the B budget or policy reserve. For obvious reasons, the amount available in the B budget was very limited. However, cabinet committees, and departments, could free up money for new programs if they were willing to cut old programs. These trade-offs were, at least in theory, encouraged in the name of flexibility, innovation, and thrift. 'Ministers who want to spend must also save.'[30]

Both PEMS and MSSD were well into the design stage before the Clark government came to power. Nevertheless, Clark and his closest advisers on the transition team found the proposed budgetary framework congenial, and the new government was quite willing to take credit for it, demonstrating that the penchant for central agency solutions had an appeal and staying power beyond the administrative-political circle closely identified with the Trudeau government. What is arguable is whether the Clark government would have undertaken the next step, to integrate policies and programs even further through a strengthening of the central agency apparatus. This is essentially what happened in January 1982. DREE as a department was effectively abolished and IT&C lost the trade function, which was moved to External Affairs. Some of DREE's program responsibilities, such as the small business and tourism subsidiary agreements with the provinces, were assigned to what remained of IT&C, which was then retitled the Department of Regional Industrial Expansion (DRIE). Responsibility for the remaining DREE subsidiary agreements was turned over to the appropriate line department, agricultural agreements to Agriculture, mining agreements to EMR, forestry agreements to Environment, and so on. There still remained the overall responsibility for the GDAs as well as the co-ordinating function of DREE, its regional development consciousness-raising role so to speak, among all government departments. These did not disappear with DREE but became the responsibility of the central agency charged with supporting the efforts and deliberations of the cabinet committee on economic development – MSED.

MSED did not, however, simply add these new responsibilities to the ones it had. In undertaking to support what now became the Cabinet Committee on Economic and Regional Development (CCERD), it too underwent an organizational transformation, a metamorphosis that stood to make it one of the more interesting innovations among the several central agencies already in place. The new Ministry of State for Economic and Regional Development (MSERD), to reflect properly its responsibility for regional development policy and for improving the 'regional responsiveness' of the federal government as a whole, was itself decentralized.

Decentralizing a Central Agency

The decentralization of MSED was accomplished through a system of regional offices, one in every province and each headed by a federal economic development co-ordinator (FEDC), an official of senior rank. These officials, with the support of a staff of twelve to twenty people, were given four main functions:
– to provide an improved regional information base for decision-making by CCERD, for use particularly in the development of regionally sensitive economic development strategies;
– to give regional officials of sector departments a better understanding of the decisions and objectives of the cabinet;
– to better co-ordinate the implementation of government decisions affecting economic development in the regions; and

– to develop regional economic development policies for consideration by cabinet.[31]
Essentially the mandate of these co-ordinators was to provide a horizontal view from the field on matters that cut across a number of
departments, a perspective that was quite different from vertical, sectoral views typically acquired within line departments. In this sense
the view of the FEDC was much closer to that of politicians seeking to
ensure equitable treatment for their constituencies or regions.

To ensure that the FEDCs would indeed have the requisite influence,
they were given a direct pipeline into CCERD through the cabinet assessment note procedure. Any proposals put to CCERD by line departments or other agencies would be reviewed by the FEDCs as to
possible political or economic ramifications. The views of the FEDC,
or FEDCs collectively, would be captured in an assessment note drafted
by staff in the operations branch of MSERD at headquarters in Ottawa
for use in cabinet deliberations. For the first time in history secret
cabinet documents were sent outside Ottawa for perusal by the regionally based officials, which led to the installation of highly secure
filing cabinets in FEDC offices and to regular night-time visits by RCMP
to ensure that the documents were not left lying about and the cabinets
kept locked. New electronic communications equipment was also installed for the transmission of messages and documents.

The seniority and hence clout of the FEDCs was established in two
ways. First, most appointees already occupied positions of senior rank.
Two in fact were previously deputy ministers of large departments.
J.D. (Doug) Love, deputy minister of Canada Employment and Immigration (CEIC) and earlier deputy at DREE, became the FEDC for Nova
Scotia; and Bruce Rawson, secretary at MSSD, became the Alberta
FEDC. Secondly, the FEDCs reported directly to the secretary of MSERD,
initially Gordon Osbaldeston. Furthermore, all ten FEDCs were deemed
to be members of the management committee, along with the three
deputy secretaries and two assistant secretaries. In this context, sheer
weight of numbers ensured that the FEDCs would have a prominent
voice. The management committee met every two months, but the
FEDCs themselves, as it turned out, ended up travelling to Ottawa on
a much more frequent basis to meet not only with MSERD officials but
also with officials of other departments and not infrequently with ministers.

The new organizational design, and the innovative role planned for
the FEDCs, originated within the machinery of government directorate

of the PCO. While many ministers and public servants knew that changes were in the offing, very few had any inkling of what the design would look like, and many were surprised by the timing and the scope of the changes. For example, Herb Gray, the minister of one of the key departments involved in the reorganization, IT&C, was not consulted and was caught completely unawares by the 12 January 1982 announcement. Outside of those in DREE, most were expecting, or at least hoping, that DREE would simply disappear and its resources be allocated to other departments. When the announcement was made there was widespread shock. One MSERD official noted that within 'the cabinet committee [CCED], ministers thought that the whole reorganization was a crock.'[32] Ministers were already resentful of the ponderous way in which the committee operated. The briefing and assessment notes from central agencies, in their view, added considerably to their paper burden. To have yet more central agency officials, this time in the form of FEDCs, involved in the vetting process would add to the paper burden and slow down further what was already a very long process of getting proposals through cabinet.

Furthermore, the proposed functions to be assigned to the FEDCs immediately aroused suspicions. The gathering of regional intelligence (shades of the regional desks in the PMO in the early 1970s) and the provision of 'a better understanding ... of the objectives of the cabinet' to 'regional officials of sector departments'[33] meant, in the eyes of individual ministers, that there would be additional meddling by central agency officials in both internal departmental matters and matters pertaining to the minister's own province. While ministers were happy to acquire the pieces left over from the dismemberment of DREE, they would much sooner have done without the cumbersome new MSERD/FEDC arrangement. Compounding matters was that many ministers disliked and distrusted Donald Johnston, the man who became minister of the new portfolio and chair of the new CCERD on 30 September 1982, replacing the more conciliatory Bud Olson. Previously president of Treasury Board, Johnston was seen as someone favouring restraint as opposed to championing the spending wishes of CCERD members.

Line department officials shared many of the same concerns. For them MSERD represented yet another central agency hurdle. Some of the strongest resistance came from within MSERD itself. Those who had been with the agency from the beginning, some three years earlier, saw the role of the agency primarily in national or sectoral terms and the arrival of the 'R' was deeply resented. Up to the time of MSERD's demise in August 1984, many in the agency, particularly in the policy branch, continued to refer to 'MSED,' studiously avoiding the 'R.'[34] With the disappearance of both DREE and IT&C, and the amalgamation of many of the remaining elements into the new DRIE, came the unhappy task of bringing together units and staff of departments that had up to that point been frequently at loggerheads with each other. Some former DREE staff ended up in MSERD, primarily in the newly created projects branch which took over responsibility for the GDAs. Other DREE staff joined the FEDC offices. Most, however, ended up in DRIE, either in headquarters in Ottawa or in the newly merged DRIE offices in the provinces.

In Ottawa circles blame (or credit) for the FEDC system tended to be assigned to De Bané who, as DREE minister, helped instigate the reorganization and apparently, while on a trip to France in 1980, had been deeply impressed by the French prefecture system.[35] Certainly in light of his earlier experiences as minister of supply and services in 1978–9, when he initiated a program to promote federal government purchases in the poorest regions of the country, and his inclination to bypass provincial governments, the French system offered a plausible model for building the regional dimension into administration. It was also thought that Bruce Rawson, the secretary of MSSD who had gone out west in the fall of 1981 to assess the federal government's overall low standing there, had had a hand in defining the role envisioned for the FEDC. Ultimately, however, most saw in the 1982 reorganization the hand of the individual thought to be the architect of the system as a whole – Michael Pitfield, clerk of the Privy Council. For most, the decentralization of MSERD represented the complete unfolding of the central agency logic in Canada, a nation, according to Colin Campbell, where government had gone furthest in 'fulfilling the canons for institutionalized executive leadership.'[36] Coupled with fascination with the new arrangement was a sense of impending doom, a feeling that the whole edifice could well collapse under the weight of its own design.

These fateful prophecies were to prove true, at least in certain respects. Two things need to be said, however. First, the implementation of the new design, in so far as the FEDC system was concerned, was accomplished with particular care. Secondly, once implemented, the FEDC system, in interacting with both MSERD headquarters and regional ministers, took on a special dynamic and a direction that was, in all likelihood, not anticipated by its designers. The special care was most evident in the personnel selected to fill the FEDC positions. Not only were the individuals reasonably senior but among the selection criteria were the requirements of good knowledge of, and connections with, the province to which the FEDC was to be assigned. Thus the Saskatchewan FEDC, Arthur Wakabayashi, a native of that province, had worked in the provincial government in the 1960s and early 1970s before moving to Ottawa. Jean Edmonds, the Manitoba FEDC, had been director general for DREE for Manitoba, was intimately familiar with the structure of the Manitoba-Ottawa GDA, and had close ties with aboriginal groups in the province. Bruce Rawson, the first FEDC to be appointed on 30 April 1982, had strong roots in Alberta and had worked for the provincial government as a deputy minister under premiers Manning and Lougheed before moving to Ottawa. Some of the FEDCs were recruited directly from provincial or municipal bureaucracies. Gordon Slade was deputy minister of fisheries in the Newfoundland government prior to becoming the FEDC in St John's in late 1982, and Normand Plante had been working for the city of Montreal as industrial commissioner before accepting his appointment as FEDC for Quebec. The FEDC offices were located either in the provincial capital or in the major business centre in the province. In Quebec and British Columbia, for example, the FEDC offices were in Montreal and Vancouver respectively. For New Brunswick, the original plan was to have the office in Fredericton, and the newly appointed FEDC, John MacNaught, had proceeded with personal housing plans on that basis. Romeo LeBlanc, however, had different ideas. DREE headquarters for the Atlantic region had been located in Moncton. There were good historical and logistical grounds, he felt, for also having the new FEDC office in that city. LeBlanc won his case. Twenty-four hours before the official announcement of his appointment, MacNaught was informed that the FEDC office would be in Moncton rather than the provincial capital.

It took some time for the various units and individuals involved in the reorganization to begin implementing the details of the new design. In the case of DRIE, many argued that the forced merger between the remaining elements of DREE and IT&C never did take.[37] Certainly many long-standing problems resulting from this merger continued to fester, and were not really resolved until DRIE itself was eliminated in 1987 by the Conservative government. In the case of MSERD and the FEDC system, the role of the FEDCs especially was far from clear. Except for specific guidelines on staffing levels, there was little guidance beyond what was contained in the prime ministerial statement of January 1982. As a result, each FEDC came to define his or her role a little differently, though this was to be expected given that each province varied in its socio-economic make-up, political climate, and the nature of the federal presence. At the same time they all had certain common tasks to perform and instruments at their disposal. There were essentially three instruments and each deserves brief discussion.

The first was the assessment note procedure noted earlier. Assembled into a summary document by staff in the operations branch of MSERD for use by ministers on CCERD, these notes were the principal means by which the FEDCs supported the continuing deliberations of this cabinet committee, primarily by sensitizing ministers to the regional implications of federal actions. In performing this function, FEDCs were expected to cultivate links with local business groups and provincial officials, as well as with federal officials of line departments based in the province. The second instrument related to the drafting and submission of a document known as the provincial economic development perspectives. These 'perspectives' were collectively part of a planning cycle of PEMS. Through his or her perspectives each FEDC provided input to the 'strategic overview' for the country as a whole prepared by the Policy Branch of MSERD. In this way CCERD would have a benchmark against which to measure proposals for development and a framework for discussing specific issues. After the overview document was discussed and then revised and approved by CCERD, it would be sent forward to the Cabinet Committee on Priorities and Planning (P&P), along with the economic and fiscal outlook from the Department of Finance as well as the overviews from the other policy sectors. At the so-called Lakes and Lodges exercise by cabinet, held in the spring at the government's retreat at Meech Lake, a locale now best known in connection with the constitutional accord of 1987, expenditure levels for each budgetary envelope would be set along with policy guidelines for their management for the coming fiscal year.

The third, and what became the single most important instrument, was the Economic and Regional Development Agreement (ERDA). These were the federal-provincial agreements, bilaterally negotiated with each province, designed to replace the expiring GDAs. They were important, not only because they were one of the few mechanisms by which the federal government could achieve direct delivery and greater visibility in the provinces, but for the FEDCs they represented the only area where they were able to influence expenditures. Essentially, as outlined in a July 1982 MSERD staff paper on 'regional fund principles,' the money orginally allocated to the GDA subsidiary agreements over the period 1977–82, a sum of slightly more than $1.9 billion, came to represent a nominal baseline for the allocation of funds for the new

ERDAs. Put differently, the envelopes for the individual GDAs were to be rolled over into envelopes for the ERDAS.

The FEDCs were *not* responsible for the design of individual programs or subsidiary agreements to be supported out of the regional fund, let alone to have the opportunity for delivering such programs. That was the responsibility of the line departments. The FEDCs did have a role, and as a consequence influence, in steering these agreements through CCERD as part of the ERDA. The basic format of each ERDA was as follows. Each contained a statement of strategic objectives agreed upon by both the federal and provincial governments, in theory derived from the perspectives document. Secondly, there would be an overall framework outlining proposed subsidiary agreements or memoranda of understanding between federal line departments and provincial agencies. The FEDCs had primary responsibility for initiating the ERDA process, if necessary by cajoling federal departments or provincial governments into putting forward proposals for new subsidiary agreements.

In doing so the FEDC needed to keep a number of objectives in mind. In place of provincial delivery of federally funded programs, as was the norm under the GDAs, the aim was 'parallel delivery.' Both federal and provincial governments would contribute to a common project, but delivery of the components would be carried out separately by each government rather than wholly through a single provincial department. In this fashion the visibility of the federal government would be enhanced, as a result of the direct delivery of federally funded components. At the same time, co-operation with the provinces would be maintained through the co-ordination of the two levels to ensure the smooth meshing of delivered components. The new strategy did not necessarily preclude more traditional forms of provincial delivery: parallel delivery was an objective rather than an absolute rule.[38] Nevertheless, it had serious implications for provincial governments, particularly the governments of the have-not provinces. As later proved to be the case, several provinces did lay off staff in areas such as mining and natural resources as federal departments used the newly available ERDA monies to fund their own programs. The trick for FEDCs contemplating the prospects of designing and successfully implementing an ERDA was to persuade the provincial government to actually consent to a new arrangement under which it stood to lose considerable financial resources.

This was not the only hurdle facing the FEDC. In developing the ERDA one further task was required: to consult with the regional minister. As spelled out in the legislation establishing MSERD and the ERDA process (Bill C-152), 'Detailed negotiations ... of any subsidiary agreement shall not be undertaken ... unless a plan for economic development to which the draft agreement relates has been approved by the Minister in concert with other Ministers.'[39] The 'other ministers' was inserted primarily to protect those who earlier had been offended by the limited consultation undertaken by DREE concerning DREE-funded activities in their own provinces. Thus, while the FEDC had the responsibility of bringing various pieces such as proposed subsidiary agreements and memoranda of understanding together into an overall package for consideration by CCERD, it was the regional minister who effectively came to enjoy veto power over both specific components and the overall agreement. In short, most FEDCs realized that they needed to involve their regional ministers in the ERDA process at a fairly early stage.

Enter the Regional Minister

All ten provinces had a designated regional minister, even those with no elected members. For three western provinces lacking elected representatives, senators occupied that role: Jack Austin in British Columbia, Bud Olson in Alberta, and Hazen Argue in Saskatchewan. Argue was minister of state responsible for the Canadian wheat Board. Austin became minister of state for social development in September 1982, replacing Senator Ray Perrault, government leader in the Senate, as minister for British Columbia. Bud Olson, while initially minister of state in charge of MSED, became seriously ill in 1981. With the advent of MSERD in 1982 he was replaced in that portfolio by Donald Johnston. In the remaining provinces there were, as before 1979, designated political ministers who were effectively in charge of patronage through the federal affairs committees.

There were some significant changes in personalities, however. In Newfoundland Donald Jamieson's departure from cabinet after the government's defeat in 1979 left a vacuum that was only partially filled by the inexperienced William Rompkey. In Nova Scotia Allan MacEachen was now joined in the ministerial ranks by former Nova Scotia premier Gerald Regan, an individual who had helped bring about MacEachen's poor showing in the 1968 leadership race. In Quebec Marc Lalonde had now come truly into his own as Jean Marchand's successor.[40] Every Thursday morning Lalonde would chair a meeting of Quebec ministers in the New Zealand Room next to the parliamentary restaurant, to consult on policies affecting Quebec and to deal with the distribution of forthcoming contracts and appointments.[41] Lalonde was quite willing to delegate authority over these matters to the other ministers who, in turn, were answerable for different areas of the province. For example, André Ouellet was responsible for the Montreal area, Pierre De Bané for the Gaspé region, and Pierre Bussières for the Quebec City region. In case of disputes between ministers or MPs, these would be settled by Lalonde directly and conclusively. His willingness to use his authority when necessary, and the fear he generally inspired, ensured that a strong hierarchical discipline within and between Quebec ministers and MPs prevailed. Only Jean Chrétien refused to acknowledge Lalonde's position and rarely attended the Thursday morning meetings.

Lalonde's authority derived not from close contact with grass-roots organizers (he had little experience at that level) or even his powerful intellect; it derived mainly from his presence as the single most important minister in the Trudeau cabinet. He was Trudeau's closest confidant, and in his position as minister of energy and later finance, Quebec ministers and MPs knew he was in a position to influence virtually any decision made by the government. When in charge of the NEP he helped ensure that the proposed Trans-Québec Maritime pipeline was included, despite opposition from senior civil servants who considered the venture uneconomic.[42] As finance minister, he restored the profile and authority of the department, which had slipped not only as a result of MacEachen's ill-fated November 1981 budget but even earlier during the 1970s with the arrival of new central agencies.[43] In this position he became known for his willingness to negotiate and cut deals with individual ministers, thereby side-stepping the different cabinet committees. Again, this helped improve his individual standing vis-à-vis other ministers. It also, as will be noted later, altered the dynamics within cabinet committees such as CCERD and limited the effectiveness of the newly introduced PEMS.

In Ontario, as in Quebec, there were a number of subregional ministers in addition to the regional minister proper, who in this case was Herb Gray, minister of IT&C. The subregional ministers included Judy Erola for northwestern Ontario, Jean-Jacques Blais for northeastern Ontario, and John Roberts for the Metro Toronto region. As well, long-time minister John Munro, representing Hamilton East, had established a well-oiled political machine that effectively dominated Hamilton and the surrounding area.[44] Gray himself represented a part of Ontario that was affected directly by many of the programs managed by his department. At the same time, events in 1980 and 1981 suggested that he was not always able to defend his region, even on those issues relating to his own portfolio. Pierre De Bané, for example, extracted a promise from Gray that special effort would be made to persuade Volkswagen to locate their new auto parts plant in the Montreal region, despite that company's strongly held view that they would be best off in southern Ontario. As well, Gray exerted little direct influence over the subregional ministers and was frequently bypassed by them.[45]

The most important new face in cabinet was the only elected minister west of Ontario, Lloyd Axworthy, member for Winnipeg–Fort Garry. In charge of CEIC, he soon became known as a highly activist minister, and more than any other minister left his imprint on the ERDA process. He did so by ensuring that his province would be the first to sign an ERDA with Ottawa. The signing of the agreement on 25 November 1983, worth over $250 million for the initial five-year period, sparked the interest of the other regional ministers, as well as MSERD officials, galvanizing them into pursuing more vigorously negotiations with provincial governments and line departments. They now had the Manitoba ERDA before them to show how it was done. Axworthy's unique role in this and other respects is treated in chapters 8 and 9. For the moment let us pay attention to the principles and practices involved in the crafting of a typical ERDA.

Creating the Economic and Regional Development Agreement

The ERDA process was preceded by the perspectives document, which in turn was accompanied by considerable spadework by the FEDCs in developing contacts with the relevant actors. These actors included not just provincial governments and client groups but also federal line departments in the region, some of which had little or no experience in working with DREE or provincial governments. Increasingly over time, it was often the federal line departments that proved most trying. By the spring of 1984, when nearly six ERDAs had been successfully completed, more than one FEDC admitted that dealing with their own government, specifically line officials, was the most difficult part of the negotiating process. Initially most FEDCs created 'regional councils' consisting of the most senior line department representatives in the province, though in many cases these officials were not very senior. These councils would meet every six to eight weeks, and for many participants it proved to be an eye-opener. In some cases they would be introduced to fellow federal employees whom they had never met, though they had been living in the same city for several years. Some FEDC offices, for example in Alberta and Manitoba, had similar councils for regional communications officers, with the view to developing a more co-ordinated federal communications strategy for the province.

The procedure in constructing an ERDA called for line departments to put forward a list of possible projects to be financed out of the regional fund for that province. In negotiating and bargaining with line departments, MSERD officials used what they referred to as a 'Dutch auction' approach, attempting to extract the maximum regional development value out of a department for the least amount of money.[46] One problem, however, in the words of one official, was that 'all the money was put on the table at once.'[47] In the overall scheme of things, the regional fund money was relatively little. However, when expenditure opportunities for anywhere from two- to five-year periods became available in the fall of 1983, under circumstances of fiscal restraint, many line departments felt it worthwhile to submit proposals. Under DREE the tack had been much different, and more disciplined. DREE provincial directors general, in negotiating GDA subsidiary agreements with provincial governments, never revealed the total amount that might be available and, further, had tended to dole out money on a much more leisurely basis.

Under the ERDA process the negotiations were, in contrast, largely with line departments whose officials knew the exact amounts available. Secondly, there were considerable time constraints and MSERD staff, especially at headquarters, were in many ways ill equipped to assess the various proposals being put forward. Many line departments, on the other hand, were familiar with the regional fund and the programs that could conceivably be funded out of it. Since January 1982 they had been responsible for many of the GDA subsidiary agreements, responsibilities they inherited with the demise of DREE. The interest of these departments, however, was not so much the continuation of these agreements but, if possible, the redirection of the funds towards support of their own programs. In many instances these were little more than continuations of existing line programs, activities that were never really conceived as regional development projects.

From the perspective of the FEDCs the ideal subsidiary agreement was one that would arise within the province itself as a result of discussions among the FEDC, the provincially based line official, and provincial government officials, and with appropriate consultations at the political level, which for the FEDC meant the regional minister. The major flaw in this ideal scenario, however, proved to be the line officials. In most cases, even when sympathetic, local line officials carried little clout with their headquarters in Ottawa. Major departments such as Transport and Agriculture, which have most of their operations based outside of Ottawa, deliberately retain most policy-making and discretionary authority in Ottawa. Officials in the field in those departments tend to carry little weight in terms of rank, even though they may have significant operational responsibilities. For example, the manager of a major airport is, at best, only at the bottom rung of the executive rank (EX) category or possibly only at the senior management (SM) level, one rank below.

In other cases, while of senior rank, the regionally based official might have little expenditure or operational authority. In the Department of the Environment, as it was then structured, there were five regional co-ordinators at the director general level (one notch down from the assistant deputy minister) who reported directly to the deputy minister.[48] They did not have any line authority over the operations in their regions, however; they could only advise the deputy. Similarly in 1981 the Department of Agriculture introduced a regional branch, headed by an official at the director level, with staff based in each province. Again, however, these regional officials had no line authority and were often outranked by the operational officials, for example scientists at local research stations, in the province. In smaller departments or units, such as the minerals branch in EMR, there really were no officials based in the provinces with whom the FEDCs could discuss plans for subsidiary agreements. In short, the FEDC had to deal far more with officials in Ottawa, and to spend more time there, than they had originally hoped or anticipated.

The moves to start the ERDA process in earnest were made at a relatively late stage – late both because most subsidiary agreements were close to expiring and because the government was well into the fourth year of its mandate. An election within the year was very likely. The memorandum to cabinet (MC) on implementing ERDAs was submitted in September 1983. This was followed by a further MC in October on 'Financing ERDAs,' which essentially reiterated the principle outlined in the July 1982 document on using the 1977–82 expenditures on GDA subsidiary agreements as a baseline for making provincial allocations. On 4 November 1983, MSERD formally requested from departments in the economic envelope written submissions on possible subsidiary agreements. Much to everyone's surprise, and to the chagrin of at least some officials in MSERD, the first ERDA, with the province of Manitoba, was signed three weeks later on 25 November 1983.

The signing of an ERDA and the signing of individual subsidiary agreements did not take place simultaneously. As under the earlier GDAs, the signing of subsidiary agreements typically followed later after several months. However, the basic outline of the subsidiary agreements, and the amount of money to be allocated to them by both the federal and provincial governments, were announced at the same time and hence had to be in place.[49] Once these commitments were part of the public record they would be difficult to undo, at least by MSERD headquarters.

In effect the 4 November request for submissions unleashed a flood of proposals from line departments, many of which had been in the works for some time, in some instances with the co-operation of the FEDCs and regional ministers. One MSERD official in the operations branch, responsible for assessing the proposals, likened the process to a Le Mans start: departments were prepared, knew what they wanted, and keen to get off the mark as quickly as possible; subsequently their proposals all crowded into the first turn simultaneously in the race for the regional fund monies.[50] MSERD staff had reasonably grounded suspicions that many of the proposals were simply off-the-shelf items that departments had been unable to fund from other sources, dusted off, and then depicted as regional programming innovations. In other instances worthwhile projects were, in the estimation of operations branch, costed far too high. In one instance an MSERD official recognized a proposal as having been previously funded under a GDA, only this time it was priced at more than three times its earlier cost.[51]

The volume of proposals, limited staff, and very limited time prevented either thorough review or tougher negotiations with the line departments. This dilemma was exacerbated by the lack of familiarity of MSERD staff, not only with the technical merits of proposals but also with their geographical context. One of the items in the proposed Manitoba ERDA was support for upgrading the rail line to the port of Churchill. The scene attendant upon the arrival of this proposal from the Department of Transport was described, apocryphally perhaps, as typifying Ottawa's lack of familiarity with the regions: 'At first no one knew where this rail line was ... Someone thought Port of Churchill might be somewhere on the west coast. When it was finally tracked down on the map, we all said: '"We're going to fund a railway to there [Hudson Bay]!?"'[52]

This item passed the hurdles and was announced as part of the

Manitoba ERDA, with the federal share being slightly over $38 million. Its significance, however, resided not only in the limited capacity of the MSERD operations staff to assess and screen the proposal but more important in the fact that the proposed subsidiary agreement was actively supported by the regional minister, Lloyd Axworthy, by the Manitoba FEDC, and by the provincial government. Indeed, officials both within Transport and Canadian National were adamantly opposed to seeing any more money spent on the line in question. While line departments were primarily responsible for submitting proposals for possible subsidiary agreements and MSERD operations staff for screening them, it was clearly the regional minister, more often than not backed by the FEDC, who determined whether or not a proposal would be supported and who would act as the catalyst for launching the ERDA process. Ultimately it was CCERD, in approving a given proposed ERDA, that would decide on which projects were to be funded. But significantly it was the regional minister from the province in question who would present the ERDA to CCERD and make the case in support of it.[53]

Essentially, the various proposed subsidiary agreements would be put on a list and the regional minister would have the opportunity to select those that appealed or to negotiate changes. The FEDC played the critical, and delicate, role of both helping the regional minister and at the same time safeguarding the process. One FEDC likened the management of the process to giving the regional minister 'a shopping cart' and ensuring that it was filled with items of reasonable quality, so that when loose money became available the minister would not 'get off the track and look silly.'[54] However, some line departments, knowing that regional ministers were involved in the selection process, would deliberately package their proposal with a view to capturing the eye of a given minister. More than one FEDC was confronted by such proposals that were often 'too cute by half.' Beyond the protective arms of the FEDC there were further constraints on regional ministers. The provinces, for example, expected that certain patterns established under the GDAs, such as expenditures on tourism development, would be continued, even if many of the programs were now going to be delivered directly by the federal government. The fact that the line departments had the formal responsibility for delivering the programs gave these departments a certain amount of leverage. Nevertheless, in specific confrontations between the regional minister and line departments and their ministers it was often the regional minister who won.

In this regard the conflict between Hazen Argue, minister for Saskatchewan (and minister responsible for the Wheat Board), and Eugene Whelan, minister of agriculture, is instructive. Whelan, in keeping with his department's national sectoral strategy, was keen to use regional fund money for livestock improvement, while Argue, echoing the interests of grain producers, was concerned primarily with such issues as soil degradation and water quality and favoured programs designed to tackle these problems. Whelan had already indicated that he did not want to renew the 'community water projects' program, funded under a GDA subsidiary agreement cost-shared between the federal Prairie Farm Rehabilitation Agency (PFRA) and the Saskatchewan government.[55] However, when the ERDA was finalized, it contained not only an 'agricultural water' subsidiary agreement, worth more than twice as much as the earlier one under the GDA, but also a 'Regina–Moose Jaw water' agreement intended to improve water quality in those communities.[56] A separate 'agricultural development' subsidiary agreement, backed by $30 million of federal money and a like amount from the provincial government, provided support for 'soil and water conservation, on-farm irrigation, crop intensification and livestock enhancement measures.'[57] Whelan's aim to subsidize primarily livestock improvement measures had been relegated to only one of four separate areas identified in the agreement.

Clearly Whelan had lost and Argue, in presenting the proposed ERDA to CCERD, had succeeded in persuading his fellow ministers that the package contained worthwhile development projects while at the same time providing a high level of federal visibility. In doing so, Argue was aided by the FEDC. Wakabayashi not only helped to assemble items for the ERDA 'shopping cart' but also provided analytical support and arguments for Argue's use. Thus, in the case of the Department of Agriculture's proposal to deliver new livestock programs on its own, the FEDC was able to question whether Agriculture really had the administrative infrastructure in place within Saskatchewan to handle these new services. The FEDC himself had certain preferences, relating primarily to the promotion of high technology, which were subsequently also favoured by Argue and which resulted in an 'advanced technology' subsidiary agreement.[58] What should be stressed, however, was that several CCERD members, for example Lloyd Axworthy and Romeo LeBlanc, had presented, or would soon present, their own proposed ERDAS. They were thus inclined to defer to the prerogative of the regional minister in determining the make-up of the ERDA. In this context, given the lack of critical assessments from the MSERD operations branch and with the support of the FEDC, reasonable arguments presented by the regional minister were likely to win out over those made by the line ministers.

Regional Ministers, ERDAs, and the Provinces

As noted, line departments and ministers were often a greater obstacle to the successful launching of an ERDA than were provincial governments. Notwithstanding the inherent difficulties of dealing with the Ottawa-based departments, the relative success in obtaining provincial co-operation still needs to be explained, particularly in light of federal-provincial tensions. The term 'relative' is used since by August 1984 only seven of the ten provinces had actually signed ERDAs, although Ontario was reported to be very close to agreement before the defeat of the Liberal government in the September 1984 election. A brief look at the names of the seven provinces provides one clue to why they succumbed to federal pressure to sign an ERDA: with the exception of Alberta they were all have-not provinces.

The 1977–82 DREE GDA allocations from the federal government, which were used as a basis for the MSERD regional fund, were dependent on provincial well-being: as can be seen in Table 1 the better-off provinces as measured by per capita income, Ontario, Alberta, and British Columbia, had received much less money under the GDAs over the five-year period than the remaining have-not provinces, both proportionately and in absolute dollars; and these figures were unlikely to change under the new ERDA regime. To put it bluntly, the have provinces stood to gain little in signing an ERDA. Quebec was in a position to gain a considerable amount, but the incumbent PQ government was understandably opposed to the new approach on several grounds. Primarily, however, it did not wish to turn over provincially delivered programs to the federal government and in fact believed that federal initiatives in the regional development area constituted intrusions into provincial jurisdiction. Above all, the Quebec government did not want to legitimize federal action by appending its signature to an Ottawa-Quebec ERDA. At the same time, the Quebec government entertained a well-justified suspicion that the federal government, in competing for the loyalties of Quebeckers, would proceed to spend the money anyway, with or without Quebec's permission.

That left the six remaining provinces, where DREE monies had played an important role in developing both the social and economic and also the political and bureaucratic infrastructure. The presence or absence

TABLE 1

GDA expenditures (1977–82), per capita income, and population
distribution by province

	Per capita income* (1984)	Population (%) (1986)	GDA (%) (1977–82)	Ratio: GDA/ population	GDA ($000) (1977–82)
Newfound-land	62.1	2.3	13.8	6.00	267
PEI	67.5	0.5	7.0	14.00	135
Nova Scotia	80.5	3.5	11.3	3.23	218
New Bruns-wick	73.7	2.8	13.3	4.75	257
Quebec	87.8	25.9	29.5	1.14	570
Ontario	109.4	35.9	5.7	0.16	110
Manitoba	93.3	4.2	5.2	1.24	112
Saskatche-wan	93.1	4.0	5.8	1.45	112
Alberta	116.3	9.3	2.0	0.21	39
British Columbia	110.5	11.4	5.8	0.51	112
Canada	100.0	100.0	100.0	1.00	$1932

SOURCE: Based on Canada, *Report of the Federal-Provincial Task Force on Regional Development Assessment*, May 1987, tables 2.9 and 2.10; Department of Regional Industrial Expansion, *General Development Agreements: Status of Subsidiary Agreements as of June 28, 1985*

* As proportion of national average: Canada equals 100.

of ERDA money loomed much more significantly in these smaller provinces, whose lagging economies were also suffering from the effects of the recession. In Newfoundland, for example, the notional amount was over $250 million. While reluctant to concede to the federal government's wish for the direct delivery of programs, the have-not provinces also realized that even if the money did not flow through provincial government coffers it would still be spent mainly in the province, and projects such as those furthering mineral exploration and reforestation represented genuine economic development activities that they could ill afford to lose. The events in Prince Edward Island in 1981, where the federal government took over programs that had been delivered by the provincial government, demonstrated that Ottawa was willing to force the issue. At the same time these events also illustrated that in substance very little changed. The same employees in Prince Edward Island were continuing to deliver the same programs from the very same offices; only now they were federal rather than provincial employees.[59]

In Nova Scotia the renewal of a GDA agricultural subsidiary agreement in October 1982 had already resulted in a certain amount of dislocation. By and large the federal government's involvement in agriculture had been restricted to research and development, with the provincial government's role oriented more towards provision of direct services to farmers. The new Canada/Nova Scotia Agri-food Development Agreement saw the federal Department of Agriculture becoming directly involved in the delivery of 'agricultural resource development,' which meant that farmers wishing assistance under this program had to apply directly to Agriculture Canada, whose officials were likely farther away than provincial offices, more rigorous in interpreting the rules, and slower to process claims.[60] These dislocations, however, could be easily blamed on the federal government. On 11 June 1984 the Nova Scotia government became the sixth province to sign an ERDA. The federal portions of the subsidiary agreement for mineral exploration and development were now delivered directly by federal departments. In the case of forestry management it meant somewhat greater spending on private woodlots than on provincial crown land, and delivery by the federal Department of Agriculture since the forestry branch of Environment Canada lacked the necessary administrative infrastructure. However, the Nova Scotia ERDA did contain the assurance that the federal government would maintain 'funding at DREE levels under the GDA.'[61]

Thus by the time the Liberals were defeated in September 1984, six of the seven have-not provinces and one have province had signed agreements with Ottawa. The flow of money may well have been the primary reason for provincial acquiescence, but it was not the only reason. The fact was that the new ERDA regime was not nearly so draconian as it originally threatened to be. The basic format, as well as the projects being supported, did not differ greatly from those under the GDAs.[62] The limited time available for putting the ERDAs together meant there was little opportunity for a thorough examination of alternative means for delivering regional programming. But in many instances it was the regional ministers – ironically the same figures who were keen on a heightened federal presence and direct delivery in the first instance – who often played a role in altering or circumventing the direct delivery rule, either to appease the provincial government or, more likely, to see the implementation of a project they favoured.

In Saskatchewan, for example, the provincial government for many years had argued for federal funding to build a pipeline to carry water from Lake Diefenbaker to the cities of Regina and Moose Jaw, largely in order to overcome water quality problems resulting from growth of algae in the uncovered transport system. However, this was a responsibility clearly under provincial jurisdiction, and the federal government had already announced in 1980 that it was no longer funding municipal infrastructure projects such as sewers and water lines.[63] Senator Argue, however, was keen to help. Support for a pipeline was out of the question, but a compromise was possible in the form of a carbon filtration plant. There was some doubt whether this plant would really have much impact on improving water quality, and there was considerable resistance within MSERD to funding projects of this type. Argue, however, insisted that it be included in the Saskatchewan ERDA; hence the $15 million 'Regina–Moose Jaw water' subsidiary agreement, with a federal share of $5 million.[64] For its part the province was delighted, both in receiving the money and in seeing the federal government bending its own rules. On other matters, such as the emphasis on water quality and soil improvement programs in the agricultural agreements, the provincial government was pleased to have Argue's help in successfully resisting increased control and direction from Eugene Whelan and the Department of Agriculture.

The coincident interests of regional ministers and provincial governments were also evident in other ERDAs. Romeo LeBlanc, expressed satisfaction with the process in that it made 'the federal position firm before approaching the provincial government' thereby 'avoiding the business of provinces going through their books to see what they could pick up' for their own programs. For the first time Fisheries and Oceans received direct funding from a subsidiary agreement, something that had eluded Romeo LeBlanc earlier under the New Brunswick GDA. By 1984 LeBlanc was no longer minister of fisheries, but the $25 million federal share of the 'fisheries development' agreement was still of direct benefit to small inshore fishermen, the mainstay of his support base over the years. The largest single item in the New Brunswick ERDA, however, was $63 million for highway construction, in good part for Route 11 into the northeast of the province. Opening up the northeast and promoting economic development there had long been one of LeBlanc's goals; for the provincial government, highway construction of any kind was the lifeblood not only of economic development but of politics as well.

In Nova Scotia a member of Allan MacEachen's 'exempt' (politically appointed) staff described the ERDA process as a 'good marriage of bureaucracy and politics.'[65] No longer were there DREE officials to interfere in the direct linkages between the minister and line departments. Thus the Nova Scotia ERDA, while resulting in a retrenchment of projects centred around Halifax, at the same time saw a continuation of projects in the Strait of Canso area, Allan MacEachen's home ground, begun under an earlier GDA subsidiary agreement. Projects under the new subsidiary agreement included wharf construction and an all-weather highway that were intended, according to the ERDA, to 'provide for a second phase of activity necessary to fully capitalize the infrastructure completed under the first agreement.'[66] Additional support for wharf construction, as well as ice-making facilities, was provided for in the 'fisheries' subsidiary agreement, for which Fisheries and Oceans received $35 million. The direct delivery programs in forestry, which featured spending on private woodlots, 'came completely out of our [MacEachen's] office.'[67]

All ERDAs, like the GDAs before them, reflected the unique conditions of each province. At the same time, unlike the GDAs, the ERDAs much more clearly reflected the predilections of each regional minister. In some cases, such as that of Manitoba to be discussed later, the influence of the regional minister was much more evident. In Quebec it was the regional minister by fiat, as Marc Lalonde simply announced that he was going to spend the money designated for the ERDA unilaterally without reference to the Quebec government.[68] But under the ERDA system even weak regional ministers had considerable influence. In other circumstances someone like Hazen Argue would likely have carried little weight either with DREE or with line departments. Now they were able to pick and choose from a number of items put in front of them, and to add their own items if they wished; and they had the assistance and support of a highly competent senior federal official based in the region who, if necessary, would steer the minister away from areas likely to cause problems or embarrassment.

Just as each province varied in its make-up, so too did the role played by the regional minister and the relations between individual ministers and their FEDCs, and this was largely due to their individual strengths and weaknesses and specific proclivities. In Alberta Senator Olson played a much less active role during this period, mainly because of health problems. As well, the amount of money allocated to the Alberta ERDA under the regional fund formula was relatively little. He did, however, take an interest in the various projects and activities targeted by the FEDC, Bruce Rawson – projects that frequently originated with the provincial government. For example, the Slave River hydro project, while owned and initiated by the provincial government, nevertheless required the co-operation and approval of several federal agencies, ranging from the Federal Environmental Assessment Review Office (FEARO) to the Canadian coastguard, and the National Energy Board, in order for it to proceed. Here the co-ordination function of the FEDC office became paramount as Rawson and his officials put in place a project management plan that would allow the project to pass over the various regulatory hurdles in a timely and orderly fashion. To save time they helped arrange joint hearings by FEARO and the Alberta Energy Resources Conservation Board. Rawson also actively lobbied, successfully, on behalf of a joint, five-year, Alberta-Canada hardwoods research and development program to be part of the Alberta ERDA, a proposal that originated with the provincial government. It became a yet further example of how the direct delivery thrust underpinning the ERDA strategy reverted to more traditional GDA-style joint delivery. It also helped explain why the Alberta government signed an ERDA with the then Liberal government in July 1984, the only have province to do so before the Conservative victory in the September election of that year. In the eyes of provincial officials the hardwoods agreement, as well as the tourism development agreement, the two main items in the ERDA, represented genuine efforts to help develop sectors that hitherto had received relatively little support.[69]

Where the FEDC office came in most useful for someone like Olson was in its role as fixer. What Alberta FEDC staff came to call the 'path finding' and 'trip wire' functions were essentially solving problems and helping individuals find their way to the appropriate federal agency, and many of these individuals came to the FEDC office on referral from Olson and, over time, other Alberta politicians, including MPs and MLAs. At one point Rawson briefed the entire PC caucus of Alberta. Individuals given help included, for example, those contemplating sales or purchases of largely American-owned companies based in Alberta who wished assurance that the Foreign Investment Review Agency (FIRA) would not cause undue delays. As well, a watching brief was maintained by Rawson and his staff on various fronts, including the faltering mega-projects. In his first year as FEDC, Rawson provided a detailed analysis and critique of where federal negotiators had gone wrong in dealing with Alberta on the Allsands tar sands oil project. This brief was not restricted to economic matters. Briefing notes, for example, were drafted on native rights, the federal communications strategy, and the Alberta government's plan to introduce hospital user fees. Rawson's previous position as secretary of the Ministry of State for Social Development led him to maintain an interest, and contacts, in the health care and social services area and to provide analysis of these issues as they arose in Alberta for the relevant deputies and ministers in Ottawa.

Of the ten FEDCs Rawson was by far the most active. He saw MSERD and the FEDC offices as an experiment, and he meant to get the most out of the experience by pushing his mandate to the limit. It was a role he could play because of his seniority and because the regional minister was relatively inactive. As well, in the absence of a substantial regional fund, he was forced to make virtue out of necessity by stressing the need of federal line departments to alter or redirect their own programs to respond to what he felt were important needs in Alberta. Thus his intense lobbying of deputies and ministers in Ottawa. In other cases, such as in Manitoba and New Brunswick, it was the regional minister who played the dominant role. In the two largest provinces, Ontario and Quebec, the FEDCs were much less important. The Ontario FEDC, Lawrence O'Toole, identified much more closely with prevailing orientations in Ottawa. In turn Herb Gray and the other Ontario ministers with regional responsibilities tended to bypass the FEDC office and deal directly with departments and agencies in Ottawa. In Quebec the regional fund was much more substantial. But there ministers and MPs, well schooled in the ways of distributing federal largesse, already had clear ideas on how they wanted to see the money spent. They were also blessed with a well-organized political network headed by Marc Lalonde for distributing monies to the different Quebec ministers and, from there, to individual MPs. Furthermore, the Montreal-based FEDC office was in the shadow of the much larger DRIE office in the same city. The DRIE office, dominated by former DREE staffers, was in a much better position to provide analytical support on Quebec development issues. Instead the Montreal FEDC office focused on specfic questions, such as possible changes in the drug patent legislation, something that the FEDC, Normand Plante, thought would benefit the Quebec economy and the Montreal area economy in particular.

If Bruce Rawson came to represent the most adventuresome and experimental of the ten FEDCs, then Doug Love in Nova Scotia was perhaps the most cautious. As a result, progress in negotiating the Nova Scotia ERDA tended to lag behind the others. But the process was also trickier because in Nova Scotia the minister ostensibly junior to Allan MacEachen, Gerald Regan, saw himself, if not dominant, certainly in control of the Halifax area. In the end MacEachen had relatively little contact with the FEDC office. A member of his exempt staff reported that during the course of ERDA negotiations there was actually much more contact between MacEachen's office and the regional DRIE office in connection with the specific subsidiary agreements on tourism and the Strait of Canso projects.[70] MacEachen, given his years of experience in dealing with federal agencies and departments, very likely had little use for the FEDC office and may have found it a hindrance. Regan, on the other hand, was a constant visitor to Love's office. One of the bright spots identified in the economic perspectives document for Nova Scotia was offshore oil and gas exploration and production. Among the projections made was that there would be considerable pressure on office space in the Halifax area, with the result that Regan and the FEDC office proposed the construction of a new office complex. To be located in downtown Halifax on the waterfront, the proposed federal complex included plans for a new art gallery and theatre. Funding for the development, which in the end was never constructed, was separate from the regional fund money under the ERDA. But the help extended to Regan, and the efforts made to channel some of the offshore-related expenditures directly into Halifax did illustrate the uses to which the FEDC office could be put by regional ministers.

Even where regional ministers failed to take advantage of the FEDC office, or contacts with the FEDC were limited, the existence of FEDC offices and the role they played were significant in themselves. Almost two decades earlier Donald Gow, a senior Ottawa civil servant turned academic, had put forward the radical notion of providing regional ministers with administrative support in the form of civil servants at the deputy level, based in the provinces, who would analyse all government policies and expenditures from a regional perspective. Gow's proposal, presented in his doctoral thesis, remained largely of academic interest;[71] there is no evidence that it had any direct impact on the MSERD design. Nevertheless, by 1984 the FEDC system had evolved into an arrangement of which Donald Gow might well have approved. The capacity of FEDCs to review A base programming expenditures was decidely limited, but for FEDCs such as Bruce Rawson it remained an important goal. Most important of all, many of the FEDCs, con-

sciously or unconsciously, became advocates of regionally defined positions. At meetings of the management committee, which took place
every two months, discussion frequently echoed the debates characterizing federal-provincial relations. The FEDCs from Alberta and Saskatchewan would complain that the Nova Scotia FEDC's support of the
federal government's offshore drilling program through PIP grants
was inappropriate; that the money could be better spent in support
of endeavours such as the tar sands project in Alberta. The fact that
many issues – energy, for example – involved mainly political decisions
or were the prerogative of a single minister reduced somewhat the
pressure on the management committee. At the same time the preponderance of FEDCs on the committee, the relative seniority of some
of the FEDCs, and the reputation of two of the FEDCs, David Bond from
British Columbia and Bruce Rawson, for being unhesitatingly blunt
in saying what they felt was amiss with Ottawa's policies did lead to
the Ottawa-based officials feeling somewhat beleaguered. This feeling
was replicated at lower levels. In the MSERD operations and policy
branches in Ottawa, the material submitted by FEDCs or their staff for
incorporation into cabinet briefing notes, for example, led MSERD
headquarters staff to voice complaints that not only the ministers but
also the FEDCs 'had gone native.' In particular Jean Edmonds from
Manitoba and Art Wakabayashi from Saskatchewan were thought to
have gone too far in providing support for their regional minister and
Gordon Slade too far in supporting the Peckford government in disputes involving fisheries, for example.

These differences and tensions were in part a reflection of the same
centre-periphery differences underpinning federal-provincial disputes; they also reflected some basic logistical and structural impedi-
ments. Operations staff, for instance, were often required to blend
and summarize ten different perspectives emanating from the ten FEDC
offices into a single two-page briefing note for cabinet. FEDC staff, in
turn, would often feel aggrieved that the nuances of the Manitoba or
Prince Edward Island position were absent from the final document
submitted to CCERD, leading to the sense that the Ottawa-based staff
was insensitive to the regions. These tensions were generated mainly
in relation to the operations and policy branches, the units that were
required to produce analyses that ultimately were national in scope.

Relations between FEDC offices and projects branch, the unit responsible for supporting the ERDA process, were much better. Originally set up to deal with the mega-projects, from 1982 onward more
than 85 per cent of staff time was actually devoted to handling the

ERDAs. The five senior analysts in this branch, each responsible for two provinces, were able to develop much greater empathy for what the FEDCs were attempting to achieve in their particular province and the difficulties they faced, and, in the words of one analyst, for 'the sensibilities of the natives.'[72] On a more practical level, projects branch had a vested interest in seeing as many ERDAs as possible completed. Like most of the FEDCs, they recognized that this meant cutting corners and compromising with regional ministers and provincial governments.

In summary, the FEDCs, singly and collectively, with and without regional ministers, found fertile ground in acting as a conduit for provincially based interests, and in identifying a host of deficiencies in the manner in which federal programs were being designed and delivered in the regions. While FEDCs such as Rawson were entrepreneurs in their own right, in the sense that they deliberately cultivated constituencies and tested the limits of their mandate, what they were able to accomplish was indicative of the vacuum existing in agencies for transmitting regional sentiments to the centre. At a minimum the FEDC was part of a system that represented the formalization of the role of regional ministers in cabinet. For some regional ministers, perhaps, the increase in leverage that resulted from this formalization was negligible; but, particularly for the weaker ministers, the formalization made a substantial difference. It gave them specific rights to participate in the distribution of regionally allocated funds, influence that went beyond the traditional prerogatives over local patronage.

The ERDAs were not the only regionally targeted programs in which regional ministers came to play a defined, quasi-formal role. Nor was MSERD the only administrative mechanism available to support those programs in which regional ministers were given a major role in the allocation of funds. To illustrate the expanded role that regional ministers enjoyed, two other programs implemented during the 1980–4 period warrant discussion. We turn now to chapter 7.

Fast-tracking Regional Expenditures: 'Special Employment' and 'Special Recovery'

Regional economic development is a field where little consensus exists among either academics or practitioners. Views on appropriate strategies range from 'the best regional policy is no regional policy' to emphasis on growth poles, industrial incentives, and infrastructure projects. For these reasons, it is difficult to render judgment on the quality and viability of instruments such as the Economic and Regional Development Agreements (ERDAs) signed in 1984. More so than in most areas of government policy, the label 'garbage-can type decision-making' easily applies: overall direction and specific criteria are vague or absent, and in the end the truly important criteria emerge only during the actual decision-making process.[1]

In the case of the ERDAs, it was during the course of negotiations that the interests and prerogatives of regional ministers ultimately became paramount. Yet the influence of officials from the Ministry of State for Economic and Regional Development (MSERD), and of the federal economic development co-ordinators (FEDCs) in particular, was not absent. They were able to ensure that the projects approved were of reasonable quality and met basic standards. The projects were in some instances rather tenuously connected with regional development. But money spent on reforestation, mineral exploration, ice-making facilities for fish plants, and the like was not necessarily wasted money. There was a sense that both the specification of the overall objectives and the programming under the ERDAs could have been better, but given the political exigencies – important exigencies relating not only to the role of regional ministers but also to federal-provincial relations and the imminence of an election – the FEDCs and the officials in the projects branch of MSERD were reasonably pleased with the results: seven of the ten ERDAs were in place by July 1984.

This sense of satisfaction, however, did not necessarily apply to other programs where regional ministers also played a major role in the allocation process. This chapter will examine two related programs. One, the Special Employment Initiative (SEI), was designed and delivered with almost no support from the bureaucracy. On a hypothetical scale measuring the integrity of the political-administrative process, the SEI would likely rank very low. The other, the Special Recovery Capital Projects Program (SRCPP), was supported through an innovative, ad hoc management team drawing personnel and expertise from both MSERD and the Department of Supply and Services. Within Ottawa circles pronunciation of the SRCPP acronym soon acquired the unfortunate intonation 'scrap,' indicative of the suspicions the program aroused about the narrow partisan intentions of its political backers. On an integrity scale, however, it would likely rank much higher than the SEI and was probably comparable to the ERDAs in terms of the quality of the projects ultimately approved. Both programs, however, highlighted the role of regional ministers and both illustrated the dilemmas in designing administrative mechanisms to support ministers in their regional capacity.

The Special Employment Initiative

The Department of Employment and Immigration (CEIC) is responsible for a veritable alphabet soup of programs designed to reduce unemployment and improve job skills within a variety of populations. During the winter months in particular, when seasonal unemployment is higher, or during times of economic recession, one of the traditional means used by government to pump money into the economy has been to channel funds through CEIC for temporary employment relief programs. During the 1980–4 period there were no less than a half-dozen separate programs ranging from Canada Works (successor to the Local Initiatives Program of the 1970s) to the Local Employment Assistance Program (LEAP), the Canada Community Services Projects program, and the Local Economic Development Assistance (LEDA) program.[2] The announcement, therefore, in the 28 June 1982 mini-budget of Finance Minister MacEachen of an 'additional allocation of $200 million ... for direct job creation programs' appeared innocuous enough, and appropriate given the severity of the recession than well under way.[3] The minister of CEIC, Lloyd Axworthy, referred to the new program as Immediate Employment Stimulation, the same title that appeared in the Supplementary Estimates.[4] Thereafter, however, the status of the program became confused. As David Crombie noted in

November during question period in the House, 'Unlike a lot of other job-creation programs which the minister has, there is very little known about this Program and it seems there is some mystery surrounding it.'[5] Axworthy increased the level of mystery by stating that 'it was not a program as such' but simply funds from the minister of finance that were allocated to a number of different departments 'to fund projects which were on the shelf.'[6]

Crombie was quite right to be suspicious. CEIC programs frequently incorporate a partisan dimension, most often in the form of involvement of MPs at the local level in the approval of projects. The design and administration of the programs themselves usually remain in the hands of CEIC officials. In the case of Immediate Employment Stimulation, or, to use the official monikers adopted in the spring of 1983, the Special Employment Initiative (SEI) and the Employment Creation Grants and Contributions (ECGC) program, the design originated directly in the offices of Lloyd Axworthy and the Prime Minister's Office (PMO). In the spring of 1982 officials from approximately a dozen departments – two people from each department, usually someone at the assistant deputy minister level and a less senior person at the director level – were summoned to the Centre block on Parliament Hill. There Denise Chong, economic policy adviser in the PMO, outlined to the gathered officials the main features of the SEI program:[7] the government wished to use a 'fast-track' method in approving employment creation projects with a high level of input from ministers. Departments were welcome to propose projects likely to lead to the generation of employment and were requested to nominate a designated individual for liaison purposes. Proposals were to be submitted *not* to CEIC, however, but directly to the regional minister of the relevant province. He or she, in turn, would either approve or reject the proposal. If approved, it would then be forwarded to a small SEI secretariat in CEIC, specially created for this purpose, for processing.

Unlike most employment programs, there was very little publicity associated with the launching of the SEI. Nor were there information booklets and application forms available from local CEIC offices, as would normally be the case. The only form, a 'quick and dirty' one hurriedly drawn up by the staff of the newly created SEI secretariat, was available solely from regional ministers who in turn disbursed them to government MPs in their province or directly to groups or individuals.[8] Publicity came into play when successful grant applications were announced by the regional minister and the MP. Significantly, on the form itself, which was the essence of simplicity, there

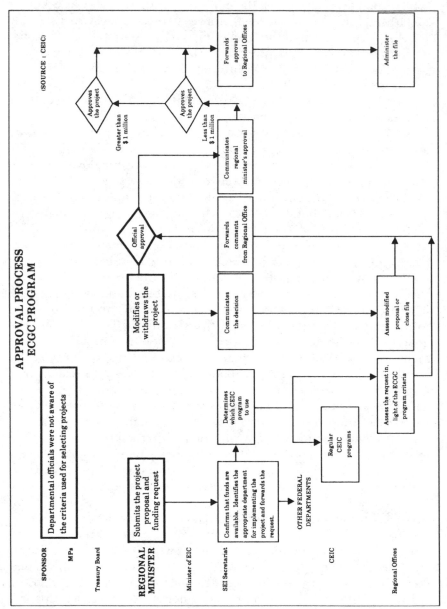

Figure 1. SEI/ECGC program approval process

was room for two signatures under the heading of approval – those of the regional minister and the minister of CEIC. The latter's signature was essentially pro forma, there to protect and reassure nervous officials in CEIC who, though recognizing that the regional minister had de facto authority over the disbursement of funds, were not convinced that he or she also had de jure authority over a program officially administered from within CEIC. The one fast rule, however – probably the only fast rule in the entire SEI program – was the requirement of the regional minister's signature on the form. Nothing else was acceptable.[9]

The approval and administrative process was examined subsequently in some detail by staff from the auditor general's office, who were simultaneously appalled and fascinated by the ingenious manner by which over $200 million of public funds was fast-tracked through the hands of regional ministers.[10] Their summary description of the process is found in Figure 1, a description which in some ways is overly elaborate. Initially the intention was to use existing departmental programs that were, in Axworthy's words, sitting 'on the shelf.' Experience in the first few months indicated, however, that this was problematic in that departments, including CEIC, had their own particular rules and standards, which at a minimum would spell delay. Hence the creation of a yet further contrivance, the Employment Creation Grants and Contributions (ECGC) program, with its own separate eligibility criteria.

The director of the SEI secretariat essentially wore two hats. First, as director of the SEI, he would determine whether a proposal, once it had been approved by the regional minister and the minister of CEIC, could best be handled by a line department such as Fisheries and Oceans, by one of the regular programs within CEIC, or failing that, through the ECGC program. After an initial experience with line departments, the second round saw the vast majority of applications routed directly to the ECGC program. Once the application landed there, the director put on his ECGC hat and assessed the proposal in light of that program's criteria. These criteria, as the auditor general later noted, had no practical effect. There were three criteria: the project was receiving substantial sums from other sources; the duration of the project was twenty-six weeks or more; and the amount requested did not exceed $250,000.[11] In order to qualify the project had only to meet *one* of the criteria. Ninety-four per cent of proposals asked for less than $250,000. All told, CEIC handled 82 per cent of all funding for projects, and approximately 70 per cent of all funds were handled through the ECGC mechanism.[12] The SEI secretariat had a full-time staff complement that never at any time exceeded five individuals. Over three thousand applications were processed; very few received more than a cursory review.

The program had an additional feature which differentiated it from the criteria and restrictions that normally apply to government programs. The Treasury Board, in its *Guide on Financial Administration for Departments and Agencies*, stipulates that all assistance for projects of a capital nature be in the form of contributions rather than grants.[13] The contributory format facilitates monitoring and control of expenditures on non-governmental projects. This rule, like many other rules, would slow considerably the disbursement of ECGC monies in so far as it took time to obtain commitment from other contributors or, worse, would make it impossible for the SEI program to be the sole funder of a project. This posed special difficulties since the majority of projects involved the construction or repair of facilities such as hockey rinks, community halls, and churches where co-sponsors willing to make the initial commitment were hard to find. As a result, Treasury Board made a special ruling on 20 September 1982, permitting SEI capital projects to be funded through grants without the normal restrictions applying.[14] Subsequently, the auditor general's office discovered that 96 per cent of funds approved for ECGC projects were indeed in the form of grants rather than contributions.[15]

In other programs, such as the Local Initiatives Project (LIP) and Canada Works, there was usually a formula used in the allocation of funds – typically the rate of unemployment in provinces or census districts in order to provide support where it was most needed. As well, particularly in the later stages of the LIP and in Canada Works, there was a well-established principle that the local MP, whether on the government side or not, would be consulted in the selection of projects in the riding. SEI was not specifically intended to help the unemployed; rather, as officials of CEIC pointed out, it was an employment creation program. Still, it was not unreasonable to assume that in provinces with elevated levels of unemployment more money would be spent.

In the event, the auditor general's office discovered that the allocation of funding by province bore little relationship to prevailing rates of unemployment. The disjuncture between SEI spending and prevailing rates of unemployment over the three-year period is evident in the data in Table 2, where percentage of total ECGC funds spent is

TABLE 2

Ratio of percentage ECGC grants to percentage in each province of total unemployed, 1982–3 to 1984–5*

	Ratio (% ECGC/ % unemployed)	Amount ($ millions)
Manitoba	2.03	10.3
New Brunswick	1.87	9.2
Quebec	1.67	78.4
Saskatchewan	1.45	5.6
PEI	1.20	0.9
Nova Scotia	1.00	5.5
Ontario	0.77	39.0
British Columbia	0.29	6.3
Newfoundland	0.27	1.2
Alberta	0.09	1.3
Canada	1.00	157.6

SOURCE: Adapted from *Report of the Auditor-General of Canada: Fiscal Year ended 31 March 1986* (Ottawa: Supply and Services 1986), exhibit 6.2

* Excludes expenditures from La Prade fund and fiscal 1985–6.

juxtaposed with the percentage of total unemployed in each province. In comparing the resulting ECGC/unemployment ratios, note that only in Nova Scotia was there an exact match between proportion of ECGC grant money and percentage unemployment. Quebec, which had less than one-third of Canada's total unemployed, nonetheless received about half the funds allotted to ECGC projects, a ratio of 1.67: 1. Newfoundland, having nearly 3 per cent of Canada's unemployed, received only 0.8 per cent of the ECGC total, making for a ratio of 0.27: 1. At the top of the list, note that provinces such as New Brunswick and Manitoba, represented by skilled and activist ministers, fared very well. The most successful province, in fact, was home to the minister whose department was responsible for delivering the SEI/ECGC program.

Opposition MPs were not informed about the grants, even those concerning projects in their own ridings, until after the fact. The complaint of Lorne Nystrom (New Democrat MP for Yorkton-Melville) to the House on 7 February 1984 illustrated the dilemma and, incidentally, provides as good a description as any of how the process worked:

I have recently found out that in Saskatchewan a program called the Immediate Employment Stimulation Program [sic] has been in existence since January 1, 1983. It is a $4 million project, and the only access to that fund is through Senator Hazen Argue. Apparently groups approach him directly, and his office then either approves or does not approve a project, and it is rubber stamped by the Minister of Employment and Immigration. Why are officials from the Department of Employment and Immigration not involved in processing the applications? Why have Members of Parliament from Saskatchewan not been informed of this $4 million slush fund in Senator Hazen Argue's office?[16]

In short, regional ministers were given free rein in disbursing ECGC funds. There was little in the way of controls or guidelines. As such SEI provided an interesting snapshot of regional ministers in action and of the differences between them. Except in Ontario and Quebec, the regional ministers directly controlled the disbursal of funds. In New Brunswick, according to an official, Romeo LeBlanc 'absolutely splintered his money,' spending small amounts in every nook and cranny of the province regardless of political affiliation.[17] Allan MacEachen, in turn, was both much slower in submitting approvals and highly secretive. Many of his projects, wharves in many cases, were located in obscure geographical locations, mostly, it was suspected, in Cape Breton. In Quebec Marc Lalonde, as always, ran a tight ship, allocating precise amounts to ministers, who in turn allocated amounts to MPs, and keeping disputes among them to a minimum. In Ontario Herb Gray was much less rigid, appearing almost afraid of his ministerial colleagues and wishing to avoid confrontation with them by giving in to their requests whenever possible. Some government MPs were denied access to the program if they failed to get along with the regional minister. However, in one instance an opposition member was allowed to participate, namely Roch Lasalle, the only Conservative member from Quebec. His participation, apparently, was contingent upon his not divulging information about the program to fellow Conservatives.

The projects funded were on the whole of the pork-barrel type – for example, the University of Manitoba benefited from grants of $125,000 for a daycare centre and $1.3 million for a sports medicine and fitness centre. In Quebec the Conseil Syndicale National (CSN), the left-oriented trade union federation, received $469,755 for a project entitled 'Operation: Changements Technologiques,' involving the employment of fifty-three short-term employees throughout the province to help make trade union organizations more sensitive to the exigencies of technological change. In neither case could it be said that there were direct connections between the minister or MP and the recipients, at least not in the sense that the latter were expected to perform a particular political service.[18] The money was handed out with the aim of creating goodwill. The CSN, for example, had no discernible connections with the Liberals. In fact since the late 1960s, when a bitter dispute erupted between the CSN and the federal government, there had been little love lost between the federal Liberals and the CSN.[19]

Where there were problems it related in part to a surfeit of money. In Quebec the SEI and ECGC appeared to be ideally suited for the direct delivery of other federal funds to Quebec citizens. One such fund, which had been lying fallow for want of means to spent it, was $200 million that had been targeted as compensation for the closure in 1978 of the La Prade heavy water plant on the St Lawrence near Drummondville.[20] In 1983 the minister responsible for the fund, Jean Chrétien as minister of energy, mines, and resources, authorized expenditure of $75 million through the SEI. The area in question, approximately one hundred miles wide centred around Drummondville and encompassing seven ridings, became the object of intense activity on the part of MPs and the minister.[21] A much greater proportion of projects in this area fell into the questionable category, including one where the local MP and members of his family became the driving force behind a proposed hockey arena and recreational centre. The centre was eventually built after several cost overruns, all of which were funded by SEI. Subsequently the MP became president and chief administrator of the complex.[22]

The most directly partisan use of SEI funds, however, occurred in Ontario. In the winter of 1983 a new organization entitled the Canadian Alliance for Italian Integration and Culture was incorporated to do charitable work in the four hundred thousand strong Italian community in the Metropolitan Toronto area, despite the presence of COSTI-IIAS, an organization that had been dispensing social services and language and citizenship courses to Italian newcomers for more than thirty years. Subsequently an organization bearing almost the identical title as the Canadian Alliance, and having the same non-profit registration number, submitted an application under the SEI to fund an operation called Alliance Community Services (ACS). The applications was successful. ACS received $583,000, and opened a storefront office at 3271 Dufferin Street in Toronto.[23] In the fall of 1983 a document came to light entitled 'A discussion paper on the integration and the Italian community's relations with the Liberal Party,' dated 29 August 1983, which stated that 'it is necessary to fund loyal and valid agencies within our community.'[24] Among the signatories of the discussion paper were some of the same individuals who were on the board of directors of the Canadian Alliance for Italian Integration and Culture, one of whom was also responsible for the application to the SEI program. Among the staff workers of the ACS were individuals who worked for Liberal candidates in federal and provincial elections, candidates such as Jim Coutts, who contested the riding of Spadina in both the by-election of 1981 and the federal election of 1984, and Michael Spensieri, who won election in 1985 as Liberal MPP.[25]

The $583,000 grant evoked strong opposition from established but cash-strapped Metro area social welfare organizations, including COSTI-IIAS. It also resulted in considerable dissension within the Italian community. Long-time supporters of COSTI-IIAS such as the Canadian Italian Business and Professional Association were particularly incensed; and even Charles Caccia, federal environment minister and member of the Italian community, was rumoured to have been opposed to the grant. Clearly a group of younger Liberal activists in the Italian community, with the help of Coutts and his connections to individuals in the PMO, were able to tap into the SEI fund to support the creation of an old-fashioned political machine. Their aim was to mobilize the Italian vote and at the same time replace a number of the incumbent Liberal MPs in the Toronto area. As the response both within and outside the Italian community demonstrated, this endeavour came at a time when not only the NDP and Conservatives were beginning to make inroads among Italians but also when most in the Italian community had become much less enamoured with machine-type politics. The grant was given with the apparent approval of John Roberts, the minister responsible for the Toronto area, but one suspects that the origins of the scheme lay elsewhere. Certainly they did not lie with the minister responsible for Ontario as a whole, Herb Gray. If anything, his lack of involvement demonstrated the lack of control he had over his Ontario ministers.

The lack of control, both political and bureaucratic, over the SEI program aroused a certain amount of consternation among cabinet ministers and even among some of the political staff in Lloyd Axworthy's own office. In most provinces many of the projects funded were ones falling under provincial jurisdiction – construction of, or repairs to, municipally owned arenas, for example. Except in Quebec, there was little protest from provincial quarters, however. Again, as in the case of the ERDAS, most provinces were happy to see the federal government spend money on municipal infrastructure and in general to see the money being pumped into provincial economies weakened by the recession.

In Quebec it was a different matter. Under the Quebec government's Intergovernmental Affairs Act, no municipality can enter directly into an agreement with Ottawa. As a result Quebec MPs, in order to spend SEI money, often entered into arrangements with municipalities whereby the local Kiwanis club, for example, would submit an application to build a community hall, and once built the hall would then be turned over to the municipality. There were also instances of local volunteer firemen's associations paving roads using ECGC grants; and in one riding three local Liberal party stalwarts put forward a scheme which would have seen several million dollars spent on a privately owned water filtration plant complete with pipelines to four or five communities. This particular scheme fell through, though not before giving the staff of the SEI secretariat some uneasy moments.[26] The Quebec government, as a result of these attempted forays into provincial jurisdiction, subsequently amended sections 20 and 21 of the Intergovernmental Affairs Act to prevent even indirect dealings by municipalities with the federal government.[27] Unfortunately this had consequences for other more straightforward CEIC programs, such as Canada Works, where the involvement of MPs in approving projects followed well-established norms with bureaucratic safeguards.

To the extent that SEI was intended as a slush fund, a pork-barrel to help buttress the electoral fortunes of those Liberal ministers and MPs able to access the fund, the results of the 1984 election suggest it was a failure. Particularly in Quebec where, it seemed, every parish church sported a new steeple or parking lot courtesy of the SEI, the results must have been a disappointment to Liberal strategists. But the SEI represented something more than traditional pork-barrelling; it also represented an effort to circumvent the bureaucracy at a time when both ministers and MPs genuinely felt a need to see government act quickly to remedy the effects of the recession. It was a feeling that capped several years of frustration in dealing with increasingly complicated administrative procedures, ironically procedures such as enhanced support by central agencies that were originally designed to provide greater political input at the cabinet level.

In short, hostility and frustration on the part of ministers and MPs were directed not only towards provincial governments but also towards the federal government's own administrative apparatus. As one official sensed, the feeling among the politicians was, 'We are going to spend the money the way we like it.'[28] The result was the SEI, a mechanism that would allow a substantial bloc of government funds to be spent with a minimum of bureaucratic interference. This, however, also meant minimal bureaucratic support. Many of the CEIC regional offices refused to become involved in the program, at best merely acting as post-boxes for the delivery of funds. Except in Manitoba, most of the FEDCs as well did not become involved in the SEI, either through choice or, more likely, because the regional ministers thought it best to keep the FEDCs and other officials in blissful ignorance. It should be noted that administrative support and guidelines were not entirely absent. As the auditor general's report indicated, although regional CEIC officials did not bother calculating the number of actual jobs created, they did attempt to monitor basic progress on capital projects.[29] As well, in the case of construction projects, the SEI secretariat did require that the sponsor of the project (i.e., the organization requesting the funds) name an architect or professional engineer. Then, on an informal basis, officials from Public Works would take a quick look at the plans. In certain provinces – Quebec and Manitoba, for example – local CEIC officials, sometimes on their own initiative, would help MPs or ministers in identifying possible projects.[30]

This limited administrative support, however, did not rescue the SEI from being seen as a particularly rank specimen among contemporary pork-barrel programs. By the winter of 1984 articles in publications such as *Maclean's* and questions in the House meant that both ministers and officials had to scramble to obscure as much as possible the origins of the program and the means used to disburse the funds.[31] In response to persistent requests from the opposition for information on the projects and the recipients, John Roberts, the minister who succeeded Lloyd Axworthy as minister of CEIC, latched on to the ingenious stratagem of simply lumping the details on SEI/ECGC funded projects with those on all projects that CEIC had funded over a four-year period, some fifty thousand projects all told of which SEI/ECGC represented approximately three thousand. These were tabled in the House on 21 February 1984. The opposition, amidst cries of outrage, were left to wade through a three-foot-high stack of computer printout, festooned with a red ribbon.[32] Vague hints of malfeasance and intimations of corruption by the opposition were never proven, though the auditor general's report delivered two years later made clear that there were definite signs of undue partisan bias in the delivery of the program.

Nonetheless, the pungent odour enveloping the program lessened considerably its credibility and limited opportunities for generating publicity and goodwill for the government.

While the SEI may have served the specific wishes of certain ministers and MPs in bringing projects to their constituencies or provinces, it also demonstrated the difficulty of delivering a credible program with limited or no bureaucratic support. At the same time, the Liberal government and individual ministers had not lost their fervour for 'fast-tracking' government expenditures. We turn now to another employment and economy-boosting program, this one launched a year after the announcement of the SEI.

Special Recovery Capital Projects

The Special Capital Projects Program (SRCPP) was first announced in the 19 April 1983 budget presented by Finance Minister Marc Lalonde. SRCPP constituted the largest single item in his overall $4.8 billion 'special recovery' program. Within six months, Lalonde projected, across the land 'Earth will be moved, steel will be rigged and concrete will be poured.'[33] In many respects SRCPP appeared to share the hallmarks of the SEI, starting with the adjective 'special.' Like the SEI, it was designed to ameliorate economic conditions stemming from the recession and to do so as quickly as possible. In the words of Tom Axworthy, 'it was your traditional new deal type capital expenditure' to create employment and to put money in the hands of consumers.[34] In this case the pouring of concrete and rigging of steel would be effected by advancing the timetable of expenditures on federal capital projects that were already in the planning stage. Like the SEI, in order to expedite the delivery of projects, normal Treasury Board procedures were suspended and ad hoc administrative arrangements put in place.[35] Once again emphasis was put on federal visibility and once more regional ministers came to the fore as key determinants of eligibility criteria and projects to be funded.

At the same time were some important differences. First, the amount of money involved in SRCPP was considerably greater – $2.4 billion as opposed to the $300 million originally allocated to the SEI. It meant that there were no actors – whether line departments, regional ministers, or MPs – who could afford *not* to be participants. SRCPP was the only new money available. Secondly, the timing, in the spring of 1983, ensured that much greater attention would be paid by the government, opposition, and the media, to the linkages between expenditures and planning for the next election. It was a time when the Liberals had only 27 per cent of popular support in the Gallup poll compared to the 52 per cent enjoyed by the Conservatives.[36] To more cynical observers, the main difference between SRCPP and the SEI was simply that the pressures to spend with a view to maximizing political advantage would be all that much greater, and that the problems associated with the SEI already coming to light would be multiplied several-fold.

The main political progenitor of SRCPP, Marc Lalonde, was fully aware of these potential problems. When first presenting a preliminary outline of the program to the political cabinet in December 1982, Lalonde, in an apparent reference to difficulties with the SEI, 'made it clear that he wasn't going to tolerate any [expletive] around on this program.'[37] He wished, above all, that a high level of credibility be maintained, mainly through strict adherence to set criteria. Nonetheless, the ministers in attendance, including Romeo LeBlanc, Herb Gray, Ed Lumley, Allan MacEachen, and Pierre De Bané, where struck by the 'regional sensitivity of projects' and, according to Donald Johnston, minister of MSERD, by the 'psychological momentum and enormous political benefits' that the infusion of substantial capital expenditures would have.[38] The political cabinet, officially a special subcommittee of the Planning and Priorities (P&P) committee of cabinet to examine budget proposals, gave approval for further consideration and the proposal was turned over for additional development to a small committee of deputy ministers, chaired by Mickey Cohen of Finance and including the secretaries of MSERD and Treasury Board and the deputy of Transport.

The initial proposal had originated within the projects branch of MSERD a few months earlier.[39] Robert Weese, director in charge of mega-projects, was contemplating the limited feasibility of most projected mega-projects, the effects of the recession, and an extensive collection of 'wish lists' based on proposed projects listed in the planning documents of line departments. He felt that capital spending widely dispersed among several projects would be an effective way of priming a sluggish economy. In memo form, his ideas circulated within MSERD and were then sent to Finance, which had earlier asked departments for creative proposals on counter-cyclical measures for inclusion in the budget. With the help of Finance officials, a proposal for expenditures on several major capital projects across the country was developed and then submitted to four key senior officials – Cohen, William Teschke, secretary to MSERD, Jack Manion, secretary to Treasury Board, and Gordon Osbaldeston, Michael Pitfield's successor as clerk of the PCO. From there the proposal went to the special sub-committee/political cabinet. In giving its approval, the subcommittee also ordered that all work undertaken on the proposed program be under the cover of budget secrecy. It now fell to the special committee of deputies (the Cohen committee), with the assistance of staff from MSERD, Finance, and Treasury board, and later a number of line de-partments, to develop criteria for the selection of projects, design a mechanism for applying the criteria and assessing proposals, and over-see the implementation of the proposals. It was decided that projects should be over $1 million in value, make a significant contribution to economic and regional development, and be ready for implementation within six months. Social projects and projects involving federal-pro-vincial co-operation were ruled out, ostensibly because of time con-straints. This also harmonized well with the federal government's stress on visibility and direct delivery.

At the end of December 1982 Finance circulated a formal request to all departments asking for proposals that fit the basic criteria. At the same time a similar request was sent to the FEDCs, asking them 'to identify ... a list of capital projects to be considered as part of a possible economic infrastructure component of the government's planning for economic recovery.'[40] Incoming proposals were loosely categorized and placed into binders. At this stage the amount of money the government was prepared to spend was not yet clear, so it was decided to create three packages of $1 billion, $2.5 billion, and $5 billion respectively. By late January staff for the committee began meeting with the sectoral *and* regional ministers.[41] Towards the end of February 1983 a priorized list of projects, with each project description occupying a single page, was submitted to the Cohen committee. From there the list went to the special cabinet subcommittee where it received approval in early March. At the same time a funding level of $2.2 billion was agreed upon. Also, about halfway through the selection process, Cohen brought in Raymond Hession, deputy minister of supply and services, to supervise the work of the staff supporting the Cohen committee. Hession became more than simply a supervisor; he became an enthu-siastic supporter of SRCPP and promoted the merits of the concept, such as the fast-track approval procedures, throughout the bureauc-racy. The group of officials working for the Cohen committee was moved into quarters in the Department of Supply and Services. After the announcement of SRCPP on 20 April 1983, the group officially be-came the SRCPP secretariat and the Cohen committee became the SRCPP

Board with Hession as chairman. As well, less than twenty-four hours before the announcement of SRCPP in the budget, an additional $200 million was added, bringing the total funding level up to $2.4 billion. Marc Lalonde, in a playful mood, had briefly waved a copy of his written text in front of news cameras. One reporter was able to capture a page of figures on film, and shortly thereafter information on the allocation of $2.2 billion to SRCPP appeared on news broadcasts. In order to allow the minister to argue that there had been no breach of budget secrecy, the figure was altered to $2.4 billion.[42]

Once the program was announced, Donald Johnston as minister for MSERD became the minister officially in charge of the program. As well, as part of the fast-track approval process, MSERD took over some of the functions normally performed by Treasury Board. Specifically, MSERD operations branch was authorized to give 'preliminary project approval' (PPA) to departments, allowing them to incur costs for design or land acquisition. Under normal Treasury Board procedures PPAs took from a minimum of two to a maximum of eight months to process. As the blurb in the SRCPP media kit stressed, the intent of the fast-track procedure was 'No Red Tape – No Delays,'[43] and by most accounts this was the case: by the end of April 1983, 96 per cent of all SRCPP projects had received their PPA.[44] The second stage, 'effective project approval' (EPA), necessary to release complete funding, was done by Treasury Board; but here too a fast-track procedure was employed. All SRCPP project submissions were designated with a large S in the top right-hand corner of each page. Such submissions, when received by Treasury Board, were given immediate priority, resulting in a turnaround time of ten days or less.[45]

By 31 March 1984 projects constituting 96 per cent of the total value of the program had received second-level, EPA, approval, and 15 per cent of funds had actually been spent. It was estimated that by end of March 1985, 60 per cent of funds would be spent, with all spending completed by end of March 1987. Most of the key decisions on large projects – and commitments to the regional ministers – were made prior to the announcement of the program in April 1983, or at least so it was thought. Many of the regional ministers were on the special subcommittee; staff of the Cohen committee had consulted with the regional ministers; and the FEDCs had been involved from the beginning in the compilation of the lists of projects. Ministers such as Romeo LeBlanc were fully aware of the program and in close communication with their FEDC. In Nova Scotia Gerald Regan and the FEDC decided on a new federal office and cultural centre complex for Halifax as a suitable project for SRCPP funding. There was ample political input and the cloak of budget secrecy was proving to be a useful mechanism for maintaining the discipline Lalonde desired. With many of the decisions already in place, it was felt momentum alone would ensure that the basic goals – such as the focus on large projects, high visibility, and expenditures solely on federal facilities – would be maintained.

The April 1983 announcement, however, brought into play several additional political forces, in particular those with needs related to the Liberal leadership race and the likelihood of an election. Liberal MPs, largely unaware of SRCPP as it was being developed but whose appetites had been whetted by the SEI program, immediately began besieging their regional ministers, the minister responsible for SRCPP, Donald Johnston, and the SRCPP offices. Furthermore, now that the overall contours of the program were evident and individual regional ministers were aware of the approximate value of their projects compared to those of their compatriots, the ministers began a second round of lobbying. In particular, a number of the projects that both MPs and ministers favoured were private sector ventures or ones requiring federal-provincial co-operation. In addition, there were demands in caucus that the criteria for making allocations across the regions be clarified. Eventually it was decided that population multiplied by the unemployment rate would be used as a rough guide, which had the benefit of skewing projects towards eastern Canada, where there were also more Liberal seats.

The pressures were exacerbated by the leadership race. One reason Lalonde persuaded the prime minister to place Donald Johnston as minister in charge of SRCPP was Johnston's image as a disciplined and honest minister, one unwilling to tolerate questionable practices in the disbursement of public funds. Johnston possessed all these qualities. He was also a candidate for the Liberal leadership. In part with the view to cultivating support among MPs, Johnston began meeting with the regional caucuses, extolling to MPs the benefits being bestowed on the Canadian economy through SRCPP. This in turn made MPs even more anxious that these benefits would find their way to their constituencies, resulting in renewed pressures on regional ministers and the SRCPP secretariat.

The pressure was greatest in Ontario. Herb Gray and his fellow ministers were unable to agree on the limited number of substantial, highly visible items that the program criteria called for. Gray, never in a strong position vis-à-vis his subregional ministers at the best of times, was forced to ask Johnston for a lump sum that he could allocate in bits and pieces to ministers and MPs in his province. He received his wish in the form of a $27.2 million package for small harbour projects. In a manner usually thought more typical of Atlantic Canada, new wharf construction and reconstruction of old ones took place in dozens of locations throughout Ontario. Lloyd Axworthy felt he deserved more money for his favoured project in downtown Winnipeg, a new NRC-Cadcam centre. In this case, after meeting directly with Lalonde and obtaining his support, he succeeded in obtaining some of the funds originally designated for Alberta. In New Brunswick LeBlanc received SRCPP funding for his long-standing endeavour, the completion of Route 11, a project essentially a responsibility of the provincial government and one that in theory should not have qualified under the initial SRCPP guidelines.[46] As well, not only in New Brunswick but in Ontario, Manitoba, Nova Scotia, and British Columbia, projects related to urban redevelopment, provincially owned canals, and sewage facilities all received federal support under SRCPP.

As with the SEI, SRCPP offered interesting vignettes on the modus operandi of individual regional ministers, including their manner of liaising with provincial governments. In Quebec Pierre De Bané combined the resources of his own department, Fisheries and Oceans, with those available under SRCPP to leave a permanent legacy on the shores of the Gulf of St Lawrence near Mont Jolie, Quebec. Struck by the fact that Quebec fishermen had only a limited presence in the Gulf fisheries and 'that it might be another 100 years before another Quebecker becomes minister [of fisheries] again,'[47] De Bané took a number of steps to improve the profile of both francophones and the federal government in fisheries. First, he repealed the authority over the administration of fisheries in Quebec that had been delegated to the Quebec government in 1922.[48] Secondly, he set his sights on having a francophone fisheries research institute located in Quebec. In order to achieve this second objective, De Bané notes, 'I used every lever I had.'[49] The primary source of leverage proved to be SRCPP. The Maurice Lamontagne Institute, one of the few francophone fisheries research institutes in the world, specializing not only in fisheries but also in oceanographic and hydrographic research, received $39.5 million from SRCPP towards the $44 million cost of the project.[50] The building was only part of the total cost. But once commitment to the building had been obtained, De Bané was able to lobby for equipment and scientific staff to make the project complete. Eventually he was able to obtain Treasury Board approval for thirty new scientists a year for five years.[51] Construction of the project began in May 1984. It officially opened in August 1986.

In Nova Scotia it was clear that MacEachen would predominate. Of the thirty-two SRCPP 'small craft harbour grants' made in Nova Scotia, eighteen went to recipient harbours in MacEachen's riding of Cape Breton Highlands–Canso, six to Coline Campbell's South West Nova riding, four to David Dingwall's riding of Cape-Breton-East Richmond, and one to MacLennan's riding of Cape Breton–The Sydneys. Only two grants went to Conservative ridings. A host of other smaller items, and some not so small, can also be linked to MacEachen, such as support to Canadian National for a rail order from Sydney Steel, an office building in downtown Sydney, as well as expansion of the coastguard college there, and development of a marine industrial park in the Strait of Canso area. Gerald Regan's riding stood to benefit primarily from the new federal office complex (a project later shelved), bridge protection piers in Halifax harbour, and the promise of two shipbuilding contracts of undetermined value.

Most interesting of all, however, was MacEachen's log-rolling with the Nova Scotia government, the results of which were arguably detrimental to the Halifax area. Specifically, MacEachen succeeded in transplanting, lock, stock and barrel, the Nova Scotia Nautical Institute, a provincial institution for marine training, from Halifax to Port Hawkesbury in Cape Breton. It was a move that precipitated considerable opposition from the students, the faculty, and the Halifax community generally;[52] but the details on the negotiations leading to the move provide rare insight into the role played by a regional minister in a province heavily dependent on federal transfers.[53]

Two weeks after SRCPP was publicly announced on 20 April 1983 MacEachen had one of his regular meetings with Nova Scotia premier John Buchanan and raised with him the issue of federal funding for the Nautical Institute. Two years earlier the provincial government had applied to Transport Canada for a $11.1 million contribution towards the construction of new facilities. No funds were available at the time, however. Now, as MacEachen indicated to the premier, it appeared that funding might be found within SRCPP. Would the prejmier be interested in having the new facility constructed in Port Hawkesbury? Buchanan reacted favourably but remained noncommittal. MacEachen, anxious not to delay matters, telexed Buchanan on 6 May, reiterating his proposal and stressing that 'I must have a response from you by noon on Tuesday [10 May 1983].'[54] The premier responded by phone. According to MacEachen's executive assistant at the time:

Again the Premier expressed his general agreement with the proposal, but for the first time he informed Mr. MacEachen that there would be an additional price to pay. The Provincial Minister of Development, Mr. Thornhill, was upset about the proposed change and felt that he could sustain the political damage only if there was an alternative benefit bequeathed on his constituency. In essence, Mr. Buchanan was saying that, if MacEachen wished to get the necessary provincial approval for the proposal, the Federal Government also would have to fund the restoration of the Shubenacadie Canal. Mr. MacEachen was a bit taken aback by this ... but he agreed to do what he could and instructed Mr. Buchanan to forward to him all available documentation on the restoration project.[55]

MacEachen put his case for funding for the Shubenacadie canal, located in Thornhill's provincial riding in the city of Dartmouth, to the special cabinet committee. By June he was able to assure Buchanan that funds for this project would be available. Details of the agreement involving the two projects were agreed to on 13 June and the official announcement of $11.1 million for the Port Hawkesbury project was made on 24 July 1983. By September, however, the Nova Scotia government had decided to up the ante, claiming in its formal submission that cost estimates for the new institute building and special equipment were now in the range of $22.5 million and that a federal contribution of $19.6 million was required. Once more, however, MacEachen was able to go back to the SRCPP fund and find an additional $4.1 million. When the province still balked, MacEachen, in a conversation with Buchanan on 30 March 1984, was able to suggest that certain components of the institute, such as the wharf complex and the fire school, could be funded from the $200 million Offshore Development Fund, created as part of the 1982 Canada–Nova Scotia Offshore Development Agreement and endowed by Ottawa.[56] Buchanan was mollified but only somewhat. He insisted that there was still $1.5 million in inflationary costs that needed to be taken into account. On 28 May 1984 MacEachen was able to promise funds to cover this item also, and on 17 August MacEachen (now senator), John Roberts, minister of CEIC, and Ron Russell, representing the Nova Scotia government, came together in Port Hawkesbury for the official signing of the federal-provincial agreement.[57] In April 1985 the first contract for construction of the institute was let. Work on the Shubenacadie canal had been under way since the previous October.[58]

MacEachen, the single most important federal minister in Nova Scotia, had his wish of a substantial project located in Cape Breton. Premier Buchanan also benefited, in so far as the federal government was now providing practically full funding for the construction of more than $20 million of provincially owned capital projects. The loser in this instance was one of the key intentions underpinning the SRCPP strategy: a high level of federal visibility through the funding of federally owned projects only and minimal provincial participation. Note also that, as various deadlines in the SRCPP loomed, MacEachen became increasingly vulnerable to Buchanan's masterful use of tactics designed to extract maximum funding from Ottawa.

The Nautical Institute and the Shubenacadie canal were not the only examples of federal-provincial co-operation or expenditure on items under provincial jurisdiction. In fact the largest expenditure of SRCPP money on a single project – $173.8 million – involved the purchase of twenty-nine CL-215 water bombers from Canadair in a 50-50 cost-sharing arrangement with six provincial governments.[59] All told, forty-one of the 160 identifiable SRCPP-funded projects involved the participation of another level of government.[60]

It would be misleading to attribute all or even most federal-provincial projects to the efforts of regional ministers. Given the obstacles posed by provincial jurisdiction in several areas, there is no doubt that the federal government would have had to come to terms with provincial governments in a number of undertakings. By the same token, there are several federal direct delivery projects that can be identified as the product of lobbying by regional ministers – the NRC-Cadcam Centre in Winnipeg and the 150 small craft harbours dotting the lake and ocean shores of Ontario and Atlantic Canada. Furthermore, many of these ventures corresponded with provincial priorities. The soil and water improvement projects in Saskatchewan, for example, were funded under the SRCPP as well as ERDA. That regional ministers, and MPs working through their ministers (mainly in Ontario and Quebec), were able to alter the parameters of the program after the initial round of decisions had been made prior to 20 April 1983 was facilitated by Lalonde's faux pas in front of reporters. The sudden addition of an extra $200 million made it easier for ministers to bring their pet projects to the fore. As well, one of the benefits of the recession was the lower than anticipated final cost estimates for several projects, thereby freeing up yet further funds.[61]

By September 1983 responsibility for decisions on SRCPP funding was turned over by the special cabinet committee to CCERD, where squab-

TABLE 3

Ratio of percentage special recovery capital projects (SRCPP)
grants to percentage of total employed in each province, 1984*

	Ratio (% SRCPP/ % unemployed)	Amount ($ millions)
P.E.I	3.16	27.3
New Brunswick	2.40	129.0
Nova Scotia	1.75	105.6
Newfoundland	1.50	75.3
Quebec	1.33	685.2
Manitoba	1.28	70.7
Ontario	0.72	397.7
British Columbia	0.58	141.3
Saskatchewan	0.53	22.3
Alberta	0.46	71.4
Canada	1.00	1725.8

SOURCE: Based on Government of Canada, *Special Recovery Capital Projects Program: The First Year* (Ottawa: Supply and Services 1984), 20–31; *Report of the Auditor-General of Canada: Fiscal Year ended 31 March 1986* (Ottawa: Supply and Services 1986), exhibit 6.2 (unemployment data)

* Does not include $693.2 million expenditure on shipbuilding.

bles between ministers continued. Lloyd Axworthy and Ed Lumley in particular were vociferous in their criticisms of Donald Johnston and his wish to keep a lid on spending. Individual ministers were, however, still able to squeeze out their favourite projects, by making direct appeals to Lalonde if necessary, as Axworthy did in the case of the NRC-Cadcam Centre. Furthermore, for Johnston it was a losing battle in the face of yet another battle, the leadership race. To maintain a reasonable level of support among his colleagues in cabinet and caucus he could not afford to be too stringent with the purse-strings. Overall discipline was clearly decaying as the prime minister entered a lame-duck phase. For Johnston, as minister of MSERD, to make any headway in enforcing expenditure constraints he needed the full backing of the prime minister, something that was not in evidence from February 1984 onward.

Table 3, using the same format as Table 2 on SEI/ECGC expenditures, presents data on the link between unemployment and SRCPP expenditures by province. The unemployment rate, as announced by Donald

Johnston, was the ostensible basis for SRCPP allocations. With the exception of Manitoba, the western provinces again did less well, even taking unemployment into account, though this time the discrepancies were not as pronounced as in the case of the SEI. And unlike the case with the SEI, under SRCPP provinces such as Prince Edward Island and Newfoundland fared much better. The data in Table 3 exclude the $693.2 million expenditure on shipbuilding. The value of individual contracts allotted out of this amount is not available. But judging from the locations of the shipyards, they tended to favour Prince Edward Island, Nova Scotia, and British Columbia, and to a lesser extent Quebec and Ontario.[62] In other words, the data in Table 3 likely underestimate the amount of SRCPP expenditures in those provinces.

One can easily sense regional ministerial influence in some of the data. It is doubtful New Brunswick would have done as well without LeBlanc's efforts; and one suspects that Manitoba did not suffer the same level of underfunding as the other western provinces largely because of the presence of Lloyd Axworthy in cabinet. Saskatchewan did not do as well, possibly because the regional minister, Senator Argue, was making life difficult for other ministers. Throughout the year 1983–4 he was publicly voicing his opposition to the government's scheme to alter the Crow's Nest Pass rate on grain shipments. One can also detect a strong sectoral overlay not only in these data but in many of the specific projects as well. The deputies of the main departments, and especially in a department like Transport, which is a heavy consumer of capital-intensive projects, were able to make their influence felt in the initial stages through their participation in the Cohen committee. Thus, over 57 per cent of SRCPP funds went to shipbuilding and transportation projects. To be sure, many of these projects were coterminous with regional ministerial preferences – highway construction in New Brunswick, for example – but neither the initial allocations as broken down by province nor the choice of projects within each provincial allocation were determined so completely by the regional ministers, as was the case with the SEI.

As well, the assessment of projects, both individually and within the context of regional and sectoral needs, was of a much higher standard. Even where the choice or location of a particular project was clearly the product of regional political influence, staff in the SRCPP secretariat were determined that the project would be of high quality, that it fall within the mandate and long-term plans of the host department, and that proper tendering procedures be followed.[63] As with the ERDAS, staff in the SRCPP secretariat, the FEDCs, and the line departments felt satisfied with the choice of projects. Certainly for the Department of Transport, SRCPP represented the advancement of departmental plans for airport expansions across the country by a number of years. Regional ministers in turn were often able to affect the priority accorded to individual projects as the initial lists were developed, as well as the specific location of projects, and, particularly with the second round of project selection, feed in their own particular choices. Compared to the SEI, regional ministerial influence may have been more limited, but within the context of a much more expensive program it still represented significant impact. Figures such as Axworthy, De Bané, LeBlanc, and MacEachen were all able to obtain important goals. Finally, a number of provincial governments, in working through or in co-operation with the regional minister, could be counted among those whose needs for capital funding were satisfied.

Federal Visibility, Regional Influence

The 1980–4 period witnessed the introduction of specific mechanisms designed to improve the standing of regional ministers. Through the ERDAs, and in special programs such as the SEI and SRCPP, regional ministers were accorded a definite role in the allocation of funds or projects administered under those programs. Particularly in developing the ERDAs and in lobbying for SRCPP projects, several ministers discovered the value of having a central agency representative, the FEDC, based directly in their province. This enhanced regional role of ministers was not restricted to their participation in these programs, however. Nor was the FEDC the only official who was able to provide ministers with a regional perspective. In March 1980 the cabinet sent out clear signals that all line departments were expected to respond more directly to the political needs of ministers. This did not necessarily mean giving in to specific requests for program alterations. Rather the expectation was one of generally being more helpful in providing information on the regional impact of different programs.

The impetus for enhancing the regional role of ministers arose out of the political and economic circumstances at the beginning of the 1980s: the constitutional crisis, the battle for the hearts and minds of Quebeckers, compounded by the most severe recession since the 1930s. The mood within cabinet and caucus was militant and expressed primarily in the renewed emphasis on visibility and direct delivery. This spirit was not restricted to the politicians. The bureaucracy at all levels saw advantage in the new visibility regime as well. The specific advantages seen in, and the meaning attached to, visibility varied considerably, however. For top-level officials in the Privy Council Office, for example, it meant further efforts to bring about greater integration and coherence across the vast array of programs delivered by the government of Canada. For officials in line departments the emphasis on direct delivery and reduced transfers to the provinces meant the possibility of increased resources for their own departments. Among ministers and MPs there was certainly support for the collective goal of affirming the federal government as the primary locus for citizen loyalty; but there was also a sense that they would now have an opportunity to affect spending and the implementation of programs much more directly. As the government proceeded with the implementation of its visibility strategy, the divergence and conflicts between these specific goals, and between politicians and civil servants, became evident. In pursuit of direct delivery, ministers and MPs were adamant in bypassing not only the provinces but also their own bureaucracy. In contrast, the PCO introduced another organizational innovation involving yet a further expansion of the central agency apparatus – a development that was anathema to both line departments and politicians. Ministers, in turn, acting in their regional capacity, frequently discovered that the introduction of programs or projects they felt to be important for the development of their province required coming to terms with the fact of provincial jurisdiction. This often spelled provincial delivery – highway construction in New Brunswick, agricultural programs in Saskatchewan, forestry programs and educational institutions in Nova Scotia. All these conflicting goals meant yet further confusion and paralysis in Ottawa-based decision-making. In this milieu there were relatively few clear winners, but it is safe to argue that among them were the regional ministers and provincial governments.

Increasing the standing and influence of regional ministers in the Ottawa executive-administrative system was not the principal goal of the visibility strategy. Yet it can be argued that it constituted the primary outcome. In terms of improving the standing and visibility of the Canadian Government as a corporate entity, many of the programs designed to do so had the opposite effect. The intricacies of the 1982 reorganization were largely lost on the Canadian public, as they were on many of the civil servants directly affected by them. In Atlantic Canada the reorganization was perceived as the elimination of a visible and recognizable entity called DREE that was replaced by a less efficient and more remote organization called DRIE.[64] The SEI program, initially kept hidden in order to serve better the cause of regional ministers and Liberal MPs, came to light amidst opposition charges of pork-barrelling and worse. SRCPP, a program that was both more innovative and backed by much better administrative support, came to be tarred by the excesses of the SEI. When SRCPP was discussed in the House it was automatically linked to the SEI. Given the confusion and secrecy surrounding the initial stages of both programs, it was difficult for opposition MPs and the press to do otherwise.[65]

SRCPP was designed both to improve the visibility of the federal government and to fulfil the needs of regional ministers. It was also clearly linked to the needs of the electoral cycle, evidenced by the fact that it was the political cabinet which approved and later supervised the program in its initial stages. But here, too, there were serious shortcomings. As well as bolstering the fortunes of individual MPs and ministers in specific ridings, it was expected that the influx of sub-stantial capital expenditures on construction would have a positive effect on the economy as a whole and in turn reflect well on the government as economic manager. The difficulty was that the fast-tracking procedures were just not fast enough. While funds were 96 per cent committed by May 1984, only about 15 per cent of funds were actually spent as of 30 March 1984. It was forecast that 60 to 64 per cent of funds would be spent by March 1985, which would have been ideal for a spring election that year.[66] As it was, the election came much earlier. James Egan, political assistant to Donald Johnston, rue-fully noted that throughout 1983–4 the only evidence of SRCPP ex-penditure was 'huge billboards [standing] proudly over vacant lots or empty patches of land for months.'[67]

The national media interpreted SRCPP as straightforward pre-elec-tion spending and made considerable play on the unofficial acronym 'SCRAPP.'[68] As a result, at an October 1983 meeting of the Liberal party's campaign preparedness committee, chaired by Senator Keith Davey, it was decided that SRCPP had failed as an election instrument and could no longer be used as a major element in the party's election strategy. The SRCPP secretariat, in devising its own communications strategy, decided to focus on local projects and local media. It was at this level that the program received its only sustained positive public-ity.[69] Again, it was also a strategy that fitted in well with the needs of individual ministers and MPs who were fortunate enough to have proj-ects in their areas.

The activities of regional ministers were also affected, both posi-tively and negatively, by the increasing chaos resulting from the organizational changes of 1982 and the role played by the minister of finance. Ministers increasingly resorted to end-runs around the cumbersome bureaucratic process in order to accomplish what they felt were important goals. CCERD itself became less disciplined. Prior to 1982, when Bud Olson was still chair of the committee, CCERD members were able to reach collective decisions. Olson was seen as an honest broker with relatively few of his own interests at stake, while MacEachen, as minister of finance, was often willing to accede to collective demands from CCERD. Johnston, Olson's successor, lacked respect and, as a leadership candidate, had a definite stake in CCERD decisions. Lalonde in turn was much more inclined to resist collective demands from CCERD calling for the expansion of the committee's envelope. At the same time he was willing to cut deals with individual ministers, a clear incentive to circumvent established procedures. Further, Lalonde's propensity to cut deals on the side was not restricted to bargaining with cabinet colleagues. Halfway through a CCERD meeting in the spring of 1984 on a proposed subsidiary agreement for the Ontario ERDA, it was announced that discussion of the topic was academic. Lalonde, who was in France at the time, had just concluded a tentative agreement over the phone directly with the treasurer of Ontario. Disgusted, some of the ministers tore their briefing documents into small pieces and, in a shower of paper, the meeting abruptly ended. Undoubtedly Lalonde's action was prompted by the inability of Herb Gray and his Ontario ministers to come to terms on what needed to be included in the ERDA. But in the end the Ontario ERDA never was signed, at least not by the Liberal federal government.

The breakdown of the rules and procedures towards the end of the Trudeau era put a premium on personal connections and the ability of ministers to use the informal levers of power. As well, some of the norms governing relations between ministers began to alter. Typically, within cabinet, ministers from the peripheries would have most of their battles with their colleagues from Ontario and Quebec. The recession, however, saw tensions between ministers where there had been relatively little conflict before. For example, MacEachen became concerned with the state of the Atlantic fisheries and fish allocations among provinces, an issue in which he had previously displayed only limited interest.[70] It is not clear whether MacEachen had a role in LeBlanc's move from the fisheries portfolio to public works, but MacEachen did support the creation of the special Task Force on Atlantic Fisheries, struck on 8 January, 1982 and headed by Michael Kirby.[71] The Kirby task force, mandated to examine the need for major restructuring in the Atlantic fisheries, which bore directly on the perennial debate over the relative efficiency of inshore versus offshore fisheries, was opposed by LeBlanc. His opposition was well founded, in the sense that the task force's conclusions and recommendations were very much weighted in favour of the large fishing firms dependent on offshore catches.[72] LeBlanc's loss of control over a sector he had dominated for nearly a decade was regarded as a significant defeat. Still, he remained the lead minister for New Brunswick and, as the allocations under SRCPP indicated, he retained the ability to exercise important influence over the allocative process. Finally, his own position on the inshore fishery appeared to be vindicated when the Kirby task force recommendations foundered on the shoals of provincial intransigence and the intense lobbying efforts of small outports in Newfoundland and the small fish-packaging companies in Nova Scotia.[73] In 1984 one of LeBlanc's protégés, Herb Breau, MP from Moncton, became fisheries minister. The new minister promptly announced a return to a policy of buying unwanted fish to maintain prices paid to fishermen, in effect returning to the pre-1982 LeBlanc era.[74]

In summary, by 1984 regional ministers were the only figures who were being served by the administrative apparatus and the policies of the Trudeau government. Large-scale initiatives such as SRCPP, while failing in their primary objectives, at the same time offered considerable benefits to individual ministers. Innovations such as the FEDC system, intended to help sensitize government as a whole to regional concerns, proved to be particularly helpful in supporting the activities of a number of regional ministers. The chaos that prevailed when the system of mirror committees, central agency monitoring, and expenditure management ceased to work effectively also offered opportunities for ministers to do end-runs around cabinet committees and even their own departments in pursuit of specific regional objectives. Large-scale goals were invariably stymied; but smaller projects such as a nautical institute or a highway in northeastern New Brunswick could still be transported through the system. It is clear that regional ministers in the late Trudeau period were responsive to local and provincial concerns primarily in the sense of having considerable influence within the Ottawa-based allocative process. They were much less prominent, however, in the design of national policies or as important symbols of their regions in the national government. They were often adept at bending or diverting elements of national policies to regional advantage, but success in this respect did not necessarily serve to bring Ottawa and the regions closer together.

Still, it is worth observing the norms prevailing in the Trudeau cabinet, which were not all that far removed from those found in the Laurier and King cabinets: when issues arose that affected a particular province the views or wishes of the minister representing that province would tend to prevail. Essentially, there was a code of mutual non-interference. As De Bané described it: 'You will not oppose my pet project and I will not interfere with yours.'[75] Thus Jack Austin was able to obtain funding for Expo 86 in British Columbia, despite misgivings by virtually the entire cabinet, including Trudeau. Ministers often obtained exemptions from policies that applied to several or all provinces. A fisheries program to buy back salmon-fishing licences undertaken during De Bané's tenure as minister was opposed in cabinet by Romeo LeBlanc. The cabinet decision taken subsequently stated that the program would not apply to New Brunswick.[76]

These norms were not unique to the 1980–4 period. Under Trudeau they had likely been in place since the early 1970s, a time when, in light of the limited success with regional desks and the like, it was decided to reaffirm some of the traditional regional responsibilities of ministers. After 1980 the focus on energy and the constitution and the implementation of the direct delivery regime resulted in individual ministers being given even greater authority over patronage and party matters.[77] And the changes introduced with the 1982 reorganization institutionalized further the role of regional ministers and in particular helped those ministers who were relatively weak.

Ultimately, however, the success of any individual minister depended on his or her innate skills and experience. The vacuum in Newfoundland resulting from Donald Jamieson's departure has been noted. Similarly in northern Ontario neither Judy Erola nor Jacques Blais was able to duplicate the stature and clout previously wielded by Robert Andras.[78] During the 1980–4 period the really successful regional ministers were those who were able to meld together the resources provided under the ERDAs and within their own departments with their own willingness to use every available conduit and arena in pursuit of regional goals. We turn now to one such example of a 'regional minister in a hurry.'

CHAPTER 8

Lloyd Axworthy:
'Regional Minister in a Hurry'

If resentment of provincial governments, distrust of the Ottawa bureaucracy, and a strong desire for more direct influence over government spending were the collective hallmarks of the 1980–4 Trudeau government, then Norman Lloyd Axworthy, MP for Winnipeg–Fort Garry and minister of the crown, likely came closest to being the man for this season in the Liberal party's history. Member of Parliament from 1979 and holding the ministerial portfolios of the Canada Employment and Immigration Commission (CEIC) from 1980 to 1983 and transport from 1983 to 1984, Lloyd Axworthy was blessed with ample native intelligence, a prodigious memory, and a profound belief in the value of the 'hands-on,' direct delivery approach to policy-making and implementation. He was deeply suspicious of large bureaucracies of any kind, yet simultaneously realized that the resources of the state, including administrative resources, were paramount if his political goals for Manitoba and the west were to be realized. This chapter focuses on Axworthy's hard-nosed efforts to mobilize the resources of the two portfolios for which he was responsible. The chapter immediately following examines his use of the two portfolios to serve his regional needs and goals in Winnipeg, Manitoba, and the west as a whole.

Born in North Battleford, Saskatchewan, of Liberal parents, Axworthy grew up in North End Winnipeg, that richly textured working and lower-middle class community, home to many of the non-British immigrant groups who settled in Winnipeg in the first half of the twentieth century. After a brief flirtation with the Conservatives in high school, resulting from an admiration of Diefenbaker's populism, and exposure to the CCF at United College, whose adherents he found too dogmatic, Axworthy ultimately found the Liberal party the most congenial for pursuing his interests in social and political activism.[1]

His political coming of age, however, came not in Canada but in the United States. He had won a Woodrow Wilson Fellowship for graduate work in political science and urban studies at Princeton University, and arrived there in 1960 at the beginning of the turmoil over civil rights. For Axworthy, intellectual pursuits became secondary unless they were directly joined to political activities. He joined the civil rights marchers in Selma, Birmingham, and Montgomery, and at Princeton briefly headed the local chapter of the radical Students for a Democratic Society.[2] The figures making the deepest impression on him, however, were the Kennedy brothers. Not only their promises to help the disadvantaged but also their political style helped bolster Axworthy's prairie populism and the lessons of his rough-and-tumble upbringing in North Winnipeg. As he allowed to a *Financial Post* reporter in 1984: 'Remember, the Kennedys were known for their activist politics – but they were also known in Massachusetts to break kneecaps to get elected.'[3]

Returning to Winnipeg, his initial forays into electoral politics were less than successful. He lost while running in the 1966 provincial election and again in the 1968 federal election, running against the venerable NDP stalwart Stanley Knowles. Axworthy did, however, improve his understanding of the ways and mores of Ottawa decision-making and internal Liberal party politics. In 1967 he became executive assistant to the newly appointed minister of consumer and corporate affairs, John Turner, and in 1968 worked on Turner's Liberal leadership campaign. He spent the subsequent year working for Paul Hellyer who, as well as minister of transport, was also responsible for the special Task Force on Housing and Urban Development. Axworthy served as executive assistant (housing), and played a key role in organizing and interpreting the task force's mandate and in drafting the final report.[4]

The lessons Axworthy drew from working for the task force, and from seeing the negative reaction that its recommendations evoked in Ottawa, are revealing. For him the task force experience raised the question of 'whether parliamentary government can act as an effective, sensitive agent of social change.'[5] The hostile reviews and the rejection by cabinet of the program that Hellyer proposed were blamed by Axworthy on a combination of 'several senior civil servants,' 'the closed interacting systems of bureaucracy and private pressure groups,' and 'certain provincial governments.'[6]

Shortly thereafter Axworthy was appointed director of the newly created Institute of Urban Studies at the University of Winnipeg. Subsidized by a $100,000 annual grant from the Canada Mortgage and Housing Corporation (CMHC), the institute offered him an ideal platform to engage in public debate and to maintain a wide range of academic and political contacts. In 1973, at the urging of Manitoba Liberal leader Izzy Asper, he contested the provincial riding of Fort Rouge and won, a seat he retained until his resignation in 1979. As Liberal MLA and director of the institute, he had first-hand experience with the workings of the Manitoba government and with the problems afflicting Winnipeg, a city that had been in steady economic decline since the mid-1920s. As one of the few Liberals in the legislature – the only one between 1977 and 1979 – he attained a high profile. At the same time he was astute enough to avoid becoming provincial Liberal leader, correctly sensing that within the polarization of Manitoba provincial politics there was little room for a left-of-centre Liberal party.

He also maintained an active role in the federal party. In 1977 he became chair of the Federal Affairs Committee for Manitoba, and throughout the 1970s in his speeches and writings sharpened the themes that were to shape his role as federal minister in the 1980s. Thus, in addressing the topic of 'managing future change,' Axworthy asked rhetorically:

> Will it be through a continuing growth of the public sector, directed by more and more crown corporations, larger civil service staff, working in close conjunction with big industrial enterprises, large labour bodies, national pressure groups, with decisions and policies emanating from some Crystal Palace in Ottawa? Or, will the management come from a decentralized system, emphasizing an increasing degree of localism, a curb on the growth of large organizations – a society that is prepared to sacrifice some of the benefits of technocratic management in order to maximize the rights of individuals to have control over their own lives?[7]

Further, he eschewed centralizing and technocratic 'civil service solutions for Western Canada' and criticized 'a senior civil service, whose only knowledge of the West comes from reading memos ... advising cabinet ministers whose own knowledge of the region is limited.'[8]

In May 1979 Axworthy won the new federal riding of Winnipeg–Fort Garry, a riding just east of the downtown core which took in part of James Richardson's old riding of Winnipeg South. He did so in an election which saw the defeat of the incumbent Liberal government and in which he became one of only two elected Liberals west of

Ontario (the other was Robert Bockstael in the neighbouring riding of Winnipeg–St Boniface). Axworthy's own margin of victory was close: fewer than five hundred votes separated him from former Conservative provincial party leader Sidney Spivak, who also had the support of James Richardson and his anti-bilingual support group, Canadians for One Canada. Axworthy, however, saw opportunity in his new position as opposition MP and in the defeat of the Liberal government: 'For the first time in fifteen years, Liberal politicians are freed from the institutional trap of government and the ossified thought of the senior mandarinate ... There is now the chance for Liberals to reach beyond the civil service network for new thoughts and to tap fresh sources of ideas.'[9] He also saw opportunities for his own self-advancement when, after Trudeau announced his resignation in November 1979, he indicated his own personal leadership ambitions.[10] At the same time he succeeded in having Winnipeg chosen as the locale for the forthcoming Liberal leadership convention, a feat that was praised in Winnipeg circles primarily for the economic benefits that would be brought to the city by visiting delegates.[11]

The defeat of the Conservatives and the calling of a new election for February 1980 put his leadership plans on hold. The consensus was that the Liberals might well be returned to power, and Axworthy, while only housing critic in the shadow cabinet, had his sights set on the energy portfolio. Of all portfolios, it was the one of greatest import to the west, and, as Axworthy well knew, his occupancy of it would clearly denote his status as western lieutenant. Whatever the actual prospects of this ambitious goal, he made energy his personal theme and in his pre-election statements outlined proposals for a Winnipeg-based crown corporation devoted to research and development of renewable energy sources.[12]

In the 1980 election Axworthy and Bockstael were again the only two Liberals elected west of Manitoba. This time, however, they were on the government side of the House, and Axworthy's margin of victory in his own riding was close to five thousand votes. When the call from the prime minister came it was not the energy portfolio that was proffered. Nor was he offered the other major portfolio that a westerner might have expected, transport. Instead he received the employment and immigration portfolio (CEIC), which included responsibility for the status of women. As well, he was asked by the prime minister to report on how best to open new lines of communication from the region to the cabinet. The portfolio, Axworthy stated, 'contrary to the public impression, is one I wanted. Between the job-creation side and the employment side and the immigration part, it is classically molded for someone who wants to be a liberal.'[13] On new lines of communication, Axworthy and Bockstael (who did not receive a portfolio) reported back to the prime minister that there was no need to 'rush to the barricades' with schemes such as proportional representation or an expanded Senate. Nor should the party again try and recruit Jack Horner type defectors, they said. The best palliative, according to Axworthy, was to make the party itself the visible link between westerners and cabinet. It was an area in which he planned for himself a principal role.[14]

Managing the Portfolio

In making the party the key link, however, Axworthy was confronted by the fact that the Liberal party in the west was both weak and lacking in resources.[15] The provincial party in Manitoba was moribund; later, when it did enjoy a revival in 1984, it was in the hands of an individual, Sharon Carstairs, who was very much Axworthy's opponent. The primary resource available to Axworthy was his ministerial portfolio, and in order to implement the items on his ambitious agenda – winning the west, fostering economic diversification in Manitoba, introducing increased autonomy for local communities, tackling the urban problems of Winnipeg, among others – he needed to assert authority over his department. This is no easy task at the best of times, and one that is rendered more difficult when regional objectives are as important as sectoral ones. In asserting his authority, and in establishing a *modus operandi* with departmental officials, Axworthy confronted much more directly than most the dilemma facing all elected officials operating under the Westminster parliamentary model: attaining control over the bureaucracy in the face of limited expertise and information on the substance and operations of the portfolio.[16] It is also a subject over which there is considerable controversy in the political science literature.

In theory the minister is ultimately accountable for all policies of his or her department and the actions of officials. The permanent officials in turn are expected to behave in neutral fashion and, in supporting the minister to the best of their ability, are supposed to offer different options on courses of action, outlining the pros and cons of each. This model, however, is rarely accepted as a description of actual practice; indeed the opposite is often taken to be the case. As popularized in the BBC television series 'Yes Minister,' the minister is usually depicted as being held captive by officials, carefully husbanded, and closeted if necessary, to ensure that he follows the path ordained by the permanent bureaucracy. The images and themes in 'Yes Minister' are reinforced in part by the academic literature on the British system, and by accounts from actual practitioners, such as *The Diaries of a Cabinet Minister* by a former minister in the Labour government, Richard Crossman.[17] In their detailed study of the budgetary process in Britain, Heclo and Wildavsky note an often prevalent attitude: 'Top civil servants often regard ministers as an unreliable breed, long on haphazard arrangements and short on appreciation for the department's continuing needs.'[18] They note that there is no obvious conspiracy among civil servants, and often their actions are motivated by what they anticipate to be the minister's needs. Yet the feeling among ministers such as Crossman is one of being cosseted by the bureaucracy with the aim of control. A wide range of practices help foster this view. For example, it is British custom for officials to monitor all phone calls made or received by the minister.

In Canada, as elsewhere, the issue of who controls whom is far from apparent. It arose most clearly when the Diefenbaker government came to power in 1957, but here the charge by Conservative ministers was that civil servants were still wedded to the Liberal scheme of things, implying that lack of ministerial control was less of a problem under the Liberals.[19] At the same time, in a 1979 book by Walter Stewart, it is argued that Mirabel airport outside Montreal and the proposed Pickering airport outside Toronto were the products of bureaucrats with an insatiable appetite for power operating with only limited political restraints.[20] In more recent times Conservative Flora MacDonald complains that, during her brief tenure as external affairs minister, she was constantly 'expected to accept the unanimous recommendation of the Department ... Seldom, if ever, was I given the luxury of multiple-choice options on matter of major import.'[21]

As a counter to the 'minister-as-captive' model, it has been suggested that the ministerial-bureaucratic relationship should be seen more in symbiotic terms. Advocates of the 'political-administration' model argue that at the level of fundamental values there is considerable common ground between the two spheres. Thus findings for a number of countries, including Canada and the United Kingdom, indicate that in the higher reaches of the bureaucracy there is considerable tolerance for, and acceptance of, the need to incorporate the values and needs of politicians in the design and implementation of policies.[22]

It is not easy to reconcile differences between different models and findings. In part they reflect the evidence on which the conclusions are based and the level of generality. Thus many of the political-administration findings are based on attitudes ascertained through surveys and apply to politicians as a class. Worth stressing is the extent to which either symbiosis or conflict can vary within and across systems.[23] In their findings for Canada, Atkinson and Coleman point out that there were important differences between civil servants based in central agencies, who, in enjoying greater contact with politicians, were also more tolerant of them, and those in line departments.[24] Equally important is that the notion of 'control' or 'dominance' tends to confuse the debate. As one of the individuals on Lloyd Axworthy's personal staff noted: 'I don't think that we ever had control as such over the department [CEIC] ... Despite this, we were still able to accomplish a hell of a lot.'[25] And an individual occupying a similar position on Allan MacEachen's personal staff stated: 'You can't control the bureaucracy; you can only influence it, to try and make it fit your needs. In fact you wouldn't *want* to control it; it is simply far too large and complicated.'[26] The key then appears to lie in the ability of ministers to mobilize the department, or elements within it, to accomplish specific goals. This can be done by various means, with or without the co-operation of officials at various levels within the department.

Relatively few studies exist of ministers and their efforts to mobilize departmental resources. One excellent study, however, by Andrew Johnson of Bryce Mackasey as minister of labour, provides valuable detail on the differing roles played by senior officials and the minister in bringing a common goal to a successful conclusion.[27] In this instance the goal was passage of the new Unemployment Insurance Act. The policy originated with a small group of civil servants, but it only received impetus when Mackasey decided to make it his personal cause, championing it within cabinet *and* within his department. Aside from the critical role played by Mackasey, it is interesting to note that the lines of opposition cut across both cabinet and the department. There were cabinet ministers who were less than keen on social policies of this type, a view that was shared by 'Old Guard' civil servants within the Unemployment Insurance Commission (UIC), then part of the Department of Labour.[28] Favouring the new policy was a coalition composed of left-wing ministers, including those from the high unemployment regions in the Atlantic provinces, newer senior officials in Labour, including the chairman of the UIC, and officials in the PCO.[29] The scheme originated with officials but throughout it was the efforts of Mackasey that proved to be crucial in maintaining support for the much more generous new UIC scheme.

Even in those instances where the impetus for new policies or the extension of old policies *appears* to lie within the bureaucracy, it should be kept in mind that it is often expedient for politicians to shift blame to civil servants, particularly when policy choices are likely to arouse public controversy. Indeed this appears to have been the case in Transport in the 1970s with the initial decision to proceed with the Pickering airport and the construction of Mirabel. In contradicting Stewart's interpretation, Sandford Borins points out that planning for Pickering was instigated by the minister of transport, Paul Hellyer, largely in response to pressure from Toronto-area Liberal MPs and ministers opposed to expansion of Malton (now Pearson) International Airport. According to Borins, Toronto ministers were also captivated by the federal largesse that would be generated by the construction of a new airport.[30] The decision to proceed with Pickering was later affirmed by Donald Jamieson, minister in 1970. At these initial stages Transport officials generally favoured expansion of Malton rather than construction of a new airport. In effect, the planning and implementation team for Pickering within Transport was created primarily in response to decisions made at the cabinet level.

Thus, while there are instances of weak ministers being captured by their departments, a more common occurrence is that of mutual dependence. Civil servants need reasonably strong ministers to promote and legitimize departmental proposals, while ministers need sympathetic and skilled civil servants who are attuned to the political needs of politicians and sensitive to the immediate context in which ministers find themselves.[31] Furthermore, conflicts over policies are just as likely to take place *among* officials and within cabinet, resulting in alliances that can easily cut across the ministerial-administrative divide.

The Axworthy Approach

Despite his avowed antipathy towards Ottawa-based officials, as minister of CEIC Lloyd Axworthy was able to make use of the expertise of civil servants who, while not necessarily sympathetic to his regional predilections, were nevertheless supportive of his aims to endow the department with more economic clout, to make it more of a participant in federal-level economic decision-making. These officials, such as the economist David Dodge who headed a task force on labour markets, were found mainly on the employment side of the department.[32] In the other major responsibility of the department, immigration, Axworthy found relatively few officials sympathetic to change. In his view the departmental emphasis here needed to be shifted from the prevailing 'enforcement mentality to one that has a much higher sense of compassion,' a shift that included an increase in the annual flow of immigrants.[33]

To this end Axworthy resorted to outside task forces and reports from special advisers, individuals whom he trusted. The initial task force, headed by Vancouver lawyer Gerald Robinson and including four other lawyers, laid stress on reforming the refugee determination process, through rewriting the immigration act if necessary, to improve due process and to broaden the grounds on which appeals could be made.[34] Significantly, the recommendations of the first task force, whose members became the Canada Employment and Immigration Advisory Council, were reinforced by a series of later reports by Robinson and other special advisers on issues arising out of the initial report. At each stage, those responsible for reports were informed that 'the sensitive issues raised ... warrant the broadest possible study and public consultation.'[35] The briefs and information on meetings with numerous church and relief agencies listed in the appendices of the reports offer ample evidence of the extent to which Axworthy and his special advisers were able to open up the immigration process to outside bodies.[36] Later, upon becoming minister of transport, Axworthy turned to longtime friends and supporters such as David Walker, his campaign manager, 'people who were more trusted by me personally by their qualities,' to undertake studies of VIA Rail and other transportation issues.[37]

Overall, Axworthy was deeply leery of the bureaucracy, and unlike the genial Bryce Mackasey a decade earlier, he tended to be crisp if not downright rude, a quality that was unlikely to engender a great deal of loyalty and enthusiasm among many civil servants. Largely because of his deeply rooted suspicions, Axworthy, much more so than any minister up to that point, came to depend on his own personal staff, and in doing so broke new ground in the annals of minister–civil servant relations in Ottawa.

Initially this involved mainly his exempt staff, individuals recruited outside of normal Public Service Commission procedures. All ministers have the right to hire half a dozen such staff to aid them in their more directly political tasks, and a time-honoured practice among many ministers is to stretch the Treasury Board rules governing such appointments as far as possible. Axworthy certainly did well in this respect; but he went much further. He hired additional personnel on the basis of 'consulting' contracts, though most of the consulting was done directly in the minister's own office. As well, the tasks assigned to his staff often went far beyond largely political matters. In addition to these political staff, Axworthy brought into his office several civil servants who were perceived to be sympathetic to his aims. These were, in effect, individuals taken away from their normal line functions, removed from the supervision of their regular superiors, and placed directly under the guidance of Axworthy and his political staff. By August 1983 there were approximately one hundred individuals working directly in the minister's offices in Ottawa and in Winnipeg.[38] Later, when Axworthy moved to the Transport portfolio, half of this staff moved with him.

J.R. Mallory, writing in the aftermath of the scandals involving the political staffs of some of the ministers in the Pearson government, noted that such staff 'deal as a matter of course with difficult policy questions which require a degree of judgement, experience, and non-partisanship which they are unlikely to possess.'[39] During Axworthy's four years as minister a number of individuals on his staff approximated this description; but the majority did not. To be sure, Axworthy put tremendous pressure on his staff and through them on civil servants. As a consequence there were often unpleasant scenes with exempt staff yelling at line officials. But these political staff were neither very useful nor lasted very long. Those who were seen as effective, by both Axworthy and line officials in terms of accomplishing set goals, and who lasted for the duration tended to be experienced, having previously worked for ministers or in the public service. Peter Smith, who joined Axworthy's staff in 1980 as his executive assistant, had worked on and off for ministers since the mid-1960s, had helped organize Turner's 1968 leadership campaign, and was for a time associate director of the School of Public Administration at Queen's University. The two 'senior policy advisers' who worked in Axworthy's Winnipeg office, Drew Cringan and Graham Dixon, were both officials in CEIC before working for him directly. Ron Collett, who joined Axworthy's staff as communications adviser in 1981, had worked on Parliament Hill and in public relations since the early 1970s. Francis McGuire, who became Axworthy's legislative assistant, had previously worked in the office of the Liberal premier of Nova Scotia, Gerald Regan, and for the Council of Maritime Premiers. Others, such as Ian Gillies, who worked in Axworthy's office both in Ottawa and in Winnipeg and who later joined the Manitoba FEDC office, had been exposed to Axworthy while studying at the University of Manitoba. Another pool of potential recruits were journalists. Ingeborg Boyens, for example, had covered Axworthy's political activities as a reporter for the *Winnipeg Free Press* before joining his staff in Ottawa, where she took responsibility for drafting many of his policy statements.

In many respects Axworthy was harder on his personal staff than on regular civil servants, which accounted in part for the high turnover among them. He also had more of them than most other ministers; at its peak in 1984 he had no less than twelve exempt staff in his Ottawa office and another five to eight based in Winnipeg, in addition to several contract employees. A sympathetic Herb Gray, Treasury Board president from 1982 to 1984, was willing to bend the rules in light of Axworthy's responsibilities for western Canada, Manitoba, and at one point, the status of women. It was the manner in which these staff were deployed that caused the greatest consternation. Essentially it was decided that line officials, at any rank, including whole units if necessary, would be short-circuited or excluded from the normal policy and administrative process if they were felt to be unsympathetic or even simply too slow in responding to requests. At issue were any policies or activities which were deemed to have an external or public impact. Thus in CEIC one issue that had relatively little external impact, though of major concern to many line officials, was office automation. It was left by and large untouched by Axworthy's people. Other issues, such as job creation programs or individual immigration permits for high-profile positions in the educational or cultural community, received close scrutiny, both in terms of the actual substance and as possible fodder for log-rolling with other ministers. Ministerial permits for immigrants, for example, were a commodity highly sought after by MPs and ministers.

Overall, efforts would be made to discover who in the departmental bureaucracy was responsible for a particular program or policy. That individual would then receive either a direct visit or a telephone call from one of Axworthy's staffers. If the line official in question was reluctant to provide information or to take advice, then he or she could well expect a call directly from Axworthy himself. Further recalcitrance could then result in instructions that decisions concerning the program would be made elsewhere. Often even these preliminary contacts would be eliminated and officials would simply be informed that all decisions on a particular program were henceforth being handled directly in the minister's office. This process of targeting specific programs, identifying the responsible officials, and making direct contact was replicated over and over in several areas. Particularly when expenditure authority was at stake, or the hiring of outside staff or consultants, the matter was likely to end up being decided in Axworthy's office. Typically individuals known to Axworthy would be hired for the project in question. In response to the query whether this constituted patronage, an Axworthy staffer explained: 'Yes it's patronage, but you have to remember that the bureaucrats have their own patronage systems [for example, links with former colleagues running their own consulting firms]. We were just trying to correct for that.'[40]

This process of bypassing officials, or taking matters out of their hands, was undertaken not necessarily because they were perceived as obstinate but just as often as a matter of simple expediency. The need for hierarchical reporting systems, in order to fulfil responsibilities to a variety of agencies such as Treasury Board and the Public Service Commission, was not at all obvious to Axworthy staffers. They simply wanted a quick answer or an advanced start-up date for a particular project. The response of individual civil servants to this bypassing of formal lines of communication varied. The most common, and one commended to their underlings by many senior officials, was twofold: first, respond the best they could under the immediate circumstances to the request of the minister; and, second, keep their immediate superior fully informed of the request and any actions taken. In this manner the integrity of the system was at least partially maintained. Officials at the different levels of the departmental hierarchy would have knowledge of the minister's interests and requests, and this knowledge in turn could be used to try and anticipate and react to the minister's future needs and intentions.[41]

In many instances officials did try and respond in positive fashion to Axworthy's demands, and when Axworthy found their efforts wanting they were genuinely hurt. Beyond this, as Axworthy's general reputation and specific stance on issues became known – for example, in CEIC it was his sympathetic stance towards natives and minority groups, in Transport his favourite issue became airline deregulation – a number of departmental employees, particularly at lower levels, used the Axworthy procedure in reverse: they would bypass their immediate superiors and let it be known in Axworthy's office that they were willing to help. They would do so often by 'brown-bagging' documents, sending material directly up to the minister's office they thought would be helpful. In many cases, of course, these involved projects high on their own personal agenda, which they felt were being thwarted by indifferent superiors. These 'brown bags' were an important source of new ideas. Usually linkages would be established and not infrequently the senders of brown bags would be invited to work directly in Axworthy's office. These unsolicited offers of help to the minister were, however, also much more problematic for line managers, for they would have little inkling of what communications transpired between the minister's office and their units.[42] They were even more likely to be left in the dark when their personnel were taken out of their regular positions and seconded into the minister's office; to boot, they were also left short-staffed.

Few officials attempted to obstruct or thwart Axworthy directly in his efforts to influence many of the department's activities. As one official in Transport reported, it was largely a matter of 'some of us being much better at rolling with the punches than others.'[43] Furthermore, in the views of several officials, the option of actively resisting Axworthy was of limited utility. Given the relatively brief tenure of ministers generally, it was better to hope that he would soon move on to another portfolio. There was also the hope that Axworthy would soon be hoisted on his own petard, a possibility that seemed likely in light of the several difficulties that dogged the minister in his first year.

These difficulties stemmed less from his management style within the department and more from his behaviour in the House, where he was seen as being far too brusque and aggressive in the give and take of parliamentary debate, and from his dealings with the National Advisory Council on the Status of Women. In a bitter public row with Doris Anderson, president of the council, Axworthy was accused of having used his influence as minister to force the cancellation of a conference on the constitution organized by the council. As a consequence, his reputation as a promoter of progressive causes suffered.[44] He was also accused of using undue influence to help his brother, a Winnipeg hotelier, obtain special dispensation from immigration authorities to bring in former drug guru Timothy Leary for a performance, a charge that in the end was never substantiated. Furthermore, his much-vaunted office staff appeared to have considerable difficulty in organizing and managing the minister's daily and weekly schedule, with the result that correspondence was frequently misplaced and public appearances cancelled at the last minute.

Yet he survived the first year, and with the experiences behind them Axworthy and his staff became more adept in dealing with the department and its myriad programs and responsibilities. Axworthy soon developed a reputation for possessing an elephantine-like memory, a capacity allowing him to 'circle back' to earlier issues, putting officials on the spot, for example, for alleged contradictions in assessing the feasibility of a program discussed several months earlier. There was also a close linkage between Axworthy's external behaviour and his actions within the department, the former often being used to stimulate responses from officials. Axworthy was an enormous consumer of public opinion poll data.[45] Very few initiatives were undertaken in the absence of relevant polls, and Winnipeg-based Angus Reid and Associates owed its meteoric rise in the world of Canadian polling firms in good part to work initially commissioned by Axworthy. Polling information would be used to justify the preparation of new programs or the modification of old ones. Programs, or program changes, would then be announced by Axworthy in speeches or press releases, typically long before the administrative details were in place and communicated to the far-flung reaches of CEIC's operations. A common Axworthy stratagem would be for the minister to inform potential clients of new programs and tell them that if they experienced any difficulties to simply contact his office directly for help. Encounters with clients would take place in meetings with various associations, community groups, or simply while mainstreeting in downtown Winnipeg. Feedback obtained in this fashion was then used to pressure officials responsible for program administration to speed up implementation or the processing of claims.

Officials, or at least some of them, were able to adapt to the Axworthy approach. One senior CEIC official, based in the Winnipeg office, described what frequently transpired when he accompanied Axworthy to community meetings or press conferences. Axworthy, who was superb in working crowds and in sensing what the audience wanted to hear, would often make on-the-spot decisions on programs concerning starting dates and eligibility. He and the official in question had worked out beforehand some simple hand signals so that when Axworthy entered uncertain waters in front of reporters or an audience he would look towards the official standing at the back of the hall who would flash 'go ahead,' 'stop,' or 'slow down' signs as appropriate.[46] In this case a sufficient level of trust had developed between them to permit this highly efficient, on-the-fly means of communication involving the target group, the minister, and the line official.

Axworthy's *modus operandi* was never fully accepted or regarded as legitimate by the majority of line officials in either of his two portfolio departments. As one stated: 'His methods were not well respected;

but then the system was not well designed to mesh with his needs.'[47] In part this involved the perennial tension between sectoral orientation and regional needs. But in addition there were specific circumstances that exacerbated the difficulties inherent in the political-administrative interface. At about the same time that Axworthy arrived as minister in March 1980, CEIC also obtained a new deputy minister, J.D. (Doug) Love.[48] The minister-deputy relationship was bound to be difficult, for the contrast between the two men could not have been sharper. Love was a studious and very careful civil servant of considerable experience. While willing to delegate authority to his officials, he was also known for not making quick decisions and for remaining relatively aloof from more practical administrative matters. He was also a believer in the value of administrative decentralization, as evidenced by his deputyship of DREE during the 1970s. Ironically, however, what Axworthy required at that point, his earlier inveighing against centralizing bureaucrats notwithstanding, was an activist deputy who knew the department and who could help him tap its resources through strong central direction. Love had neither the knowledge of the department nor the inclination to intervene.

The need for active intervention from the top lay in the fact that CEIC was, and still is, for administrative purposes, a highly decentralized department. While basic policies and programs are laid down at the centre, their implementation rests almost entirely with the ten regional directors general based in each of the provinces. Each director general is thus directly responsible for the implementation and supervision of the four primary functions of CEIC – unemployment insurance, employment services, immigration, and special programs such as the Canadian Jobs Strategy – while the assistant deputy ministers responsible for these four functional areas have virtually no line authority over the directors general. As a result there can be considerable variation from region to region in the delivery of programs.[49]

Prior to Love, CEIC had had highly active deputies who made it their job to familiarize themselves with departmental operations – for example, Allan Gotlieb from 1973 to 1976 and Jack Manion from 1976 to late 1979. Manion in particular knew the department well, having worked his way up in Employment as a junior civil servant. He would constantly visit the regions, often arriving in outlying CEIC offices with little notice and asking penetrating questions about program administration. It was through this means that problems of co-ordination and consistency resulting from the decentralized structure could be kept under control. And it was this style that was crucial if changes were to be implemented and rapidly diffused throughout the department. That was not Love's style, however, and very quickly Axworthy and his team decided that the deputy would be unlikely to be of much help to them. Meetings would be scheduled with other officials, for example, assistant deputy ministers such as David Dodge, which under normal circumstances would be organized by the deputy. As well, officials were surprised, and somewhat discomfited, to find members of Axworthy's exempt staff present at routine administrative meetings which previously had been restricted to civil servants only. Two years later Love retired, afterwards to become the Nova Scotia FEDC, and was replaced by Gaetan Lussier, previously deputy at Agriculture, who had a reputation as an astute, energetic, and highly dedicated manager. Yet the arrival of this much more hands-on manager did little to alter Axworthy's approach. He continued to ignore the deputy, leaving him to cope on the basis of information on Axworthy's interventions that filtered back up the hierarchy, and to administer those areas such as office automation in which Axworthy had little interest.

As is the practice of any sound deputy, both Love and Lussier avoided direct confrontations with their precocious minister. The one area where there was tension, however, and where the deputies resisted pressure, related to the protection of departmental personnel. It was one thing for a minister to bypass line officials, it was another matter to demand peremptorily that officials be removed or shifted. In the case of Axworthy, this issue came to be focused on the alleged uncooperative behaviour and attitudes of the director general of the Manitoba region, Jack Vanderloo. An official who had started his career with the old Department of Citizenship and Immigration, and who himself had emigrated from the Netherlands in the 1950s, Vanderloo came to represent to Axworthy many of the department's precepts that he felt to be wrong or outdated. This long-serving administrator was deemed by Axworthy to be reactive rather than proactive in dealing with unemployment among minorities and the handicapped, and reluctant to come to grips with the different attitudes and needs of third world immigrants and refugees arriving in Canada in ever-increasing numbers. Worse, in Axworthy's eyes Vanderloo was administratively responsible for all CEIC activities in the minister's own province! Within a few months Axworthy was demanding that a new director general be found for Manitoba. Love resisted. Matters came to a head in the spring of 1982, however, when internal memos were leaked to the press that seemed to imply that Vanderloo and at least one other senior official in Manitoba were deliberately countermanding official departmental policy on affirmative action. Axworthy in turn stated that he was ordering an immediate investigation by his deputy minister into the matter.[50] By the end of August, Vanderloo had moved to a new position in auditing at CEIC headquarters in Ottawa.

When Axworthy moved to Transport in August 1983 he took a good part of his staff, including line officials seconded to his office, with him. Senior Transport officials, in expressing concern over the arrival of the Axworthy contingent, were informed that the paperwork from Treasury Board authorizing the unorthodox procedure would arrive shortly. As in CEIC, Axworthy staffers began making incursions into the bowels of the bureaucracy, making connections and bypassing higher-level officials. Yet, interestingly, the relationship between Axworthy and the deputy was relatively good, in the sense that there was relatively little overt conflict between them. The reason for this, as suggested by one Axworthy staffer,[51] was that they had a common goal: both wanted to rein in and enhance control over the operations of the three separate 'modal administrations' for ground, air, and marine transportation. Their motives for wishing greater control differed, of course. Axworthy had his regional priorities, while the deputy, Ramsay Withers, was interested in asserting greater control in the long term over costs, primarily in what has traditionally been the most troublesome branch of the department, the air transport administration.[52]

It is within the three 'administrations' of Transport that most of the administrative power lies, and given the size of the department the assistant deputy ministers heading them have responsibilities that easily exceed those of many deputies in other departments. The administrations are also highly insular with little interaction between them. As well, the department contained a major regulatory agency, the Canadian Transportation Commission (CTC), and was responsible for two of Canada's more prominent crown corporations, Canadian National Railways (CN) and Air Canada. Efforts made in the early 1970s to reorganize the department, to provide the top with greater authority and high-level policy analysis capability, had enjoyed little success.[53]

Axworthy had had previous dealings with Transport, and with Air Canada and CN, for transportation issues are deeply embedded in all aspects of the western Canadian economy and its politics. As he noted retrospectively, 'Transport was kind of a hardware-oriented department ... The capacity for policy development was virtually non-existent and secondly some of the policies we wanted to produce were running counter to what the traditional policies of the department had been.'[54] Thus in August 1983 Axworthy's staff knew that while changes in transportation policies could potentially have much greater impact on the west than most of those in CEIC, Transport would also be a much harder nut to crack. There was a further consideration. They knew that they were entering what was likely the last year of the government's mandate. Time was at a premium, which increased pressure to use high-handed means to pry control over valued resources away from the 'hardware types' in the three modal administrations of Transport.

Little time was wasted. Control over expenditures was centralized directly in the minister's office by having the minister reserve final decision on all contracts over $10,000. Thus in the case of seven major contracts put out to tender by the department's air administration, ranging in value from $159,386 to $1,389,329, in each instance the bidder recommended by line officials was passed over by Axworthy and the contract directed instead 'to companies ranked anywhere from second to fifth.'[55] The minister's prerogative extended to travel by civil servants: plans for attendance at conferences on international shipping or air safety, which officials felt was crucial for the department, were cancelled by suspicious staff in Axworthy's office. The task of auditing Ports Canada, a crown corporation for which Transport is responsible, was taken away from the auditor general and assigned to a Winnipeg-based private-sector appointee.[56] Treasury Board rules concerning expenditures on ministerial staff, rules that were already stretched, went completely by the board after 1 April 1984. By the time Axworthy left office on 17 September after the Liberal defeat, his staff budget for the full fiscal year 1984–5 had already been overspent by more than 70 per cent.[57] And once again a number of lower-level officials deemed sympathetic were brought into the minister's office.[58]

It was in the air administration and the air transport division of the CTC where the greatest pressure was applied, and where the greatest friction occurred. Action was taken on a whole range of issues, beginning with the elimination of the 50 cents charge on baggage carts at Canadian airports. Many of the same outside consultants who had worked on immigration or employment-related projects were now asked to apply their knowledge to transportation issues. For example, law professor Ed Ratushny, who had served on the immigration task force and prepared special reports on the refugee status determination process, now turned his hand to developing air transport accessibility standards for disabled and elderly persons.[59] The largest single issue affecting the air administration and the CTC was the possibility of deregulating air transport, a prospect towards which officials were lukewarm at best. Axworthy concluded that the documents on this issue, prepared by Transport officials for submission to cabinet, contained views diametrically opposed to his own.[60] An avowedly free market concept originating south of the border, deregulation nonetheless fitted easily into the minister's populist framework, for the concept's appeal was primarily in the much lower fares generated for consumers.[61]

In order to help break the departmental mindset, as well as control, Axworthy organized academic-type seminars in the department, involving both political staff and line officials and bringing in academic specialists such as William Stanbury, who had long favoured deregulation.[62] Arguing conflict of interest, Axworthy demanded that all members of the CTC return their free air passes on Air Canada and other airlines.[63] Further, in September 1983 he ordered that the CTC hold hearings to 'consider in a comprehensive manner domestic fare policy.'[64] The Winnipeg lawyer Morris Kaufman was appointed by Axworthy to represent consumer interests before the CTC. In a move to stimulate cross-border traffic, Axworthy struck a direct relationship with the US assistant secretary of transportation, and when negotiations began between Transport Canada and American officials on liberalizing rules governing cross-border traffic, a member of Axworthy's staff sat in on the talks 'to ensure that policy would be carried out at the bargaining table.'[65] Even before the CTC made its report, which recommended partial moves towards a deregulated environment, Axworthy had invited People's Express, the airline progeny spawned by deregulation in the United States, to begin flights from selected Canadian airports such as Mirabel to US destinations.

The actual move to deregulation and the abolition of the CTC did not arrive until much later – after the Liberals were defeated. But it can be safely argued that Axworthy had been instrumental in initiating the process.[66] New rules concerning rights of access to air transport by handicapped people were also implemented, not by Axworthy but by his successor, Donald Mazankowski. But again Axworthy can be credited for having instigated them.[67] His impact on employment and immigration policies was less clear, despite having a much longer tenure in CEIC. Originally his agenda included reform of the unemployment insurance system, a goal that never really even reached the planning stages.[68] But here other events intervened, primarily the recession, which forced Axworthy and the department to concentrate on a variety of makeshift employment programs and on very basic tasks such as processing the rapidly escalating number of claims for UIC.

Overall, however, these policy goals in Transport and CEIC were not necessarily Axworthy's most important objectives. For him the main reason for mobilizing and pressuring the staff in the two portfolios was to use the available resources for regional purposes. How these resources were used to the benefit of the west, and in particular Winnipeg and Manitoba, and how they were used to bolster Axworthy's narrow electoral base in the riding of Winnipeg–Fort Garry, is the subject of the next chapter.

CHAPTER 9

The Manitoba Network: Regional Representation in Action

In Ottawa circles, Axworthy will likely remain forever known for having created a virtual parallel departmental secretariat, a political bureaucracy whose primary function was to displace or directly control several activities normally left to line department managers. Axworthy is not the first minister in the annals of cabinet government to have done so.[1] Interestingly, however, the closest example to Axworthy's brand of political administration occurred several decades earlier and in a different setting. The individual in question, Lloyd George, British prime minister from 1916 to 1922, 'is said to have been the only minister of modern times who could defeat the obstinacy even of treasury officials. Usually, however, he preferred to circumvent them. He carried his private secretaries with him from one department to another ..., culminating, when he was prime minister, in the creation of a duplicate civil service dependent on himself, the "Garden Suburb." '[2] Lloyd George's 'Garden Suburb' was located in the back garden of 10 Downing Street. In Axworthy's case, however, the equivalent was spread out over no less than four separate offices, two in Ottawa and two in Winnipeg, for it should be kept in mind that Axworthy's political agenda was shaped primarily by his regional sensibilities. As an official in CEIC noted: 'In dealing with Lloyd we soon came to understand his priorities: what was for Winnipeg, what was for Manitoba, and what was for the west, in that order.'[3] During his four-year tenure as minister it was clear that proposals were ranked and judged largely by these three priorities.

Three separate strategies or sets of projects came to be identified with these priorities. First and foremost was the redevelopment of downtown Winnipeg through a framework entitled the 'Core Area Initiative,' supported by a tri-government agency specially created for that purpose. Secondly, there were a number of projects relating to the economic and social well-being of the northern half of the province, including aid for natives and transportation centres such as the port of Churchill on Hudson Bay, Manitoba's only direct access to ocean transport. Thirdly, there was the aim of the transformation of the western Canadian economy as a whole by means of economic diversification and supported by the Western Development Fund created in 1980. Some programs, such as economic diversification, were able to serve all three priorities while others were targeted specifically towards the Core initiative. Each of the three priorities warrants discussion. As well, attention must be paid not only to Axworthy's use of his department but also to arenas such as cabinet and cabinet committees in which influence was exercised.

Regional Priorities

The Western Development Fund

Announced in the October 1980 budget by Finance Minister Allan MacEachen, the $4 billion Western Development Fund, of which $2 billion was to be allocated over the subsequent three years, was targeted towards improving western transportation systems, particularly as related to ports and grain-handling, and to 'initiatives relating to industrial diversification.' It was by far the most promising harbinger of Axworthy's influence over future expenditures, for the announcement appeared to contain all the commitments Axworthy had been pressing on the federal cabinet over the previous six months; and decisions on which projects were to be funded, it seemed, would be made directly by the newly struck cabinet committee on western affairs, of which Axworthy was chairman.[4]

Both the fund and the Western Affairs Committee had been created at the urging of Axworthy, with the help of Bud Olson and Tom Axworthy, Lloyd's brother who worked in the prime minister's office. The fund, claimed Axworthy, constituted new money that would be quite separate from previously announced expenditures for rail-line rehabilitation. Generally, it was depicted as a quid pro quo for the National Energy Program, representing a commitment on the part of the federal government to return to the west a large proportion of energy revenues collected by Ottawa.[5] The Western Affairs Committee was the only cabinet committee with geographically defined responsibilities. Chaired by Axworthy and with a membership of thirteen, including the ministers of Transport, DREE, and Industry, Trade and Commerce (IT&C), it became the primary arena for ventilating western concerns. Perspectives and views developed in meeting of the committee were then injected by Axworthy himself into the deliberations of other committees, such as Economic and Regional Development (CCERD) and Priorities and Planning (P&P).

After the initial flurry of public excitement, however, the status of the fund and the committee remained ambiguous, at least until November 1981 when Allan MacEachen announced that the fund would be chopped by more than half, from $4 billion to $1.5 over five years.[6] Furthermore, the $1.5 billion would be spent primarily on improving the rail system and secondarily on native economic development; and while the Western Affairs Committee would provide advice on how policies were to be developed, it never did attain direct expenditure control under PEMS over what remained of the fund. The failure of the fund was clearly linked to the failure of the federal government to reach an energy pricing agreement with the western provinces. As well, it reflected a loss by Axworthy within cabinet: at a meeting of the P&P committee in March 1981, he was bested by Eugene Whelan, minister of agriculture, and Jean-Luc Pépin, transport minister, over the disposition of the money that remained in the fund.[7] Not until he took over the transport portfolio in 1983 did he have direct access to the funds available for rail improvements. In this instance they involved expenditures on the implementation of the Western Grain Transportation Act (Bill C-155), the legislation that spelled the end of the eighty-six-year Crow's Nest Pass rate for grain transport. Abolition of the Crow rate altered a major historical birthright of western farmers. It would mean an increase in the rates to be paid by farmers, combined with higher direct subsidies to the railways.[8] It was a change unlikely to engender a great deal of popularity for any minister let alone one from the region most directly affected. However, by August 1983 the basic die of the Crow legislation had already been cast under Pépin. It fell to Axworthy to make last-minute adjustments in the hope of making it more palatable to affected groups and to push the legislation through the House.

While the Crow issue received plenty of discussion in the Western Affairs Committee, Axworthy's main role while still minister of CEIC was to appear before public groups in western Canada to defend the government's policy and to extol the virtues of changing the rate.[9] His own preferences were not strongly in evidence in either the draft legislation Pépin proposed in early 1982 or in the final legislation. But then agriculture was not Axworthy's strongest suit, and a well-defined position on the highly emotional issue more likely than not would have resulted in additional difficulties.[10] As well, by December 1981, within cabinet and the PMO 'changing the Crow' was outranked only by the National Energy Program and the constitution as policy issues considered to be of the highest priority.[11] It was clear, therefore, that Axworthy was expected to toe the line and help communicate government policies to the constituency for which he claimed a major responsibility. Thus Peter Smith, at that time executive assistant to Axworthy, was given the task of maintaining contact with Winnipeg-based newspapers on the Crow issue.[12] The expenditures that Axworthy was able to influence in relation to the Crow lay primarily in the lavish advertising budget that was used to sell the benefits of the new legislation. Extensive use was made of billboards, newspaper and magazine advertisements, and television spots throughout the summer of 1984, all of them featuring Axworthy himself.

Thus on the two most important issues affecting the west as a whole Axworthy had limited influence. He lost the battle over the Western Development Fund and had limited impact on the final version of the Crow legislation. In the case of the latter, Quebec ministers and the Quebec caucus actually had more influence, ensuring that subsidies would go to the railways rather than to farmers, thereby safeguarding the Quebec livestock industry and limiting the expansion of that sector in western Canada. Only the western grain co-operatives appeared to be reconciled to the final result. Axworthy's primary contribution to the legislation was a more generous safety net for western farmers, specifically a provision tying increases in freight rates charged to farmers to the actual price of wheat.[13]

There really were no other vehicles that Axworthy could use to effect a broad western strategy. The only remaining resource was his own portfolio, CEIC, and while offering opportunities for substantial discretionary spending, these could be stretched only so far. By default Winnipeg and Manitoba became the single most important targets, and the aim of Axworthy and his staff became the identification of indigenous projects that could be promoted or new projects that could be planted on Manitoba soil.

Manitoba Regional Development Programs

Evidence on how programs administered by CEIC could be shaped in order to maximize benefits for the minister's own province was provided in the examination of the Special Employment Initiative (SEI) in chapter 7. It will be recalled that in comparing the ratios of SEI expenditures to unemployment rates, Manitoba received more than twice as much funding as would be warranted on the basis of the unemployment rate alone. In this respect it easily outranked the other provinces (Table 2). Yet the amount of money involved, a little over $10 million, was relatively small compared to total federal expenditures made in the province over the four-year period. The question then is whether the SEI program was indicative of a broader pattern of influence. At the same time, while Axworthy's portfolios may well have been key in providing the resources, the actual delivery of the programs would not have been possible without the co-operation of other agencies and governments. Attention needs to be paid, therefore, to the coalitions that developed over time that supported Axworthy in his efforts to bring federal monies to the province.

The first major issue affecting Manitoba and Axworthy was the renewal of the various subsidiary agreements under the Canada-Manitoba General Development Agreement (GDA), a number of which were about to expire and one of which, the Manitoba Northlands Agreement, was of substantial size. Originally signed in 1976 with total expenditures of nearly $163 million, this subsidiary agreement was intended to stimulate economic growth and social development above the 53rd parallel with particular emphasis on native communities. While both the design and the results fell short of what the originators of the project in the Manitoba government had hoped for,[14] it was still by far the largest single item in the Manitoba GDA.

Renewal of the agreement was affected by two factors, however. First, the original agreement had been signed by the NDP government under Ed Schreyer. When negotiations for renewal began the NDP was no longer in power, having been replaced by the Conservatives under Sterling Lyon. The conservatives were less enthusiastic about the goals underpinning the original Northlands agreement, in part because they had much less of an electoral constituency in that part of the province. As well, they were set on obtaining funds to upgrade the provincially owned Manitoba Forestry Resources Limited (Manfor) complex at The Pas with a view to then selling it off to the private sector. Secondly, the new DREE minister, Pierre De Bané, had made federal credit and visibility a personal crusade and, in giving examples of DREE projects where such visibility was lacking, he pointed specifically to the Northlands agreement.[15] He also let it be known that he was opposed to providing funds for the Manfor complex. By November 1981, however, the Lyon government was defeated; a year later a new agreement was in place committing Ottawa and Manitoba to combined expenditures of $186 million, with the federal government contributing $125 million. The primary difference between the original Northlands agreement and the new one, according to Axworthy, was that the new pact focused on 'local economic growth' and provided 'northerners, particularly those in remote and native communities, with the skills, training and support systems needed for their full participation in future growth and job opportunities.'[16]

The other new feature in the agreement was increased emphasis on direct delivery: $86 million of the federal money was to be spent in this fashion, and it was unlikely a coincidence that most of this direct delivery would be accomplished through CEIC. Without doubt this feature, aside from giving Axworthy much greater control, helped alleviate De Bané's concerns on the federal visibility score. The other critical factor was the argument put by Axworthy to both De Bané and CCERD: the new NDP government under Howard Pawley was potentially the only friendly government in western Canada and Ottawa should do all it could to cultivate good relations.[17] It was a theme that Axworthy was to repeat again and again, and not only in Ottawa circles. In slightly revised form it was floated before the local media, with emphasis put on how close co-operation between the two governments was a highly effective means of bringing federal money to Manitoba.

The Pawley government was initially reluctant to see the federal government becoming more prominent in the delivery of programs at the expense of already established provincial agencies such as the Manitoba Department of Northern Affairs. Nonetheless, the Manitoba government realized that continuation of expenditures in the northern part of the province was crucial. While containing less than 10 per cent of the total provincial population, all five provincial seats in the area were held by the NDP.[18] Given their slim majority in the legislature, this was an important consideration. Furthermore, in reviewing the state of negotiations between Ottawa and other provinces, Manitoba officials, the premier, and the Manitoba minister of industry, trade and technology noted that none of the others appeared to be having much luck negotiating renewals other than on very small items. Finally, Axworthy pointed to the new ERDA approach looming on the horizon. While this promised more in the way of direct delivery, Axworthy did commit himself to protecting the province's interest as much as possible, and specifically to funding activities in northern Manitoba. Thus the stage was set for the next round of negotiations, this time involving an entire array of subsidiary agreements as well as a replacement for the overall GDA umbrella set to expire at the end of March 1984.

The Manitoba Economic and Regional Development Agreement

Chapter 6 noted how the federal approach to regional development was premised on the following priorities: parallel delivery, involving direct delivery by each level of government of different components relating to the same overall objective; joint delivery through a joint federal-provincial management team; and provincial delivery of federally funded projects. The last was to be avoided unless absolutely necessary. It had also been the primary means for the delivery of subsidiary agreements under the GDAs. The federal government's reversal of priorities under the new Economic and Regional Development Agreements (ERDAs) was bound to make negotiations difficult with the provinces.

In this light, Manitoba's signing of the agreement on 25 November 1983 was remarkable; and it was remarkable not necessarily because the province acceded – the weight of the federal government's fiscal capacity would likely have ensured this in the long term – but because the signing was well ahead of schedule, a full four months before the GDA was due to expire. Indeed, the formal signing had to be re-enacted on 4 January 1984 because the legislation creating the Ministry of State for Economic and Regional Development (MSERD) and endowing the minister, Donald Johnston, with legal authority received neither third reading nor royal assent until December 1983. The significance of the Manitoba ERDA went beyond the rapid pace with which it was negotiated. As the first ERDA, it set not only the tone but also the format of negotiations with the other provinces. It also provided an interesting case study of the conditions that allowed the federal and Manitoba governments to overcome the obstacles of direct delivery and to do so in a highly expeditious and mutually advantageous fashion.

Negotiations began in the spring of 1983 at a meeting involving Axworthy, Donald Johnston, and Wilson Parasiuk, Manitoba minister of energy and mines, who had also been involved in the negotiation of the original GDA under DREE in the mid-1970s. Axworthy and Johnston indicated that they were quite content to see Manitoba as the first province to sign an ERDA. Parasiuk and officials in the cabinet secretariat took this as a sign of encouragement. Shortly thereafter the Manitoba government consciously decided to move as quickly as possible. As a senior Manitoba official noted, 'While we were uncomfortable with direct delivery, it was felt that our interests were best served by not balking.'[19] Specifically, by being first the Manitoba government was not bound by what the other provinces received in their agreements. In subsequent meetings Axworthy provided additional evidence of the importance of moving quickly – namely, confidential CCERD documents that appeared to indicate a signing bonus of $40 million to the first province to sign an ERDA. Furthermore, upon becoming transport minister Axworthy was able to up the ante further, promising redeployment of A-base funding within his portfolio favouring Manitoba, in particular funds for refurbishing and upgrading Winnipeg international airport.

The Manitoba government put forward its list of priorities, headed by the port of Churchill and the rail line servicing it, agriculture, and cultural industries. These proved acceptable to Axworthy. He in turn indicated that for him the transportation component, particularly as it related to Winnipeg, was most important. By the late summer of 1983 the pace picked up considerably. There would be weekly Friday afternoon meetings held in the Manitoba Legislative Building with federal economic development co-ordinator (FEDC) Jean Edmonds, Bill Grogan also from her office, Jim Eldridge, deputy secretary to the Manitoba cabinet for federal-provincial relations, Axworthy himself, and other Manitoba ministers and officials as needed. As far as the participants were concerned, the basic outline of the ERDA had been settled; what needed to be worked out were the details.

The details, however, were no easy matter, primarily, as Axworthy explained, because of the need to appease interests within CCERD and in his own department. Donald Johnston, chairman of CCERD, wanted to preserve as much as possible the letter and spirit of the direct delivery approach. Quebec ministers, specifically Marc Lalonde and Jean Chrétien, were highly critical of the total federal costs of the package. Axworthy conveyed to Manitoba officials the gist of his tribulations with Department of Transport officials and Quebec ministers. At no time, however, was there a sense that Axworthy or the staff from the FEDC office might have been dissimulating to gain advantage. Indeed, the opposite was the case, with one Manitoba official commenting that in his several years of government service he had never seen such co-operation and forthright sharing of information among federal and provincial officials.[20] Manitoba officials and politicians commiserated with Axworthy, and in drafting both the ERDA and the various subsidiary agreements care was taken to describe activities

TABLE 4

Overview of Canada-Manitoba Economic Development Agreements

		Financial commitment ($ million)		
Agreement	Status	Federal	Provincial	Total
Canada-Manitoba Economic and Regional Development Agreement (ERDA)	Effective 04/01/84			
1. Economic development planning	Effective 04/01/84	1.50	1.50	3.00
2. Mineral development	Effective 01/04/84	14.80	9.90	24.70
3. Transportation development	Effective 01/04/84	111.61	26.05	137.66
4. Port of Churchill	Effective 01/04/84	38.06	55.09	93.15
5. Urban bus	Effective 04/06/84	25.00	25.00	50.00
6. Communications and cultural enterprises	Effective 11/06/84	13.00	8.00	21.00
7. Agri-food development	Effective 30/05/84	23.00	15.30	38.30
8. Forest renewal	Effective 15/03/84	13.58	13.58	27.16
Total		$240.55	$154.42	$394.97

SOURCE: Canada-Manitoba Economic and Regional Development Agreement, status as of 11 June 1984

and funding sources for each in terms of parallel delivery. Axworthy also stressed the need to spell out each agreement in full detail, not necessarily to make it more saleable to CCERD but to protect it, noting: 'I'm not going to be here forever; we have to build in safeguards.'[21]

The end result was an ERDA with combined direct expenditure commitments of nearly $400 million. As the overview in Table 4 shows, the Manitoba government achieved most of its objectives, including funding for the port of Churchill and cultural industries and new agreements in agriculture and forestry. By the time all the subsidiary agreements and memoranda of understanding had been signed by 11 June 1984, the package was in excess of three hundred legal-sized pages, much of it single-spaced.

The good rapport among the politicians and Manitoba and federal

officials, including not only those in the FEDC office but also the regional executive director of the Manitoba DRIE office, Cliff Mackay,
and a local CEIC official, R.A. (Bob) Morin, is what made the ERDA
possible. The bargaining among them were facilitated by what J.S.
Dupré describes as 'trust ties,' the lubricant critical in making Canadian executive federalism function effectively and at the same time so
often lacking.[22] It was a rapport that was in part a function of close
proximity. The Manitoba Legislative Building had been home to Axworthy for six years, and its spacious quarters housed the offices of
many of the senior officials responsible for economic development
programs and federal-provincial relations. Officials and the politicians
of all three parties knew each other intimately. As Axworthy put it:
'The important thing to understand is that I know all these guys.'[23]

Yet while the Manitoba-based participants marvelled at the degree
of co-operation among themselves, they were at the same time struck
by the complexities of the bargaining taking place *within* the federal
government. The trust ties evident between the Manitoba-based participants were clearly lacking among many of the ministers and departments in Ottawa. Complicated deals involving Axworthy, DRIE
minister Ed Lumley, and Lalonde, often with the view to disengaging
Johnston from the process, would be arranged and then come unstuck,
sometimes because of conflicts between Johnston and Lumley, at other
times because of difficulties between Axworthy and Quebec ministers
such as Chrétien. Axworthy also had difficulties with his officials in
Transport. Since a major portion of funds to be spent under the ERDA
(more than half as it later turned out) would be on transportation
subsidiary agreements, both Axworthy and the Manitoba government
were anxious that those responsible on the federal side for managing
these projects be based in the province. Officials in Transport Canada,
however, wanted to retain management authority directly in Ottawa,
arguing that there were no officials with sufficient seniority located
in Manitoba. Indeed Transport officials would have preferred to have
seen no federal support at all for many of the projects in the proposed
agreements. As it turned out, the two subsidiary agreements were
implemented but were managed from Ottawa.

Transport officials had a certain amount of difficulty with the proposed $111 million 'Subsidiary Agreement on Transportation Devel-
opment,' the bulk of which, $101 million, was slated for the restoration
and expansion of airport facilities, mainly in Winnipeg but also in
Brandon and Thompson. Plans for these projects had long been in
place but, prior to Axworthy's arrival in the transport portfolio, had

received much lower priority. Advancing the timetable was achieved by redeploying A-base budgetary resources away from projects elsewhere; and making airport improvements part of a federal-provincial agreement helped ensure that alteration of priorities would be much more difficult in the future.

Both the redeployment of funds and the lack of flexibility entailed by the subsidiary agreement were sources of considerable concern on the part of Transport officials. What irked officials even more, however – in this case officials in the surface administration of Transport Canada – was funding for the port of Churchill rail line. Beginning as a supply centre for the fur trade in the early eighteenth century, the port's importance by 1980 was based almost entirely on its status as a grain-shipping port and as Manitoba's sole seaport for ocean-going vessels. In this respect, however, it faced considerable difficulty, primarily because of a highly restrictive shipping season, only ninety days for non-ice-strengthened ships. The rail line servicing the port also had limitations in the form of weight restrictions because of the fragility of discontinuous permafrost zones. As a consequence Churchill never has figured prominently as a grain port, on average handling less than 3 per cent annually of total Canadian grain exports.[24]

Both CN and surface administration officials questioned further support for either the port or the rail line. Between 1973 and 1981 close to $20 million had been spent on port improvements yet the facility continued to lose money. Only once during that period did the port exceed the 715,000-tonne break-even point.[25] But for Manitoba the port had symbolic significance as its only seaport, providing a sense of independence from western and Great Lakes shipping points. Beyond grain handling it also had broader economic significance. It is a major resupply centre for the Keewatin District of northern Manitoba and was visualized as an important tourism centre with potential for development. Throughout the 1970s the Western Premiers' Conference regularly stated their belief in the importance of Churchill to the economy of western Canada. In June 1983 the Manitoba legislature passed a resolution urging the federal government both to upgrade the port and to force the Canadian Wheat Board to ship more grain through it.

Transport officials opposed putting more money into Churchill. CN, however, went even further. Shortly after Axworthy had taken on the transport portfolio, he received a visit from CN executives, and, much to his astonishment, among the issues raised was the suggestion that the minister give serious consideration to closing down the line entirely.[26] The suggestion did little to raise the crown corporation's standing in Axworthy's eyes as to either their political acumen or their willingness to help him in his quest to promote economic development in the west. It also recalled a furore involving CN the previous year when it appeared that the corporation was about to move its prairie regional headquarters from Winnipeg to Edmonton. At that time Axworthy, in the face of public criticism from Pawley and Parasiuk, stated his intention to resign from cabinet if CN were to leave Winnipeg.[27] If anything, opposition from his officials and CN strengthened Axworthy's resolve. In the event, improvements to the line and the port were at the top of the priorities of the Pawley government; without an agreement on Churchill there would be no ERDA. The final subsidiary agreement saw the federal government contributing $38 million and Manitoba $55 million.[28] Each government contributed $19 million directly to CN for rail-bed improvements and refurbishing of rolling stock. The federal government, mainly through Ports Canada, spent $14.75 million on port facilities, including dredging, dust control and asbestos removal in grain elevators, and a new tugboat, as well as $2.8 million on the upgrading of the Churchill airport. The largest single contribution, $35.59 million, came from Manitoba for the construction of a two-hundred-mile hydro line to eliminate the port's dependence on oil-fired generators.

The agreement itself was a model of co-ordinated parallel delivery. The only jointly delivered project was the combined contribution of $38 million to CN, and in this instance it was a federal crown agency that was responsible for delivery. The expectations on what CN was supposed to actually deliver were spelled out in considerable detail. All other activities, except for a few joint studies, were to be delivered separately by each government, including program administration and communications. The other subsidiary agreements were similarly structured to make them suitable for the direct delivery regime so important to the MSERD minister and staff in MSERD headquarters. At the same time the fine print in a number of the agreements reveals a certain amount of cross-subsidization between the federal and provincial categories. Thus in the Churchill agreement, in order to protect Manitoba Hydro from losses on the new transmission line, it was agreed that the 'the Federal Government users of electricity will continue to pay diesel electric rates for traditional consumption for an 8 year period,'[29] a subsidy that was estimated to be worth at least $12 million.

Most of the other subsidiary agreements, on forest renewal, mineral development, and cultural industries for example, were equally detailed and similarly well-crafted in allocating discrete components to the two separate levels of government for delivery. The one agreement where this level of detail was lacking concerned urban bus development signed in 4 June 1984. Other than indicating that each government would spend a total of $25 million on five technological areas of bus development, there were no details on which agency or government would actually undertake the research. When the Mulroney government came to power three months later it was a simple matter for them to ignore the agreement, given the absence of any specific requirements or performance criteria.

On the whole Axworthy was closely involved in all phases of the Manitoba ERDA, from the initial stage of developing specific agreements, to negotiating the details, and finally to announcing the good news of the agreement to the press. His imprint was to be found not only in the contents of the agreements but also in the overall amount allocated to Manitoba under ERDA relative to other provinces. In comparison with its western neighbour, Saskatchewan, Manitoba received more than twice as much federal funding under the ERDA, $240.55 million for a five-year period as of 31 August 1984, compared to $103.79 million for Saskatchewan.[30] The cost-sharing arrangements in the Manitoba ERDA were also more generous, with the federal government providing 57 per cent of combined federal-provincial spending compared to only 45 per cent in Saskatchewan.

Of course, ERDA funding was based, at least notionally, on DREE allocations between 1977 and 1982; and DREE funding levels in turn had been based on relative needs and development potential as assessed in the mid-1970s on the basis of per capita income and provincial fiscal capacity, among other factors. This could, in part, have accounted for the more generous funding level for Manitoba. But historical DREE funding patterns indicate that Saskatchewan generally received more, not less, than Manitoba. This can be seen in Table 5, where average annual funding for the two GDA periods (1974–9 and 1979–84) and funding for the ERDA period (1984–9) are compared. Keep in mind that it is the 1984–9 ERDA whose initiation can be attributed to Axworthy's efforts. Note that for the first GDA period the per capita dollar amount for Manitoba and Saskatchewan is almost identical. For the second period Saskatchewan received $4 per capita per year more, possibly reflecting the fact that up to that point cabinet representation in the person of Otto Lang was likely much stronger. For the ERDA period, however, the Manitoba annual average more than triples to $43 per capita, while that for Saskatchewan drops to $16. With the exception

TABLE 5

GDA/ERDA $ per capita expenditures by province and territory, 1974–89*

	1974–9	1979–84	1984–9†
Newfoundland	126	74	80
PEI‡	400	165	124
Nova Scotia	49	58	57
New Brunswick	82	66	57
Quebec	17	16	13
Ontario	2	3	3
Manitoba	15	14	43
Saskatchewan	15	19	16
Alberta	5	3	4
British Columbia	3	8	12
Yukon/NWT	–	12	–
Canada	16	14	14

SOURCE: Adapted from Government of Canada, *Report of the Federal-Provincial Task Force on Regional Development Assessment* (May 1987), Table 8
* Average federal expenditures in 1981 constant dollars for fiscal years in each five-year period
† Estimated for the period 1987–9
‡ PEI comprehensive development plan prior to 1983–4

of British Columbia, the ERDA allocations for the other provinces either dropped somewhat or stayed at approximately the same level.

A similar pattern emerges using somewhat different data, in this case the relative share of GDA and ERDA expenditures over time. Table 6 compares the percentage distribution of GDA expenditures (1977–82)[31] with that for ERDA expenditures (commitments up to 1987). Note that Manitoba's share of the total amount more than doubled. The only other province to do nearly as well was British Columbia. In this case credit must be given to the Conservative government and the ministers and MPs from that province who were instrumental in seeing a generous forestry agreement ($150 million federal money) incorporated into the British Columbia ERDA in the spring of 1985. In short, there is evidence that ministers from Quebec had ample reason to feel chagrined. Essentially Manitoba vaulted past Quebec in terms of funding relative to population, achieving a level of federal regional development aid comparable to that for some of the Atlantic provinces.

Thus the 'Manitoba first' strategy pursued by Axworthy and the

TABLE 6

Historical GDA and ERDA allocations by province (percentages)

	Population (%)	GDA* (%)	ERDA† (%)
Newfoundland	2.3	13.8	10.9
PEI	0.5	7.0	4.2
Nova Scotia	3.5	11.3	11.3
New Brunswick	2.8	13.3	9.6
Quebec	25.9	29.5	24.4
Ontario	35.9	5.7	5.6
Manitoba	4.2	5.2	11.7
Saskatchewan	4.0	5.8	6.9
Alberta	9.3	2.0	3.4
British Columbia	11.4	5.8	12.0
Canada	100.0	100.0	100.0

SOURCE: Adapted from Government of Canada, *Report of the Federal-Provincial Task Force on Regional Development Assessment* (May 1987), Table 2.10
* Distribution of total DREE expenditures on subsidiary agreements from 1977 to 1982
† Distribution of total ERDA commitments as of 14 January 1987

provincial government bore considerable fruit. However, the Manitoba ERDA and the welfare of the northern half of the province were not Axworthy's only or even primary concerns. The largest single portion of his energies, and a considerable portion of the various CEIC programs for which he was responsible, were targeted towards the area he knew best, metropolitan Winnipeg.

The Core Area Initiative

The call for renewal and redevelopment of downtown areas in response to urban decay and changing economic circumstances is a common theme throughout North America. As a major urban centre Winnipeg had certainly not been immune to pressures, from politicians, developers, citizen groups, and various combinations thereof, to tackle problems and opportunities resulting from urban decline. However, while Winnipeg's urban problems were compelling they were not overwhelming. First, although Winnipeg grew in size over the years its rate of growth was much lower than that of other major cities.

Essentially, it had reached its economic zenith in the early part of the twentieth century; thereafter its importance as the major transportation, commercial, and industrial centre of the west gradually declined.[32] Second, as an urban centre Winnipeg is still relatively sparsely populated. Land, even in the downtown core, is plentiful. Third, Winnipeg has had in place since 1972 'Unicity,' a single-tier government incorporating what was previously the city of Winnipeg and eleven surrounding communities.[33] This promised to facilitate city-wide urban planning and the possibility of greater resources being brought to bear on specific problems, such as those of the downtown core.

The manner and rate, however, of tackling these urban problems throughout the 1970s were a disappointment to a number of people. A large-scale development in the downtown area south of Portage Avenue by the Trizec Corporation remained only partially completed. As David Walker, a friend and academic colleague of Axworthy, pointed out, this development had drawn considerably on the city government's financial resources, much more so than the city planners had first anticipated.[34] Axworthy, and individuals such as Walker, while not necessarily anti-development, definitely had a populist cast of mind on urban redevelopment issues, one that incorporated a concern for the problems facing the numerous native people in the city and for the need to preserve the character and ethnic diversity of downtown neighbourhoods. Several years of analysing Winnipeg's problems had given Axworthy ample opportunity to develop ideas on what needed to be done. In his view the answer to Winnipeg's problem of stagnant growth lay in redeveloping the downtown core, and this was best accomplished through closely integrated redevelopment of both residential and commercial sections.

The notion of an integrated downtown redevelopment scheme also provided an ideal vehicle for linking together several diverse projects that Axworthy hoped to bring to Winnipeg. One of the failings of James Richardson as regional minister had been his inability to capitalize on the items that he had succeeded in bringing to the city. For example, one of his prize catches, the Royal Canadian Mint, was placed on the outskirts of the city. It remains unconnected with any other development or activity. For Axworthy, it offered a lesson on how *not* to exploit pork-barrelling opportunities. In his view, 'the key to prosperity in Winnipeg lay at the centre' not in the peripheries, and different projects brought together could constitute something more than the sum of their parts.[35] It was in this fashion that the idea of the Core Area Initiative was born.

The initiative had one additional advantage for Axworthy. In early 1980 relations between the provincial government and Axworthy, and with the federal government as a whole, were difficult if not impossible, as evidenced by the stalled negotiations over the Northlands agreement and Premier Lyon's implacable hostility to Trudeau's Charter of Rights. The city of Winnipeg and its mayor Bill Norrie offered an opportunity to bypass the Lyon government. With the help of Jean Edmonds, who in 1980 was still regional director of DREE for Manitoba, Axworthy found $32 million originally allocated for urban native economic development. With the promise of money in hand Axworthy approached the mayor, indicating that the money could be used to help revitalize the downtown area and suggesting that the city match the amount. The province in turn, Axworthy informed Norrie, could then be asked for a like amount so that the costs would be divided equally among the three levels of government. Axworthy intimated that there was at least another $50 to $60 million in federal funding that could be tapped for the proposed redevelopment.

By 29 May 1980 Axworthy, Norrie, and Gerry Mercier, Manitoba minister for urban affairs, had agreed to co-operate in the development of a common strategy and in the identification of specific projects to be undertaken. They also settled on a name for the strategy – the Winnipeg Core Area Initiative (CAI). On 22 September the three signed a memorandum of understanding (MOU) outlining the objectives, potential programs, and financial arrangements, and agreed to the formation of a policy committee consisting of themselves. As well, the MOU specified the area to be bounded by CAI development plans.[36] The area was centred directly north of Portage Avenue and included the historic but rundown market and exchange areas as well as China town, the CN East Yards, and neighbourhoods along Logan and Selkirk avenues. But the boundaries were stretched to include the Osborne Village area on the other side of the Assiniboine River and Provencher Boulevard in St Boniface. Osborne Village and Provencher Boulevard were located, respectively, in Axworthy's and Bockstael's ridings.

Arguing that it was good business to put up $32 million and that the city would never be able to undertake the project alone without federal help, Norrie persuaded his executive council and city council to support the CAI.[37] The CAI proposal lacked certain features that some thought were crucial to any downtown redevelopment scheme – namely, the removal of the CPR rail yards from the area north of Portage.[38] Yet given the scope of the CAI, a project that would eventually lead to the largest single land expropriation in Winnipeg history,

there was surprisingly little criticism. Its acceptance at this stage represented an important achievement for Axworthy. After several years
of inaction, work was finally beginning on downtown redevelopment,
and he had managed to instigate it essentially by contributing only
one-third the cost of the basic project. For Bill Norrie, approval of
the CAI and his membership on the three-person policy committee
made him a major player in a significant project. This fact, along with
the project itself, put him in good stead in facing the electorate in the
mayoralty race in November of that year. Indeed, it became the major
plank in his election platform.

The honeymoon spirit between Axworthy and Norrie was soon broken, however. The provincial government belatedly realized the import of the three-way cost-sharing arrangement: that the city and
province combined would pay two-thirds of the costs. Then in early
November the federal minister of housing, Paul Cosgrove, announced
the termination of the federal Community Services Contribution Program (CSCP), which had provided Canadian municipalities with approximately $400 million funding for sewers and other capital
expenditures over the period 1978–80. In a meeting at the Legislative
Building, Premier Lyon informed Norrie that, with the ending of the
CSCP, the city of Winnipeg stood to lose $40 million over the next five
years, implying that Norrie had likely been duped by Axworthy; that
instead of gaining an infusion of $32 million, the city would actually
suffer a net loss of $8 million. Norrie, in a blind fury, publicly an-
nounced that the loss of CSCP funding could well spell the end of the
CAI.[39] In a private meeting with Norrie, Axworthy attempted to allay
the mayor's concerns, arguing that the $32 million DREE funding was
indeed new money and that CSCP funds would continue to be available
but in the form of new programs. A few days later Axworthy was able
to announce a federal loan subsidy from Canada Mortgage and Housing Corporation for an $8 million senior citizens' housing complex.
He was also able to point out that two weeks earlier he had been able
to announce the arrival of the Petro-Canada subsidiary, Enertech Canada (later called Canertech), mandated to research renewable energy
sources with an annual expenditure budget of $20 million a year, and
that the planned location for it would likely be in the city's designated
core area.[40]

Norrie stayed the course, and the province, which had also been
threatening to withdraw from the CAI, eventually dropped the issue
of the CSCP termination. The mayor had already staked a good part
of his reputation on the benefits that would be brought about through

implementation of the CAI; it was too awkward to back out now. In January 1981 public meetings were held and more than sixty proposals were put before the three-member policy committee. By May the federal cabinet Committee on Economic Development gave its approval to the $32 million federal commitment, and on 3 June 1981 the policy committee released its 'Proposed Winnipeg Core Area Initiative.' It outlined plans for an industrial park for small high-technology industries in the Logan Avenue area, reconstruction of the market square area, a variety of programs to create jobs for three thousand core area residents, redevelopment of the CN East Yard, park development in the Portage North area, and aid to commercial activity along Provencher Boulevard and Osborne Street and in Chinatown. The proposal also provided for the creation of a CAI office and a management board consisting of three senior civil servants from each level of government, and for the appointment of a general manager. By October 1981 all three governments had formally approved the tri-level arrangement, and Larry Boland, previously development manager of Harbourfront in Toronto, became the first general manager.[41]

Although the plan received criticism – for example, Howard Pawley, NDP leader of the opposition, complained that the CAI represented 'a victory for building over people'[42] – it also received considerable support among a variety of constituencies. Thus one NDP city councillor, Magnus Eliason, said he was 'quite agreeably pleased' with the plan and the executive director of the Social Planning council of Winnipeg, Tim Sale, while expressing concern over implementation and management, nevertheless approved the general thrust of the proposal.[42] The bitterness generated over the earlier funding dispute continued to rankle in the mayor, however.[43] He also felt, with some justification, that Axworthy was likely to be his main competitor in vying for control over the project and in garnering credit for its achievements.

Axworthy, quite rightfully, saw the project as his, in the sense that without the initial push and the $32 million in DREE funding it would not have come about. He moved quickly to assert his presence, and in seeking to establish control, the value of the numerous resources within CEIC soon became apparent. One of his political assistants, Francis McGuire, was given the task of ensuring that the various proposals that called for training and job creation within the core area would have direct access to existing CEIC programs, such as the Local Economic Development Agencies (LEDA) program. Axworthy also announced the possibility of the core being home to a new National Research Council (NRC) research centre, a project the need for which had been discussed for several years in Manitoba scientific circles. And in October 1981 Axworthy was able to announce that Air Canada would be constructing, in the North Portage area of the core, a $65 million computer centre, a facility that would eventually employ upwards of one thousand people.

Approximately 40 per cent of total funding of CAI projects was handled directly by the core area office, drawing on the $96 million tri-level fund. The remaining funding, beyond the $96 million base budget, was delivered directly by the three governments involved, and on the federal side CEIC became the single most important agency in delivering funded programs. Thus, of the close to $57 million that was spent on the education, training, and employment component of the CAI up to September 1985, $43 million came from the federal government and virtually all of it passed through CEIC.[45] The various CEIC programs targeted towards the core area were delivered under the rubric of a Special Needs Employment Strategy, which in turn was co-ordinated through a Special Needs Office established by CEIC in the core area.[46] CEIC funds were also used for capital projects. For example, a $700,000 grant from the SEI was used to transform a former service station in the Osborne Village area into a 250-seat performing arts theatre as well as for renovations to Augustine United Church. CHMC was the other major source for capital projects. In May 1983 Axworthy was able to obtain funding from the Special Recovery Capital Projects Program (SRCPP) for the long-awaited NRC 'Institute for Manufacturing Technology' (NRC-Cadcam Centre).[47]

The ability to use CEIC programs for the good of the CAI provided considerable influence over its direction. Many of the grants went to groups headed by individuals who were close political associates of Axworthy, or at least known and trusted by him. Thus Gordon Vidal, executive director of the Riverborne Development Association that was the recipient of the $700,000 SEI grant, had worked previously in Axworthy's constituency office. The association, a 450-member volunteer citizens group, also received a $450,000 grant directly from the CAI for the purchase of the former service station, as well as further grants from the CEIC under the Canada Community Development Projects program, from the Solicitor General's Department for a crime prevention program, and $120,000 from the secretary of state for the 'general administration' of the association in order to allow it, according to Vidal, to respond to government-funded programs under the CAI.[48]

Since many of the projects approved and funded by the CAI board

were contingent upon complementary funding from the federal government, this provided Axworthy with considerable influence over
virtually all CAI activities. His preferences and intentions were made
known through a variety of means. David Walker became his chief
trouble-shooter, staying in touch with the numerous people employed
by the CAI and relaying news of progress or difficulties to Axworthy.
Several of the staff hired directly by and working for the CAI office
were generally considered to be Axworthy appointees. Indeed, by 1984
the term 'Lloyd's boys' in reference to CAI staff appeared frequently
in the local media.[49] The federal representatives on the CAI board
would be in continual contact, both with Axworthy's senior policy
advisers based in Winnipeg, such as John Conlin and later Graham
Dixon, and with Axworthy himself. In Axworthy's absence, Dixon
would often act in his place at meetings of the policy committee.

The prominent role played by Axworthy and his staff created considerable tension between Norrie and Axworthy. In the eyes of Axworthy and his workers, the mayor began taking on all the
characteristics of a full-blown villain. In effect, however, they likely
misunderstood the position of the mayor and the extent to which city
council as a whole was apprehensive about Axworthy's activities. As
with any large-scale project, there were more than enough issues to
generate dissension: protests from businesses over expropriation of
their land, disputes over the balance between industrial development
and preservation of residential homes in the Logan Avenue area, ac-
cusations concerning possible speculation in assembling land for the
Air Canada building, and questions about the efficacy of the CAI training and employment generation programs that were being put in place.[50]
Despite his difficulties with council, the mayor did succeed in obtaining
approval for items such as the land assembly for the Air Canada building, an item crucial to the further development of the North Portage
area.

The effects of the cooling of relations between Axworthy and the
city were countered by the election of the NDP government under
Howard Pawley in November 1981. Gerry Mercier was replaced by the
new minister of urban affairs, Eugene Kostyra, as the provincial representative on the policy committee. Axworthy was in a good position
to press for help in furthering his own initiatives in downtown Winnipeg, given his support of provincial priorities in the Northlands
agreement. The provincial government in turn was aware that Axworthy was indeed capable of bringing new federal money to Manitoba, money that would in other circumstances have been spent

elsewhere. In the event, some of city council's animosity towards Axworthy was redirected towards the provincial government. Kostyra, in turn, would come to Axworthy's defence when the latter came under criticism for placing excessive funding into CAI projects located in his own riding.[51]

The greatest controversy occurred in April 1983. Axworthy released plans to redevelop the remainder of the North Portage area with a large-scale development, estimated to cost anywhere from $100 to $400 million. The proposal, which contained plans for a new arena, the new NRC research centre, a new CBC building, and a hotel among other items, was put to representatives of the city and the urban affairs minister, Eugene Kostyra.[52] Axworthy indicated that he wanted to see work begin as soon as possible. As was the case with the original CAI proposal, the initial source of funding would be the federal government, and in this instance it would be funds from the SRCP program.

Even at the best of times Axworthy was not a man to dally. With the fast-tracking features of SRCPP, however, there was all the more reason to hurry. Within a few days of the proposal's presentation at a closed meeting on 22 April the city began receiving ultimatums. Axworthy aide John Conlin, stating bluntly that 'We're not going to sit around and wait for the city to have meetings until hell freezes over,' gave the city until 6 May to indicate agreement in principle.[53] City council in turn pondered the several implications of the proposal, such as the effects of the new arena on the existing Winnipeg arena, and the possibility that part of the original CAI fund would be redirected towards the new project. Despite the deadline, and pressure from the provincial government, the city declined to commit itself to either the arena or the initiation of expropriations. A few days later, however, Axworthy, Norrie, and Kostyra struck a compromise whereby a tri-level intergovernmental task force composed of officials would examine the area and develop proposals.[54] It was also tacitly agreed that the idea of a new arena would be dropped. The task force recommendation later that summer called for a complex consisting of an enclosed mall, a science centre surrounding the previously announced NRC-Cadcam Centre, the rerouting of Portage Avenue, and more than one thousand rental housing units. It also recommended the creation of a tri-level crown corporation called the North Portage Development Corporation to handle all development and financing for the various phases of the project, financing that was estimated to be at least $300 million with $156 coming from the private sector. The formal signing of the documents creating the corporation and appointing its directors finally took place in December 1983, though not before a certain amount of additional public cajoling from Axworthy's staff had taken place.[55]

By 1984 the pressures on both Axworthy and the CAI increased. The local press, despite Axworthy's assiduous courting of it, was becoming increasingly hostile.[56] Certainly Axworthy's predilections for mixing patronage with pork-barrelling, a dangerous mixture at the best of times, provided media such as the *Winnipeg Free Press* with ample fodder. Within the CAI office, staff found the atmosphere deteriorating as the exigencies of the looming election battle resulted in increasing pressure both to put projects in the area encompassed by Axworthy's riding and to place more of Axworthy's people in key positions. At the same time, sensing that Axworthy could well lose the upcoming constituency battle with well-known provincial Conservative Louis (Bud) Sherman, Norrie applied pressure of his own. Matters came to a head in the summer of 1984 over the replacement for Boland, the CAI executive director, who had resigned earlier in June. Axworthy and the new provincial minister of urban affairs, Mary Beth Dolin, had settled upon another former director of the Institute of Urban Affairs, Christine McKee, to take over the position. Norrie, however, dragged his feet, and by early September he was openly accusing Axworthy and the provincial government of making an 'Ottawa style patronage appointment.'[57]

Norrie won this particular battle; McKee did not get the job. It went instead to an inside employee, Jim August, who had been employment co-ordinator for the CAI. Four days before the federal election Axworthy and Dolin announced an agreement that would have seen the federal and provincial governments spend an additional $64 million on the CAI. It was, however, an agreement struck without Norrie's knowledge and consent, and the mayor made quick work of denouncing it.[58] The deal was never consummated. Furthermore, a number of items in the CAI were subsequently reduced in scope or frozen, and several of the employment creation programs funded mainly through the CEIC were not renewed when funding ended. One of the jewels in Axworthy's scheme for reshaping the downtown landscape, the NRC-Cadcam Centre, though completed, sat unoccupied for more than two years. Too late to prevent its construction, the new Conservative government and Axworthy's successor as federal representative on the CAI policy committee, Jake Epp, were adamant in not spending the annual $20 million operating costs necessary to make it operational.[59]

Yet the physical landscape, and to a degree the social and commercial contours of the central core of the city, had been irrevocably reshaped. The momentum of Axworthy's initiative continued right to the end of the decade as the offspring of the CAI, the North Portage Development Corporation, proceeded with the construction of a $400 million hotel-shopping-residential complex on the North Portage site. The selection and placement of specific buildings and the implementation of particular employment programs were the product more of opportunity than any grand design. Yet their existence can be attributed largely to the energies of Lloyd Axworthy, his capacity to harness the resources of the federal government, and his unique ability to use those resources to lever still more funding from provincial and civic authorities. It is perhaps also a mark of the times that the clearest imprint of Axworthy's legacy as western minister is concentrated almost entirely in a few square blocks of downtown Winnipeg.

The Manitoba Network

By various estimates Axworthy brought between $500 and $800 million in federal expenditure to Manitoba during his four-year tenure as minister in the Trudeau cabinet, disbursements that likely would not have occurred in his absence.[60] These were not only for items under the Manitoba ERDA and the CAI but for a variety of other projects, ranging from the $13 million Max Bell athletic complex at the University of Manitoba and the $8 million South Winnipeg Training Centre to numerous small grants for organizations such as the Winnipeg Symphony Orchestra, 'to avert staff layoffs,' and the Royal Winnipeg Ballet. They also included a million dollars from the federal government's centres of excellence program for the Urban Studies Institute at his alma mater and new Winnipeg-based CEIC computer facilities servicing western Canada.[61]

Thus on the measure of monetary benefits alone Axworthy easily outranked earlier Manitoba cabinet representatives such as James Richardson and Gordon Churchill, and compared favourably with such contemporary regional stalwarts as Romeo LeBlanc and Allan J. MacEachen, figures who had been at the game much longer. Yet while Axworthy acted as catalyst in helping to obtain federal largesse for Manitoba, most of the projects would not have been possible without the help of other participants. Of equal significance, therefore, is the informal coalition he brought together, drawing on participants from the city and provincial governments and a number of federal officials based in Manitoba. It was in many ways a fluid and unstable coalition, and help from participants was often given grudgingly; but it was an effective coalition nonetheless, one capable of doing battle with opposing forces based in the federal bureaucracy, the cabinet, and the Liberal party itself.

One of the dilemmas any cabinet minister faces, even when money is available, is that the spending of it often requires surmounting barriers external to the federal government proper. For Axworthy, to embark on the renewal of the Winnipeg downtown core meant eliciting the co-operation of the city of Winnipeg and the Manitoba provincial government. He proceeded by first striking a deal with Norrie on the CAI, which he then used to pressure the provincial government for additional financial support. The bloom on the Axworthy-Norrie alliance faded rather quickly, but this union was soon replaced by a much more durable one between Axworthy and the NDP government after November 1981. Working closely with Axworthy, provincial ministers such as Parasiuk, Kostyra, and Dolin, as well as Pawley himself, supported and indeed helped devise strategies to maximize federal expenditures within the province. Axworthy received ample provincial support for his initiatives in Winnipeg; the province in turn received funding for its initiatives in northern Manitoba under the ERDA; and both sides praised each other publicly for the mutual assistance rendered. They also supported each other publicly when controversies arose, such as over the provincial government's much criticized payroll tax scheme introduced in 1982.[62]

Facilitating the activities of Axworthy and provincial politicians was an informal network of officials who knew and trusted each other. Provincial senior civil servants such as Eldridge, E.J. Robertson, deputy minister of industry, trade and technology, and Michael Decter, secretary to cabinet and the cabinet Committee on Economic Development, played a critical role in developing the 'Manitoba first strategy' for the ERDA negotiations, adapting their insights from working with DREE GDAs to the new federal direct delivery regime. At the federal level there was, first and foremost, Jean Edmonds. In her capacity as DREE regional director she found the initial money that allowed Axworthy to launch the CAI. Later, as the Manitoba FEDC, she contributed her own expertise to the careful assembly of the ERDA. Her own philosophy on regional development, which stressed the compatibility between economic efficiency and well-designed regional policies, put her at odds with senior officials in the policy branch of MSERD in Ottawa. It was, however, a philosophy that was readily accepted by Axworthy and the Manitoba provincial government.

Over time a number of other Winnipeg-based federal officials in

CEIC and other departments proved to be helpful adjuncts to Axworthy in his efforts. Two of Axworthy's senior policy advisers in Winnipeg, Drew Cringan and Graham Dixon, began as regular employees of CEIC. Dixon, for example, was manager of the main CEIC office for the metropolitan Winnipeg area until 1982 and in this capacity announced in June 1981 that his office was 'dead serious about the employment aspects' of the CAI. 'We'll have to answer to the community for what we do.'[63] The help of these officials was in many ways crucial. CEIC was responsible for the physical delivery of many of the components of the CAI. While some funding, such as that under the SEI program, was delivered to groups largely outside the purview of normal CEIC channels, other items such as the operation of the CEIC Special Needs Office of the CAI required the full co-operation of CEIC staff.

Actual decisions on the funding of specific projects were made by the nine-member management committee composed in equal parts of civic, provincial, and federal officials. For obvious reasons the federal representatives, which included R.A. Morin from CEIC and J. Cliff Mackay, regional executive director of the Manitoba DRIE office, had to be well attuned to the political winds blowing from the Axworthy camp.[64] They were more than passive emissaries, however. They made sincere efforts to make the CAI a reality, in some instances by stretching existing program criteria to make projects eligible, in other instances by addressing public gatherings on the merits of the CAI. Mackay also played an important role in drafting parts of ERDA subsidiary agreements that depended on DRIE for delivery.

Within the CAI itself Axworthy's views had considerable weight, in part because many of the staff had obtained their positions as a result of Axworthy's influence. Some, such as Matthew Kiernan, at one point assistant general manager of the CAI, tended to be identified as Axworthy supporters. Others, such as Jim August, who subsequently became general manager, were seen as more neutral. There were relatively few who were identified as having strong links with either the city or the provincial government. At the same time there were often good working relationships between CAI and provincial officials. Thus Kiernan and Decter, who was also on the CAI board, knew each other well and after leaving the employ of the CAI and provincial government respectively joined together to form a consulting firm.[65]

The ties were much weaker with the business community which, according to Axworthy, was largely Tory in any event. Here the aim was simply to get their respect. 'Whether they liked me didn't matter.'[66]

To this end he helped obtain funding for a new business administration building at the University of Manitoba. As well, as part of the subsidiary agreement on transportation development, the University of Manitoba received $7 million from the federal government and CN towards the costs of a new transportation institute.[67] At the same time he took pains to represent the mainstays of Winnipeg's manufacturing sector, such as Boeing, Bristol Aerospace, and Standard Aero, as well as the interests of several smaller firms in Winnipeg's clothing and textile industry. One major battle he fought in cabinet on behalf of Boeing involved a scheme being promoted by De Bané, which would have seen Airbus Industrie of Europe constructing a plant in the Eastern Townships of Quebec to build aircraft wings, the purchase of Airbus aircraft by Air Canada, and the early retirement of a good part of Air Canada's fleet of Boeing 727s and DC-9s. The scheme came to naught but not before causing Boeing and the aerospace industry in Winnipeg some anguish.[68]

Axworthy's most direct tie with the Winnipeg business community was through Izzy Asper, his former mentor. At one point Axworthy's office lobbied extensively on behalf of Honeycomb Telephone, a company controlled in part by Asper, for the right to provide cellular radio-telephone service on a nation-wide basis, which was eventually awarded to Montreal-based Cantel Incorporated. But overall, in Axworthy's view, government was not simply a facilitator but the creator of economic activity. Without the stimulus of government action there would be little activity on the part of the private sector. The unfolding of the CAI, culminating with the North Portage development, was for Axworthy ample proof of the validity of his beliefs.

The network extended beyond Manitoba. At the same time, opposition to Axworthy's activities was not restricted to Ottawa or Quebec but could also be found in Manitoba itself. In Ottawa Axworthy's efforts on behalf of Manitoba received support from other ministers in cabinet, ministers who by and large also represented provinces or regions outside of the central Canadian core. De Bané, LeBlanc, and MacEachen were among those Axworthy considered to be in sympathy with his aims, and all of them readily traded program items with each other and generally provided mutual support.[69] Axworthy's closest ally in cabinet, however, was Ed Lumley, who became DRIE minister in 1982. The two were seat-mates in the House of Commons, and while there would often spend their time concocting schemes for the mutual exchange of program resources.[70] Not infrequently, after one of their negotiating sessions in the House, CEIC and DRIE officials in Winnipeg would simultaneously receive telexes providing appropriate instruction on particular projects. Given that DRIE was responsible for a number of the projects funded under the CAI, Lumley's co-operation was important.

Opposition to Axworthy came primarily from the Quebec caucus and in particular from Chrétien. Within the P&P and Social Development committees of cabinet, for example, in response to Axworthy's pleas for special consideration for Manitoba, Chrétien would constantly remind him, 'send us no seats, no money.' The source of the conflict between the two men is not clear, but certainly by 1983 it was obvious that Axworthy would not be supporting Chrétien for the Liberal leadership. But the tension with Chrétien also proved to be a point of division within Manitoba. There were distinct rifts between Axworthy and the new provincial Liberal leader selected in 1982, Sharon Carstairs. No help was forthcoming from the Axworthy team when Carstairs ran, unsuccessfully, in a provincial by-election in 1984 in a riding encompassed by Axworthy's federal constituency. Prior to the federal Liberal leadership convention in 1984 Axworthy and Carstairs were in open opposition at a meeting of Manitoba delegates, the former supporting John Turner and the latter Chrétien. Also arrayed against Axworthy were Otto Lang, former federal agriculture and transport minister, and his wife Adrienne. The couple had gravitated east to Winnipeg from Saskatchewan after Lang's defeat there in 1979.[71]

Divisions within the Manitoba Liberal community were evident elsewhere. Robert Bockstael, holding the neighbouring Liberal seat of St Boniface, by 1984 had become deeply embittered over his failure to enter cabinet, a fate for which he held Axworthy partially responsible. While not voicing his views publicly, he did indicate to Axworthy his unhappiness over both the lack of a cabinet position and the allocation of federal largesse.[72] Axworthy and his staff, in turn, suspected Bockstael of providing the Quebec caucus with details of Manitoba's success in obtaining federal money, information which could be used against Axworthy in his battles in cabinet.

In short, the alliances favouring Axworthy on the one hand, and opposing him on the other, cut across both government and party lines. While Axworthy effectively controlled the Liberal party in Manitoba, primarily by virtue of his control over the Manitoba federal affairs committee, in many ways the Manitoba party was a much less reliable ally than the NDP provincial government.

Using the Network: Strategy, Tactics, and Resources

Some of the deals struck by Axworthy, such as those made with Lumley over their desk in the House, were consummated with remarkable rapidity. Yet success in attaining most of the larger objectives, such as the Air Canada building, was no easy matter, and in fact required months and often years of detailed work. The primary arena was cabinet and its committees, and it was here that Axworthy focused much of his energy in debating with his cabinet colleagues the merits of his numerous proposals affecting western Canada. Thus Jean-Luc Pépin, Axworthy's predecessor in the transport portfolio, recalls that in the Western Affairs Committee of cabinet, which met weekly on Tuesday mornings, he was subjected to almost 'continuous supervision' by Axworthy and his aides.[73] Yet whatever Axworthy's skill and energy in cabinet debate, it was of limited utility when the numbers, usually in the form of a solid phalanx of Quebec ministers, were arrayed against him. Axworthy was well aware of these odds and vowed to use his own acumen and resources to overcome them.[74]

One particular resource he used to good effect in cabinet discussions was public opinion data, garnered mainly through his connection with Angus Reid, the Winnipeg-based pollster. The development of an electoral technocracy under Keith Davey in the 1960s and 1970s, in support of the party leader, meant control over public opinion data was centralized within the PMO; and early on Martin Goldfarb from Toronto had effectively established himself as the Trudeau government's principal source of polling data. Polling information, obtained both in party-commissioned polls and those done for government departments, was then used by the PMO to help ensure the prime minister's influence within caucus and cabinet. Access to polling data was closely guarded. Among ministers only Marc Lalonde and André Ouellet had regular access to these data.[75]

Axworthy clearly recognized the need to counteract this monopoly. As one of Axworthy's political advisers explained: 'Goldfarb had then, and I'm sure still does have the notion that we might as well continue to write off the prairies. Well, if the pollster for the prime minister and the party starts with that premise, what can the people supporting the only western minister and a scraggly band of senators do but fight?'[76] To do battle effectively meant obtaining the services of their own pollster, in this case Angus Reid, who was fully aware of the role he played in relation to Axworthy and of the impact his data had on the distribution of influence within cabinet:

That was the key as to why this fragmentation [of cabinet] occurred. He wanted to use me as a minister under a ministerial system ... If everyone's getting the stuff from Goldfarb – let's say Goldfarb's going to be flying up mainly to see the prime minister and a couple of key members of cabinet. Let's say they all come from Ontario or Quebec. Here's Lloyd Axworthy and for some strange reason ... [his] pollster keeps coming back and saying well this issue doesn't really matter in the west. Lloyd's agenda is a little different. He's looking to build up a base of support in the west. So he needs to have someone that he can turn to independent of the guy whose evidence is viewed as authoritative.[77]

Polling data, independent of those provided by Goldfarb, were used not only in cabinet discussions. In most cases considerable preparatory work would be undertaken by Axworthy and his staff to 'pre-sell' proposals to cabinet committee members before these actually arrived in the committee for discussion and decision. In addition, the needs and predilections of individual members would be assessed, departmental resources conceivably meeting those needs identified, and then appropriate approaches made either by Axworthy himself or through exempt staff. The items used for log-rolling would often be very simple, for example a ministerial permit to expedite the entry into Canada of a nanny for a minister's relative. The money available under the SEI program, and the flexibility associated with the use of ECGC grants, were particularly valuable in negotiating with ministerial colleagues. Axworthy's responsibility for the SEI was also useful in a broader sense. As he informed his cabinet colleagues, the unorthodox and somewhat questionable means used to deliver the program, involving the virtual complete circumvention of the administrative apparatus, put him at considerable peril. Ministers, he said, should therefore be grateful for the political risks he was carrying on their behalf.

A major project such as the Air Canada computer centre entailed pressure applied in a number of arenas. The decision to construct the facility and to place it in Winnipeg was essentially made by Air Canada management and then ratified by the Air Canada board of directors. There was never a government directive as such. At the time, the crown corporation was contemplating the consolidation of its various computer installations located in different office buildings in Winnipeg in a single location; and that location was most likely to be in Montreal where Air Canada headquarters were located. Axworthy let it be known directly to Claude Taylor, then Air Canada president, that his support in cabinet to allow Air Canada to draw further on its line of credit, essentially its only source of capital funding, was contingent upon the new facility being placed in Winnipeg. Additional signals were sent through Pépin, who was subjected to considerable pressure over the issue in the Western Affairs committee. As well, two members of the Air Canada board of directors with good connections to Axworthy, Izzy Asper and Lorna Marsden, a prominent Toronto area Liberal and later senator, were used in lobbying for the Winnipeg site. Subsequently Air Canada, duly sensitive to the earlier controversies over the shift of maintenance facilities to Montreal in the 1960s, announced not only that Winnipeg would remain the primary centre for its computer facilities but that the new building would be located within the city core, becoming a major building block in the CAI development.

Once a commitment had been obtained from cabinet or a crown corporation, the task then became one of ensuring that plans were translated into concrete reality. As James Richardson discovered earlier with the commitment made to CAE to place defence work in Winnipeg, a decision made one day can easily be reversed the next, and until the actual project is in place nothing is certain. When the new facility does open its doors, the task then is to ensure that the minister receives maximum credit. In Winnipeg a major responsibility of Axworthy's political staff was to organize press conferences and generally to liaise with the media. In one instance, shortly after the opening of the new senior citizens' complex supported by CMHC, a huge sign appeared outside the complex, ostensibly from the newly installed residents, thanking the Honourable Lloyd Axworthy for his efforts in making the project a reality. An Axworthy aide explained: 'We paid for the sign, of course. People just don't do that sort of thing on their own.'[78] Similarly, two Orion buses for the handicapped, funded by Transport Canada under an experimental program, were emblazoned with the minister's name in bold lettering. More than a year after the defeat of the Liberal government the buses still sported Axworthy's name while trundling through Winnipeg Streets. The new austerity measures introduced by the Conservative government has precluded repainting of the vehicles.

In pursuing any project of substance, such as the Air Canada computer centre, efforts were made not only to appeal to affected constituencies but to use those constituencies to help apply pressure on the relevant authorities. Thus in the case of the NRC-Cadcam Centre, scientists in the local universities were asked to write letters to the appropriate agencies in Ottawa and generally to lobby on behalf of a new NRC facility for Manitoba. In this instance the support was mutual. Discussions over the need for such a facility had been continuing for several years within Manitoba scientific circles, and Axworthy had little difficulty in finding either the arguments needed to justify the project or the additional lobbying effort.

The core of energetic workers and helpers in Manitoba and Ottawa was frequently referred to as the 'Axworthy machine.' As a descriptive term it was misleading, however, particularly in light of the well-oiled and long-lived political machines in many of the large cities in the United States.[79] As an organization, it was under considerable tension and dependent almost entirely on the resources of the two portfolios headed by Axworthy. Even among Axworthy's close supporters there was often bitter conflict. Axworthy was furious, for example, when Izzy Asper pre-empted Axworthy in announcing the new Air Canada computer centre and then attempted to claim credit for it. The split between Axworthy and the provincial Liberal leader, Sharon Carstairs, has already been noted.

The 'machine' was centred entirely around Axworthy himself and a small nucleus of loyal supporters whom he had known for several years, such as Morris Kaufman, a Winnipeg lawyer and city councillor, and David Walker, his campaign manager and chief trouble-shooter. The rest of the machine, as it existed over Axworthy's four-year term as minister, was made possible only by the resources inherent in Axworthy's position as a minister of the crown, a small army of one hundred or so exempt staff, contract employees, and permanent civil servants seconded to his office.

Prior to becoming minister, Axworthy had achieved a certain status within the Liberal party as an example of one of those rare species: a western Liberal successfully elected at both the provincial and federal levels. But within the national party as a whole he had at best limited clout, even during his tenure as minister. For example, Keith Davey successfully resisted pressure that Liberal party advertising be channelled to ad agencies in Vancouver and Winnipeg favoured by Axworthy. The advertising contracts these agencies did receive were ones given by Transport Canada at Axworthy's insistence.[80] Angus Reid, with whom David Walker was affiliated for a time, did not begin receiving Liberal party contracts until after John Turner became Liberal Leader. Prior to that, however, it did receive all of Transport Canada's public opinion polling contracts that were let during Axworthy's tenure as transport minister.[81] Indeed, without the initial help provided by Axworthy it is unlikely that the Reid firm would have eventually become one of the five largest polling firms in Canada.

Axworthy truly came into his own as a major figure within both cabinet and the party with the selection of John Turner as Liberal party leader in June 1984. Axworthy, co-chairman of the Turner leadership campaign, was given responsibility for the Wheat Board as well as the Department of Transport and was designated chief western lieutenant in Turner's revamped and much smaller cabinet. In taking an approach reminiscent of Mackenzie King, Turner decided to limit the number of regional ministers but to give each broader responsibilities. Thus, in addition to Axworthy being confirmed for the west as a whole, Herb Gray retained responsibility for Ontario, André Ouellet, replacing Marc Lalonde, became Quebec lieutenant, and Gerald Regan was made responsible for Atlantic Canada.

Within the Turner cabinet Axworthy enjoyed considerably more influence. This leverage, in combination with the loosening of expenditure controls that normally occurs during an election campaign, allowed Axworthy to announce projects simply on obtaining a commitment from the prime minister and before receiving approval from the appropriate cabinet committee or from Treasury Board. This heightened authority, however, was a relatively short-lived state of affairs, ending with the Liberal defeat in September 1984. With the defeat Axworthy also lost the perquisites of office, including all the staff and the resources constituting the basis of the 'Axworthy machine.' The machine had, in fact, been able to do little to deliver Manitoba, let alone the west, for the Liberal party. But it did protect Axworthy's own seat from the Conservative landslide. In his riding of Winnipeg–Fort Garry he defeated the favoured Conservative candidate, Bud Sherman, by 2354 votes.

Representation in Action

The case of Lloyd Axworthy brings into sharp relief a number of features of the regional minister system as it existed in the 1980–4 period. More so than with most ministers, it brought out the sharp clash in values between, on the one hand, a minister bent on skewing departmental activities towards regional concerns and, on the other, regular line department officials oriented towards servicing in an equitable manner what they perceived as several constituencies, and doing so according to set rules and using set hierarchical authority systems. Secondly, Axworthy demonstrated that, with the application of sufficient insight and at times brute force, the elaborate central agency system designed in part to help keep errant ministers under control could be easily circumvented, and indeed that parts of it, such as MSERD's FEDC office, could be used for a minister's own purposes.

The Axworthy case also illustrated the peculiar advantages, at least for the minister in question, of regional underrepresentation. While Quebec, in the person of Marc Lalonde, demonstrated the potency of an authoritative minister in charge of a large but cohesive and single-minded caucus, Axworthy demonstrated the benefits of being the sole elected minister without the encumbrance of a regional caucus. Further, as underscored by the discussion of the Manitoba network, the Axworthy case is also noteworthy for the informal alliance that arose within Manitoba which cut across all three levels of government, encompassing the minister, the Manitoba FEDC office, the provincial government, and the Winnipeg city government. In many respects the Manitoba coalition can be compared to state-based coalitions in the United States, typically centred around one or both senators and including the state government.[82] Thus, even within the tight confines of Canadian interstate federalism, potentially significant interstices can be filled by federal politicians, pressing regional concerns on cabinet and the bureaucracy, concerns often incorporating provincial government objectives. Furthermore, though it is claimed that 'cabinet solidarity and strong parties make it impossible for regional cabinet ministers to muster cross-party support on regional matters,'[83] within Manitoba the Axworthy coalition easily crossed party lines.

Finally, Axworthy was far from shy in making publicly known not only his accomplishments for Manitoba but also his differences with cabinet colleagues. Roger Gibbins has noted that in Canada the norms of cabinet solidarity and secrecy limit the capacity of ministers to represent regional interests. 'Because decisions are taken in secret, representation cannot be seen in action.' Hence 'the minister may appear to be an apologist for decisions that adversely affect the region he represents, rather than an effective territorial representative.'[84] Axworthy would overcome this convention in a number of ways, sometimes by publicly indicating that he had lost a given dispute with Quebec ministers – in being forced to scrap plans for an aerospace training centre, for example. Much more frequently the technique of 'unnamed sources' would be used to outline the details of battles that Axworthy was engaged in with the bureaucracy or other ministers.[85] At other times he would pronounce his willingness to carry the Manitoba flag to Ottawa in doing battle over issues such as transfer payments.

Through his adroit use of the media – he would arrive in Winnipeg from Ottawa on Thursday evenings in time for his announcements to appear in the *Winnipeg Free Press* weekend edition – he ensured that the Manitoba public knew where he stood vis-à-vis the status quo in Ottawa.

Ultimately, however, despite seeing himself as western lieutenant, Axworthy was a regional minister in a very narrow sense: his accomplishments, significant to be sure, accrued primarily to a few square miles of downtown Winnipeg. While he played an important role in ensuring that Manitoba as a whole, and particularly northern Manitoba, received considerably more under federal regional development programs than the other western provinces, this related as much to the need to log-roll with the provincial NDP government as with his own inclinations. His preoccupation with the CAI, and with placing projects in his own riding, stemmed in part from his familiarity with Winnipeg and its urban problems and his personal commitment to urban renewal with a human focus. But it also stemmed from the crucial need to protect his precarious electoral base in Winnipeg–Fort Garry. In all likelihood these two factors played a major role in Winnipeg becoming the primary beneficiary of the federal largesse that Axworthy was able to direct to the west. While the literature on federalism suggests that the move to national office will often result in politicians taking on a broader, more national orientation,[86] the Axworthy case suggests that such as a move does not necessarily result in the discarding of a preoccupation with local concerns.

Once more, this relates to the problem of electoral vulnerability and the need to do all one can to protect slim electoral margins. Axworthy was not alone in this: Allan MacEachen and Donald Jamieson are further examples of politicians who faced similar electoral pressures. There is also the vulnerability of the minister's position as minister and of the government itself. Just as Pierre De Bané felt that there might not be another minister from Quebec in the fisheries portfolio for quite some time, thereby justifying the use of the portfolio for the benefit of the Gaspé region, Axworthy openly stressed to provincial politicians and officials the need to move quickly in extracting maximum benefits out of the ERDA. As he noted, it was quite possible that neither he nor the Liberal government might last beyond the next election.

In many ways Axworthy's personality, his willingness to play rough, and the position in which he found himself as sole elected minister from the west made him a unique case. Yet the pressures that conditioned much of his behaviour, principally those arising out of the vagaries of the Canadian electoral system and the difficulties in dealing with the bureaucracy, are ones that face most cabinet ministers. Simply put, Axworthy's rush to do as much as he could for Winnipeg and Manitoba within a limited time span revealed the nature of those pressures, and the contradictions and tensions inherent in the political-administrative interface, in a much starker manner than usual.

CHAPTER 10

Regional Politics and Regional Development: The Mulroney Approach

Examination of the 1980–4 period revealed the activities of regional ministers openly pursuing projects for their province and showed considerable tension between ministers and civil servants. It can be argued, however, that events in this period were unique. It is rare to find a contemporary regional minister such as Lloyd Axworthy so transparent in his pursuit of regional goals. The coincidence of the worst economic downturn since the depression with the heightened impetus towards direct delivery, in good part a result of the constitutional impasse, can also be seen as atypical. It could well be, therefore, that the last Trudeau government constituted an exception to the overall trend towards the attrition of regional ministerial influence, and that the unusual circumstances of that period are unlikely to repeat themselves in the near future.

This line of thinking is premature, however. As this chapter and the one following will demonstrate, the government of Brian Mulroney, elected by a landslide in September 1984 and re-elected in 1988, continued the pattern set by the previous Liberal government. Despite the explicit efforts of Prime Minister Mulroney to suppress the regional proclivities of ministers, the Conservative cabinet was soon subject to regional fissures and dissension. Within two years the government had resurrected the Liberal practice of formally designating a 'political minister' for each province and had also created its own set of regional agencies to enhance the standing of ministers, and of the government as a whole, in the peripheries. Admittedly, the shape and character of the regional minister system under Mulroney differed from that under the Liberals, a function largely of prime ministerial style. There were fewer ministers exercising regional clout compared to 1980–4, but at the same time these figures – ministers such as Donald Mazankowski and John Crosbie – possessed more influence than did comparable ministers under the Liberals; and they were able to exercise that influence in terrains extending beyond their own provinces. Furthermore, for the first time in several years the venerable title 'Quebec lieutenant' came to be used regularly and publicly to refer to the 'political minister' for that province. At a minimum, the continuation of the regional minister system under Mulroney testifies to its durability in Canadian political life. At the same time, the role of prime ministerial leadership and style of governance continued to be important in determining the specific form of regional ministerial influence.

The Initial Approach: 'No More André Ouellets'

One of the themes of Mulroney's 1984 campaign was the excessive patronage and pork-barrelling of the Liberals and how he would ensure that regional barons such as André Ouellet, former minister for the Montreal area, would be 'no more.'[1] Under the Liberals, regional ministers were the primary link in the distribution of patronage through their control of the federal affairs committee in their province, a right they had established after their battles with Trudeau over the role of the regional desks within the Prime Minister's Office (PMO). Under the new scheme of things, however, patronage was to be based more on consultations with the non-elected rank and file rather than ministers and MPs, with final decision-making centralized in Ottawa. The new system came to be centred on 'provincial advisory committees' chaired by non-elected Conservative notables in each of the provinces. Significantly these chairpersons were appointed by the PMO before the election and *before* Mulroney tendered invitations to prospective ministers to join his cabinet.[2] In other words, there was a deliberate effort to ensure that Liberal history would not repeat itself.

Blame or credit for attempting to circumscribe the more overtly political and regional role of ministers, however, should not be restricted to Mulroney or the new Conservative regime as a whole. Prime Minister John Turner, who presided over the interregnum between Trudeau and Mulroney, had already abolished the two main ministries of state, the Ministry of State for Economic and Regional Development (MSERD) and the Ministry of State for Social Development (MSSD). His aim had been to simplify cabinet decision-making through the elimination of a substantial layer of bureaucracy represented by these agencies. The effect, however, was to undercut the administrative support enjoyed by at least some regional ministers. The disappearance of MSERD meant that the role of the federal economic development co-ordinators (FEDCs), the mainstay of regional ministers in helping to develop the Economic and Regional Development Agreements (ER-DAs), was much reduced. The FEDCs now reported to a small unit submerged within the Department of Regional Industrial Expansion (DRIE) and no longer had a direct reporting relationship to the Cabinet Committee on Regional and Economic Expansion (CCERD). The as-sessment note procedure and mirror committees of senior civil serv-ants for cabinet committees had also been eliminated by the Turner reforms.

By late summer of 1984 the ERDA process had been largely completed, although three ERDAs remained unsigned. With the elimination of MSERD, formal responsibility for regional development policy was now vested in a junior minister within DRIE. The only continuing regional development effort was the Industrial Regional Development Program (IRDP) of DRIE, a program which had drawn criticism for placing a disproportionate amount of its support in Ontario rather than in the less affluent peripheral provinces.[3] Thus at the beginning of the Mul-roney mandate there were few ongoing activities that lent themselves to the promotion of regional causes either in themselves or at the behest of regional ministers.

An additional factor lay within the bureaucracy itself. On the one hand, the bureaucracy was uneasy with Mulroney's intent to provide a more clear-cut political direction to government departments, as underlined by his pre-election promise that 'in a Tory government the Minister will run his department. And any Deputy Minister who doesn't understand that will have a career notable for its brevity.'[4] On the other hand, many civil servants, particularly those at the higher echelons, welcomed what they felt was the new government's more 'national orientation' towards matters of policy and organizational de-sign. Terms such as 'direct delivery' and 'regional responsiveness,' shibboleths of the 1980–4 period, were for many civil servants code words for undue politicization of program design and delivery, and they welcomed any moves that would keep the forces of regionalism at bay.[5] Also welcomed was a disinclination by Mulroney to resurrect the central agencies abolished by John Turner, those entities that had made life so difficult for line departments and older, established agen-cies such as the Treasury Board Secretariat. In addition, the Minis-terial Task Force on Program Review,[6] chaired by the deputy prime minister, Erik Nielsen (the Nielsen task force), had the support, and in fact drew extensively on the expertise of, many senior civil servants. In short, to the extent that the agenda of the Mulroney government was discernible, there was ample support among the senior levels of the bureaucracy for those parts of the agenda that stressed leaner and at the same time more sectorally oriented programs.

A second factor concerned Mulroney's approach to federal-provincial relations – namely, his stated intent to avoid the confrontations so characteristic of the Trudeau era and to build a consensus with the provinces on major goals.[7] Also implied in his view of federalism was the devolution of many of the regional activities of the federal government to the provinces. This obviously would mean less opportunity for federal ministers to act as regional or provincial spokespersons in so far as co-operation with the provinces would entail enhanced recognition of the provinces as representatives of regional interests. It also implied less in the way of direct delivery of programs, the mechanism that had proved so providential for Liberal cabinet ministers. Finally, there was the new crop of ministers themselves. Much of the power and influence of regional ministers under Trudeau was derived from their ability to come to grips with their portfolio and to use it to service their regions. This was in good part a function of experience, a commodity that most ministers in the Mulroney cabinet clearly lacked. Thus on no less than five counts – limited access to the patronage machinery, reduction of administrative support for regional matters, Mulroney's more 'national orientation' and more conciliatory approach to federal-provincial relations, and the lack of ministerial experience – there appeared to be little that would promote a continuation of the regional minister system as it existed under the Liberals.

These strictures on the regional dimension in federal government programs, and the emphasis given to the national dimension, became apparent in a number of the moves made in the fall and winter of 1984–5. Several projects dear to the hearts of former Liberal regional stalwarts were either closed down, such as the two heavy water plants in Cape Breton, or frozen, such as the NRC-Cadcam centre in downtown Winnipeg. And in the case of Montreal, as André Ouellet, the target of Mulroney's opprobrium, put it: 'There is no doubt we [had] used our strong influence to support companies in our area with government contracts ... We didn't do it by breaking any rules, but crown corporations knew they had a social responsibility here. The Conservatives don't seem to have this political desire.'[8]

. On a broader level, DRIE minister Sinclair Stevens served notice of the government's intention to transfer to the provinces much of the responsibility for the IRDP, reserving for the federal government only control over grants to large national and multinational firms.[9] At about the same time, finance minister Michael Wilson, as part of his budget address, declared his government's intention to begin removing obstacles to the growth and competitiveness of the Canadian economy, such as the inefficient use of regional development incentives and the regulatory framework governing sectors like the highly regulated transportation industry.[10] In July 1985 the Department of Transport released a position paper outlining, in its own words, 'sweeping revisions to Canada's transportation policy.' Its proposals featured 'Less regulation, leading to less government interference' and 'Greater reliance on competition and market forces.'[11] Provincial premiers, attending their annual get-together later that summer, quickly recognized that these proposals would undermine a variety of subsidies and regulations protecting access of local manufacturers and shippers to cheap transportation, and duly fired off a communiqué stressing that 'commercial viability of transportation links must be balanced with regional economic development objectives.'[12] There was no evidence that federal ministers from provinces likely to be affected by these policy changes had been consulted by Transport or had expressed concern.

The tenor of the federal government's new thrust was reflected in the attitudes of many of the ministers. The minister of finance was clearly interested in reducing the government's fiscal commitments in a variety of areas and in rendering the national economy more efficient by allowing greater play to market forces. But some of these same views were evident among ministers from the peripheral provinces. Thus Tom McMillan, minister of tourism and later environment, reflecting on previous Liberal excesses stated: 'The good old days were the bad old days ... Regional ministers looked after their riding to the detriment of the rest of their region ... There's more to life and politics than the ego massaging of the old regional baron system.'[13]

Within DRIE, the profile of the unit responsible for regional development and the ERDAs slipped further. There was no longer even a junior minister for regional development, and beginning in October 1985 the assistant deputy minister (ADM) in charge of the departmental unit for regional development began reporting to the associate deputy minister rather than directly to the deputy. By early 1986 the unit in question, and the ADM position, had disappeared altogether, having been merged with the branch responsible for overall policy. These policy initiatives and organizational changes were undertaken in part in response to what the bureaucracy felt were the wishes of the new regime; but they also represented a working out of the preferences held by many of the senior officials themselves. Within DRIE, which had absorbed several former MSERD policy staff, there had long been resistance to the forced amalgamation back in January 1982 of the remnants of the Department of Regional Economic Expansion (DREE) with the Department of Industry, Trade, and Commerce (IT&C). Many in IT&C and in the then Ministry of State for Economic Development (MSED) resented having to take responsibility for regional issues.

In Transport there were long-standing views on the need to rationalize the branch-line system in western Canada and on the need to overhaul the ramshackle system of transportation subsidies for Atlantic Canada, views which found ample expression in the *Freedom to Move* document.[14] Furthermore, in the case of Transport, officials were happy to respond to a request by their new minister, Donald Mazankowski, for 'complete records for each of the past four years of all aspects of the minister's office including ... the current employment of all former exempt, seconded or contractual staff anywhere in Transport Canada.'[15] Within a short time they were able to provide the minister with 'two huge black briefing books' on the financial and staffing arrangements for the period covering Lloyd Axworthy's tenure in the portfolio.[16]

In short, the stripping away of what could be termed the regional dimension broadly defined from government programs and departmental organization was done in part at the initiative of officials themselves. To the extent, however, that they thought these initiatives were consistent with the government's future political needs they were likely misguided, for at the very time that these initiatives were being undertaken many ministers and government MPs were beginning to discover the presence, and consequently the needs, of their regional constituencies.

The Resurgence of the Regional Dimension

The regional dimension, in fact, was never far beneath the apparently calm political waters in Ottawa. Indeed, disturbances and minor eruptions began rippling the surface almost from the beginning. Within two months of the 1984 election victory the traditional rivalry between Sydney Steel Corporation (Sysco) in Cape Breton, Nova Scotia, and Algoma Steel in Sault Ste Marie, Ontario, manifested itself in a well-publicized dispute between Elmer MacKay from Nova Scotia, the solicitor-general, and James Kelleher from northwestern Ontario, minister for international trade. One of the election promises made by MacKay was that Sysco would become the exclusive supplier of steel rail to Canadian National (CN). When MacKay discovered that CN had placed a $12 million order with Algoma Steel, he rebuked the crown corporation for doing so and asked that the order, and all subsequent orders, be placed with Sysco. Canadian National duly obliged and publicly announced on 24 October 1984 that it would from then on purchase all its rail from the Nova Scotia mill. Along with protests from Ontario Liberals and Algoma Steel, Kelleher himself indicated in a press release that he was 'very concerned' about the awarding of the contract to Sysco.[17] Following a meeting a week later involving MacKay, Kelleher, CN president Maurice LeClair, and transport minister Donald Mazankowski, a joint statement let it be known that it was 'in the national interest' to have both steel mills supply rail to CN.[18] The dispute continued to simmer, however, and subsequently it was agreed that Sysco would receive 80 per cent of all CN rail orders. As well, much to the ire of Algoma Steel management, Sysco received a federal contribution of $110 million three years later towards the modernization of the provincially owned steel mill, subject to the proviso that Sysco's new universal mill would not make products other than steel rail.[19]

The issue of CN rail orders was, however, only the first of a number of regional disputes that began to place strains on the political and organizational capacities of the Mulroney cabinet. Among the legacies from the Trudeau government were the three unsigned ERDAs with Quebec, Ontario, and British Columbia. The Ontario agreement was nearly complete and only the intervention of the election in September had prevented its implementation. Thus the agreement signed in early November 1984 did not differ significantly from what had been negotiated earlier, except for a softening of the federal government's direct delivery stance.[20] In the case of Quebec, the Liberal government had, in the spring of 1984, announced the unilateral direct delivery of all federal regional development programs. By December 1984 the Conservative government, largely at the behest of the prime minister, had succeeded in negotiating an ERDA with the Quebec government, in part by agreeing to provincial delivery of most of the proposed subsidiary agreements and in part by boosting the overall commitment to $1.57 billion, half of that coming from federal sources.[21]

The Mulroney government had also succeeded in negotiating a tentative agreement with British Columbia in late November 1984. However, when British Columbia premier William Bennett heard the details of the Quebec ERDA he demanded equal treatment – to wit, the same amount on a per capita basis, which would have meant a total amount exceeding $600 million and more than three times the size of the Alberta ERDA signed under the Liberals. In the end the province obtained most of what it wanted: that is, $575 million on a 50–50 cost-shared basis, the major portion of it in the form of an extremely generous forestry agreement worth a total of $300 million. The five-year agreement came about through the efforts of the two British Columbia ministers, fisheries minister John Fraser and energy minister Pat Carney, the latter vice chair of the Cabinet Committee on Economic and Regional Development (CCERD), buttressed by pressure from the nineteen-member British Columbia caucus. They managed to overcome resistance from the minister responsible for the ERDA, Sinclair Stevens, who was inclined to bargain harder with the British Columbia government with the aim of stretching the forestry agreement out over ten years.[22]

The disagreement in cabinet over the British Columbia ERDA was kept relatively quiet. This was not true, however, for another dispute in which Stevens found himself in the winter of 1985. In this instance it involved a personage no less than the prime minister and a demand to DRIE from Domtar Inc. for a $100 million grant to modernize a paper mill located in Windsor, Quebec. Stevens initially rejected the demand, stating that the program supporting modernization projects of this sort was no longer in effect. This response, however, unleashed considerable criticism in the Quebec press, from the Quebec government, and, not least, from the Quebec Conservative caucus. The prime minister, confronted by the altercation upon returning from a Caribbean holiday, stated that while he was not willing to hand out a blank cheque to the company, he would nonetheless entertain some form of federal aid for the mill. After negotiations with the company and the Quebec government, the federal government was able to provide Domtar with an interest-free loan of $150 million.[23]

Sinclair Stevens himself was not above taking into account the needs of certain regions he felt were hard done by. Although having no connection with Cape Breton – he held a Toronto area riding and was generally identified as a Bay Street entrepreneur – he nevertheless began taking a special interest in that particular economically disadvantaged part of Nova Scotia. In part to compensate for the closure of the two heavy water plants, the May 1985 budget announced the launching of the Enterprise Cape Breton program, which provided, among other items, for 50 per cent tax credits to foster private sector investment in tourism, agriculture, fisheries, and manufacturing and processing industries in that region.[24] After pressure from the other Atlantic provinces, and ministers from those provinces, the same theme but rather different incentives appeared in the February 1986 budget in the form of the Atlantic Enterprise Program, featuring loan guarantees up to $1 billion and interest rate buydowns of up to 6 per cent for new private sector initiatives in the region.[25]

By the spring of 1986 it was clear that in a number of instances ministers from various provinces were able to make their voices heard and influence felt within cabinet on regional issues. There was, however, no formal recognition of regional ministers as such, nor were there any formal mechanisms in place to deal with regional matters. This was soon to change. In late 1985, after the closure of a Gulf Canada oil refinery in east end Montreal had evoked protests, including a public condemnation from one of the less successful cabinet ministers in the Mulroney government, Suzanne Blais-Grenier,[26] a special six-member cabinet committee chaired by Robert de Cotret was struck to review the economic development prospects of the Montreal area.[27] Then in July 1986, at a special meeting of the cabinet in western Canada, the prime minister announced the appointment of special 'political ministers,' one for each province. According to Mulroney, 'These men and women will have primary responsibility of improving the Government's direct consultations with the people, with the party, with the ordinary voters, to bring to our attention in a political way those concerns that can best be addressed most effectively at the federal level.'[28] In Ontario and Quebec, he stated, the designated political ministers, Michael Wilson and Marcel Masse respectively, 'each will head a committee of political ministers from his province, as it was decided that one minister each could not adequately deal with the two largest provinces.'[29]

The task of these political ministers to communicate with citizens in the regions was put to a severe test in the fall of 1986 when the Mulroney cabinet faced its first major decision of a zero-sum nature. In this case it was the awarding of the $1.3 billion CF-18 maintenance contract to Quebec-based Canadair, the former crown corporation now owned by Bombardier Limited of Quebec, rather than to either Bristol Aerospace in Winnipeg or the IMP Group in Nova Scotia.[30] What made the task of the Manitoba regional minister, Jake Epp, particularly difficult was the apparent fact that the team of civil servants evaluating the bids had rated the one from Bristol Aerospace as significantly cheaper and technically superior.[31] The Conservative government was faced with the dilemma of appearing to contradict openly the advice of an interdepartmental team of civil servants, a dilemma that the Liberals had managed to avoid seven years earlier when faced with the initial decision to acquire the CF-18. As Atkinson and Nossal argue, the political costs involved in appearing to use a primarily political rationale in making decisions of such magnitude can be very high indeed.[32] Largely as compensation, Epp was able to announce in January 1987 a $200 million maintenance contract for the older and technologically less sophisticated CF-5 fighter aircraft.[33] Later, as both political minister and minister of health and welfare, Epp announced on 8 October 1987 the construction of a $93 million disease control laboratory in Winnipeg, a project that at least some Conservative MPs felt should have been located in Ottawa. Epp, in justifying the extra costs entailed by the Winnipeg location, stated that, 'It fits very clearly into our concept of developing the country. You build the regions.'[34] Both the CF-5 contract and the disease laboratory were seen, however, as relatively poor compensation for the loss of the much more sizeable CF-18 contract and did little to allay fears on the part of the Manitoba government that Winnipeg was losing its position as a major transportation centre and as a nucleus for expertise in aerospace, particularly given the additional loss that July of the Winnipeg VIA Rail maintenance facility to Vancouver.[35]

The more significant development, however, was the creation of no less than three separate agencies for regional development purposes with total expenditure commitments in excess of $2.2 billion over a five-year period. During the summer of 1987 the government announced the creation of the Atlantic Canada Opportunities Agency (ACOA), the Northern Ontario Development Board (Fed-Nor), and the Western Diversification Strategy/Office (WDO) for the direct delivery of federal regional development programs. All three agencies were given a quasi-autonomous status, but ACOA attained the most independent position. Not quite a crown corporation but not a line department either, it was headed by a president, whereas the chief civil servant in WDO was appointed as a deputy minister.[36] Fed-Nor, an agency reporting to DRIE, received its own secretariat based in Sault Ste Marie administered by an official at the director level. Each agency, however, was assigned a senior minister from the relevant region: McKnight was made responsible for WDO, Kelleher for Fed-Nor, and Senator Lowell Murray for ACOA with John Crosbie reporting for the agency to the House of Commons. DRIE lost most of its direct regional responsibilities, except those for southern Ontario and Quebec, and was combined with the Ministry of State for Science and Technology under a new moniker, the Department of Industry, Science, and Technology (IST). Both ACOA and WDO also took over from DRIE/IST responsibility for all except the ERDA tourism subsidiary agreements. As well, ACOA took over what remained of the IRDP and the Enterprise Cape Breton and Atlantic Enterprise programs. The FEDCs for western and Atlantic Canada, formerly reporting to DRIE, were now attached to WDO and ACOA respectively. In keeping with the corporate motif with which ACOA was endowed, the FEDCs were now called vice presidents in charge of the provincial offices. The deputy of the new WDO, Bruce Rawson, was formerly FEDC for Alberta. In the case of ACOA, it was announced that an advisory committee of all six ministers from the Atlantic region would play a role in providing policy direction to this new agency.

Finally, in the realm of patronage, in early February 1988 the prime minister, under pressure from ministers as well as the caucus, dismissed the chairs and dismantled the provincial advisory committees, thereby virtually eliminating the non-elected Conservative party members from the decision-making process. Control over patronage was turned over to the political minister for each province who, in making patronage recommendations to Ottawa, was now to be advised by a representative from the provincial caucus and the Conservative campaign chairperson from their province. According to Jeffrey Simpson, 'This troika system is only a slight modification of the system of "political ministers" used by the Liberals, a system Mr. Mulroney once insisted his party would never use.'[37] Thus, from an initial effort to stymie the rebirth of regional ministers, by restricting access to patronage and by declining to resurrect the administrative support mechanisms abolished by John Turner, and from an initial position of wanting to turn over to the provinces all responsibilities for regional policy, the Mulroney cabinet had apparently come full circle.

From Replication to Innovation

It would be misleading, however, to see this development as mere replication of the system under the Liberals. While there were similarities, there were also crucial differences. In the area of similarities one of the more interesting parallels concerned the willingness of individual ministers to log-roll with provincial governments or to accede on the issue of direct federal delivery when it became expedient to do so. Under Trudeau, for example, Lloyd Axworthy from Manitoba and Allan MacEachen from Nova Scotia were quite adept at striking reciprocal deals with provincial governments, mutually beneficial arrangements that often drew the ire of fellow ministers and civil servants in Ottawa.

In continuing the tradition, Elmer MacKay, the political minister for Nova Scotia, became instrumental in obtaining a variety of new facilities and aid for projects in his constituency of Central Nova, including a federally funded court-house, a federal government loan guarantee for 85 per cent of a $100 million loan towards the costs of the $127 million Westray coal-mine, and an investment by DRIE of $100 million in rescuing the Trenton railcar works.[38] As well, MacKay proved highly proficient in facilitating mutually beneficial deals between Ottawa and the Nova Scotia government. The Westray coal-mine, for example, was fully supported by the premier and the Nova Scotia minister of industry, trade, and technology, Donald Cameron, whose riding also happened to be in Pictou County.[39] As well, a $200 million loan made to Nova Scotia in 1982 as part of the Canada–Nova Scotia Offshore Agreement was transformed into a direct grant by the Mulroney government in 1984. Decisions on which projects were to be funded out of the grant were, according to the Nova Scotia minister of development, Roland Thornhill, subject to 'an informal type of arrangement' between the two governments.[40] At least $17 million was spent directly in MacKay's own riding, mainly on roads. The remainder was spent on projects largely unrelated to offshore development, including a ferry terminal, a free-trade zone in Sydney, housing, a sewer line to a Dartmouth suburban housing development, and a traffic control system in Halifax-Dartmouth.[41]

In the striking of this 'informal type of arrangement' concerning the offshore fund, some of the projects to which the Nova Scotia government had been previously committed were dropped, projects based on understandings arrived at between Premier John Buchanan and former Liberal minister MacEachen. Thus the promised fire training school, wharf facilities, and marine electronics equipment for MacEachen's parting gift to Cape Breton in 1984, the Port Hawkesbury Nautical Institute, to be paid for out of the offshore fund, were never acquired.[42] The only promise to MacEachen on offshore monies on which the Nova Scotia government made good was funding for the expansion of St Martha's Hospital in Antigonish, in MacEachen's former riding.

The Political Management of Regional Development

A major innovation was the design of the three new development agencies. These agencies resurrected one of the themes identified with the previous Liberal regime, direct delivery, but significantly they also incorporated features intended to prevent excessive politicization of the delivery process and, in the case of ACOA, highlighted the pan-regional role assigned to one minister, Senator Lowell Murray.

Of the three, Fed-Nor early on took on the most distinctly political cast: the advisory board for the agency was composed of eleven members, one from each of the eleven federal electoral districts in northern Ontario; all eight members of the board initially appointed had ties directly either with the responsible minister, James Kelleher, or with the federal or provincial Conservative party; and the chairman of the advisory board, Leo Bernier, was a former member of the Ontario Conservative cabinet of William Davis.[43] This arrangement, claims Christopher Waddell, was intended to 'provide ample opportunity for political involvement in the determination of the projects.'[44] A subsequent analysis by the Ontario Ministry of Intergovernmental Affairs concluded that 'electoral considerations were fundamental in its creation,' and lamented the lack of criteria in the agency's budget for the expenditure of funds and the fact that 'unilateral federal delivery of Fed-Nor will prohibit piggy-backing of Ontario programs ... for greater effectiveness.'[45] In the case of WDO, final decisions on overall spending priorities were made by a ministerial committee of western ministers, in which Mazankowski and McKnight were acknowledged to have primary influence.[46] As with Fed-Nor, the affected provincial governments expressed concern over the fact that all decision-making on grants was to be handled by the federal government directly.[47]

The agency to which the greatest attention was given, and which subsequently stimulated the creation of Fed-Nor and WDO, was ACOA, first promised in the speech from the throne on 1 October 1986. Given the importance of regional development programs in particular and the dependence of the Atlantic region generally on federal expenditures, expectations were that ACOA would be the agency most subject to pressure by individual MPs, provincial governments, and regional ministers. Likely for that very reason, the agency was both designed and implemented with a view to preserving as much as possible the integrity of the agency's means of evaluating individual applications and at the same time to meeting the needs of federal visibility and the electoral needs of ministers.

The idea of the agency was first promoted by New Brunswick premier Richard Hatfield, who forwarded to the prime minister a five-page outline of the basic concept for ACOA developed by regional development specialist Donald Savoie. Subsequently Savoie was retained by the federal government to provide a detailed proposal. Working in the Treasury Board office and after consulting widely within the Atlantic region, Savoie presented his report in April 1987 to a small committee consisting of two PMO officials, Charles McMillan and Fred Doucet, and chaired by Dalton Camp of the Privy Council Office (PCO). Camp, eminence grise within the party, had been brought into the government's inner circle in 1986 to help restore the government's public credibility and to bring order to its disintegrating political agenda. While officially in the PCO, he spent much of his time in the PMO. In his report Savoie reviewed previous regional development efforts in the region and focused on the failed marriage between DREE and IT&C, the importance of *new* small and medium-sized businesses in fostering future growth, and the lack of an entrepreneurial climate in the Atlantic region. He also touched on the problem of direct involvement of politicians in regional development policy: on the one hand, ministers from the regions were often key in promoting federal support for regional development, he said, but on the other hand, their direct involvement frequently resulted in the backing of proposals with high profile but limited value.[48] In his recommendations Savoie proposed the creation of a 'stand apart agency operating in full autonomy from any one federal department and with easy and unencumbered access to effective decision-making authority in Ottawa (Cabinet and Cabinet committees).'[49] This agency would be responsible for managing an Atlantic Canada Investment Fund, a pool of at least $250 million in investment capital to be used to support new business enterprises in the region. One of his main recommendations, however, was that actual programs drawing on the fund should be delivered by the provinces. Furthermore, the agency should have the ability, and clout, to assess all new or revised federal programs bearing on the region.[50]

Savoie's report struck two basic chords, one positive and one negative. Dalton Camp in particular was fully aware that ACOA could not be allowed to lapse into a simple slush fund. Savoie's caveats about protecting the new agency from the predacious instincts of not only regional ministers but also MPs and provincial MLAs were well taken by the three-member committee. Charges made at the time of ACOA's announcement that it would become highly politicized simply reinforced this view.[51] However, the committee rejected Savoie's proposal that the delivery of programs, including decisions on specific projects, be left to the provinces. The government was about to enter the final year before a likely election, and hence direct delivery and visibility became of paramount importance. Under these circumstances the specific electoral needs of the government and of the five elected ministers from the region could not be ignored. John Crosbie explained in the House: 'One of the issues, of course, about program delivery, is who gets the credit for it. We want to be sure that the federal Government is going to get credit for the programs involving 100 percent federal money or 75 percent federal money.'[52] Furthermore, as Senator Murray noted in addressing the House of Commons committee on the merits of the new ACOA legislation, 'What is different about this is that this bill will give Atlantic Ministers, Members of Parliament and others, as it were, a department of their own, with resources, with the ability to do research, to bring together information, to carry out this advocacy role, pursuing and promoting the interests of the region in the system.'[53]

The end result was a stand-alone agency along the lines recommended by Savoie but, contrary to Savoie's advice and much to the chagrin of the Atlantic premiers,[54] delivering its own programs and controlled largely by the Atlantic ministers. The required discipline in turn was provided by the non-elected minister for the agency, Lowell Murray, senator for Ontario but originally from Cape Breton, and by the president of the agency, Donald McPhail, a seasoned civil servant, former ambassador to West Germany, and at one time assistant deputy minister in DREE.[55] The task of McPhail was to put the new agency in place with a staff who were competent but also committed to the Atlantic region. The leitmotif of the agency became one of simplifying and streamlining procedures and of reaching the widest possible clientele of small and medium-sized business entrepreneurs.[56]

The task of Murray was to provide overall political direction while at the same time limiting as much as possible political interference in the actual operations of the agency. During his tenure as ACOA minister from June 1987 until August 1988, Murray succeeded in doing precisely that. By all accounts he managed to restrict the six Atlantic ministers to discussions of overall policy rather than individual projects and to minimize diversion of the $1.05 billion fund away from ACOA's primary mandate of providing direct support to small and medium-sized business, despite efforts by some ministers to the contrary. MacKay, for example, in order to oblige Premier Buchanan then facing a provincial election, was anxious to see ACOA money transferred to the province of Nova Scotia to help with the clean-up of Halifax harbour, a request that was strongly resisted by Murray. At the same time Murray did not rule out other possible sources of federal funding for provincial infrastructure projects.[57] Also significant was the composition of the ACOA advisory board. Unlike WDO, which had no advisory board, or Fed-Nor, whose board was populated entirely by Conservatives, the ACOA board had a much more nuanced partisan shading. Selected in part by the four regional ministers in consultation with the provincial premiers, the initial board consisted of four provincial civil servants and fifteen business people. According to Agar Adamson, only six of the nineteen board members were known Conservatives, four were considered Liberal, and the rest neutral.[58] After four meetings Donald Deacon, board member from Prince Edward Island and former Liberal MPP in Ontario, was able to say that the board was more interested in discussing policy initiatives than the merits of individual cases, and, he stated, 'I have been very impressed with Senator Murray. I honestly think he has done everything he can.'[59]

By June 1988, despite the stalling of the ACOA legislation (Bill C-103) in the Liberal-dominated Senate and some delays in putting the administrative apparatus in place to handle the flood of applications that arrived from February onward, the agency had issued $18 million in grants as part of the new ACOA Action Program. As if to emphasize the non-partisan nature of the allocation process, the ACOA office in Nova Scotia released a detailed riding-by-riding breakdown for the province of the number of applications received and approved, the data showing a success rate of between 18.4 and 36.7 per cent and no apparent link between success and Conservative incumbency.[60] Applications for less than $1 million were handled by the provincial ACOA office, for between $1 and $5 million by ACOA headquarters in Moncton, and for amounts over $5 million to a maximum of $20 million directly by the minister.

By October 1988 the agency had awarded several hundred grants, ranging in size from $1875 for a feasibility study on renovating a residential home into a country inn to $7.1 million for improving the Baie Verte asbestos mine in Newfoundland.[61] A high proportion of the small and medium-sized grants were for tourism-related enterprises such as motels and hunting lodges. Smaller grants were often made in support of local craft enterprises. For example, an applicant in Boutiliers Point, Nova Scotia, received a $4560 grant 'to bring her candy business out of the craft markets and into permanent quarters in her home. She will be building a separate kitchen for the manufacture of her truffles and other confections.'[62] While decisions on all small and medium-sized grants were made by local ACOA account executives, the local MP did have the opportunity to make the official announcement. Indeed, all successful applicants were required to leave responsibility of the announcement to the agency, which in turn ensured that the relevant MP had input into formulating the press release or could participate in more elaborate presentations. As well, numerous meetings were organized throughout the region at which business people and interested parties could ask questions about the program and meet not only with ACOA officials but with the minister or local MP and occasionally ACOA board members as well.

In summary, Senator Murray, as minister of ACOA, essentially performed a co-ordinating and control function for the Atlantic region, both in limiting undue partisan influence and in preserving direct delivery. As he himself put it to ACOA staff, 'I can make the hard decisions these other guys [elected minsters] can't.'[63] Through this means he was able to generate a modicum of overall credibility while at the same time allowing ministers and MPs to garner some of the credit and goodwill, both for the overall success of the program and for bringing specific projects to their riding.

This state of affairs was not to last, however. With the prospects of a fall election increasingly likely by the late summer of 1988, the five elected ministers became more vocal about their needs for resources to defend their seats, pointedly noting Murray's safe position in the Senate. In August the prime minister asked the senator to step down, a request to which Murray readily acquiesced but which nonetheless evoked an angry response from Dalton Camp, who made his displeasure known to Mulroney and others in the PMO. With Murray's departure and the arrival of Gerald Merrithew, minister for New Brunswick, as his successor, partisan calculations and ministerial influence became much more obvious. The period covered by the election campaign, 26 September to 20 November 1988, saw the announcement of $155.9 million in grants.[64] During this period $106 million in grants and interest rate subsidies had been awarded to Newfoundland applicants, leading to opposition charges of 'political pressure' exerted on ACOA staff by John Crosbie.[65] There was also a preponderance of large grants among those announced, $100.5 million being allocated to just twenty-five items, sizeable projects that were much more likely to come up for ministerial review and decision. For example, grant and interest rate reduction packages such as the $7.1

million one to the Baie Verte mine and the $5.9 million one to Corner Brook Pulp and Paper Limited in Newfoundland would have been decided at the ministerial level.[66] ACOA did not release a province-by-province breakdown of expenditure commitments. The pattern of announcements, however, suggested that a preponderance of large projects ended up in Newfoundland, including the largest single grant of $8.5 million, a contribution towards a fisheries research centre at Memorial University.[67] During the overall ten-month period covering the implementation of its Action Program ACOA committed itself to $427 million in grant assistance and an additional $165 million to be covered by its interest rate buydown or loan insurance program.[68] In other words, close to half of its five-year $1.05 billion budget had been committed during the first year.

Yet the infusion of numerous small and medium-sized grants – the average grant was $154,000 and the overall approval rate 65 per cent (and between 70 to 80 per cent for grants under $200,000)[69] – throughout the region forestalled major criticism of ACOA. The test of this was the fact that during the election campaign neither of the two opposition leaders, John Turner and Ed Broadbent, recommended abolishing any of the three agencies. Indeed, during the election campaign Turner, arguing that 'regional development policies are the glue that holds our nation together,' proposed allocating more funds to all three development agencies – an additional $1.5 billion – and the establishment of a special ministry to co-ordinate their activities.[70]

The political management of WDO followed a roughly similar pattern. While there were some selective interventions in particular cases by ministers such as Mazankowski, on the whole the agency and its four provincial offices were left to themselves to develop and apply criteria in assessing proposals, criteria related primarily to the business viability of projects and the avoidance of funding enterprises that would compete with and undermine existing ones in the region. The direction provided by the western ministers affected mainly the allocation between provinces and the overall level of WDO funding made available for expenditure during its first year. Early on it was decided that special emphasis would be placed on British Columbia, a province where a number of ridings were at stake and where Conservative support was considered soft. By October 1988 $113 million of the $234.3 million in grants and loans allocated on a provincial basis had been put into that province.[71] Initially Manitoba lagged considerably behind the other provinces, having received by May 1988 only $525,824 from the fund.[72] By October, however, Manitoba had received $34.5 million while the overall amount committed to the region as a whole was $383.3 million, representing close to a third of the $1.2 billion five-year fund.[73]

The three development agencies covered most of the country except for southern Ontario and Quebec. The creation of Fed-Nor and WDO came about largely in response to requests from Kelleher and Mazankowski after ACOA had been announced in October 1986.[74] No such requests for a special agency came from Quebec ministers, and regional development responsibilities for the province remained with the new IST department. But the urge of Quebec ministers to become more involved in direct delivery and to be closer to the clientele was not lacking, however. By the fall of 1987 IST, under its minister Robert de Cotret, began planning for a series of regional development offices in Quebec's outlying regions that would be under the direct control of the federal government. Under the terms of the 1984 ERDA, most of the federal regional development money was being channelled through Quebec government administrative channels. Arguing that these programs 'have not shown good results,' De Cotret stated: 'We now favour a totally different approach, of decentralized, region-based intervention.'[75] By December 1988 he had initiated a series of public 'consultations.' 'Our intention is to create consultative bodies that would tell the Government what it is that people in these regions really need. We are considering real decentralization here. No more heavy-handed bureaucrats telling the people what is good for them.'[76]

The response from the Quebec government was both swift and predictable. The action of the federal government in acting alone, stated Gil Rémillard, the Quebec minister of intergovernmental affairs, was 'unacceptable.'[77] And Robert Bourassa warned the prime minister directly that Quebec was adamantly opposed to 'any significant change in the way Quebec and Ottawa now co-operate.'[78] 'Hard and tight' negotiations, in Bourassa's words, followed over the next several months until agreement was finally reached in early June, resulting in a hastily called press conference on 9 June at which Mulroney and Bourassa announced jointly the signing of a $970 million five-year agreement, with more than half the funding to be provided by the federal government.[79] According to Rémillard, the collaboration framework established by the two governments 'will ensure cooperation based on a real partnership with the utmost respect for the jurisdiction of both governments.'[80] The agreement provided not only development support for the outlying regions but included $330 million for the 'central regions,' which also opened the door to incentive grants in the Montreal area, as originally recommended by the special task force on Montreal, recommendations that De Cotret had rejected two years earlier.

By coincidence the signing of the agreement came just days before two scheduled by-elections, one federal and one provincial, both on the same day and in contiguous districts in the Lac St Jean region. In the campaigns for both, the prime minister and the premier made numerous commitments to the area. The centre-piece was a promised $45 million road, to be paid for under the regional development agreement, which would link Lac St Jean to the James Bay region where the provincial government was planning to construct $30 billion worth of hydroelectric projects over the next twenty years.[81] There was little doubt that the exigencies of the federal Lac St Jean by-election, which saw a close confrère of the prime minister, Lucien Bouchard, elected, and the broader need of the Mulroney government to forge close ties with the Bourassa government, resulted in the initial impulse towards direct delivery transformed into a co-operative agreement under which the Quebec government would be responsible for delivery of most programs.

Overall, the three development agencies, and the special arrangements made for Quebec, represented efforts to manage politically a difficult area, where controversy over appropriate strategies and inappropriate political influence was rife but where it was important to ensure that regional ministers were given a strong sense of participation, a sense that they were important actors in directing developments affecting their province and were seen as such in front of provincial citizenries. In the case of Quebec, however, it was also clear that, under the right political circumstances, the policy of direct delivery could be altered to something much less draconian in order to assuage provincial government concerns.

From Tugboats to Offshore Oil: Organization, Hierarchy, and Regional Influence in the Mulroney Cabinet

Regional development, the topic examined in the previous chapter, was not the only area in which ministerial influence in the Mulroney cabinet was evident. Without much difficulty one can find additional examples where there was clear exercise of ministerial prerogative: the redirection by Donald Mazankowski of a tugboat construction contract from a firm in Kingston, Ontario, to one in Manitoba; the scheduling of the royal visit to ensure a full day in the town of Kindersley, home to William McKnight, minister for Saskatchewan and in charge of WDO; and the announcement by John Crosbie, minister of transport in 1987 and minister for Newfoundland, of several projects such as wharf improvements during a by-election in St John's–East.[1] But this sort of behaviour has been part and parcel of Canadian politics for decades and is not unexpected. At the same time, these activities are likely indicative of the broader influence enjoyed by these individuals and point to what may be by far the most significant development: under Mulroney certain regional ministers became much more influential than comparable figures under the Liberals. One can discern the emergence of at least three major figures whose influence extends beyond their immediate provinces, a development that bears more than passing resemblance to the system of regional notables under Mackenzie King.

Donald Mazankowski became a dominant force both in cabinet as deputy prime minister and in virtually all matters pertaining to western Canada, while John Crosbie and Lowell Murray came to play a similar role for Atlantic Canada. Taking over the deputy prime ministership (DPM) from Erik Nielsen in 1986, Mazankowski moved the DPM office into the Langevin Block (the same building housing the PMO and PCO), greatly expanded both the staff complement and the scope of the office, and generally transformed the position into a far more potent entity than it had ever been under any previous occupant.[2] He became, in corporate terms, the equivalent of a chief executive officer, responsible for managing the government's political agenda, with Mulroney as chairman of the board.[3] By early 1989 Mazankowski, like C.D. Howe before him, began being referred to as 'minister of everything.' He was seen as directly responsible for placing members of his own political network, close friends and protégés such as Harvie Andre, Doug Lewis, and Charles Mayer, into important portfolios and onto key cabinet committees.[4] Thus by the end of the first term of the Mulroney government Mazankowski had clearly established himself at the apex of a hierarchy of regional ministers in the west; and those ministers lower in the hierarchy, such as McKnight, who were reasonably powerful in their own right, recognized and deferred to Mazankowski's authority.

There was more tension among the ministers from Atlantic Canada, but from the beginning of the mandate Crosbie stood well above the other elected ministers through sheer force of personality and a high level of competence in managing his portfolios. Indeed, he was able to make his influence felt before the 1984 election when he essentially spelled out for Brian Mulroney the terms of the agreement in principle on Newfoundland's right of ownership to offshore energy resources. This agreement, signed with considerable fanfare between Mulroney and the Newfoundland premier, Brian Peckford, in June 1984, became the basis for the Atlantic accord later signed between Ottawa and Newfoundland.[5] Crosbie was also able to dictate who from among Newfoundland MPs would *not* sit in cabinet when he effectively vetoed a possible appointment for his rival James McGrath, who had been fisheries minister in the Clark government.

Aside from the fact that he performed well in the portfolios assigned to him, at a time when a number of other Conservative ministers were less than stellar in this regard, Crosbie also drew on a Newfoundland tradition of having strong ministers in Ottawa, which had been established by predecessors such as Jack Pickersgill and Donald Jamieson. In re-establishing this role, which had lapsed with Jamieson's departure in 1979, Crosbie demonstrated the importance of strong representation for the Newfoundland government in the conduct of intergovernmental relations across a wide array of issues. As an official in the Newfoundland Intergovernmental Affairs Secretariat stressed: when Crosbie and the Conservatives came to power in September 1984, 'Our whole tactics changed, everything was [now] channelled through his office. Instead of direct telexes to the prime minister or going to the press, we would prepare detailed briefing books for Crosbie. Crosbie [in turn] would visit us in our offices and tell us what was possible in Ottawa.'6 In the eyes of the Newfoundland government he was seen as an able, intelligent, and very determined minister who was capable of protecting Newfoundland's interests in crucial areas. In contrast, 'During the early eighties there was an attempt made to use Rompkey [junior Liberal minister], to keep him informed. But he was not considered effective. In considering strategy vis-à-vis Ottawa, Rompkey was a weak path. He had no influence at all over the offshore or fisheries.'7

While Crosbie may have been the most powerful Atlantic minister, he was not the only one; the minister playing an equally important, albeit rather different role was Senator Lowell Murray. As senator from Ontario and minister in charge of federal-provincial relations, Murray had no specific electoral obligations to the region. He was, however, thoroughly familiar with the region's problems and its politics, and precisely because he had no particular obligations he was able to take on a role for the Atlantic region in some respects akin to that of a Quebec lieutenant. A trusted confidant of the prime minister, he saw his task as maintaining order among the five elected Atlantic ministers and, in particular, as ensuring the successful launching of ACOA, taking care that the new agency would not succumb to the numerous pressures, not only from ministers but also from MPs, provincial governments, and provincial MLAs.

Mazankowski and Crosbie, and to a lesser extent Murray and Michael Wilson, in his capacity as finance minister rather than minister for Ontario, have played a crucial role on major issues, and this was most evident on decisions concerning funding support for energy projects. In the six-month lead-up to the 1988 election the federal government announced support for a series of energy mega-projects, including the Hibernia oilfield offshore of Newfoundland, the Fort McMurray tar sands project of the Other Six Leases Operation (OSLO) consortium in Alberta led by Imperial Oil, the Husky heavy oil upgrader in Lloydminster, and the Vancouver Island natural gas pipeline.8 All three oil projects are considered risky propositions, viable only if there is a significant increase in the world price of oil when the product comes on stream.9 The Vancouver Island pipeline is also problematic, its viability dependent on several pulp mills committing themselves to natural gas. Of the three western projects, however, the Husky upgrader is clearly the least viable. Without the support of Mazankowski, who argued its case on the basis of equal standing with Newfoundland, it is unlikely that it would have attracted government funding. The upgrader, whose operations will straddle the Alberta-Saskatchewan border, fitted well the electoral needs of both Mazankowski and McKnight, a close friend of Mazankowski and minister in charge of WDO. Prominent at the press conference on 2 September 1988 in Lloydminster were the two ministers and the premiers of the two provinces, whose governments were also making a significant contribution to the project. Absent, however, was the federal minister of energy, Marcel Masse.[10] It is worth recalling that under the Trudeau regime energy was handled directly by the minister of energy, and the occupants of that portfolio, in particular Marc Lalonde, brooked little interference from other ministers acting in either their sectoral or regional capacities.

As noted, Crosbie played a significant role in striking the Atlantic accord; later he played an equally significant role in obtaining federal government backing for the development of Hibernia, negotiating the details with both the Newfoundland government and the companies involved. The $5.2 billion development, announced on 18 July 1988 in St John's by the prime minister and the Newfoundland premier, will cost the federal government at least $3.175 billion in direct grants and loan guarantees.[11] Earlier in his role as minister of transport Crosbie negotiated directly with the Newfoundland premier over the proposed closing of the CN owned and operated Terra Transport, which provided rail, trucking, and intercity bus services in that province. Up to $850 million was offered as compensation to the province for major road improvements.[12]

Crosbie's influence was also evident in the international arena, specifically in relation to the Canada-France fisheries treaty. The tentative pact struck by External Affairs officials with France to resolve the dispute over French access to Northern cod stocks initially caught Crosbie offguard. The deal was then vehemently attacked by both Peckford and Crosbie, and the eventual scuttling of the January 1987 deal was likely due as much to Crosbie's threat to resign as to Peckford's protests.[13] Of significance was not only Crosbie's ability to veto the proposed treaty by using the ultimate threat – his resignation – but also the fact that he was willing to go public with his opposition to a particular federal action. A fisheries agreement that was bad for Newfoundland would be signed only 'over our dead bodies,' according to Crosbie in a speech in St John's in which he threatened the resignation of the entire Newfoundland caucus.[14] Earlier in the House during an emergency debate on the issue Crosbie stated that the lack of consultation with the Newfoundland government and the industry 'was unacceptable, as far as I'm concerned,' and that an apology from the federal government was in order.[15] An apology was duly conveyed to Peckford by the deputy prime minister, Donald Mazankowski.

Government Organization and Prime Ministerial Style

The particular shape of the regional minister system in the Mulroney cabinet – domination by a few figures rather than power diluted among a larger number as under Trudeau – can be attributed to a number of factors. First, there were the obvious lack of experience and limited political connections among the vast majority of the new recruits to the 1984 cabinet. Mazankowski and Crosbie, both seasoned political veterans, had previous ministerial experience as well as considerable clout within the party. But equally important was the prime minister's approach towards governance and politics generally. Mulroney's brokerage, transactional orientation made individual actors, as opposed to the system, much more important.[16] Under the Liberals the process was more formal and structured. Areas of responsibility were assigned to cabinet committees, which under the Program Expenditure Management System (PEMS) also had expenditure authority. And with respect to programs such as the development of the ERDAs, each regional minister was ensured a role in the initiation and approval of projects in their province. Under the Conservatives the process became much more actor-driven, frequently involving informal, one-on-one relationships between individual ministers. It was a style practised, and actively encouraged, by Mulroney, who loves nothing better than consulting over the phone with a wide group of acquaintances and striking informal arrangements with single individuals or within small groups. He is also prone to surround himself with persons whom he trusts and has known for a long time. As is well documented by the chaos that appeared to reign in the early period of his government, and within the PMO in particular, this style of governance did not easily lend itself to the smooth functioning of a highly complex administrative apparatus.[17]

The machinery of government, and the organization of cabinet business, did adapt, however, to the Mulroney transactional approach. The deputy prime minister's office (DPMO) under Mazankowski was strengthened and took over much of the day-to-day conduct of government business. Mulroney applied himself more to broader issues in the national and international arena and the PMO was reorganized by a new chief of staff, Derek Burney, a twenty-five year veteran civil servant, who ensured clear lines of communication and responsibility. Dalton Camp, from an office close to that of the prime minister, provided regular political advice and liaison with the PCO, the agency which has traditionally had primary responsibility for supplying administrative support to cabinet but from which Mulroney had distanced himself. The recruitment of professionals like Burney notwithstanding, Mulroney as well as many of his ministers continued to distrust the senior civil service and this was reflected in the relative decline of the PCO, as indicated by the limited participation of the clerk of the PCO in regular briefings held for the prime minister, and the strengthening of both the PMO and, especially, the DPMO.

The impact of the prime minister's influence was directly evident in the organization of cabinet and the manner in which cabinet business was conducted. Cabinet as a whole and cabinet committees, as well as PEMS, became much less important. While the Mulroney cabinet expanded in size – to forty by 1990 – it became at the same time little more than a 'mini-caucus' of Conservative MPs.[18] Key committees such as CCERD began meeting much less frequently. In a major departure from PEMS, in a number of committees the practice developed of approving new projects 'in principle' but leaving the minister in question with the responsibility of finding financing for his or her proposal in direct dealings with the minister of finance or the prime minister or both. Thus Elmer MacKay, in seeking help for the failing Trenton Rail Car works in his riding, was able to obtain funds directly from the prime minister.[19] For obvious reasons this practice encourages informal negotiations between ministers, thereby reinforcing the pattern of one-on-one interaction and the bypassing of cabinet committees.

The formal cabinet committee structure inherited from the Trudeau era became more peripheral to cabinet decision-making. But this did not mean all cabinet committees declined. One informal committee that did become central to the decision-making process, and which did not exist previously, was the Operations Committee headed by the deputy prime minister.[20] Responsible for managing the work plan of government with respect to emerging issues, its membership included the chairs of the three major sectoral committees – CCERD, social development, and defence and foreign policy – as well as the prime minister's chief of staff, the minister and deputy minister of finance, secretary of Treasury Board, and the clerk of the PCO. Other ministers attended when issues concerning their portfolio arose. When first struck in 1986, the Operations Committee was regarded as subcommittee of the Priorities and Planning (P&P) Committee without expenditure authority. Yet, as Peter Aucoin noted in early 1988, 'it is at the sessions of the committee that the ministers involved tackle the matter of budgetary resources. It is here that the trade-offs are made between these key ministers, rather than in Priorities and Planning or in the sectoral committees.'[21] It was in this committee that decisions on energy projects, for example, were made.

By January 1989 the 'Ops Committee,' as it came to be called, had gained formal status as one of the two key committees in cabinet, the other being the newly created Expenditure Review Committee, of which Mazankowski was made the vice-chair.[22] The Ops Committee normally met on Monday mornings and debated issues likely to be controversial before they were discussed in the P&P Committee meeting on Tuesdays. In formal terms the P&P Committee, chaired by the prime minister, remains the premier committee of cabinet. But for all intents and purposes the Ops Committee had become the de facto inner cabinet, the gatekeeper to P&P with all the influence over agenda setting that such a role implies, one of the ironies being that the prime minister was not even a member of the committee.

One of the innovations brought to policy matters and the management of individual portfolios by the Conservatives was the upgrading of ministers' exempt staff, and one of the key positions was now 'chief of staff.' As the highest-ranking political staff member, he or she was expected to be far more than the minister's executive assistant and enjoyed a salary comparable to that of a deputy minister. Designed to act as a counterweight to the influence of the permanent bureaucracy, it was hoped that the position would be filled by experienced people from the private sector with a high level of expertise in the mandate encompassed by the minister's portfolio and with a high level of commitment to the goals espoused by the Conservative party. Subsequent experience proved that individuals combining partisan commitment and expertise were a rare commodity. According to Gordon Osbaldeston, 30 to 40 per cent of the chiefs of staff performed work equivalent to that of executive assistants in the previous government, albeit now at a much higher rate of pay; in a further 30 per cent of cases these political figures 'created substantial problems.'[23] As the recruitment of Burney as Mulroney's own chief of staff demonstrated, the really competent individuals were more often than not to be found within the ranks of the civil service rather than in the private sector.

For incoming ministers such as Crosbie, who had a good sense of their objectives and regional responsibilities, and knew whom they wanted as their political staff, the more flexible rules on recruiting partisan staff proved helpful. Thus early on Crosbie acquired experienced staff – for example, lawyers such as Henry Brown and Malcolm Rowe – to help him in his liaison work with other ministers and the Newfoundland government and, importantly, to help him in the 'surveillance' function, scanning cabinet documents to see what was on the horizon. The flexibility in recruitment of political staff was further enhanced by administrative reforms gradually implemented in 1986 in the form of the Increased Ministerial Authority and Accountability (IMAA) initiative. Stemming in part from the Nielsen task force report, IMAA saw the delegation of a significant amount of Treasury Board authority over personnel and financial matters to individual departments.[24] Among other things, this allowed ministers to greatly expand the size of their exempt staff without having to refer to Treasury Board rules.

However, for inexperienced ministers this flexibility was of little help. The choices they made in recruiting staff were sometimes inappropriate, in the sense that the new staff had, in many instances, no knowledge or understanding of the machinery of government or the political-administrative process. In terms of helping their minister in mobilizing the department for regional purposes or in scanning cabinet documents for important issues or opportunities affecting their minister, these political staffers were far less helpful than, for example, the FEDCs had been under the Liberals, regular civil servants but mandated to help ministers in their regional capacity. Furthermore, in the case of inexperienced ministers, an effort was made by the PMO to place their own selections into ministers' offices. This was done in part to assist new cabinet ministers but also in the hope of attaining a measure of centralized political control to be exercised via the PMO.

Unfortunately the PMO in the first two years had more than enough difficulty co-ordinating its own internal activities, let alone those in individual ministerial offices. Effective centralized political control, when it arrived, came two years later and in a rather different form. Up to that point Mazankowski had been trying to bring some order to the chaos of erupting scandals and ministers following their own agenda. In Mazankowski's eyes the crisis came in late 1986 when Michel Côté, minister responsible for Canada Post, informed the Conservative caucus of major changes in postal rates and termination of home delivery in new subdivisions only three hours before he announced them in the House. There was a near revolt among Conservative backbenchers. It was shortly after this episode that the Ops Committee was formed; henceforth, upon direct orders from the prime minister to all cabinet members, any announcement or change of any significance had to be cleared first through Mazankowski and the Ops Committee.[25]

Those ministers who had the requisite experience and ability were able to exploit at the outset the political resources and new flexibility made available and to establish themselves in their departments. They were also more likely to end up on the key cabinet committees. It was not surprising therefore that a few ministers did quite well and several did not. Even when the prime minister resurrected the formal title of 'political minister' and the recognition that went with it, this did not alter the basic pattern of regional ministerial influence set during the first two years of the government. Clearly the history of regional representation, from Clifford Sifton, through Jimmy Gardiner and C.D. Howe, to Mazankowski, has demonstrated that the *sine qua non* of a strong regional minister is the capacity to give direction to one's department. It can be seen as indicating a more general ability to manage several complex activities and a variety of constituencies. At the same time, the mobilization of one's portfolio is a necessary prerequisite to being able to use departmental resources to service regional constituencies and to wield influence around and beyond the cabinet table.

In the Mulroney cabinet there have been several ministers who were not really able to come to terms with their portfolios for regional purposes or who were simply not interested in the regional role. In the case of the latter, the senior minister from Saskatchewan, Ray Hnatyshyn, was offered the mantle of political minister for that province. He declined and the position went instead to McKnight. Both Kelleher and Gerald Merrithew, junior minister of forestry, proved to be disappointing in their portfolios, and neither was seen to be effective as a political organizer. Kelleher, in fact, was defeated in the 1988 election while Merrithew lost the ACOA portfolio in 1989. By February 1990 Merrithew was also forced to share his duties as political minister for New Brunswick with the much younger Bernard Valcourt. Valcourt, despite an impaired driving conviction following a motorcycle accident in 1989, had nonetheless shown considerable acumen in his brief career as minister of consumer and corporate affairs as well as flair for political organizing in northern New Brunswick. These basic qualities no doubt contributed to his rapid political rehabilitation, as signified by his being made minister of fisheries and at the same time co-regional minister for the province. Elsewhere, limited experience and lack of close connections with regional economic and political constituencies probably account for the rather limited profile that Pat Carney achieved as spokesperson in cabinet for British Columbia. John Fraser, who did have better connections, particularly with the provincial Social Credit party, had his career as regional minister for that province prematurely ended by the tainted tuna scandal during his brief tenure in the fisheries portfolio.

Some cabinet members were able to do reasonably well despite limitations as ministers. MacKay, who was less than adroit in his handling of the Solicitor General portfolio before being moved to the safer post of minister of national revenue, was able to bring several benefits to his riding, and to a lesser extent Nova Scotia, mainly as a result of prime ministerial obligations. MacKay provided support to Mulroney during the 1982 leadership race and gave up his seat to the leader in 1983. MacKay was also close to Nova Scotia premier John Buchanan, who by the spring of 1989 led the only Conservative provincial government in the Atlantic region and who had also provided support for the federal government's free trade initiative. The five Conservatives returned to Ottawa from Nova Scotia in the 1988 election also represented a somewhat higher success rate, at least in comparison with Newfoundland and Prince Edward Island.

The minister from whom much was expected was Jake Epp, minister from Manitoba. One of the more senior members of the cabinet, he invariably drew comparisons with his precocious predecessor as regional minister, Lloyd Axworthy. But in this respect he proved wanting. He was clearly out-manoeuvred on the CF-18 decision, apparently believing that the cabinet meeting in November 1986 would decide the issue on technical merits, notwithstanding a number of signs indicating that a commitment to Bombadier and Canadair had already been made months earlier. Crucially, the loss of the contract was as much a symbolic as an economic defeat, given that it struck at Manitoba's single most important high-technology sector. Also the 1984 freezing of construction of the NRC-Cadcam Centre and the closure of Canertech were seen as unwarranted vindictiveness, aimed, to be sure, at Lloyd Axworthy, but ultimately harming a province that had elected a majority of Conservative MPs. Epp's inability to protect Manitoba from these cuts and to deliver new projects proved frustrating to other Tory MPs in the province, and partially as a consequence he was unable to maintain discipline over them. When Epp concurred with the site selection panel for the new disease control laboratory, which recommended placing the facility near the University of Manitoba Health

Sciences Centre, Leo Duguay, MP for St Boniface, complained bitterly, and in public, that the project should at a minimum have been put into a Conservative riding.[26] Ultimately, however, Epp was a man with strong moral and religious scruples. This did not mean he considered the pursuit of regional interests less than ethical, but rather that a number of issues crucial to his health portfolio and touching on major moral concerns became important preoccupations in their own right. As a consequence there was less time left for regional matters.

Mulroney and the Quebec Lieutenancy

Ever since the early death of Macdonald's trusted Quebec colleague George-Etienne Cartier, Conservative leaders have had considerable difficulty in finding suitable candidates for the position of chief lieutenant for Quebec, an individual who would represent Quebec's interest within cabinet, provide advice on developments in that province, manage the party machinery, and ultimately, deliver the support of the Quebec electorate. The failure of both Borden and Diefenbaker has been seen largely as their failure to deal with the Quebec lieutenancy. In turn, the relative success of the Liberals has been seen in part to lie in the fact that leaders such as Laurier, St Laurent, and Trudeau, having roots in the province, had much less need for a strong supporting figure, although even Laurier felt the need to recruit Israel Tarte as his chief political organizer. In the case of Trudeau, men such as Jean Marchand and Marc Lalonde, while not perhaps in the same mould as Ernest Lapointe, nevertheless played key roles as chief organizers and disciplinarians for the province and within the Quebec caucus.

In 1984 Brian Mulroney was probably the first Conservative prime minister from the province of Quebec who had a close affinity with its largely francophone population. For this reason it seemed he did not need a Quebec lieutenant, and his early interventions in the affairs of other federal departments in matters affecting Quebec and his later close involvement in striking the Meech Lake Accord seemed to bear this out. In doing so, however, Mulroney was also risking one of the precepts of his office – namely, the prime minister should be seen as a national figure, standing above the fray of regional and local interests. There were also pronounced logistical problems in having the prime minister devoting considerable attention to the details of Quebec affairs. As well, the problems attending the behaviour and practices of some of the neophyte Quebec ministers, who lacked both ministerial and political experience, threatened to engulf Mulroney himself. It was only natural, therefore, that the 1986 reorganization of the PMO and the naming of political ministers for each of the provinces would also involve the naming of a special figure for Quebec who would act as organizer, confidant, and trouble-shooter.

The initial choice of Marcel Masse was logical on a number of grounds. Unlike most ministers from Quebec, he was a known figure and had been a member of Union Nationale governments in Quebec during the 1960s. He also represented an important element in the coalition that had brought the Conservatives electoral victory in 1984. While much of this success could be attributed to Mulroney directly – the perception of his having strong Quebec roots – it also was because of tacit support from traditional nationalist forces in Quebec, which for a time had found a home in the Parti Québécois (PQ). As regional minister Masse did not prove up to the task, however, being much more interested in the substance and perquisites of his portfolio of Communications and lacking a taste for the nitty-gritty of political organizing in the trenches of Quebec politics. Instead, a number of other ministers filled at least partially the subsequent void: De Cotret established, if not a following, then at least respect in his work as DRIE minister; and Benoît Bouchard, in turn, established a reputation as astute political organizer, responsible for single-handedly raising Conservative party membership in Quebec from 29,000 to 65,000 over a one-year period.[27] Then, in the spring of 1988 Mulroney persuaded long-time friend and former PQ activist Lucien Bouchard to leave his post as ambassador to France and join the cabinet as secretary of state. Bouchard, a classmate of Mulroney at Laval, had been credited as having been the single most important influence in shaping the prime minister's views on Quebec nationalism in the post-1980 period. Bouchard's credentials as, in his own words, 'a bona-fide Quebec nationalist,'[28] also provided Mulroney with a crucial instrument in cementing links with the political élite on both sides of the Quebec national assembly. In June 1988 at the time of the Lac St Jean by-election, Bouchard received the blessing of both Robert Bourassa and PQ House leader, Guy Chevrette.[29]

Even before his election to the House, Bouchard made evident his authority within the Mulroney government. In early June 1988 he declared his intention of ensuring a Montreal-area location for the federal government's proposed new space agency.[30] Later, after it was announced the agency would indeed be located there, and various municipalities in the area were vying for it, Bouchard, as one of the 'two powerful cabinet godfathers' for the south shore region was instrumental in having the town of St Hubert selected as the site.[31] The other 'godfather' was André Bourbeau, the provincial manpower minister. Bouchard also took the lead on issues of direct concern to Quebec, specifically on the implementation of the Official Languages Act (Bill C-72), where he reached an agreement with the Quebec government outlining the limits on the application of the act within Quebec.[32] When Bourassa invoked the 'notwithstanding' clause in the constitution and introduced new legislation outlawing bilingual signs, after the Supreme Court of Canada had struck down Quebec's original language law on signs, Bouchard indicated his approval of the Quebec premier's action, openly contradicting Mulroney's position on the issue.[33]

Yet Bouchard's position as Quebec lieutenant designate did not spell control over the party's machinery within the province. In part the other Bouchard (Benoît), by dint of hard work and having a touch for grass-roots politicking, had already established a proprietary interest in this area. More decisively, as revealed at the time of the Lac St Jean by-election, Lucien Bouchard was both uncomfortable and ill-equipped to deal with the glad-handing and mainstreeting entailed by electoral politics. As a consequence, he remained as a sort of spiritual godfather for Quebec, while the detail and work involved in political organizing has been left more to street-smart politicians such as Benoît Bouchard. Lucien Bouchard was neither the political fixer along the lines of Jean Marchand, nor the all-powerful and authoritarian disciplinarian in the mould of Marc Lalonde.

For a few months, however, Bouchard's role as Quebec's representative in Ottawa crystalized into a position of singular importance. In February 1990 he officially replaced Masse as political minister for Quebec and, in the crucial period leading up the Meech Lake ratification deadline of 23 June, continually and publicly affirmed Quebec's right not to be isolated and to have its minimum demands outlined in the accord accepted without change. At one point he indicated that Canada might need to choose between Quebec and Newfoundland, asking 'Canada without Quebec, what would that be?'[34] Bouchard's dramatic performance came to a head in the month of May. The all-party Commons committee examining the ways and means of rescuing the accord, headed by the Conservative MP from Quebec, Jean Charest, presented a menu of possible options to be considered by the government and the first ministers, including the possibility of wording in the constitution to ensure that the 'distinct society' clause would

not override the Charter of Rights. For Bouchard this was unacceptable; by 22 May he had resigned from both the cabinet and the caucus.
In July of that year, a month after the fatal sinking of the Meech Lake
Accord, Bouchard, six other Tory MPs from Quebec, and one Liberal
announced the formation of the Bloc Québecois, a party with the sole
aim of fighting on behalf of Quebec within Parliament. If Mulroney's
hopes had been that in Bouchard he had found the modern version
of a Cartier or a Lapointe, they were forever destroyed by Bouchard's
abrupt departure. Mulroney had inherited instead, it appeared, the
ghost of Frederick Monk, Robert Borden's nemesis of some eighty
years before.

Bouchard's abrupt exit, however, did not lead to mass defections
on the part of Quebec MPs or ministers. Most continued to express
loyalty to Mulroney. Benoît Bouchard, who beforehand had also publicly questioned his role in Ottawa and the party should Meech Lake
fail, in turn accepted the position of Quebec lieutenant. Furthermore,
even at an earlier stage, the lack of a single, all-powerful figure failed
to hamper the ability of the Quebec caucus to formulate common
goals and to present a unified front on practically all issues, not just
Meech Lake. As Alex Kindy, MP for Calgary Northeast, noted: 'The
Quebeckers stick together and 90 per cent of the time they get what
they want. I wish the other provinces would do the same.'[35] Representing 37 per cent of the Conservative caucus, the sixty-two-member
Quebec contingent elected in the 1988 election built on their experiences of the previous term and came to enjoy an influence easily rivalling that of the Quebec caucus in the previous Liberal government.
The latter actually constituted a majority of caucus members, but the
Quebec Conservative grouping, by virtue of having a single point of
view developed at their Tuesday night meetings, in contrast to the
unformed opinions of the other provincial caucuses, was able to dominate meetings of the full caucus. Equally important, Tory MPs from
the other provinces accepted the role that the Quebec wing of the
party had established and the rationale for it. According to Donald
Blenkarn, MP for a Toronto-area riding, 'In the old days, we were a
one-culture party and that is why we were never in government ...
Now we're the two culture party.'[36]

The 1988 election had also seen the election of MPs from Quebec
better suited for service in cabinet, such as Gilles Loiselle and Jean
Corbeil, both of whom entered the cabinet in January 1989. Loiselle,
for example, a moderate nationalist, had served as a senior civil servant
in the Quebec government during the PQ years. His entry into cabinet

also affirmed the essential aim of the Mulroney approach to national reconciliation: striking an alliance with moderate nationalist forces in Quebec. Unlike Lucien Bouchard, however, Loiselle stayed with Mulroney, and not just up to the death of Meech Lake but well beyond. After the cabinet shuffle of January 1989, more than 28 per cent of ministers were from Quebec. The western contingent of ministers was slightly smaller, 25 per cent of cabinet membership. But, under the tutelage of Mazankowski, it occupied many of the key portfolios and positions within the two most important cabinet committees. In short, two regions – Quebec and the west – had come to represent the primary loci of power within cabinet.

The Electoral Aftermath

The changes brought about by the 1988 election results went beyond increasing the strength of Quebec within cabinet. It also signalled the decline of influence of certain other provinces and regions. As Tom McMillan, former minister from Prince Edward Island, where all four government MPs went down to defeat, stated: 'My biggest regret as a Prince Edward Islander, quite apart from the situation as it affects me, is that my province won't be in the forums in which priorities are set and resources are distributed.'[37] One of the first regions to feel the effects, however, was northwestern Ontario where James Kelleher had lost his seat. The understanding arrived at in cabinet establishing the conditions for providing federal support to Sysco – funds for its modernization were to be used only for improving rail production facilities, not those for structural steel, so as not to undercut Algoma in its markets[38] – essentially became a dead letter. Kelleher was no longer in cabinet to remind colleagues of the 1987 agreement. Elmer MacKay, re-elected in his Nova Scotia riding and defender of Sysco's interests, simply indicated that he could not recall any federal agreement; and Premier Buchanan, keenly interested in protecting funds for the provincially owned mill, also said he had 'never seen any such document.'[39]

The broader effects of changes in the electoral map and the relative weight of cabinet ministers could be seen early in 1989 with the expenditure-reduction exercise and the striking of the Expenditure Review Committee of cabinet. With the election behind them and the free trade legislation safely through the House, the government turned to the problem of the deficit. Since it was at the beginning of the electoral cycle, there was now an opportunity to reduce expenditures and introduce tax reforms with the view of enhancing revenues before pressures for spending proposals began building up again. When the results of the committee's deliberations were announced in the February budget and later in April with the tabling of the Estimates, one thing was evident: while the overall cuts were more limited in scope than anticipated, the actual cuts were most likely to be found where the Conservatives had suffered a decline in support, or where representation in cabinet was weak, or where both applicd.[40]

The heaviest single cut relative to population fell upon Prince Edward Island with the closure of the Canadian Forces air base at Summerside; the province had failed to elect a single Conservative and had a Liberal government. The other major air base scheduled for closing was located in a Conservative riding but in a province, Manitoba, where the party had lost two seats and whose minister, Jake Epp, had already lost previous battles in cabinet. A number of smaller bases – radar installations scattered throughout the country – were also scheduled for closing, and the two air bases had long been targeted by military planners as expendable. The air base closures, however, were more likely linked to the political vulnerability in which the locales found themselves than to any rational planning. The other major defence cutback, the shelving of plans to proceed with the construction of a fleet of nuclear-powered submarines, had little in the way of a regional impact. The only potential loser was the Saint John shipyard, which in the event had already been blessed with several years of work in the form of contracts for all twelve of the new frigates.

The broader effects of expenditure reductions were felt most strongly in Atlantic Canada. There the cuts, in combination with reduced unemployment insurance benefits and a sharp downturn in the fishing industry – a result of lower prices and reductions in fish quotas – helped exacerbate a widely held impression that the region was being ill done by. The Estimates tabled in April indicated a 24 per cent increase in ACOA spending for the fiscal year 1989–90, a consequence primarily of the grant commitments made prior to the election the previous fall. At the same time, however, Michael Wilson indicated that after 1990 funds available for regional development, and specifically for ACOA, would be reduced. In May 1989 Elmer MacKay, the new minister in charge of ACOA, announced that funding for the agency was being 'reprofiled': the $1.05 billion ACOA fund would be stretched out over a seven-year period rather than five years as first announced in 1988.[41] As well, ACOA officials announced changes in eligibility requirements with a view to putting greater emphasis on smaller projects. Projects costing over $200,000 were eligible only for interest rate buy-downs and loan insurance. After much complaint the level was raised to $500,000 for certain projects.

Underpinning the changes and the 'reprofiling' of ACOA's budget were the 1988 election results. Nova Scotia had sent only five Tory MPs where more were expected. Newfoundland, where the bulk of major project grants ended up, sent only two. And the ridings which had received some of the most substantial grants, Cape Breton–Highlands–Canso in Nova Scotia and Baie Verte and Cornerbrook in Newfoundland, had fallen to the Liberals. Despite the relatively poor election results, ministers and MPs still felt aggrieved in not having had more direct influence over ACOA spending. Furthermore, figures such as Bernard Valcourt, who became minister in 1989, were unhappy with ACOA's apparent neglect of the more rural areas in the Atlantic region and lack of support for infrastructure projects such as new roads. The changes, therefore, reflected the realignment of political forces: Wilson was permitted to trim back future budgetary expenditures on regional development; MacKay, minister for Nova Scotia, was made responsible for ACOA. In turn, MacKay took a more directly partisan approach. In appointing new Nova Scotia representatives to the advisory board, he chose four known Conservatives with close ties to either himself or the premier or both. In July rumours began surfacing over impending changes in ACOA's internal management; and a few weeks later McPhail, under attack from both officials in Finance and ministers from the region, left the ACOA presidency.[42]

In a separate but related development, negotiations over the renewal of the numerous subsidiary agreements under the ERDAs, most of which had expired on 31 March 1989, remained stalled, largely because the federal government was seeking to reduce both its absolute level of funding and its proportion of the cost-sharing arrangements.[43] Then, in a move that caught both provincial and ACOA officials offguard, the junior minister of tourism in Ottawa, Thomas Hockin, announced that the IST department would not be renewing the tourism subsidiary agreements with the provinces.[44] The remaining forty-four subsidiary agreements were the responsibility of ACOA, but officials there were working under direct orders from the cabinet's Expenditure Review Committee not to renew certain agreements and to seek increased provincial contributions. While some changes reflected efforts to provide the Nova Scotia minister with more direct leverage over ACOA, and while the prime minister was pointing to the overall increase in the level of transfer payments to the Atlantic region, the dominant impression was one of the region's declining influence within the circles that mattered in Ottawa.[45]

In examining the expenditure reduction exercise it is also important to note which sectors and regions remained relatively untouched. Among the areas which escaped the effects of the exercise was agriculture, the portfolio for which was in the hands of Mazankowski and which was of primary importance to the west. Energy also escaped relatively unscathed, although federal financial support for the OSLO project was deemed to be inadequate by the Alberta government and Imperial Oil, but, significantly, the Husky heavy oil upgrader in Lloydminster, a project of considerable importance to both Mazankowski and McKnight, actually benefited from a $51 million increase.[46] Also significant was the fact that pressures to spend money continued unabated, the best efforts of Finance Minister Wilson and his officials notwithstanding. The Expenditure Review Committee, which was effectively controlled by Mazankowski, and the committee ostensibly concerned with *reviewing* expenditures as opposed to making new expenditures, began dispensing money in early June 1989 from a special 'priorities fund' for those new projects considered to be of the utmost importance.[47]

Parochialism and Political Vulnerability

In many ways the Mulroney cabinet is testimony to the continuity and durability of the regional minister system in Canadian political life; and in certain respects it represents a return to the less troubled Mackenzie King period: that is, a limited number of major figures dominate large regions and operate within a system in which a premium is placed on brokerage-based connections and transactions. Despite initial efforts by both the prime minister and the bureaucracy to minimize the regional dimension in Ottawa decision-making, within two years the Mulroney government had come to adopt a system of ten regional ministers, each one having control over patronage and considerable say over matters directly affecting their province.

The Mulroney cabinet provided instances aplenty of regional ministerial influence and of ways of designing administrative arrangements to take into account the political needs of ministers. Not only was the system of ten 'political ministers' resurrected, but three special regional development agencies were created to give ministers opportunity to affect regional programming, and to be seen doing so, in the relevant regions. As well, the technique of resorting to appointments from the Senate for regional purposes was given a novel twist by having Senator Lowell Murray take special responsibility for ensuring the success of ACOA and maintaining discipline among the Atlantic ministers. Mazankowski provided the most clear-cut example of a minister using his portfolio, his clout within cabinet, and his network of close friends and colleagues in cabinet to ensure maximum benefits for the west and for Alberta in particular. Demands for a special regional development agency for the Atlantic region gave Mazankowski the opportunity to demand similar treatment for the west.[48] Hence the WDO initiative. Similarly, he succeeded in making support for Hibernia contingent upon like support for western mega-projects.

John Crosbie, in turn, showed a remarkable capacity to influence the activities not just of his own portfolios but also those of other ministers in areas that were deemed crucial to the well-being of Newfoundland. While his star dimmed after Newfoundland dropped from four government members in 1984 to two in 1988, he still retained control over all fisheries matters affecting the east coast. By the spring of 1989 it was openly acknowledged by fishing industry sources and in the press that quotas for various fish stocks and the allocations between inshore and offshore fishermen were being set directly by Crosbie rather than the minister of DFO, Thomas Siddon.[49] In his protégé Ross Reid, the new MP for St John's East, parliamentary secretary to the fisheries minister, and former official in the PMO, Crosbie had an efficient means of monitoring the activities of that department. Furthermore, as minister of international trade since March 1988, Crosbie already enjoyed considerable influence on the conduct of negotiations over the tricky Canada-France boundary dispute. When agreement between the two countries was finally struck in the spring of 1989, it was Crosbie who answered questions in the House on the effects of the agreement on allocations for east coast fishermen.[50] Similarly, in February of the same year it was Crosbie who announced the reductions in quotas for species such as the northern cod, resulting from the much more rapid depletion of those stocks than scientists had predicted. In doing so, Crosbie stressed that the brunt of the cuts were to be borne by the large offshore fishing trawlers based mainly in Nova Scotia. The quota for the largely Newfoundland-based inshore fishermen remained unchanged from the previous year. 'We're dealing with thousands of human beings, who live and breathe and need jobs,' he noted.[51] By the same token, in the aftermath of the April 1989 budget Crosbie became the primary, or certainly the most visible, cabinet member defending the government's record with respect to Atlantic Canada.[52]

The Mulroney government also provided illustrations of how cabinet and cabinet appointments could be used to bolster the party and individual candidates in regions of the country where electoral support was considered weak. In the last cabinet shuffle preceding the 1988 election, Gerry St Germain, MP for Mission–St Moody in British Columbia, became minister of state for forestry, a promotion that was seen as a response to the party's weak standings in public opinion polls in that province.[53] Similarly, the entry into cabinet of two new junior ministers, John McDermid from the Toronto area and Shirley Martin from the Niagara peninsula, who were made ministers of state for housing and transport respectively, was clearly linked to the fact that they represented ridings in regions considered vulnerable to electoral change.[54]

Such appointments can be seen as largely symbolic in nature, intended to convey an impression of an enhanced presence of the affected region or province in Ottawa. As Mulroney stated in the case of St Germain: 'I hope British Columbians will be pleased.'[55] Junior ministers, if only because they are both junior to the senior minister in the portfolio and inexperienced, cannot be expected to have serious clout. But even the limited status of a junior portfolio places the occupant a rung or two above the mass of regular MPs in the competition for scarce resources. The very limited resources available within the minor portfolio of minister of state for fitness and amateur sport did not prevent the minister, Jean Charest, from finding funds to support two separate track meets in his own riding of Sherbrooke, Quebec.[56]

The use of cabinet appointments to help bolster electoral support points to a more fundamental and inescapable factor, one that has shaped cabinet formation and the behaviour of individual ministers since confederation: the vulnerability of MPs, ministers, and prime ministers alike to personal electoral defeat. As pointed out earlier, the level of electoral competition is much higher in Canada than elsewhere, which in practical terms means that the likelihood of being defeated in one's own riding, even if the government as a whole is re-elected, is from three to five times higher than in the United States or Britain. In the 1988 elections in the United States, for example, the rates for both personal incumbency and party continuity for the House of Representatives were over 98 per cent; for the Senate the rates were over 85 per cent.[57] In the same month, in the Canadian federal election, the personal incumbency rate for the House of Commons was only slightly over 60 per cent; for party continuity (that is, the same party retaining the seat) it was approximately 75 per cent.[58] Among members of the Canadian federal cabinet, six went down to defeat, including James Kelleher from Sault Ste Marie, Flora Macdonald from Kingston–The Islands, Stewart McInnes from Halifax, Thomas McMillan from Prince Edward Island, Ray Hnatyshyn from Saskatoon, and the newly promoted Gerry St Germain from British Columbia.

The manner in which the free trade issue was played out in different regions, having a negative effect in the Atlantic Region and northwestern Ontario while having a positive effect in Quebec, no doubt goes some way to account for the defeat of Kelleher, McInnes, and McMillan. Yet it is telling that, with the possible exception of Kelleher, none of the defeated ministers were particularly noteworthy for having a pronounced regional perspective on issues or in making maximum use of their portfolios for regional or local purposes. Hnatyshyn eschewed the role; MacDonald, in heading the portfolio of employment and immigration, made explicit that, unlike her Liberal predecessors, she was going to minimize use of employment creation programs for partisan purposes; and McMillan had made clear early in his tenure as minister his negative views on 'the old regional baron system.'[59] McInnes, in a revealing comment during his campaign for re-election in the riding of Halifax, admitted to his failure to protect a major project in the riding from government cutbacks: '[With] the stop in the restoration work at the Citadel Hill, my government made a mistake.'[60] Extensive use of government resources to shore up one's riding is no guarantee of success, as demonstrated by Kelleher's efforts, yet in certain instances it likely can make a difference. The case of Lloyd Axworthy in Winnipeg in 1984 is one such example.

Electoral vulnerability, or certainly the perceptions and beliefs concerning one's political mortality, ultimately is a factor shaping the role played by the government as a whole. Essentially government becomes susceptible to a variety of local forces, and nowhere was this more evident than in the case of Lucien Bouchard's entry into federal politics in 1988. According to Alain Chiasson, a development officer employed by the region, the federal by-election in Lac St Jean, as well as the nearby provincial by-election, provided 'a golden opportunity to draw some attention on the issue,' the issue being the construction of the $45 million road.[61] 'Politicians are always more receptive, and more readily accessible to the regions, when they are on the campaign trail,' he explained. 'The political context was just perfect, so we decided to organize a big push.'[62] The riding and surrounding area duly received a pledge, directly from the prime minister, of a new road. But it was not only the new road and a variety of other future benefits for the riding to which the government succumbed; there was also the broader request of the Quebec provincial government that Ottawa refrain from extending its involvement in the direct delivery of regional development projects. As noted, the by-election was the catalyst that forced De Cotret to give up his own particular schemes for regional development and instead to come to terms with the Quebec government on a co-operative five-year agreement. This agreement essentially preserved the status quo of provincial dominance in the design and delivery of such programs.

The need not only to win a by-election in the final year of the government's mandate, but to do so on behalf of a high-profile minister who was potentially the next *chef du Québec*, made local and provincial factors unusually prominent. Yet this example of using the electoral process to local advantage is illustrative of the instrumentality of Quebec political attitudes, something that to a lesser extent is also true of the rest of the country. Evidence reveals that in Canada as a whole the level of partisan identification has generally been lower than in other countries.[63] While this has not led to high levels of electoral instability or the fragmentation of the party system, there has been a pattern of periodic sudden shifts – the Conservative landslides in 1958 and 1984, for example – a high level of turnover in individual seats, and frequent intervals of minority government.[64] The re-election of the Conservative government in 1988 marked the first time in thirty-five years that a party had won back-to-back majority governments, an achievement that had continually eluded the Liberals under both Pearson and Trudeau.

In most elections Quebec has often been the crucial variable in making or breaking a majority government, not only because of the large numbers of seats at stake but also because of the possibility of the wholesale turnover of seats on a scale that occurs but rarely in Ontario, for example. Thus in 1984 the largest block of seats lost by the Liberals was in Quebec. Furthermore, in recent years a good proportion of ridings in Quebec tend to be open question marks. Prior to the 1988 election the twenty-five or so ridings in the Quebec City region were all considered to be highly competitive, with electoral margins of one thousand votes or less.[65] The hypothesis that Quebec voters are more likely to defect from the party they voted for previously is given credence by the data displayed in Table 7 drawn from

TABLE 7

Vote in 1984 of all who voted Liberal in 1980 by language and residency (percentages)

	Quebec francophones	Non-Quebec francophones	All anglophones
Liberal	44.4	64.3	54.8
Conservative	51.9	28.6	36.7
NDP	3.7	7.1	8.5
Total	100.0	100.0	100.0
(N)	(295)	(70)	(496)

SOURCE: 1984 national election survey

the 1984 national election survey. Francophones resident in Quebec who had voted Liberal in 1980 were much more likely to vote Conservative in 1984 than either francophones or anglophones outside of Quebec. The issue of whether Quebec voters are more calculating and instrumental in their voting habits, or indeed whether they are more likely to vote as a block, cannot be settled here.[66] But certainly the greater potential of substantial shifts in that province creates a context in which leaders of both major political parties must pay careful heed to Quebec interests at both the constituency and provincial level.

It is also clear, however, that the party in power, and individual cabinet ministers in particular, also pay close heed to local and regional interests elsewhere, as evidenced by the anxiety of Mazankowski and McKnight to have the financial commitment for the Husky heavy oil upgrader in place before the election and the many efforts of MacKay on behalf of the riding of Central Nova. MacKay, like many ministers before him, demonstrated the highly parochial nature of many regional ministers and their frequent reluctance to deal with regional obligations outside of their particular area of the province. At one point, on the steps of Rideau Hall after the January 1989 cabinet shuffle, the prime minister stated that, in the absence of elected members from Prince Edward Island, MacKay would become the designated minister for that province. Later, when questioned about his new role, MacKay disavowed knowledge of having acquired such a responsibility, and there was no sign of his involvement in subsequent developments affecting the Island.[67] At the same time, the interests of broader regions were not necessarily neglected. Mazankowski, for example, with the assistance of McKnight, was able to find $27 million from the Western Diversification Fund to support the Action Committee on Western Canadian Low-Sulphur Coal, a project that essentially subsidized the transportation of western coal to Ontario to make it competitive with US coal and that was of benefit to all three of the westernmost provinces.[68]

Yet while adept in providing support for these essentially regional projects and in finding resources within the Ottawa system, ministers in the Mulroney government proved much less adept in developing their own autonomous regional agenda. Most of the projects promoted by regional ministers tended to be of long standing, and ones favoured by provincial governments. The Vancouver Island Pipeline, OSLO, Hibernia, increased market opportunities for western coal, and the like were all projects whose place on the political agenda was due much more to long-term lobbying by provincial interests and governments than to any independent initiative developed by regional ministers. Ministers may have been crucial in obtaining the necessary financial commitment from the federal cabinet but they were essentially acting in response to cues originating with provincial governments. In some instances provincial government prompting took the form of direct instructions and tutelage from the premier to the minister in question. In the case of MacKay, for example, Premier Buchanan would continually ride herd on the minister and remind him of his obligations, particularly when the minister showed signs of flagging or bending to arguments within cabinet on issues such as financial support for provincially owned Sysco.[69] In other instances ministers may have had their own political agenda. Nonetheless, given that particular projects loomed so large and were of such importance in the provincial scheme of things, they had but little choice but to provide open support to the provincial government in efforts to obtain federal assistance. Even had he wished to – which he certainly did not – for Crosbie it would have been political suicide to have provided less than full support for Hibernia.

Finally, it is worth noting the continuation of a practice that became evident at the time of the last Trudeau cabinet – namely, cabinet ministers openly and publicly indicating their differences with other ministers or even the prime minister in the name of protecting regional interests. Examples of this practice would be MacKay and Kelleher's drawn-out battle over the fates of steel mills in their respective provinces, the issue being settled only by Kelleher's electoral defeat; Crosbie's threat to resign and his demand for an apology from the government – which he received – over its handling of the Canada-France fisheries dispute; and Lucien Bouchard's stance on the importance of the notwithstanding clause in the constitution for protecting Quebec interests, a position that was exactly opposite to that of the prime minister. These were the most obvious examples, but one can find numerous lesser ones where ministers as well as individual MPs make clear to local constituencies their success in prying away from some other province or region a valued project or contract. Gerald Merrithew, for example, pointed with pride to the fact that all six of the second batch of frigates would be built in Saint John, New Brunswick, rather than being split with Quebec yards.[70]

Like their immediate predecessors in the last Trudeau cabinet, regional ministers under Mulroney were certainly more prominent and more powerful than their counterparts in the Pearson cabinets and in the first decade of the Trudeau era. While not enjoying the same level of support for provincially based activities, such as the help of the FEDCs and a designated role in the ERDA process provided during the 1982–4 period, Conservative ministers acting in their regional capacities did have certain informal powers as well as the support of specific agencies such as ACOA and WDO. The present-day cabinet may not represent the regional powerhouse it was under Laurier or King. Certainly regional ministers are less visible than they once were. Nor do ministers appear to perform the role they once did in linking regional interests with the centre or in defending unpopular government policies in the regions, a distinction generally attributed to ministers in the cabinets of Macdonald, King, and Laurier. Lucien Bouchard, while Quebec's man in Ottawa, was definitely not Ottawa's man in Quebec. Nonetheless, by giving voice and weight in cabinet to provincial concerns, present-day ministers acting in their regional capacity have increasingly come to represent a decentralizing force within the Ottawa executive-administrative system.

CHAPTER 12

Conclusion

This study began with the proposition that the role of the modern regional minister has been both undervalued and, contrary to received understanding, has actually become more important in crucial respects. I have sought to demonstrate the validity of this proposition by two means: by offering a reinterpretation of past practices, arguing that the halcyon days of cabinets composed of 'regional notables ... who powerfully asserted the needs of their provinces at the highest political level in the land'[1] were not always what they seemed; and by showing, through an examination of regional ministers in recent decades and with reference to specific case studies, that regional ministerial influence has been evident in a variety of domains. To be sure, cabinets composed of regional notables did exist: the Macdonald and Laurier cabinets and the Mackenzie King cabinet from 1935 to 1948, to give examples. But there were also cabinets in the earlier period that were flawed, badly so in some instances: the cabinets of Borden, Bennett, and even King during his first nine years as prime minister, to cite those cases where representation from provinces was incomplete or where the key representative from Quebec was either absent, incompetent, or lacking the confidence of significant political constituencies in Quebec. To the extent that broad characterizations of the past lead one to assume a smooth linear decline from earlier times to the present, they have likely led to misleading inferences.

More important, the highly variable role played by regional ministers both within specific cabinets and over time needs to be underscored. Even during the heyday of the King cabinet, which featured prominent regional figures such as Jimmy Gardiner, Ernest Lapointe, and C.D. Howe, representatives from provinces such as Alberta and Prince Edward Island were largely absent. Other provincial representatives, such as Angus L. MacDonald, premier of Nova Scotia before entering cabinet, found efforts on behalf of their province unavailing. It was during Laurier's time that provincial representation was likely more closely balanced, power more evenly divided, and, inter alia, consociational norms evolved that gave ministers effective veto over those policies directly affecting their province. In the post-1935 King cabinet, although Gardiner and Howe exercised influence well beyond their own province, this came at the expense of other provinces and their ministers. The ill-fated Stuart Garson, minister for Manitoba, was one such minister who suffered. Some regions lost, others gained. As well, a number of ministers, while paying close heed to the needs of their riding, played at best only a limited role in promoting the interests of their province. The deportment of Charles Tupper and W.S. Fielding, representatives from Nova Scotia in the Macdonald and Laurier cabinets respectively, provides a useful illustration in this regard.

The role, thus, was highly variable; and the term 'regional' itself contracted and expanded over time. In some instances it came to be understood as concerning largely local matters – the riding and perhaps immediate environs, combined with greater claim to goods and patronage compared to lesser ministers and mere MPs from elsewhere in the province; at other times it came to mean the province, such as during Laurier's time; and during the King era of the 1930s and 1940s, some ministers did indeed represent broad regions, the Canadian west in the case of Gardiner. At the same time one should keep in mind the relative size of provinces and regions. Ontario rarely had a single regional minister, although Howe came closest to occupying such a position. Yet to hold sway over a good portion of it – northwestern Ontario, for example – is significant in itself. To be minister for Quebec is a considerable achievement, given the typically large number of government MPs from that province and the size of the territory. It also points to the inherent obstacles that any aspirant to the Quebec lieutenancy must overcome in order to have authority over such a large caucus and to the difficulties that any prime minister faces in selecting and promoting a figure who commands both authority over the Quebec wing and the trust of the prime minister.

In short, any assessment of regional influence within the contemporary cabinet must be conducted in light of the long-term variability in the regional minister role. The advent of television and electioneering techniques focusing on the national leader of each party, beginning with John Diefenbaker in 1957, certainly eroded the standing of regional figures in the parties. In addition, during the 1960s regional ministers came to be overshadowed by the major rifts between Ottawa and the provinces, and especially between Ottawa and Quebec, and by the drama of first ministers' conferences. All of this also helps explain the neglect by political scientists in recent years of the regional dimension in cabinet decision-making. The increasing importance of federal-provincial summitry, the arrival of the institutionalized cabinet in the 1970s, and Pierre Trudeau's distrust of colleagues with independent power bases further impeded the efforts of ministers intent on representing regional interests and likely did lead to the attrition of regional influence.

Yet in many ways this attrition can be seen as a temporary phenomenon. By the mid-1970s the regional desks within the Prime Minister's Office had been eliminated, and the role of regional ministers as the 'political' or 'lead' minister for their respective province reaffirmed, including their control over patronage. More important, they were able to extend their influence into hitherto unexploited areas. The Treasury Board deconcentration scheme of 1975, which gave ministers specific opportunities to lobby for substantial government facilities to be located in their province or riding, is but one example. This pattern of expanding influence continued into the 1990s, and during the Mulroney era came to include significant control over the launching of new energy mega-projects.

There are, and will continue to be, major differences with the past. Contemporary regional ministers do have a lower profile than their predecessors, and in good part this relates to the decline of party. It is now rare for a present-day minister to carry a great deal of weight or even to have played much of a role in the party at the provincial level. Even federally their role within the party has typically been limited prior to their arrival in cabinet. Their power and cultivation of support bases often does not develop until after they gain access to the resources of their department, including perquisites such as exempt staff. In the present era individuals in cabinet who can be considered important as regional ministers more often than not arrived at their position through the skilful deployment of their portfolios: Romeo LeBlanc as minister of fisheries, Allan J. MacEachen as House leader, Lloyd Axworthy as minister of employment and immigration and later transport, and Donald Mazankowski as 'minister of everything.' In the past prominent figures such as Sifton, Gardiner, and Howe were more than simply adept in managing their departmental responsibilities. But at present the crucial resource is the ministerial portfolio. Party is still important, but primarily as one of the arenas in which ministers jockey for position and influence. Jimmy Gardiner's influence during the heyday of the King cabinet, David Smith points out, 'rested on the twin pillars of Commander of Agriculture *and* lieutenant of the Liberal party.'[2] And his party lieutenancy derived primarily from his position as former premier of Saskatchewan, chief Liberal organizer for western Canada, and operator of the most efficient political machine in the country. The contrast with someone like Axworthy – whose machine was primarily local, less stable, and made possible almost entirely by the resources available through his portfolio – could not be sharper.

Ministers in general may now have a lower profile compared to earlier times. Yet ironically over the past decade one can find a number of instances where ministers have flouted the long-standing norms of cabinet secrecy and solidarity, without any apparent harm to their careers. In 1981 ministers from Ontario and Quebec were in open dispute over the location of a Volkswagen parts plant. Lloyd Axworthy, while defending the government on some issues, such as the need to change the Crow's Nest Pass freight rate, at the same time became adroit in conveying to the citizens of Manitoba his differences with cabinet colleagues on a variety of issues. In the Mulroney cabinet the dispute between James Kelleher and Elmer MacKay over rail orders for steel plants located in their respective provinces cropped up regularly in news reports over a four-year period, and neither minister was averse to making public his particular side of the issue. John Crosbie, in turn, displayed no hesitation in publicly condemning his own government over alleged mishandling of the fisheries negotiations with France. As well, ministers in the Mulroney government were willing to criticize openly officials whom they felt were thwarting their objectives. Thus Elmer MacKay had little compunction in lambasting 'a couple of bureaucrats who won't know a coal mine if they fell over one or fell into one,' when officials in the Department of Industry, Science, and Technology declined to authorize funding for a coalmine in his riding, on the grounds of high costs and, indirectly, safety.[3] A hundred years earlier Charles Hibbert Tupper, in reproaching the deputy minister of railways for failing to let coal contracts to Tupper's constituents in the same area of Pictou county, at least confined his criticism of officials to personal correspondence with Prime Minister Macdonald.

In noting contrasts with the past, attention should be drawn to changes in the nature of Quebec representation within cabinet. The lack of such representation, specifically the lack of a dependable *chef* for that province, has led to the undoing of a number of cabinets, not least the Diefenbaker government of 1957–63. Yet even in those governments in which Quebec francophone figures played a prominent role, such as Lapointe in the King cabinet, they tended still to be underrepresented and excluded from economic portfolios. It was not until the 1960s under Lester Pearson that Quebec francophones obtained slight overrepresentation in cabinet relative to colleagues from other regions,[4] a pattern that has been maintained under Trudeau and Mulroney and which faltered only under Joe Clark when there was a paucity of elected Conservatives from Quebec in the 1979 election. Equally important, beginning with Trudeau, francophone Quebeckers have regularly come to occupy economic portfolios, including finance, energy, and Treasury Board. Combined with the remarkable cohesion of the Quebec caucus and the disciplined hierarchy generally prevailing among Quebec ministers, the unity and the effectiveness in achieving goals that Quebec ministers have demonstrated have given genuine meaning to the expression 'French power in Ottawa.' It is a development that is perhaps as important and formidable as it is unheralded. While attention has been focused on the need to bring Quebec into the constitutional fold, relatively little notice is taken of the remarkable changes that have been effected at the level of the federal cabinet. At the same time, it also explains the reluctance of Quebec to embrace Senate reform in so far as an elected Senate, in which the smaller provinces enjoy overrepresentation, could derogate power and influence from cabinet.

Of course, cabinet is not the only arena in Ottawa in which strong regional influences can be found. In the early post-confederation period, when party discipline was weak, the existence of several 'loose fish' made the prime minister, in seeking a workable parliamentary majority, much more sensitive to regional concerns.[5] Over time the development of rigid party discipline reduced the power of these regional enclaves in the Commons. The 1960s, however, saw the revival of regional caucuses and in particular that of the Quebec caucus. Since then they have become an important source of pressures and ideas as well as a significant resource for regional ministers.[6] Regional ministers must pay heed to the concerns presented to them by MPs and the provincial caucus as a whole. At the same time, being able to count on the unbroken support of the provincial caucus can be a powerful weapon within caucus at large and within cabinet. Ultimately, it is within cabinet that the crucial and final decisions are made, and in this sense the regional ministers stand at the apex of a system of regional representation that has its base within the Commons.

Developments in cabinet size and structure should not be ignored. The size of cabinet has gown considerably since the days of King, and Jeffrey Simpson's characterization of the present-day cabinet as a 'mini-caucus' draws attention to the fact that it is in the cabinet committees, and in only certain committees at that, where the truly important bargaining takes place.[7] In the later Trudeau cabinet it was membership in the Planning and Priorities and Economic and Regional Development committees that largely determined one's standing. Under Mulroney these committees, while still important, came to be superseded by the Operations and Expenditure Review committees. It was within the Ops Committee, whose existence was formalized only in January 1989, that proposals for presentation to P&P were screened and the government's future agenda largely determined. It is not without significance that those ministers formally designated as the lead minister for their province are also on these more important committees.

Shaping the Regional Minister Role

If the regional ministerial function can be seen as a constant in Canadian political life, three factors can be identified as important in shaping the regional role of ministers at any given time. First is simply individual personality. Some ministers become unusually prominent because they have both the will and the capacity to cultivate the role of regional spokesperson. The point is fairly obvious, but it does underscore the need to recognize the distinctiveness of each figure. Axworthy, therefore, was unique in the same sense that Howe and Gardiner were unique as individuals and not just because of particular circumstances. Secondly, there is the matter of the electoral system and electoral vulnerability. The point has been made both in this book and by others that by a variety of measures, the much lower proportion of safe seats in Canada for example, Canadian elections are much more competitive than elsewhere: ministers are susceptible to electoral defeat in their own ridings, even when the incumbent government is reelected. It is important in so far as it helps explain ministers' preoccupation with pork-barrelling, not necessarily on behalf of the province but more for their own particular corner of their province. A number of writers have commented on the persistence of localism in

Canadian politics: electoral competitiveness is both a manifestation of this localism and a reinforcer of it.

The third factor shaping the position of regional ministers past and present is the broader role played by the prime minister. In the first instance the prime minister determines the allocation of portfolios to individuals, though here he is constrained by what the election results bring forward in the way of raw material, particularly from the regions. As prime ministers from Macdonald onwards have frequently rued, the material is often far from adequate. Secondly, the prime minister determines the extent to which the role is made explicit as well as the scope of the role. Macdonald, for example, tended to restrict ministers largely to patronage while Laurier and King were more inclined to leave certain policy matters to their ministers, inasmuch as they related to regional concerns. Further, there is the issue of style generally, and of policy paradigms specifically, adopted by the prime minister. Here the difference between Trudeau and Mulroney provides a useful study in contrasts. The rational management paradigm of Trudeau and the brokerage paradigm of Mulroney led under the former to formalization of the regional minister role within the administrative-executive system, and under the latter to its largely informal development.[8] The 1980–4 period, which saw the rational management philosophy reach its zenith, also saw formal administrative support extended even to relatively weak regional ministers. Subsequently, the less formal allocation of regional duties to ministers under Mulroney has seen a few ministers dominate while others have done less well.

The Centrality of Regional Ministers

There is danger in viewing all ministerial behaviour through the lenses of the regional minister model. Much like a small child with a hammer, who sees everywhere nails requiring attention, it is possible to see the presence of regional ministers in every cubby-hole of Canadian politics. It is important therefore to establish those areas and conditions in and under which regional ministers are indeed influential. It also raises the broader question of centrality, whether regional ministers operate largely on the margins or whether they make their presence felt, in their regional capacity, where the truly momentous decisions are made.

In this study it was noted that in the case of very large projects, such as the initial decision to acquire the CF-18 fighter aircraft, when the options are limited and when the bureaucratic agencies involved in the decision are united, there is a lower likelihood of the decision being based primarily on regional criteria. Even so, in the case of the CF-18 acquisition there was still considerable log-rolling in order to make the decision more palatable to Quebec ministers and MPs. However, the case of the CF-18 maintenance contract, let to Canadair Limited by the Mulroney government on manifestly more political grounds, suggests that regional factors can and do play a role in fairly substantial decisions.

Substantial as these projects may be, there is one area where it is more difficult to detect the exercise of regional influence, except in the most general way; this is in transfer payments to both provinces and individuals. Keith Banting's comments on the effect of federalism on redistributive social policies likely also holds true for the role of regional ministers. Banting notes that federalism in Canada 'has not significantly altered ... redistributive goals, and has not diverted significant resources away from redistribution between individuals through the income security system.'[9] In similar fashion, little evidence exists of ministers having tapped directly into the social transfer system for regional purposes. To put it differently: while the fortunes of provinces and specific ridings can vary dramatically in terms of regional development grants, discretionary projects, and defence expenditures with the arrival and departure of cabinet representatives, this is not the case with respect to old age pensions to individuals or transfer payments to provinces under Established Programs Financing (EPF), the Canada Assistance Plan, or the fiscal equalization program. Thus for the fiscal year 1988–9 over $54 billion of the $133 billion total federal budget was allocated to transfers to persons ($30 billion) and transfers to other levels of government ($24 billion), with old age security benefits securing the largest single amount ($15 billion). Discounting public debt charges ($33 billion), this represents more than half of total budgetary expenditures.[10] The category of 'major subsidies and transfers' – which includes expenditures on agriculture ($2.6 billion), industrial and regional development ($1.6 billion), and job creation and training ($1.8 billion), $11.2 billion all told[11] – contains those items that are much more susceptible to the machinations of regional ministers. To a lesser extent this also holds true for payments to crown corporations ($4.4 billion), national defence ($11 billion), and international development assistance ($2.8 billion).[12]

To the extent that regional ministers are involved in income transfer programs, they generally tend to be supportive of them. MacEachen, for example, as minister of health during the 1960s, was instrumental in steering the medicare legislation through cabinet, preserving the intent of universality and accessibility of the program in the face of strong opposition from the right wing in cabinet. This kind of influence is different, however, from being able to direct disproportionate benefits to a particular province. The exception is likely the Unemployment Insurance Program (UIC), where eligibility requirements and duration of benefits are regionally tailored, and where periodic revisions in the regulations are subject to a degree of regional minister input. Certainly proposals for the removal of the special UIC provisions for fishermen are vehemently opposed by ministers and MPs from the affected areas. Yet to the extent that the overall level of social expenditures may be pushed upward through the efforts of regional ministers, it should be noted that in comparative terms Canadian expenditures on social welfare, while higher than those of the United States on a per capita basis, still fall short of the levels obtaining in many of the north European countries.[13] Furthermore, in the one area where ministers from the peripheries would have a direct interest in pushing up expenditures – regional development – Canada has consistently spent less than, for example, Great Britain,[14] a country which is unitary rather than federal and where the concept of regional ministers is largely alien.

The above discussion of budgetary categories provides only a rough indicator of the possible outer reaches of regional ministerial influence. Furthermore, within the more likely budgetary categories such as 'major subsidies' it should not be thought that all or even a majority of expenditures are discretionary or that they would not have taken place without the intervention of a minister. It is in the character of many of the projects targeted by regional ministers that they are deemed necessary, by line officials often, or would have been put in place in any event. What distinguishes them as special projects is that the minister in question has managed to have them located in his or her province or, better yet, in his or her riding, or to have advanced the timetable for their construction, frequently at additional cost. Thus, the $93 million disease control laboratory obtained for Winnipeg by Jake Epp had long been in the planning stages. As Epp conceded, there were extra unspecified costs in having it in Winnipeg rather than in Ottawa; it is these costs that can be properly considered the regional ministerial premium as it were. While one can point to specific projects or expenditures that would never have existed or been made without such ministerial intervention – the NCR-Cadcam Centre in

Winnipeg, the continued operation of heavy water plants in Cape Breton, the Lac St Jean highway in Quebec – these are perhaps not as common as projects already in the planning stages and deemed necessary by line departments but which end up being located in particular locations for largely political reasons.

At the same time it is worth mentioning the phenomenon of expenditures that are *not* made precisely because of the realization that regional factors will inflate costs to unmanageable levels. In 1988 Transport Minister John Crosbie cancelled the purchase of 130 new double-decker rail cars for VIA Rail because the original estimate of $2.2 billion grew by more than $500 million as a result of plans to split production of the cars between UTDC in Ontario and Bombardier in Quebec. A much more cost-effective means would have seen the two companies bid against each other. However, the fact that ministers from neither Ontario nor Quebec would have tolerated having the entire project go to the one province or the other effectively precluded such a strategy.[15] As well, it is conceivable that, in light of the earlier CF-18 maintenance contract, neither corporation had been willing to engage in a competition for fear of having the result later overturned by a cabinet decision.

In summary, it is quite possible that the clout of regional ministers is found primarily on the margin. It is, however, still a good-sized margin, one that could conceivably expand in the future. As successive ministers of finance succeed in reducing the cash outlays to the provinces under equalization and EPF, and in clawing back old age allowances from better-off pensioners, this may leave more room for discretionary, project-oriented expenditures. As well, there is the lingering proposal of the Royal Commission on Economic Union (the Macdonald Commission) to increase 'administrative support for regional ministers.' In their words: 'We wish to strengthen this dimension of our institutional arrangements.'[16] Should this recommendation be adopted, it would over time likely enhance the capacity of ministers to analyse, and subsequently to influence, an even broader range of expenditures than at present. As noted in this study, with the decline of patronage as an instrument of political mobilization, ministers have increasingly turned to block expenditures as an alternative, and since the mid-1960s the opportunities for influencing such expenditures have increased. In short, there is likelihood that in future their role in this area will expand rather than contract.

While the efforts of ministers on regional issues may affect only a minority of total expenditures, the same cannot be said for the proportion of time they actually devote to those concerns. The 1912 Murray report commented on the extraordinary amount of cabinet business devoted to matters such as 'the acceptance of a tender for the erection of a pump, the promotion of a clerk from one grade to another, and the appointment of a lighthouse keeper or an exciseman.'[17] These were all matters in which ministers from the affected regions had a clear interest. What is remarkable is how little has changed over the intervening years. The order-in-council instrument, which requires – at least in theory – the collective approval of cabinet for even the most minor action of ministers and whose use Murray recommended be sharply curtailed, is still in place. Ministers such as Lloyd Axworthy readily admit that the vast majority of their time was spent on regional concerns.[18] Sectorally oriented ministers such as Jean-Luc Pépin, in turn, complain that more than half their time was spent fending off the imprecations of regional ministers.[19] Donald Savoie, academic, civil servant, and close observer of federal policy-making, writes: 'Anyone who has attended a cabinet or cabinet committee meeting – particularly the Economic Development Committee – knows full well that the clash of regional interests dominates the discussion.'[20] Savoie further notes that cabinet tends to be populated by 'process participants,' ministers who 'take particular delight in striking deals ... Projects are what matters and the more the better. They will look to their own departments to come up with specific projects for their own ridings or for the regions for which they are responsible.'[21] In contrast, those ministers labelled as 'departmental participants,' that is, prone to push their department's goals and interests as defined by officials, are in a minority. 'In any event, ministers suffering from departmentalitis are quickly spotted by their colleagues and they will find it more difficult to be heard in cabinet.'[22]

The regional predilections of ministers and the sectoral responsibilities of departments lie at the heart of what is referred to as the clash of 'space versus function.'[23] Line department officials, responding to what they see as important national constituencies, often find it difficult to focus the attention of their minister on sectoral issues or to prevent him or her from diverting monies from a national program to a regional project. The case of Axworthy, discussed in detail in chapters 8 and 9, brings out most explicitly the depth of feelings generated by both sides on the issue. The same tensions were evident in the portfolios managed by Romeo LeBlanc and Pierre De Bané, and were also evident in the Mulroney cabinet. For example, shortly after his departure from the Privy Council Office in the summer of 1989,

Dalton Camp, adviser to the prime minister and proponent of regional development, had some less than kind words for 'the small bores in Finance, Treasury Board, and latterly in the Prime Minister's office, who have opposed ACOA from the outset.' This was in connection with the cuts in ACOA's budget and the alleged 'shabby' removal of Donald McPhail, president of the agency.[24]

Yet, as in the case of the possible impact on overall expenditures, one should not overestimate the extent of differences between political heads and their permanent staff. Departments and departmental officials, as a result of long experience, are able to adapt themselves to a degree to the regional needs of ministers. In Transport, for example, officials will take pains to put extra monies into the minister's home province, sprucing up lighthouses and wharves for an Atlantic minister, grain elevators and branch lines for a western minister. Furthermore, a minister's preoccupation with regional matters can also give freer rein to officials in those domains where a few regional interests are at stake. In CEIC, for example, Axworthy and his staff were content to leave the issue of office automation mainly to officials. As well, regional and departmental needs are not always incompatible. Again with Transport, when Crosbie became minister in 1986 officials in the marine administration of the department heralded the move, seeing it as an opportunity to obtain a stronger profile and more resources relative to the air and surface administrations.[25] The previous ministerial incumbents, Axworthy and Mazankowski, had been from the west; Crosbie was the first minister from the Atlantic since Donald Jamieson in the early seventies.

These efforts of line officials notwithstanding, in recent years they have proved insufficient in the eyes of ministers. The past decade has witnessed both Liberal and Conservative governments seeking ways to circumvent the existing machinery and to develop programs and alternative mechanisms to serve the regional needs of cabinet. A number of such programs, mechanisms, and agencies were examined in this study: the Economic and Regional Development Agreements (ER-DAs), the Special Employment Initiative (SEI), the Special Recovery Capital Projects Program (SRCPP), and the three regional development agencies established under Mulroney – ACOA, the Western Diversification Office/Strategy (WDO), and the Northern Ontario Development Agency (Fed-Nor). These agencies and programs have had varied success. They have provided regional ministers with more influence over a greater range of expenditures; but at the same time they frequently threaten to bring the government as a whole into disrepute, as was the case with the SEI, or prove difficult to manage, as was true of the SRCPP. Indeed SRCPP, with its specially designed fast-track procedures to expedite approval of major projects through Treasury Board, was not quite fast enough to match the speed of the electoral cycle.

It is the tension between the electoral cycle and the need to plan and administer carefully that is particularly problematic. The electoral needs of ministers and government MPs provide the impetus for establishing agencies such as ACOA in the first instance. Yet to avoid destroying the credibility of the government both within and outside the region through wanton or highly partisan expenditures, the implementation of the agency and its programs has to be carefully managed. This the minister responsible for ACOA, Senator Lowell Murray, and ACOA officials managed to do, at least initially and at the expense of delaying the start of the ACOA 'action' program. But in the final run-up to the election, ministerial pressures resulted in a vast increase in grants awarded, administrative mechanisms not coping, and multi-million-dollar grants being made to favoured ridings in the region. In the post-election phase, ACOA's budget, under fire from Finance, was substantially reduced and the agency's programs reorganized. As the next election campaign begins to loom there will likely be renewed pressures to replenish resources and, once again, hasty and unplanned expenditures will be made to fit the perceived electoral needs of ministers and government MPs. Under these circumstances the design and delivery of regional development programs is probably less than optimal. Equally important, as evidenced by Dalton Camp's bitter recriminations, the pattern of sudden expenditure increases and decreases feeds the prejudices of both Ottawa-based officials and regional ministers.

Intrastate Federalism, Cabinet, and Senate Reform

It is not only the connection between ministerial needs and the electoral cycle that proves problematic. So, too, is the link between regional ministers and provincial governments. In the literature on the representation of regional interests in central institutions, a distinction is drawn between provincialist and centralist versions of intrastate federalism.[26] The former entails direct provincial representation in central institutions, for example, the direct provincial appointment of senators; the latter involves 'making the central government more responsive to territorial diversities in ways which bypass provincial governments.'[27] As its label implies, this type of intrastate federalism is intended to be centralizing in its effects, linking Ottawa and the peripheries more tightly together at the expense of provincial government influence.

Clearly the efforts of the 1980–4 Trudeau government at direct delivery through ERDAS, SRCPP, and the like, giving ministers opportunities to establish direct links with regional constituencies and to bypass provincial governments, fit the definition of centralist intrastate federalism. As for the Mulroney government, it also retained direct delivery in fields such as regional development. Yet, the centralist label notwithstanding, the actual effects of direct delivery have been in many ways profoundly decentralizing. Within some of the affected agencies, for example the Ministry of State for Economic and Regional Development (MSERD), the same tensions characterizing federal-provincial relations over issues such as energy reappeared in the form of debates between MSERD's federal economic development co-ordinators (FEDCs) and its Ottawa-based officials. Furthermore, the thrust towards direct delivery was frequently transformed into something more akin to provincial delivery in which the rules were bent to accommodate provincial demands. Numerous instances of this could be found within the ERDAS, within the SRCPP, and, under Mulroney, most concretely in the regional development agreement struck with Quebec in the summer of 1988.

The reason for the thwarting of direct delivery relates in part to the complexities of modern federalism. There are very few areas in which the federal government can act unilaterally, and unilateral action is what direct delivery essentially implies. Invariably Ottawa finds itself having to come to grips with provincial government jurisdiction. Equally important, however, the pressures to circumvent the rules of the direct delivery regime frequently come from the regional ministers, even in instances where the federal government could conceivably act on its own or when ministers were often keenest in adopting direct delivery in the first instance. Federal-provincial tension frequently spells stalemate and ministers often see it in their interest to remove the obstacles to the flow of money into their provinces or regions, particularly if a favoured project is at stake. If the problem can be resolved by allowing provincial governments to participate in the delivery of programs, then expediency may well demand that the principle of visibility and direct delivery be suspended. Even where direct delivery is maintained, the projects in question are often ones that are already high on the agenda of provincial governments.

This brings us to a decisive point: the capacity of provincial governments to bring pressure on the federal government through regional ministers. The evidence suggests that the federal cabinet does have much more of an intrastate character than is generally conceded, despite the absence of direct partisan links and the limited mobility of senior politicians between the two levels of government. Even under conditions of adversity vis-à-vis specific provinces, federal ministers are still capable of acting as spear-carriers for provincial governments. Thus in 1981, when the federal Liberals and the Parti Québécois were locked in mortal combat, the Quebec federal Liberal caucus and its ministers actively lobbied on behalf of a Montreal location for the Volkswagen parts factory, a project initially espoused by the Quebec government.

One of the most striking phenomena, however, is the extensive log-rolling and in some instances the development of distinct alliances between regional ministers and provincial governments, regardless of party affiliation. The case of Lloyd Axworthy presents the clearest example of a coalition of political interests based in Manitoba that involved participants from federal, provincial, and municipal governments. The Axworthy network was the most obvious illustration from the 1980–4 period, but there were several other ministers equally adept in the art of federal-provincial log-rolling. Romeo LeBlanc, throughout his career as minister, was in close contact with Richard Hatfield, Conservative premier of New Brunswick. Allan MacEachen was past master in striking reciprocal deals with Nova Scotia premiers, as well as with cabinet colleagues, in order to ensure that desired projects, ranging from oil refineries to nautical institutes, were placed in Cape Breton. In the Trudeau government it appears that the link between the minister for the province and the premier was carefully protected. According to LeBlanc, it was standard practice for the regional minister to be invited to meetings between the premier and federal line ministers. And, LeBlanc recalls, at such meetings there were instances when he sided with Hatfield on an issue rather than with his cabinet colleague.[28] The existence of these cross-partisan linkages undermines, at least in part, the widely accepted tenet that in Canada 'Cabinet solidarity and strong parties make it impossible for regional cabinet ministers to muster cross-party support on regional matters.'[29]

The motives of regional ministers in pressing provincial interests can be traced in the first instance to the need to protect their riding. As one minister put it: 'the constituency is where the rubber meets the road.'[30] The much higher level of electoral vulnerability in Canada

compared to elsewhere has been noted. As illustrated by the arrangement between MacKay and the Nova Scotia government concerning
the disposition of the $200 million offshore development fund, federal-
provincial log-rolling can be an ideal way of servicing one's riding:
new roads in Pictou County for MacKay, a variety of infrastructure
projects elsewhere in the province. Such arrangements also demonstrate that federal leaders are often just as regionally centred, parochial even, as their provincial counterparts.

It might appear then that regional ministers take their cues from
provincial governments and that at best they are mere conduits for
provincial input into federal policy-making. This is not wholly accurate. Provincial governments are not the only source of information
or cues. The media in Canada, and particularly the print media, are
provincially based, oriented towards provincial audiences, and have
been shown to play an important role in setting the political agenda.[31]
Business interests and the people employed by them, as Jake Epp discovered in the case of the aerospace industry in Manitoba, can make
their presence felt in various ways, including direct visits to the regional minister. Business associations are frequently organized on a
provincial basis or, in the case of national associations, strongly con-
federal in structure to allow provincial branches considerable autonomy. This development is more pronounced in Canada than in other
federations if only because of the particular distribution of powers
between federal and provincial governments.[32] Finally, regional ministers, despite their propensity to look after their own riding first, still
identify with their province and are interested in its well-being. LeBlanc,
for example, readily admits that even on national decisions only re-
motely affecting his province, 'my concern as New Brunswicker actually clouded my judgement a little bit.'[33]

Even in their capacity as conduit, the minister still plays a crucial
role. In Manitoba, when Axworthy ceased to be minister, provincial
fortunes dropped precipitously. Similarly, in Newfoundland the arrival
of John Crosbie as the province's voice in cabinet was perceived to
make a world of difference, at least in the eyes of officials, with respect
to fisheries and offshore resources. Furthermore, Crosbie did not simply convey provincial views to Ottawa; he also provided Newfoundland
officials with insights into the opportunities and roadblocks existing
within the Ottawa system. In Prince Edward Island it is unlikely that
the Canadian forces base at Summerside would have suffered the in-
dignity of sudden closure – the economic equivalent in Ontario of
shutting down the General Motors plant in Oshawa – had the province

enjoyed reasonably strong representation in cabinet. In short, regional ministers are an important part of the equation in determining success or failure in protecting or promoting the province's interests within Ottawa circles and especially within cabinet. That the provinces do indeed consider this important is reflected in their concern over representation in the House of Commons and their resistance to any moves in the direction of a system providing greater voter equality. As John Courtney writes:

> Given the emphasis placed on the cabinet as the principal federal representational institution, any change to the formula for redistributing the seats among the provinces is in practical terms almost out of the question. Indeed with the acceptance of the unanimity amendment provision (s. 41) of the Constitution Act, 1982, the consent of all provinces and of both houses of parliament would be needed to alter or abandon the senatorial floor guarantee for Commons representation. It is impossible to conceive of any of the smaller provinces agreeing to end their inflated protection of parliamentary seats when that provides them with a virtually assured presence at the cabinet table.[34]

For the majority of provinces, including all four in the Atlantic region that depend upon Ottawa for close to half their revenues, the success in extracting funding beyond the basic transfer payments is in part based on the presence of strong representation in cabinet. At the same time, in their position as interlocutors, regional ministers are frequently able to put their own imprint on the project or program, whether in the form of direct benefits for their riding or simply in the design and delivery of a program that fits with their conception of what is good or desirable for their province or broader region. In so far as they, and most often they alone, are responsible for representing the claims of others to cabinet, cabinet committees, or individual ministers, they are often in a position to mould the ultimate decision, either by throwing their weight behind an issue or by soft-pedalling it. Beyond this, entrepreneurial regional ministers can exercise a great deal of influence by exploiting the opportunities that often exist in the interstices between various government programs and jurisdictions. Over the past decade several regional ministers have flourished, possibly because of, rather than despite, the intractability of the administrative state and the competitive nature of modern federalism.

Yet there still remains the all-important question of regional ministers' effectiveness, not necessarily in the delivery of benefits to their regions but in linking regional populations more closely with the centre, of being able to defend unpopular government policies, and in ensuring support for the broader goals of government and for the government itself at election time. This, after all, was the quality attributed to the cabinets of Macdonald, Laurier, and King. On the one hand, in the Trudeau and Mulroney cabinets there have been examples of several ministers preoccupied with channelling federal largesse primarily to their own ridings. On the other hand, it has been argued that the broader, nation-building efforts of a minister such as Mazankowski have been appreciated by neither Conservative provincial governments nor voters in western Canada, at least not in the sense of enhancing the legitimacy of the federal government and central institutions.[35] Mazankowski and others appear to lack stature in comparison both with present-day premiers and with past ministers such as Gardiner and Lapointe. Lucien Bouchard, during his brief tenure as minister, likely did enjoy relatively greater prominence within Quebec; but at the same time, in representing Quebec interests in Ottawa, he was uncompromising, public, and incautious to a degree that Lapointe or virtually any of his predecessors would never have attempted.[36] Certainly federal ministers are vulnerable to charges by provincial politicians that they did little either to promote the Meech Lake Accord in their regions, for example, or to take a stronger national stand.[37] The limited conciliation between Ottawa, Quebec, and some of the provincial governments that did occur prior to the death of the Meech Lake Accord can be attributed primarily to the role played by Mulroney himself. It is in their perceived failure to play a major role in bringing the regions into a larger, shared sense of national identity that the difference between traditional and contemporary regional ministers remains most evident.

This important lacuna suggests there may well be a need for institutional change, at least in order to provide a more visible presence of the regions at the centre. With the stillborn 1990 'first ministers' agreement,' it appears, notwithstanding the failure of the Meech Lake Accord, that in the long run Senate reform is still the most likely vehicle to bring about such an improvement.[38] Whether a newly revised and elected Senate will succeed in doing so is problematic, if only because of the host of contingent factors that have a bearing on the desired outcome. In a reformed Senate, even seemingly minor institutional features can have unpredictable effects.[39] Certainly, the Triple

E proposal (equal, elected, and effective), as originally recommended by the Alberta government, by entrenching an inherent clash between an 'independent' chamber and parliamentary government would lead, at worst, to frequent constitutional crisis and stalemate and, at a minimum, to erosion of cabinet authority and thus reduction in the power of regional ministers. Furthermore, elected senators who have power but no responsibility are unlikely to develop strong loyalties to central governing institutions.

Yet an elected Senate is not necessarily incompatible with cabinet government. Certainly the 1990 first ministers' agreement was intent in reconciling the two. Thus, for example, the proposal for an elected Senate made by the Royal Commission on the Economic Union in 1985 would allow senators to hold portfolios and enter cabinet as full members, and thus be formally integrated into our system of parliamentary government, something that would not be possible under the Triple E scheme.[40] According to Peter Aucoin, this approach, including senatorial appointment to cabinet, would actually strengthen both the overall status of the Senate and the role of cabinet as a regionally representative body: 'Precisely because partisanship and party government would encompass the Senate, the appointment of Senators to the cabinet would enhance its role. In fact, this could be extended so that the cabinet included at least one senator from each province ... A cabinet including a number of senators should serve to reinforce not just the form but the substance of the original purpose of regional representation in the cabinet.'[41]

Especially if the complementary proposal of proportional representation (PR) were to be used in electing senators, it would provide prospective regional ministers from the second chamber with a broader and more stable base from which to develop their assessments of provincial and regional needs and to press their claims in cabinet. In particular it would break the straitjacket in which many regional ministers currently find themselves of being dependent on a very narrow and often highly competitive electoral constituency, with all the attendant pressures to engage in parochial behaviour. It would also give them greater freedom to develop policy positions independent of those put forward by provincial governments yet still sensitive to the concerns of provincial populations. This alone might lead both to more visible as well as more substantive representation of regional interests. Furthermore, PR would greatly reduce the likelihood of any one province lacking government members in the Senate and hence representation in cabinet.

Whether politicians from the regions will take advantage of such new institutional arrangements to develop a broader and more independent perspective on provincial issues, and to play a more integrative role, must necessarily remain a matter of speculation. Specific outcomes, desirable or otherwise, depend on more than institutional design. Individual proclivities and beliefs of politicians need to be taken into account, and developments within the electorate, particularly in western Canada, may well so seriously undermine the standing of the mainline parties that even with PR there may be a paucity of elected senators of the government party who could enter cabinet.

These several caveats notwithstanding, the one remaining constant is likely the fact of regional sentiments and interests continuing to make themselves felt in the exercise of executive leadership and administration at the federal level. Furthermore, with the temporary suspension of all formal first ministers' conferences in the aftermath of Meech Lake, and the willingness of most Quebec Conservatives to remain both in the government caucus and in cabinet, this means that in the short term cabinet will likely become more, not less, important as an instrument of national conciliation. As well, despite the increasing Americanization of Canadian politics – with the judicialization of rights, for example, or the possibility of adopting direct democracy procedures such as the referendum – it is improbable that Canada will abandon the basic Westminster model of cabinet government altogether. The prospect remains strong, therefore, that the cabinet as we know it will continue to stand at the apex of federal government institutions. Equally likely, this body will continue to be thoroughly alive to the myriad pressures and nuances involved in the representation of regional interests.

Notes

Chapter One

1 Alan C. Cairns, *From Interstate to Intrastate Federalism in Canada* (Kingston: Institute of Intergovernmental Relations 1979), 6

2 D.V. Smiley, *Canada in Question: Federalism in the Eighties* (Toronto: McGraw-Hill Ryerson 1980), 134

3 A. Paul Pross, 'Space, Function, and Interest: The Problem of Legitimacy in the Canadian State' in O.P. Dwivedi, ed., *The Administrative State in Canada: Essays for J.E. Hodgetts* (Toronto: University of Toronto Press 1982), 122

4 J.R. Mallory, 'The Macdonald Commission,' *Canadian Journal of Political Science* 19 (September 1986): 609. Certainly in press reports on the distribution of patronage plums, items ranging from clam-fishing licences in Nova Scotia to tugboat contracts in western Canada, the 'senior' or 'political' ministers for those provinces appear to figure prominently. For example, see 'Clams for the taking,' *Globe and Mail*, 30 January 1986: A6; 'Taxpayers miss boat in reversed decision over contract for tug,' ibid., 13 February 1986: A13.

5 See, for example, Peter McCormick, Ernest C. Manning, and Gordon Gibson, 'Regional Representation in Canada' in J. Paul Johnston and Harvey E. Pasis, eds., *Representation and Electoral Systems: Canadian Perspectives* (Scarborough: Prentice-Hall 1990), 95–106. Their earlier work formed the basis for the Alberta government's Triple E Senate proposal ('equal, elected, and effective'). Government of Alberta, *Report of the Alberta Select Special Committee on Senate Reform* (Edmonton: Plains Publishing, March 1985)

6 David E. Smith, *The Regional Decline of a National Party: Liberals on the Prairies* (Toronto: University of Toronto Press 1981), 138

7 D.V. Smiley and R.L. Watts, *Intrastate Federalism in Canada*: Vol. 39, Research Studies of the Royal Commission on the Economic Union and

Development Prospects for Canada (Toronto: University of Toronto
Press 1985), 82

8 Smiley, *Canada in Question*; Richard Simeon, *Federal-Provincial Diplomacy: The Making of Recent Policy in Canada* (Toronto: University of Toronto Press 1972); see especially the latter's comments on the limited role of cabinet in accommodating provincial interests, 27–9.

9 Roger Gibbins, *Regionalism: Territorial Politics in Canada and the United States* (Toronto: Butterworth 1982), 67

10 Frederick J. Fletcher, 'Mass Media and Parliamentary Elections in Canada,' *Legislative Studies Quarterly* 12 (August 1987): 366

11 J.S. Dupré, 'The Workability of Executive Federalism in Canada' in H. Bakvis and W. Chandler, eds., *Federalism and the Role of the State* (Toronto: University of Toronto Press 1987), 238–9; Pross, 'Space, Function, and Interest,' 107–29

12 This Framework is based loosely on, and adapted from, the one used by Simeon in *Federal-Provincial Diplomacy*, 12–16.

13 Herman Bakvis, 'Regional Politics and Policy in the Mulroney Cabinet, 1984–88: Towards a Theory of the Regional Minister System in Canada,' *Canadian Public Policy* 15 (June 1989): 121–34

14 For a discussion of different definitions of 'regions' in Canada, see Janine Brodie, *The Political Economy of Canadian Regionalism* (Toronto: Harcourt Brace Jovanovich 1990), ch. 1.

15 See, for example, M.J. Trebilcock, M. Chandler, M. Gunderson, P. Halpern, and J. Quinn, *The Political Economy of Business Bailouts*, vol. 1 (Toronto: Ontario Economic Council 1985), 261–3.

16 Eric A. Nordlinger, *On the Autonomy of the Democratic State* (Cambridge, MA: Harvard University Press 1981), 130–2

17 Simeon, *Federal-Provincial Diplomacy*, 124–45

18 On central agencies and PEMS, see Colin Campbell, *Governments under Stress: Political Executives and Key Bureaucrats in Washington, London, and Ottawa* (Toronto: University of Toronto Press 1983), 77–99, 147–66, 194–200.

19 For a detailed examination of the budgetary process, see Donald J. Savoie, *The Politics of Public Spending in Canada* (Toronto: University of Toronto Press 1990).

20 Paul G. Thomas, 'The Role of National Party Caucuses' in P. Aucoin, ed., *Party Government and Regional Representation in Canada*: Vol. 36, Research Studies of the Royal Commission on the Economic Union and Development Prospects for Canada (Toronto: University of Toronto Press 1985), 69–136

21 J.A.A. Lovink, 'Is Canadian Politics too Competitive?' *Canadian Journal of Political Science* 6 (September 1973): 341–79

22 C.E.S. Franks, *The Parliament of Canada* (Toronto: University of Toronto Press 1987), 75–9

23 Cairns, *From Interstate to Intrastate Federalism*

24 For much of Canada's history all eleven governments have actively guarded and promoted their autonomy and jurisdictional authority, which in the last two decades has led to a relatively permanent state of 'competitive' federalism, in which federal and provincial governments are embraced in continual conflict. The title, and the contents, of David Milne's book, *Tug of War: Ottawa and the Provinces under Trudeau and Mulroney* (Toronto: Lorimer 1986), capture the full flavour of this embrace, a state of affairs most Canadian political scientists attribute to our constitutional framework; see, for example, Alan C. Cairns, 'The Governments and Societies of Canadian Federalism,' *Canadian Journal of Political Science* 10 (1977): 695–726. Garth Stevenson is among a minority stressing the predominant role of provincial and American economic interests in strengthening the role of the provinces (*Unfilled Union: Canadian Federalism and National Unity*, 3rd ed. [Toronto: Gage 1989]. For a view challenging the province-building thesis, see R.A. Young, Philippe Faucher, and André Blais, 'The Concept of Province-Building: A Critique,' *Canadian Journal of Political Science* 17 (December 1984): 783–818. Regardless, there is little doubt that the present constitutional framework structures the conduct of federal-provincial affairs.

25 Kenneth McRoberts, 'Unilaterism, Bilateralism and Multilateralism: Approaches to Canadian Federalism' in R. Simeon, ed., *Intergovernmental Relations*: Vol. 63, Research Studies of the Royal Commission on the Economic Union and Development Prospects for Canada (Toronto: University of Toronto Press 1985), 71–129

26 See the listing of nearly three-hundred federal-provincial activities for which line departments have primary responsibility in *Federal-Provincial Programs and Activities: A Descriptive Inventory* (Ottawa: Government of Canada, Federal-Provincial Relations Office 1984).

27 Industrial development programs are the most prominent of these but they also include social programs such as unemployment insurance. See Peter Aucoin and Herman Bakvis, *The Centralization-Decentralization Conundrum* (Halifax: Institute for Research on Public Policy 1988).

28 Andrew F. Johnson, 'A Minister as an Agent of Policy Change: The Case of Unemployment Insurance in the Seventies,' *Canadian Public Administration* 24 (Winter 1981), 612–33

29 David R. Mayhew, *Congress: The Electoral Connection* (New Haven: Yale University Press 1974), 55

30 J.R. Mallory, 'The Minister's Office Staff: An Unreformed Part of the Public Service,' *Canadian Public Administration* 10 (Spring 1967): 29

31 Johnson, 'A Minister as an Agent of Policy Change,' 617

32 Smiley, *Canada in Question*, 136–7; Gibbins, *Regionalism*, 140–3

33 According to Donald Savoie, 'Among the countries currently classified by the United Nations as "industrialized market economies," Canada is surely one of the most highly regionalized and its economy is accordingly one of the most badly fragmented.' *Regional Economic Development:*

Canada's Search for Solutions (Toronto: University of Toronto Press 1986), 3; see also Stevenson, *Unfilled Union*, esp. ch. 4; O.F.G. Sitwell and N.R.M. Seifried, *The Regional Structure of the Canadian Economy* (Toronto: Methuen 1984); on the attitudinal dimension, see D.J. Elkins and R. Simeon, *Small Worlds: Provinces and Parties in Canadian Political Life* (Toronto: Methuen 1980).

34 Thomas O. Hueglin, 'The Politics of Fragmentation in an Age of Scarcity,' *Canadian Journal of Political Science* 20 (June 1987): 235–64

35 Alan C. Cairns, 'The Embedded State: State-Society Relations in Canada' in K. Banting, ed. *State and Society: Canada in Comparative Perspective*: Vol. 31, Research Studies of the Royal Commission on the Economic Union and Development Prospects for Canada (Toronto: University of Toronto Press 1985), 53–86

36 Savoie, *Politics of Public Spending*, 196

Chapter Two

1 On the difference between 'inter-' and 'intrastate' federalism, see Alan C. Cairns, *From Interstate to Intrastate Federalism in Canada* (Kingston: Institute of Intergovernmental Relations 1979); and D.V. Smiley and R.L. Watts, *Intrastate Federalism in Canada*: Vol. 39, Research Studies of the Royal Commission on the Economic Union and Development Prospects for Canada (Toronto: University of Toronto Press 1985).

2 P.B. Waite, *The Life and Times of Confederation, 1864–1867: Politics, Newspapers, and the Union of British North America* (Toronto: University of Toronto Press 1962), 116

3 Jean Hamelin, *The First Years of Confederation*, quoted in D.V. Smiley, 'Central Institutions' in S.M. Beck and I. Bernier, eds. *Canada and the New Constitution: The Unfinished Agenda* (Montreal: Institute for Research on Public Policy 1983), 29

4 W.L. Morton, 'The Cabinet of 1867' in F.W. Gibson, ed. *Cabinet Formation and Bicultural Relations* (Ottawa: Studies of the Royal Commission on Bilingualism and Biculturalism 1970), vol. 6: 5

5 P.B. Waite, *Canada 1874–1896: Arduous Destiny* (Toronto: McClelland and Stewart 1971), 54–6

6 See Kenneth D. McRae, ed., *Consociational Democracy: Political Accommodation in Segmented Societies* (Toronto: McClelland and Stewart 1974), esp. the contributions by McRae, 'Consociational Democracy and the Canadian Political System,' 238–61, and S.J.R. Noel, 'Consociational Democracy and Canadian Federalism,' 262–8. See also Arend Lijphart, *Democracy in Plural Societies* (New Haven: Yale University Press 1977) on the consociational democracy theme generally.

7 Morton, 'The Cabinet of 1867,' 16. This 'over-representation' of the maritimes (one post to a population of 150,000 compared to one to 260,000 for the country as a whole) was necessary in light of the considerable opposition to confederation in those two provinces, their relative wealth,

and ultimately, the necessity of their inclusion in order to make confederation possible. But, as Morton points out, there was more to the equation than this, namely certain compensations for English Conservatives in Ontario and French Canadians in Quebec. The former held, in addition to the prime ministership, three of what were considered to be among the weightier portfolios – justice (also held by Macdonald), public works, and the post office – and two minor portfolios (all told four ministers, including Macdonald). The latter had only three representatives in cabinet compared to the four they had typically enjoyed prior to 1867 in the ministries of the Province of Canada. However, George-Etienne Cartier was the second-ranking minister in cabinet and, as well, he determined the appointment of the other two ministers. Beyond this, under confederation French Canadians enjoyed full control of the province of Quebec (with certain limitations designed to protect the English-language minority) and were given fixed representation in the Commons and in the Senate.

8 See also Norman McL. Rogers, 'Federal Influences on the Canadian Cabinet,' *Canadian Bar Review* 11 (February 1933): 103–21.

9 Escott M. Reid, 'The Rise of National Parties in Canada' in H.G. Thorburn, ed., *Party Politics in Canada*, 4th ed. (Scarborough: Prentice-Hall 1979), 12–20. Confederation itself caused a certain amount of blurring of party lines where they did exist. Thus in Quebec, where the lines between the *Bleus* and the *Rouges* were clearly drawn, there were supporters of confederation on both sides.

10 See David E. Smith, 'Party Government, Representation and National Integration in Canada' in P. Aucoin, ed., *Party Government and Regional Representation in Canada*: Vol. 36, Research Studies of the Royal Commission on the Economic Union and Development Prospects for Canada (Toronto: University of Toronto Press 1985), 1–68.

11 Morton, 'The Cabinet of 1867,' 2

12 Gordon Stewart, 'John A. Macdonald's Greatest Triumph,' *Canadian Historical Review* 63 (1982): 22. By 1871 Macdonald had begun to lay claim to crown authority to justify patronage appointments. In the United States, while the practice of patronage was widespread, it was never justified as a right stemming from the country's constitution.

13 Gordon T. Stewart, *The Origins of Canadian Politics: A Comparative Approach* (Vancouver: University of British Columbia Press 1986), 26

14 Gordon Stewart, 'Political Patronage under Macdonald and Laurier 1878–1911,' *American Review of Canadian Studies* 10 (1980), 3–21

15 Stewart, *Origins of Canadian Politics*, 78

16 O.D. Skelton, *Life and Letters of Sir Wilfrid Laurier*, quoted in Frederick W. Gibson, 'Conclusions' in Gibson, ed., *Cabinet Formation*, 171

17 Stewart, *Origins of Canadian Politics*, 72. Control over positions such as judgeships was absolutely crucial since these officials had authority to adjudicate things like electoral lists, recounts, and so on.

18 P.B. Waite, 'Becoming Canadians: Ottawa's Relations with Maritimers in

the First and Twenty-first Years of Confederation' in R.K. Carty and
W.P. Ward, eds., *National Politics and Community in Canada* (Vancouver:
University of British Columbia Press 1986), 162

19 J. Murray Beck, *Joseph Howe, Volume 2: The Briton Becomes Canadian 1849–
1873* (Montreal: McGill-Queen's University Press 1983), 16

20 Quoted in Waite, 'Becoming Canadians,' 162

21 Stewart, 'Macdonald's Greatest Triumph,' 21

22 Macdonald, quoted in J.E. Hodgetts, *The Canadian Public Service: A
Physiology of Government 1867–1970* (Toronto: University of Toronto Press
1973), 44

23 According to Brian Young, 'Although Confederation lent idealism to his
acts, Cartier was always a tough infighter, party organizer and patronage
broker with a clear idea of what most people wanted in politics.' And
further, 'As early as the 1850s all administrative decisions in the Montreal
region, and appointment of judges, militia officers, customs officials,
school inspectors, and even prison chaplains, crossed Cartier's desk.'
George-Etienne Cartier: Montreal Bourgeois (Montreal: McGill-Queen's
University Press 1981), 70

24 Tilley had been appointed lieutenant-governor of New Bruswick in 1873
and for that reason had largely removed himself from politics. He re-
entered the cabinet in 1878 but with reduced influence given that only
five of the sixteen New Brunswick seats went Conservative in 1878. In
Nova Scotia, Tilley's chief rivals, Joseph Howe and Jonathan McCully,
were both dead by the time of the second Macdonald cabinet. Donald G.
Creighton, 'The Cabinet of 1878' in Gibson, ed., *Cabinet Formation*, 21–2

25 Beck, *Joseph Howe*, 264–5

26 Quoted in Waite, 'Becoming Canadians,' 161

27 John English, 'The "French Lieutenant" in Ottawa' in Carty and Ward,
eds., *National Politics and Community*, 184–200

28 Morton, 'The Cabinet of 1867,' 8, 17

29 Creighton 'The Cabinet of 1878,' 19–36

30 J.A. Chapleau, who had entered the cabinet in 1882 after his stint as
Quebec premier, complained to Macdonald in 1888 about the lack of
Quebec involvement in national issues. Macdonald pointed out that
Quebec had four major departments, including, from a patronage
perspective, the lucrative secretary of state, with its new printing office,
implying that this was really all that Quebec could conceivably want. The
relevant letters are found in Joseph Pope, *Correspondence of Sir John A.
Macdonald 1840–1891* cited in Stewart, 'Macdonald's Greatest Triumph,' 31,
n. 110. Macdonald's behaviour, however, can in part be explained by his
concern to manage the conflict between Chapleau and Langevin;
certainly he did not want to improve Chapleau's position at Langevin's
expense. See Barbara Fraser, 'Political Career of Sir Hector Louis
Langevin,' *Canadian Historical Review* 62 (June 1961): 121.

31 See Ralph Heintzman, 'The Political Culture of Quebec, 1840–1960,'
Canadian Journal of Political Science 16 (March 1983): 3–59.

32 Quoted in Hodgetts, *The Canadian Public Service*, 45
33 Federal control was originally secured in 1885 with the passage of the franchise bill. See Stewart, 'Macdonald's Greatest Triumph.' Control over the franchise reverted back to the federal government in 1917.
34 John T. Saywell, 'The Cabinet of 1896' in Gibson ed. *Cabinet Formation*, 38-9
35 Ibid., 42-3
36 Ibid., 44-5
37 Fraser, 'Sir Hector Louis Langevin,' 127-8
38 Stewart, 'Political Patronage under Macdonald and Laurier,' 11
39 Quoted in William A. Matheson, 'The Cabinet and the Canadian Bureaucracy' in Kenneth Kernaghan, ed., *Public Administration in Canada*, 3rd ed (Toronto: Methuen 1977), 264-5
40 Jeffrey Simpson, *Spoils of Power: The Politics of Patronage* (Toronto: Collins 1988), 112
41 Ibid., 112, 109-10
42 Up to that point there had been 'indirect' representation from the west to ensure the federal character of the cabinet. For example, in 1872 George-Etienne Cartier sat for the constituency of Provencher, Manitoba, and Francis Hincks, minister of finance, for the constituency of Vancouver, although both men were from central Canada and Cartier was regarded as the Quebec minister. Macdonald himself represented western Canada between 1878 and 1882 by holding seats first in Manitoba and then in Victoria, British Columbia. Rogers, 'Federal Influences,' 108-9
43 Waite, *Canada 1874-1896*, 128-9, 147-50
44 Ibid., 128-9
45 Simpson, *Spoils of Power*, 112
46 Ibid., 112-13
47 David E. Smith, *The Regional Decline of a National Party: Liberals on the Prairies* (Toronto: University of Toronto Press 1981), 10
48 Ibid., 16-17
49 D.J. Hall, *Clifford Sifton, Volume 2: A Lonely Eminence 1901-1929* (Vancouver: University of British Columbia Press 1985), ch. 8
50 J.E. Hodgetts, *Pioneer Public Service: An Administrative History of the United Canadas, 1841-1867* (Toronto: University of Toronto Press 1955)
51 John English, *The Decline of Politics: The Conservatives and the Party System 1901-20* (Toronto: University of Toronto Press 1977), 14
52 Parliament of Canada, *Report on the Organization of the Public Service of Canada* by Sir George Murray, Sessional Paper No. 57a (Ottawa: C.H. Parmelee 1912), 9
53 J.E. Hodgetts, William McCloskey, Reginald Whitaker, and V. Seymour Wilson, *The Biography of an Institution: The Civil Service Commission of Canada 1908-1967* (Montreal: McGill-Queen's University Press 1972), 21 n.31
54 P.B. Waite, *The Man from Halifax: Sir John Thompson, Prime Minister* (Toronto: University of Toronto Press 1985), 145

55 Robert MacGregor Dawson, *The Civil Service of Canada* (London: Oxford University Press 1929), 40
56 Waite, *Canada 1874–1896*, 20
57 Hodgetts et al., *Biography of an Institution*, 9–14
58 For example, the Civil Service Act of 1882, passed in response to the recommendations of the Royal Commission to Inquire into the Organization of the Civil Service Commission of 1880–1, struck a board of examiners to prepare lists of eligible candidates 'from which ministers might make appointments.' The Civil Service Amendment Act of 1908 gave power to the Civil Service Commission both to examine and to recruit new civil servants, but its jurisdiction was restricted to certain parts of the inside service. Royal Commission on Bilingualism and Biculturalism, *Report* Book 3A (Ottawa: Queen's Printer 1969), 99–100
59 Simpson, *Spoils of Power*, 113
60 After 1911 urbanization and industrialization in Ontario made patronage there a less critical factor in electoral success. In Quebec, however, where the French-speaking population still tended to be excluded from large commercial enterprises and the realm of banking and finance and confined to low-status occupations and the free professions, patronage continued to be an important part of social, and economic as well as political life. Heintzman, 'The Political Culture of Quebec, esp. 10–18
61 Morton, 'The Cabinet of 1867,' 13
62 Parliament of Canada, *Report on the Organization of the Public Service of Canada*, 7–8
63 J.R. Mallory, 'Cabinets and Councils in Canada,' *Public Law*, Autumn 1957: 236
64 Matheson, 'The Cabinet and the Canadian Bureaucracy,' 266
65 Quoted in Waite, *Canada 1874–1896*, 220
66 Ibid.
67 Waite, *The Man From Halifax*, 107–12. On the railway mess, J.M. Beck, *Politics of Nova Scotia*, Vol. 1: *1710–1896* (Tantallon, NS: Four East 1985), 192–213.
68 The institution was the Dorchester penitentiary. Disregarding the four political nominees, Thompson appointed instead the deputy warden, the candidate considered most competent, to the vacant position. Waite, *The Man from Halifax*, 191
69 Ibid., 412
70 See Hall, *Lonely Eminence*; ch. 8.
71 Langevin himself had hoped, and to a degree even expected, that Riel would be spared the gallows. All three Quebec ministers – Langevin, Chapleau, and Caron – supported the government throughout the crisis. For their efforts they were burned in effigy 'day and night' in Montreal and Quebec City. Fraser, 'Sir Hector Louis Langevin,' 119–20
72 Stewart, *Origins of Canadian Politics*; Reginald Whitaker, 'Between Patronage and Bureaucracy: Democratic Politics in Transition,' *Journal of Canadian Studies* 22 (Summer 1987): 55–71

73 Stewart, *Origins of Canadian Politics*, 83; F.H. Leacy, ed., *Historical Statistics of Canada*, 2nd ed (Ottawa: Statistics Canada 1983), Series D1-7

74 Leacy, ed., *Historical Statistics*, series D1-7

75 See, for example, Vincent Lemieux, *Le patronage politique: une étude comparative* (Québec: Presses de l'Université Laval 1977).

76 R.A. Young in '"And the People Will Sink into Despair": Reconstruction in New Brunswick, 1942–52,' *Canadian Historical Review* 69 (1988): 127–66, uses the model to good effect to explain the failure of post–World War Two reconstruction policies in New Brunswick. He notes, however, that while clientele structures were especially pervasive and deep in the timber trade, they tended to be shallower in the areas of fisheries and agriculture. In third world systems – in Africa, for example – the reciprocal exchange process tends to be embedded in a system of values according superior status to the patron and generally a high level of trust among all participants. René Lemarchand, 'The State, the Parallel Economy, and the Changing Structure of Patronage Systems' in D. Rothchild and N. Chazan, eds., *The Precarious Balance: State and Society in Africa* (Boulder: Westview 1988), 149–70.

77 Whitaker, 'Between Patronage and Bureaucracy,' 63

78 An amendment to the Senate and House of Commons Act, assented to on 3 August 1931, meant that MPs were no longer required to seek re-election when appointed to an office in the ministry. Government of Canada, *Guide to Canadian Ministries since Confederation, July 1, 1867–February 1, 1982* (Ottawa: Supply and Services 1982), 90

79 Jeffrey Simpson, for example, provides several examples of premiers and ministers who tried to stem or alter the patronage tide, usually enjoying only limited success. Simpson, *Spoils of Power*, passim

80 In a sense Fielding did not need to do much to help Nova Scotia during his first stint in cabinet as minister of finance under Laurier. The province, along with the rest of the country, was just entering a sustained period of economic growth and prosperity, something for which Fielding claimed considerable credit. In 1896 he did help the Nova Scotia government recover $671,000 in railway grants, an issue on which previous Conservative governments had earlier refused to act. From 1921 onward, however (again as minister of finance, this time under King), when the maritimes suffered economic decline he was unsympathetic, refusing 'to acknowledge any basis for Maritime complaints.' See J.M. Beck, *Politics of Nova Scotia, Volume 2: 1896–1988* (Tantallon, NS: Four East 1988), 98; also 19, 28–30, 107.

81 Gibson, 'Conclusions,' 175–6

Chapter Three

1 John English, *The Decline of Politics: The Conservatives and the Party System 1901–20* (Toronto: University of Toronto Press 1977), 48

2 John English, 'The "French Lieutenant" in Ottawa' in R.K. Carty and W.P. Ward, eds., *National Politics and Community in Canada* (Vancouver: University of British Columbia Press 1986), 186–92

3 The following section on Borden's government is based largely on the accounts in English, *Decline of Politics*.

4 As well, Hazen was New Brunswick premier at a time when the province was steeped in corruption. See Arthur T. Doyle, *Front Benches and Back Rooms: A Story of Corruption, Muckraking, Raw Partisanship and Intrigue in New Brunswick* (Toronto: Green Tree Publishing 1976).

5 Ibid., 76–7

6 See the accounts in Heath MacQuarrie, 'The Formation of Borden's First Cabinet,' *Canadian Journal of Economics and Political Science* 23 (1957): 90–104; English, *Decline of Politics*; and Roger Graham 'The Cabinet of 1911' in F.W. Gibson, ed., *Cabinet Formation and Bicultural Relations* (Ottawa: Studies of the Royal Commission on Bilingualism and Biculturalism 1970), vol. 6: 5.

7 Ronald G. Haycock, *Sam Hughes: The Public Career of a Controversial Canadian, 1885–1916* (Waterloo: Wilfrid Laurier University Press 1986)

8 Jeffrey Simpson, *Spoils of Power: The Politics of Patronage* (Toronto: Collins 1988), 124

9 Ibid.

10 English, *Decline of Politics*, 100

11 J.E. Hodgetts, William McCloskey, Reginald Whitaker, and V. Seymour Wilson, *The Biography of an Institution: The Civil Service Commission of Canada 1908–1967* (Montreal: McGill-Queen's University Press 1972), 45–62

12 See John H. Thompson, *The Harvests of War: The Prairie West, 1914–1918* (Toronto: McClelland and Stewart 1978).

13 For example, the gross value of the production of iron and steel had more than tripled and that for the manufacturing of transport equipment nearly quadrupled between 1910 and 1920. See F.H. Leacy, ed., *Historical Statistics of Canada*, 2nd ed. (Ottawa: Statistics Canada 1983), series R354–9, R399–404.

14 Robert Craig Brown and Ramsay Cook, *Canada 1896–1921: A Nation Transformed* (Toronto: McClelland and Stewart 1974), 98–9

15 Reginald Whitaker, 'Between Patronage and Bureaucracy: Democratic Politics in Transition,' *Journal of Canadian Studies* 22 (Summer 1987): 64

16 H.V. Nelles, 'Public Ownership of Electrical Utilities in Manitoba and Ontario,' *Canadian Historical Review* 57 (1976): 461–85

17 J. Murray Beck, *The Pendulum of Power: Canada's Federal Elections* (Scarborough: Prentice-Hall 1968), 158

18 On the Maritime Rights Movement, see Ernest R. Forbes, *The Maritime Rights Movement, 1919–1927: A Study in Canadian Regionalism* (Montreal: McGill-Queen's University Press 1979).

19 In Quebec it was in rural farming areas that the Conservatives, with their promise of protection and home markets, made gains, especially among

dairy farmers, because of heavy foreign competition from New Zealand, among others. Beck, *Pendulum of Power*, 200

20 English, 'The "French Lieutenant" in Ottawa,' 185

21 David E. Smith, 'Cabinet and Commons in the Era of James G. Gardiner' in John C. Courtney, ed., *The Canadian House of Commons: Essays in Honour of Norman Ward* (Calgary: University of Calgary Press 1985), 77. For a detailed account of Gardiner's career, see Norman Ward and David E. Smith, *Jimmy Gardiner: Relentless Liberal* (Toronto: University of Toronto Press 1990).

22 Smith, 'Cabinet and Commons,' 78

23 Quoted in Gibson, 'The Cabinet of 1935' in Gibson, ed., *Cabinet Formation*, 122

24 Ibid., 126–7

25 Smith, 'Cabinet and Commons,' 70

26 Ibid., 76–7

27 Irving Abella and Harold Troper, *None Is too Many: Canada and the Jews of Europe, 1933–1948* (Toronto: Lester and Orpen Dennys 1982), 17–20, 41–3. At the time the Immigration Branch was part of the Department of Mines and Resources, of which Crerar was the minister. Abella and Troper note that Lapointe himself was not anti-semitic; merely highly sensitive to the political forces in Quebec that were so disposed, including above all Duplessis and the Union Nationale.

28 Quoted in Ann Gomer Sunahara, *The Politics of Racism: The Uprooting of Japanese Canadians during the Second World War* (Toronto: Lorimer 1981), 148

29 Ibid., 149

30 J.L. Granatstein, 'King and His Cabinet: The War Years' in John English and J.O. Stubbs eds., *Mackenzie King: Widening the Debate* (Toronto: Macmillian of Canada 1977), 176; Sunahara, *The Politics of Racism*, 140

31 Alan C. Cairns, *From Interstate to Intrastate Federalism in Canada* (Kingston: Institute of Intergovernmental Relations 1979), 6

32 The finance portfolio has been held by Nova Scotians seven times since confederation.

33 J.L. Ralston, when he re-entered the cabinet in 1939 as minister of finance, did so as a member from PEI. However, by that time he had become identified with the Montreal business and financial community.

34 Quoted in Gibson, 'The cabinet of 1935,' 118

35 Ernest R. Forbes, 'Consolidating Disparity: The Maritimes and the Industrialization of Canada during the Second World War,' *Acadiensis* 16 (1986): 3–26. A.L. Macdonald apparently was highly uncomfortable in Ottawa and did not fare well in either cabinet or the Commons. See John Hawkins, *The Life and Times of Angus L.* (Windsor, NS: Lancelot 1969), 214–34.

36 Rogers, 'Federal influences,' 113

37 *Report of the Royal Commission on Bilingualism and Biculturalism*, Book 3A, 101

38 As J.E. Hodgetts and O.P. Dwivedi note, there is little hard data on provincial government employment levels in the pre-war period (*Provincial Governments as Employers: A Survey of Public Personnel Administration in Canada's Provinces* [Montreal: McGill-Queen's University Press 1974], 2); Harvey Rich cites data showing that the size of the Ontario civil service more than doubled from 1915 to 1934 (from 2817 to 7013) ('Higher Civil Servants in Ontario: A Case Study of an Administrative Elite,' PhD. dissertation, University of California [Berkeley 1973], 38); over the same period the federal civil service grew from 29,000 to 40,000 (Leacy, ed., *Historical Statistics of Canada*, series Y211–N59). It is safe to assume, therefore, that the rate of growth in provincial employment was much higher. At the same time, hiring practices were far looser than those at the federal level, easily lending themselves to patronage purposes as evidenced by the 'Gardiner machine' in Saskatchewan.

39 Ralph Heintzman, 'The Political Culture of Quebec, 1840–1960,' *Canadian Journal of Political Science* 16 (March 1983): 33

40 Simpson, *Spoils of Power*, 135

41 Reginald Whitaker, *The Government Party: Organizing and Financing the Liberal Party of Canada 1930–58* (Toronto: University of Toronto Press 1977), 13

42 Ibid., 15

43 Ibid., 61–6

44 Ibid.

45 Ibid., 118, 127

46 J.L. Granatstein, *The Ottawa Men: The Civil Service Mandarins, 1935–1957* (Toronto: Oxford University Press 1982), ch. 3

47 Hodgetts et al., *Biography of an Institution*, 105–8

48 Ibid.

49 J.S. Dupré, 'The Workability of Executive Federalism in Canada' in H. Bakvis and W.M. Chandler, eds., *Federalism and the Role of the State* (Toronto: University of Toronto Press 1987), 238

50 Simpson, *Spoils of Power*, 134–5

51 Whitaker, *The Government Party*, 89

52 Quoted in ibid.

53 Quoted in Report, *Royal Commission on Bilingualism and Biculturalism*, Book 3A, 105–6

54 Ibid., 106–7

55 Forbes, 'Consolidating Disparity,' 12

56 Significantly, J.L. Ralston, who had re-entered the cabinet in 1939 as a member from PEI, 'waged a systematic campaign for the ferry [to replace one that had sunk earlier] and other Island causes *but only after his resignation from the cabinet in 1944*.' Ibid., 11 (italics added).

Chapter Four

1 J.L. Granatstein, *The Ottawa Men: The Civil Service Mandarins, 1935–1957* (Toronto: Oxford University Press 1982), Passim
2 Ibid., 254
3 See Robert M. Campbell, *Grand Illusions: The Politics of the Keynesian Experience in Canada, 1945–1975* (Peterborough, Ont: Broadview Press 1987).
4 Dale C. Thompson, 'The Cabinet of 1948' in F.W. Gibson, ed., *Cabinet Formation and Bicultural Relations* (Ottawa: Studies of the Royal Commission on Bilingualism and Biculturalism 1970), vol. 6: 143–54
5 Ibid., 151
6 Quoted in David E. Smith, 'Cabinet and Commons in the Era of James G. Gardiner' in John C. Courtney, ed., *The Canadian House of Commons: Essays in Honour of Norman Ward* (Calgary: University of Calgary Press 1985), 80
7 Ibid.
8 Robert Bothwell and William Kilbourn, *C.D. Howe: A Biography* (Toronto: McClelland and Stewart 1979), 263, 278, 324, 326
9 Interview with J. Murray Beck, professor emeritus, Dalhousie University, Halifax, 9 August 1989. These special provisions were made by cabinet order in 1953 and were strongly resisted by the bureaucracy. Leslie A. Pal, *State, Class, and Bureaucracy: Canadian Unemployment Insurance and Public Policy* (Kingston and Montreal: McGill-Queen's University Press 1988), 111–12
10 Reginald Whitaker, *The Government Party: Organizing and Financing the Liberal Party of Canada 1930–58* (Toronto: University of Toronto Press 1977), 182. Mayhew's demotion, it should be noted, came largely at the urging of Sinclair. Mayhew subsequently became ambassador to Japan.
11 Bothwell and Kilbourn, *C.D. Howe*, 247
12 Granatstein, *The Ottawa Men*, 223
13 See J.R. Mallory, 'The Five Faces of Federalism' in J.P. Meekison, ed., *Canadian Federalism: Myth or Reality* (Toronto: Methuen 1977), 24–6
14 Whitaker, *The Government Party*, 406–14
15 David E. Smith, *The Regional Decline of a National Party: Liberals on the Prairies* (Toronto: University of Toronto Press 1981), 56
16 David E. Smith, 'Party Government, Representation, and National Integration in Canada' in Peter Aucoin, ed., *Party Government and Regional Representation in Canada*: Vol. 36, Research Studies of the Royal Commission on the Economic Union and Development Prospects for Canada (Toronto: University of Toronto Press 1985), 1–68; R.K Carty, 'Three Canadian Party Systems' in George Perlin, ed., *Party Democracy in Canada: The Politics of National Party Conventions* (Scarborough: Prentice-Hall 1988), 24–8
17 Granatstein *The Ottawa Men*, 266–72
18 See, for example, George Perlin, *The Tory Syndrome: Leadership Politics in*

the Progressive Conservative Party (Montreal: McGill-Queen's University Press 1980).

19 Marc La Terreur, *Les tribulations des Conservateurs au Québec: de Bennett à Diefenbaker* (Quebec: Les Presses de l'Université Laval 1973)

20 Perlin, *The Tory Syndrome*, 63

21 Margaret Conrad, *George Nowlan: Maritime Conservative in National Politics* (Toronto: University of Toronto Press 1986), 180–1

22 Ibid., 249

23 Ibid., 246

24 Anthony G.S. Careless, *Initiative and Response: The Adaptation of Canadian Federalism to Regional Economic Development* (Montreal: McGill-Queen's University Press 1977-), 33; Thomas J. Courchene, *Economic Management and the Division of Powers*: Vol. 67, Research Studies of the Royal Commission on the Economic Union and Development Prospects for Canada (Toronto: University of Toronto Press 1986), 147

25 Careless, *Initiative and Response*, 71–6

26 Ibid., 73

27 Ibid., 110

28 Conrad, *George Nowlan*, 272

29 Colin Campbell, 'Cabinet Committees in Canada: Pressures and Dysfunctions Stemming from the Representational Imperative' in Thomas T. Mackie and Brian W. Hogwood, eds., *Unlocking the Cabinet: Cabinet Structures in Comparative Perspective* (London: Sage 1985), 64

30 There is a vast literature on the Quiet Revolution and its effect on Canadian federalism. For a most useful treatment of the topic, see Kenneth McRoberts, *Quebec: Social Change and Political Crisis* (Toronto: McClelland and Stewart 1988).

31 Tom Kent, *A Public Purpose: An Experience of Liberal Opposition and Canadian Government* (Kingston and Montreal: McGill-Queen's University Press 1988), 229

32 *Royal Commission on Bilingualism and Biculturalism*, Book III (3A) (Ottawa: Queen's Printer 1969), chs. 5, 6 and 7

33 John English, 'The "French Lieutenant" in Ottawa' in R. Kenneth Carty and W. Peter Ward, eds., *National Politics and Community in Canada* (Vancouver: University of British Columbia Press 1986), 194–6

34 Richard Simeon, *Federal-Provincial Diplomacy: The Making of Recent Policy in Canada* (Toronto: University of Toronto Press 1972)

35 Bruce G. Pollard, *Managing the Interface: Intergovernmental Affairs Agencies in Canada* (Kingston: Institute of Intergovernmental Relations 186), 11

36 Marsha A. Chandler and William M. Chandler, *Public Policy and Provincial Politics* (Toronto: McGraw-Hill Ryerson 1979), 9. For criticism of their findings, see R.A. Young, Philippe Faucher, and André Blais, 'The Concept of Province-Building: A Critique,' *Canadian Journal of Political Science* 17 (December 1984): 783–818.

37 Careless, *Initiative and Response*, 110–11; Conrad, *George Nowlan*, 248

38 Smith, *The Regional Decline of a National Party*, 53
39 Ibid., 57
40 Gordon Robertson, 'The Changing Role of the Privy Council Office,'
    Canadian Public Administration 14 (Fall 1971): 489–90; Kent, *A Public Purpose*,
    221–8
41 J. Stefan Dupré, 'The Workability of Executive Federalism in Canada' in
    H. Bakvis and W.M. Chandler, eds., *Federalism and the Role of the State*
    (Toronto: University of Toronto Press 1987), 238–40; Colin Campbell,
    *Governments under Stress: Political Executives and Key Bureaucrats in
    Washington, London, and Ottawa* (Toronto: University of Toronto Press
    1983), ch. 4
42 *Report of the Royal Commission on Government Organization* (Ottawa:
    Queen's Printer 1962). See also Peter Aucoin and Herman Bakvis, *The
    Centralization-Decentralization Conundrum: Organization and Management in
    the Canadian Government* (Halifax: Institute for Research on Public Policy
    1988), 2.
43 Aucoin and Bakvis, *The Centralization-Decentralization Conundrum*, 46–7
44 Careless, *Initiative and Response*, 130
45 Ibid., 79
46 Ibid., 114
47 Simeon *Federal-Provincial Diplomacy* 57–58

Chapter Five

 1 Gordon Robertson, 'The Changing Role of the Privy Council Office,'
    Canadian Public Administration 14 (Fall 1971): 491–2
 2 P.E.Trudeau, *Federalism and the French Canadians* (Toronto: Macmillan
    1968), 203
 3 Peter Aucoin, 'Organizational Change in the Machinery of Canadian
    Government: From Rational Management to Brokerage Politics,'
    Canadian Journal of Political Science 19 (March 1986): 8; Richard D. French,
    'The Privy Council Office: Support for Cabinet Decision-Making' in
    Richard Schultz et al., eds., *The Canadian Political Process* (Toronto: Holt,
    Rinehart and Winston 1979), 365
 4 Peter Aucoin and Richard French, *Knowlege, Power and Public Policy*
    (Ottawa: Science Council of Canada 1974), 12
 5 Aucoin, 'Organizational Change,' 9
 6 Mitchell Sharp, 'Decision-Making in the Federal Cabinet,' *Canadian
    Public Administration* 19 (Spring 1976): 3
 7 Robertson, 'The Changing Role of the Privy Council Office,' Table 1,
    492. The number of full cabinet meetings actually dropped from 139 to 75
    over this period, but this was small compensation when committee
    meetings increased from 120 to 311.
 8 Quoted in George Radwanski, *Trudeau* (Toronto: Macmillan 1978), 188

9 David E. Smith, *The Decline of a National Party: Liberals on the Prairies* (Toronto: University of Toronto Press 1981), 75–82

10 Quoted in ibid., 76

11 A.R. O'Brien [National Director of the Liberal Party] quoted in ibid., 84

12 Donald J. Savoie, *Regional Economic Development: Canada's Search for Solutions* (Toronto: University of Toronto Press 1986), 42

13 Ibid., ch. 4

14 Anthony G.S. Careless, *Initiative and Response: The Adaptation of Candian Federalism to Regional Economic Development* (Montreal: McGill-Queen's University Press 1977), 86, 131–2

15 Bruce D. Macnaughton and Conrad J. Winn, 'Economic Policy and Electoral Self Interest: The Allocations of the Department of Regional Economic Expansion,' *Canadian Public Policy* 7 (1981): 318–27

16 Colin Campbell, 'Cabinet Committees in Canada: Pressures and Dysfunctions Stemming from the Representational Imperative' in Thomas T. Mackie and Brian W. Hogwood, eds., *Unlocking the Cabinet: Cabinet Structures in Comparative Perspective* (London: Sage 1985), 67. The actual composition of committees was kept secret until 1979. However, Campbell and George J. Szablowski in *The Superbureaucrats: Structure and Behaviour in Central Agencies* (Toronto: Macmillan 1979) were able to ascertain committee memberships through interviews.

17 Joseph Wearing, *The L-Shaped Party: The Liberal Party of Canada 1958–1980* (Toronto: McGraw-Hill Ryerson 1981), 135

18 Aucoin, 'Organizational Change,' 14

19 There was actually a net gain from Quebec eastward, from sixty-three Liberal seats in 1968 to sixty-six in 1972.

20 Wearing, *The L-Shaped Party*, 154–5. The Political Planning Committee would meet weekly for up to an hour and a half.

21 Smith, *Regional Decline of a National Party*, 104

22 For a critical overview of the joint submissions of the western premiers on 'Capital Financing and Regional Financial Institutions,' 'Economic and Industrial Development Opportunities,' and 'Transportation,' and on the limited capacity of the federal government to respond to the proposals of the premiers, see Kenneth H. Norrie, 'Some Comments on Prairie Economic Alienation,' *Canadian Public Policy* 2 (1976): 211–24.

23 For example, the Liberal Party 'Conference on Western Objectives,' held in Vancouver just prior to the WEOC in Calgary, was ignored by the Western media, and its impact on the WEOC itself 'was scarcely discernible.' See Smith, *Regional Decline of a National Party*, 105.

24 Careless, *Initiative and Response*, esp. ch. 10

25 Donald J. Savoie, *Federal-Provincial Collaboration: The Canada–New Brunswick General Development Agreement* (Montreal: McGill-Queen's University Press 1981), 25–7

26 Savoie, *Regional Ecomomic Development* 44–7

27 J.D. Love, 'The Continuing Relevance of DREE Decentralization,' *Canadian Public Administration* 30 (Fall 1987): 443–4

28 Savoie, *Federal-Provincial Collaboration*, 29. In what was in some ways a precursor of the GDA approach, Prince Edward Island and Ottawa had already signed in 1969 a fifteen year comprehensive development plan supported by ARDA-FRED money.

29 Donald J. Savoie, 'The General Development Agreement Approach and the Bureaucratization of Provincial Governments in the Atlantic Provinces,' *Canadian Public Administration* 24 (1981): 116–31

30 S.J.R. Noel, 'Patrons and Clients in Canadian Politics,' paper presented to the annual meeting of the Canadian Political Science Association, Quebec City, June 1976, 23–4

31 Savoie, *Federal-Provincial Collaboration*, 105

32 Ibid., 48–52, 85–8; '$ Millions in fisheries aid "In Limbo",' *Telegraph Journal* (Saint John, NB, 11 February 1977: 3; interview, Romeo LeBlanc, Ottawa, 25 March 1986. Similar problems arose with a proposed Ottawa–New Brunswick forestry agreement.

33 This is the position taken by Love, 'The Continuing Relevance of DREE Decentralization,' 442–3.

34 Quoted in William A. Matheson, 'The Cabinet and the Canadian Bureaucracy' in Kenneth Kernaghan, ed., *Public Administration in Canada*, 3rd ed. (Toronto: Methuen 1980), 278

35 Campbell, 'Cabinet Committees in Canada,' 69

36 Peter Aucoin and Herman Bakvis, *The Centralization-Decentralization Conundrum: Organization and Management in The Canadian Government* (Halifax: Institute for Research on Public Policy 1988), 48

37 Sandford F. Borins, *The Language of the Skies: The Bilingual Air Traffic Control Conflict in Canada* (Montreal: McGill-Queen's University Press 1983), 132

38 Ibid., 42, 50–1. The deputy minister in place at the beginning of the dispute, O.G. Stoner, was replaced on 1 May 1976 by Sylvan Cloutier, who did play an important role. He in turn bypassed William Huck, chief air administrator (equivalent of assistant deputy minister), and dealt directly with the director general in charge of civil aviation, Walter McLeish, the individual who likely played the most critical role in eventually resolving the dispute.

39 'MacEachen leads the left,' *Chronicle-Herald*, 29 February 1968; Grit minister got "fair share" for his native Newfoundland,' *Globe and Mail*, 20 November 1986: A14

40 J.A.A. Lovink, 'Is Canadian Politics too Competitive?' *Canadian Journal of Political Science* 6 (1973): 341–79. There are a number of ways to measure the extent of electoral competition, but one basic indicator alone illustrates the difference quite dramatically. For the period from 1953 to 1965 the percentage of 'no-change' seats in the US House of

Representatives was 78.2; in the UK House of Commons, 77.0; in the Canadian House of Commons, 23.6.

41 'Marchand faces uphill fight to save Quebec City seat,' *Ottawa Journal*, 28 September 1972

42 'Carroll chosen to contest seat,' *Cape Breton Post* (Sydney, NS), 21 May 1949: 3

43 'McEachen [*sic*] viewed Ottawa strongman,' ibid., 10 October 1963: 6

44 He became past master in pre-empting the announcements of other ministers, for example announcing a CN rail order for hopper cars to the Eastern Car Company in Trenton, Nova Scotia, before the minister of the responsible department, Transport, was even aware of it. 'MacEachen stole the thunder,' ibid., 25 February 1964: 6

45 Sandford F. Borins, *Investments in Failure: Five Government Corporations That Cost the Canadian Taxpayers Billions* (Toronto: Methuen 1986), 10–13. Originally there were four contending proposals, including ones by Imperial Oil and the Dynamic Power Corporation. The Western Deuterium proposal was favoured by the departments of Finance and Industry, Trade and Commerce, and Atomic Energy of Canada Limited. The claim that Pearson and MacEachen played a predominant role is made by Paul Hellyer who participated in the debate in cabinet. According to Judy LaMarsh, evidence of the special influence MacEachen had over the prime minister was that of the two photographs Pearson had in his office: one was of his wife, Maryon, the other was of himself with MacEachen. See *Memoirs of a Bird in a Gilded Cage* (Toronto: McClelland and Stewart 1968), 168.

46 For example, 'WE DID IT! Heavy water comes to C.B.: $30,000,000 plant to be built at Glace Bay' *Cape Breton Post*, 3 December 1963: 1; 'More attention from Ottawa says MacEachen,' ibid., 30 May 1964; 'N.S. heavy water potential not yet tapped,' ibid., 2 May 1967: 1

47 Borins, *Investments in Failure*, 119

48 Allan Tupper, 'Public Enterprise as Social Welfare: The Case of the Cape Breton Development Corporation,' *Canadian Public Policy* 4 (1978): 540–1

49 'Minister defends federal government,' *Cape Breton Post*, 24 June 1968: 12

50 'MacEachen hurt by showing,' *Chronicle-Herald* (Halifax, NS), 8 April 1968: 1; 'Contest left deep scars in Atlantic area,' ibid., 9 April 1968: 1

51 'The Cape Breton hero of the Liberal minority survival,' *Globe and Mail*, 25 June 1973: 9

52 Borins, *Investments in Failure*, 121

53 'The Cape Breton hero,' 9

54 Interview, Romeo LeBlanc, Ottawa 25 March 1986

55 Fisheries had been a separate department until 1969 when it was joined with Forestry. In 1971 both units became part of the newly created Department of the Environment. In 1979 Fisheries once more became a separate department entitled Department of Fisheries and Oceans.

56 'LeBlanc: he was never dull,' *Chronicle-Herald*, 1 October 1982: 1
57 Romeo LeBlanc interview, 25 March 1986. Excellent accounts of LeBlanc as 'minister of fishermen' and his specific policies can be found in A. Paul Pross and Susan McCorquodale, *Economic Resurgence and the Constitutional Agenda: The Case of the East Coast Fisheries* (Kingston: Institute of Intergovernmental Relations 1987), esp. 31-5, 85-91.
58 LeBlanc interview, 25 March 1986
59 LeBlanc, quoted in 'LeBlanc urges fishermen to organize,' *Chronicle-Herald*, 23 October 1974: 1
60 'LeBlanc announces herring subsidy plan,' *Telgraph Journal* (Saint John, NB), 10 April 1976: 3
61 R.D.S. Macdonald, 'Inshore Fishing Interests on the Atlantic Coast: Their Response to Extended Jurisdiction by Canada,' *Marine Policy* 3 (July 1979): 171-89. Pross and McCorquodale, *Economic Resurgence*, 89-90
62 'LeBlanc agrees to MFU proposal,' *Telegraph Journal*, 29 December 1978: 4
63 See 'Leblanc [sic] aide les pêcheurs avant les compagnies,' *Le Soleil* (Quebec City), 2 novembre 1978: A12. Thus while the overall participation rate of licensed fishermen in the Atlantic fisheries rose from 36,464 in 1974 to 60,032 by 1980, the number of Nova Scotia fishermen over this period grew only slightly, from 10,460 to 11,432, See Susan McCorquodale, 'The Management of a Common Property Resource: Fisheries Policy in Atlantic Canada' in Michael M. Atkinson and Marsha A. Chandler, eds., *The Politics of Canadian Public Policy* (Toronto: University of Toronto Press 1983), Table 2, 154. The overall increase in licensed fishermen occurred mainly in Newfoundland. Given LeBlanc's sympathy for a 'social fishery,' one would have expected close links between the minister and the Newfoundland government. This was not the case, however, a fact that Pross and McCorquodale attribute to LeBlanc's aggressive defence of federal jursidiction and caustic rhetoric. See *Economic Resurgence and the Constitutional Agenda*, 32.
64 LeBlanc interview, 25 March 1986; 'LeBlanc creates new Gulf fishery region,' *Telegraph Journal*, 26 September 1980: 5
65 For example, 'LNG deal to create "thousands" of jobs,' *Chronicle-Herald*, 17 December 1977: 1; 'Peat-fired plant for North N.B.?' *Telegraph Journal*, 11 January 1978
66 LeBlanc interview 25 March 1986
67 'LeBlanc creates new Gulf fishery region,' 5
68 LeBlanc interview, 25 March 1986
69 Ibid.
70 Relations between MacEachen and G.I. Smith, who succeeded Stanfield as Conservative leader and premier in 1967, were more acrimonious, a result stemming primarily from the difficulties over the DLC heavy water plant. As a result MacEachean participated in the 1971 provincial election campaign, actively supporting Regan. This help, however, was not

repeated in subsequent elections, either for Regan or for his successor, Sandy Cameron.

71 'Minister defends federal Government'

72 As David Smith notes: 'Modern Canadian politics is characterized more by patronage at the top of the party hierarchy than at the bottom.' 'Party Government, Representation and National Integration in Canada,' 53

73 R. MacGregor Dawson, *The Government of Canada*, 5th ed. rev. by Norman Ward (Toronto: University of Toronto Press 1970), 476–8

74 S.J.R. Noel, 'Dividing the Spoils: The Old and New Rules of Patronage in Canadian Politics,' *Journal of Canadian Studies* 22 (1987): 89–91

75 For an examination of both programs, see Robert S. Best, 'Youth Policy' in G. Bruce Doern and V. Seymour Wilson, eds., *Issues in Canadian Public Policy* (Toronto: Macmillan of Canada 1974), 137–65

76 Donald E. Blake, 'LIP and Partisanship: An Analysis of the Local Initiatives Program,' *Canadian Public Policy* 2 (1976): 19–20

77 Ibid., 25

78 Careless, *Initiative and Response*, 86, 173–5; 'Marchand: Tout l'est du Québec deviendra une région designée,' *La Presse* (Montreal), 30 janvier 1969: 8

79 Savoie, *Regional Economic Development*, 42; 'Marchand's campaign fiery but Wagner gets the limelight,' *Montreal Star*, 25 October 1972

80 Macnaughton and Winn, 'Economic Policy and Electoral Self Interest,' 321

81 'Marchand's campaign fiery'; also 'Marchand faces uphill fight to save Quebec City seat, *Ottawa Journal*, 28 September 1972: 14

82 'Quebec: cash or crash,' *Ottawa Citizen*, 15 December 1970: 1; 'Marchand inaugure à Montréal un nouveau bureau de son ministère,' *La Presse*, 6 février 1971; 'Dans un an, Montréal ne sera plus zone désignée,' *La Presse*, 20 juin 1972; Savoie, *Regional Economic Development*, 40–2. To be sure, conditions attached to grants made in this region were more restrictive. For example, grants were limited to 10 per cent of approved capital costs compared to limits ranging from 25 to 35 per cent in other regions.

83 'The highway that Don built may lead back to Ottawa,' *Globe and Mail*, 4 October 1972: 8

84 Newfoundland Subagreements: Highways, 1974–5, 1975–6, 1976–81, 'General Development Agreements: Status of subsidiary agreements as of June 28, 1985,' mimeographed (Ottawa: Department of Regional Industrial Expansion 1985). The federal share of the $137 million total was $121 million.

85 Interviewee No. 41, St John's Newfoundland, 27 February 1986

86 Quoted in 'Powerful cabinet voice Trudeau would listen to,' *Globe and Mail*, 20 November 1986: A14

87 Savoie, *Regional Economic Development*, 57

88 Ibid., 60–1

89 Atlantic Provinces Economic Council, 'Analysis of the Reorganization

for Economic Development' (Halifax 1982), 13–14. The actual proportion spent in the Atlantic provinces never exceeded 53 per cent, reached in the early 1970s.

90 Love, 'The Continuing Relevance of DREE Decentralization,' 438

91 Kenneth Kernaghan, 'Representative and Responsive Bureaucracy: Implications for Canadian Regionalism' in Peter Aucoin, ed., *Regional Responsiveness and the National Administrative State*: Vol. 37, Research Studies of the Royal Commission on the Economic Union and Development Prospects for Canada (Toronto: University of Toronto Press 1985), 36

92 Interviewee No. 58, Ottawa, 25 February 1987

93 Kernaghan, 'Representative and Responsive Bureaucracy,' 36, 38

94 Interviewee No. 51, Ottawa, 4 April 1986

95 In 1979 the new president of Treasury Board, Sinclair Stevens, announced the deferral or outright cancellation of thirteen of the projects originally announced by Chrétien. Some, though not all, were reactivated when the Liberals returned in 1980. See Savoie, *Regional Economic Development*, 97.

96 Kernaghan, 'Representative and Responsive Bureaucracy,' 38

97 'Probe asked in job move to Shediac,' *Telegraph Journal*, 24 January 1978: 1

98 LeBlanc interview, 25 March 1986

99 Interviewee No. 80, former exempt staff member in the office of Allan J. MacEachen, Interview, Halifax, 29 February 1988

100 'Taxpayers casualties in DVA move: Relocation cost $65.7 million and climbing,' *Globe and Mail*, 29 October 1983: 1

101 Kernaghan, 'Representative and Responsive Bureaucracy,' 37

102 LeBlanc interview, 25 March 1986

103 W.M. Dobell, 'Defence Procurement Contracts and Industrial Offset Packages,' *International Perspectives* (January/February 1981): 14

104 John M. Treddenick, 'The Arms Race and Military Keynesianism,' *Canadian Public Policy* 11 (1985): 77–92

105 Dobell, 'Defence procurement contracts,' 15

106 Department of Supply and Services, 'Request for Proposal' for New Fighter Acquisition Program (1977), quoted in Michael M. Atkinson and Kim Richard Nossal, 'Bureaucratic Politics and the New Fighter Aircraft Decisions,' *Canadian Public Administration* 24 (Winter 1981): 549, 539–43

107 Dobell 'Defence procurement contracts,' 15

108 Atkinson and Nossal, 'Bureaucratic Politics and the New Fighter Aircraft Decisions,' 552–60

109 Dobell, 'Defence procurement contracts,' 17–18

110 Atkinson and Nossal, 'Bureaucratic Politics and the New Fighter Aircraft Decisions,' 557–62. Only IT&C raised major objections when, at a relatively late stage, it suddenly became aware that one of their programs, the administration of the defence production sharing arrangements with the United States, stood to be adversely affected by

the way the industrial benefits articles were calculated. This difficulty had been ironed out, however, by the time the proposed contracts were submitted to the Clark government in November 1979.

111 Dobell, 'Defence procurement,' 17. The reduced commitment involved changing the originally proposed $750 million loan and grant rescue package for Chrysler to a $200 million guarantee.

112 Ibid.

113 'CAF given $4.3 million by court,' Globe and Mail, 6 August 1982: B10; 'CAF Industries Limited awarded $4.3 million over broken federal promise,' Winnipeg Free Press, 5 August 1982: 1, 4

114 'Taxpayers casualties in DVA move'

115 John W. Langford, 'Air Canada' in Allan Tupper and G. Bruce Doern, eds., Public Corporations and Public Policy in Canada (Montreal: Institute for Research on Public Policy 1981), 267–9

Chapter Six

1 G. Bruce Doern, 'The Mega-Project Episode and the Formulation of Canadian Economic Development Policy,' Canadian Public Administration 26 (Summer 1983): 222

2 See Keith Banting and Richard Simeon, eds., And No One Cheered: Federalism, Democracy and the Constitution Act (Toronto: Methuen 1983); David Milne, Tug of War: Ottawa and the Provinces under Trudeau and Mulroney (Toronto: Lorimer 1986); Kenneth McRoberts, 'Unilateralism, Bilateralism and Multilateralism: Approaches to Canadian Federalism' in Richard Simeon, ed., Intergovernmental Relations: Vol. 63, Research Studies of the Royal Commission on the Economic Union and Development Prospects for Canada (Toronto: University of Toronto Press 1985), 71–129; Ron Graham, One-Eyed Kings: Promise and Illusion in Canadian Politics (Don Mills: Totem 1987).

3 Bruce G. Pollard, Managing the Interface: Intergovernmental Affairs Agencies in Canada (Kingston: Institute of Intergovernmental Relations 1986), ch. 3

4 Department of Finance, 'Federal-Provincial Fiscal Arrangements in the Eighties: A Submission to the Parliamentary Task Force on the Federal-Provincial Fiscal Arrangements by the Honourable Allan J. MacEachen, Deputy Prime Minister and Minister of Finance,' 23 April 1981: 33–9

5 Report of the Parliamentary Task Force on Federal-Provincial Fiscal Arrangements, August 1981, Fiscal Federalism in Canada (Ottawa: Supply and Services 1981), esp. ch. 10

6 Canada, Statement on Economic Development for Canada in the 1980s (Ottawa: November 1981)

7 Doern, 'The Mega-Project Episode,' 223

8 Canada, Major Canadian Projects: Major Canadian Opportunities, Report to the Major Projects Task Force on Major Capital Projects in Canada to the Year 2000 (Ottawa: Supply and Services 1981) cited in ibid., 223

9 Doern, 'The Mega-Project Espisode, ' 235
10 G. Bruce Doern and Glen Toner, *The Politics of Energy: The Development and Implementation of the NEP* (Toronto: Methuen 1985), 30–2
11 Ibid., 114
12 Herman Bakvis and William M. Chandler, 'The Future of Federalism' in H. Bakvis and W. Chandler eds., *Federalism and the Role of the State* (Toronto: University of Toronto Press 1987), 306–18
13 See, for example, J. Stefan Dupré, David M. Cameron, Graeme H. McKechnie, and Theodore B. Rotenberg, *Federalism and Policy Development: The Case of Adult Occupational Training in Ontario* (Toronto: University of Toronto Press 1973).
14 Pierre De Bané interview, Ottawa, 2 April 1986
15 Donald J. Savoie, *Regional Economic Development: Canada's Search for Solutions* (Toronto: University of Toronto Press 1986), 67–9
16 'Ottawa plans major changes in cost-sharing,' *Globe and Mail*, 13 August 1981: 1
17 Ibid., 2
18 Signed in 1969, the plan preceded the GDAs signed with the nine other provinces and actually constituted the model for the GDA approach as implemented in 1974.
19 Savoie, *Regional Economic Development*, 71–2. In actual terms most of the employees involved in these programs continued to work as before, and in the same offices, except now they were working for, and paid by, the federal government. See, for example, 'Feds take over funding of transport centre,' *The Guardian* (Charlottetown), 15 October 1981: 1; 'DREE to hire 7,' ibid., 30 October 1981: 3; 'Ottawa hiring Islanders to help with programs,' ibid., 31 October 1981: 1.
20 Savoie, *Regional Economic Development*, 71–2; '$10-million program announced: Seed money to be spread over decade,' *Telegraph Journal*, 24 October 1981: 4
21 'General Development Agreements (GDAs): Status of Subsidiary Agreements as of June 28, 1985' (Ottawa: Department of Regional Industrial Expansion, mimeographed)
22 De Bané interview, 2 April 1986
23 Savoie, *Regional Economic Development*, 73
24 Office of the Prime Minister, press release, 12 January 1982
25 G. Bruce Doern and Richard Phidd, 'Economic Management in Canada: Some Implications of the Board of Economic Development Ministers and the Lambert Report,' paper presented to the Canadian Political Science Association annual meeting, Saskatoon, May 1979
26 Proposed order-in-council, section 18, Ministries and Ministers of State Act (Ottawa: Privy Council Office 1978) quoted in Richard D. French, *How Ottawa Decides: Planning and Industrial Policy-Making 1968–1980* (Toronto: Lorimer 1980), 124–5
27 Peter Aucoin and Herman Bakvis, 'Regional Responsiveness and

Government Organization: The Case of Regional Economic Development Policy in Canada' in P. Aucoin, ed., *Regional Responsiveness and the National Administrative State*: Vol. 37, Research Studies of the Royal Commission on the Economic Union and Development Prospects for Canada (Toronto: University of Toronto Press 1985), 67

28 French, *How Ottawa Decides*, 129

29 The inner cabinet, part of a scheme to streamline cabinet operations, consisted of the chairpersons of cabinet committees, ministers in charge of central agencies, and regional ministers where a region was not already represented under the first two headings. Region was broadly defined. There were no ministers from Nova Scotia and New Brunswick, for example. Decisions taken by each cabinet committee were considered to be final and could be appealed to the inner cabinet only under special circumstances and with the permission of the prime minister. As Richard French notes, however, almost from the beginning most politically sensitive decisions ended up in the inner cabinet. See ibid., 135–6

30 Canada, Department of Finance, *The New Expenditure Management System: A Paper Outlining the Envelope System for Allocating and Controlling Expenditures of the Government of Canada* (Ottawa, December 1979) 7, quoted in ibid., 139

31 Office of the Prime Minister, press release, 12 January 1982; for further details see Peter Aucoin and Herman Bakvis, 'Organizational Differentiation and Integration: The Case of Regional Development Policy in Canada,' *Canadian Public Administration* 27 (Fall 1984): 348–71.

32 Interviewee No. 22, senior MSERD official (projects branch), Ottawa, 26 April 1984

33 Office of the Prime Minister, press release, 12 January 1982

34 Aucoin and Bakvis, 'Regional Responsiveness and Government Organization,' 82

35 Interviewee No. 24, senior official, MSERD (projects branch), Ottawa, 26 April 1984

36 Colin Campbell, *Governments under Stress: Political Executives and Key Bureaucrats in Washington, London, and Ottawa* (Toronto: University of Toronto Press 1983), 351

37 G. Bruce Doern, 'The Political Administration of Government Reorganization: The Merger of DREE and ITC,' *Canadian Public Administration* 30 (Spring 1987): 34–56

38 Federal Economic Development Co-ordinator's Office, Manitoba 'Glossary' (Winnipeg: mimeographed undated)

39 Canada, House of Commons, *Bill C-152: An Act respecting the organization of the Government of Canada and matters related or incidental thereto*, first reading, 15 May 1983, section 35: 24

40 'Marc Lalonde: the strong man grows stronger,' *Globe and Mail*, 16 July 1983: 1, 4

41 Jeffrey Simpson, 'The Two Trudeaus: Federal Patronage in Quebec, 1968–84,' *Journal of Canadian Studies* 22 (1987): 102
42 'Lalonde wants pipeline rerouted to serve 250,000 more Quebecers,' *Gazette* (Montreal), 20 October 1981: 1; Doern and Toner, *The Politics of Energy*, 42
43 R.A. Young, 'Business and Budgeting: Recent Proposals for Reforming the Revenue Budgeting Process,' *Canadian Public Policy* 9 (September 1983): 347–61
44 Henry Jacek, 'John Munro and the Hamilton East Liberals: Anatomy of a Modern Political Machine' in Bill Freeman and Marsha Hewitt, eds., *Their Town: The Mafia, the Media and the Party Machine* (Toronto: Lorimer 1979), 62–73
45 Harold Crookell, 'The Volkswagen Duty Remission Plan' in Mark C. Baetz and Donald H. Thain, eds., *Canadian Cases in Business-Government Relations* (Toronto: Methuen 1985), 145–60. On Gray's relations with other Ontario ministers see Paul G. Thomas, 'The Role of National Party Caucuses' in Peter Aucoin, ed., *Party Government and Regional Representation in Canada*: Vol. 36, Research Studies of the Royal Commission on the Economic Union and Development Prospects for Canada (Toronto: University of Toronto Press 1985), 103–4.
46 The various guidelines and precedures were outlined in a memorandum to cabinet (that is for CCERD) on 'Implementing ERDAS' in September 1983.
47 Interviewee No. 20, official in MSERD (operations branch), Ottawa, 26 April 1984
48 For details on decentralization in this department see M. Paul Brown, 'Environment Canada and the Pursuit of Administrative Decentralization,' *Canadian Public Administration* 29 (Summer 1986): 218–36.
49 To take an example, the 'Canada/Saskatchewan Economic and Regional Development Agreement,' signed 30 January 1984, subsection 4.1(d), states that the 'Ministers' shall 'establish a Course of Action for the next fiscal year to identify specific development opportunities for implementation pursuant to the priorities in Schedule "A" ...' The *Course of Action, 1984/85* released at the same time specified dates and events such as 'By April 1, 1984, the federal minister of Energy, Mines and Resouces and the provincial Minister of Energy and Mines will sign the Canada/Saskatchewan Subsidiary Agreement on Mineral Development which will focus on geoscientific activity designed to delineate new targets for exploration.' The timetable was not rigidly adhered to (e.g., the minerals agreement was not actually signed until 16 May 1984), but it did indicate basic understanding among federal and provincial officials of what subsidiary agreements were agreed to and the dollar amounts involved.
50 Interviewee No. 6, MSERD official (operations branch), Ottawa, 6 November 1983
51 Interviewee No. 20, 26 April 1984

52 Interviewee No. 6, 6 November 1983
53 Not all regional ministers were members of CCERD, but they would nonetheless be present for the presentation and discussion of their ERDA.
54 Interviewee No. 10 (FEDC), 20 February 1984
55 'Interim Water Agreement,' signed by the Government of Canada and the Government of Saskatchewan, 17 May 1979, terminating 31 March 1984. The federal government contributed $7.9 million and the Saskatchewan government $7.35 million.
56 These were eventually signed, respectively, 7 August 1984 ($16 million) and 1 May 1984 ($5 million), both terminating 3 March 1989.
57 Signed 7 August 1984
58 Signed 31 August 1984 with a scheduled termination date of 31 March 1989. Both governments contributed $16.6 million toward funding research and development on advanced technology at Saskatchewan universities and the Saskatchewan Research Council.
59 This involved Phase III of the PEI 'comprehensive development plan' originally signed in 1969. Savoie, *Regional Economic Development*, 71; see also note 19 supra.
60 The agreement was signed 5 October 1982 and terminated 31 March 1986. The earlier DREE subsidiary agreement had actually expired a year earlier but was allowed to run for one more year until the new agreement was in place. Under the new agreement the province was responsible for 'land development' and the federal government for 'agricultural resource development, technology acceleration, technology development and market development.' The federal share of the $48.3 million agreement was $23.3 million, which was less generous than the close to $30 million of the $48.2 million total it provided under the 1976 agricultural agreement.
61 Savoie, *Regional Ecomonic Development*, 84
62 Ibid., 81
63 In November 1980 the federal housing minister, Paul Cosgrove, had announced the termination of the Community Services Contribution Program, which had provided municipalities with more than $400 million in federal funding for sewers and other capital expenditures over the period 1978–80.
64 Signed 1 May 1984
65 Interviewee No. 80, former exempt staff member, office of Allan MacEachen, 29 February 1988
66 Canada/Nova Scotia Economic and Regional Development Agreement, 11 June 1984. Quoted in Savoie, *Regional Economic Development*, 84. The federal share of this $28 million subsidiary agreement was $19.6 million.
67 Ibid.
68 'A défaut d'entente, Ottawa injecte $109 millions dans le développement régional,' *Le devoir*, 5 juin 1984; 1, 8; 'Ottawa to go it alone on spending of Quebec job funds,' *Globe and Mail*, 5 June 1984: 3

69 Alberta's hardwood resource constitutes 40 per cent of the total wood volume in the province, but at the time of the agreement less than 1 per cent of this resource was being used. Exploitation of this resource was something that had been favoured by the Alberta government. 'Canada-Alberta Forestry Policy Framework,' Appendix A, draft, Edmonton, 1984. The 'Tourism Development Agreement' (signed 13 May 1985) provided, among other things, support for improved transportation facilities (e.g., microwave landing systems at the Jasper-Hinton airport, financial help to feeder airlines, reopening of the VIA rail link with Jasper, and highway completion and bridge construction), support that was seen as a welcome change from the cutbacks that had been imposed earlier by Transport Canada.

70 Interviewee No. 80, 29 February 1988

71 Donald Gow, 'Canadian Federal Administrative and Political Institutions: A Role Analysis,' PhD dissertation, Queen's University 1967; an abridged version containing the key recommendations is also available: Donald Gow, *Rebuilding Canada's Bureaucracy*, edited by E.R. Black and M.J. Prince (Kingston: School of Public Administration 1976).

72 Interviewee No. 23, MSERD official (project branch), Ottawa, 26 April 1984

Chapter Seven

1 The garbage can model was developed by Micheal D. Cohen, James G. March, and Johan P. Olson, 'A Garbage Can Model of Organizational Choice,' *Administrative Science Quarterly* 17 (1972): 1–25. For Canadian applications of the model see Michael M. Atkinson and Richard A. Powers, 'Inside the Industrial Policy Garbage Can: Selective Subsidies to Business in Canada,' *Canadian Public Policy* 13 (1987): 208–17.

2 Details on these programs can be found in Canada, *Job Creation Programs, An Overview, 1983* (Ottawa: Canada Employment and Immigration Commission 1983). Curiously it makes no reference to the Special Employment Initiative.

3 Budget Papers, 'Supplementary Information and Notice of Ways and Means Motion on the Budget.' Tabled in House of Commons 28 June 1982: 31

4 Canada, *Supplementary Estimates (B), 1982–83* Employment and Immigration, 38

5 House of Commons, *Debates*, 16 November 1982: 20,695

6 Ibid.

7 Interviewee No. 72, CFIC official, Ottawa, 30 July 1987. Among Chong's duties in the PMO was the responsibility 'to harmonize government policy with political strategy,' ('Women around the Prime Minister,' *Chatelaine*, August 1982: 67). Whether she was actually responsible for designing the SEI remains unclear. In the event, the scheme would have required the approval of the political cabinet, and, given that money from the La

Prade fund was also delivered under the aegis of the SFI, both Marc
Lalonde and Jean Chrétien would have had to be involved.

8 Interviewee No. 72

9 Ibid.

10 Interviews, officials (four), Office of the Auditor General, Ottawa, 5 June
1987

11 *Report of the Auditor General of Canada: Fiscal Year Ended 31 March 1986*
(Ottawa: Supply and Services Canada 1986), para. 6.28

12 Ibid., para. 6.29. The 82 and 70 per cent figures were estimates provided
by staff in the auditor general's office.

13 Chapter 9.4. The policy on using contributions rather than grants for
capital projects was adopted in 1977 upon recommendation of the House
of Commons Public Accounts Committee, cited in ibid., paras. 6.34 and
6.35.

14 Treasury Board Minute No. 784672, cited in ibid., paras. 6.25 and 6.36

15 Ibid., para. 6.36

16 House of Commons *Debates*, 7 February 1984: 1148

17 Interviewee No. 72

18 The MP for the riding in which CSN headquarters were located, who was
also parliamentary secretary for public works, did send to the CSN a 'liste
des candidats en quête de travail' whom he hoped might be hired for
the project. It was not a requirement, however, and none of the
individuals on the list were in fact hired. Letter from Jean-Claude
Malépart to CSN, 18 July 1983. Interviewee No. 125, senior CSN official,
Montreal, 10 June 1989

19 See David Kwavnick, 'Pressure Group Demands and the Struggle for
Organizational Status,' *Canadian Journal of Political Science* 3 (1970): 56–72.

20 'La Prade: Ottawa gardera le contrôle des $200 millions,' *La Presse* 22
March 1982: A4

21 Jeffrey Simpson, *The Spoils of Power: The Politics of Patronage* (Toronto:
Collins 1988), 343

22 *Report of the Auditor General of Canada: Fiscal Year ended 31 March 1986*, paras.
6.93 through 6.96

23 See Ian Waddell (MP, Vancouver-Kingsway), House of Commons,
Debates, 13 February 1984: 1319, and 14 February 1984: 1364–8; 'Italians in
Toronto,' *Globe and Mail*, 22 October 1984: M3

24 Waddell, House of Commons, *Debates*, 13 February 1984: 1319

25 Ibid., 14 February 1984: 1365: 'Italians in Toronto'

26 Interviewee No. 72

27 The act was amended so that no school-board, municipal corporation,
and the like could 'circumvent the prohibition [to 'negotiate or enter
into an agreement with the Government of Canada'] by permitting or
tolerating that it be affected by an agreement made between a third
person and a government, a department or an agency contemplated in
said subparagraph.' Government of Quebec, 'Act Respecting the

Ministère des Affaires intergouvernementales,' *Statutes of Québec 1984*, ch. 27 c. M-21, s. 20, am.: 464

28 Interviewee No. 72

29 *Report of the Auditor General of Canada: Fiscal Year ended 31 March 1986*, para. 6.43

30 For example, in the case of the CSN project, the CSN was initially approached by an official from the local CEIC office. In Manitoba, the home province of the minister responsible for the SEI, Lloyd Axworthy, officials had little choice but to help promote the program, particularly in Winnipeg (see ch. 8).

31 For example, 'The cost of job-making,' *Maclean's*, 6 February 1984: 6, 8

32 'Liberal MPS given 91% of job fund, NDP says,' *Globe and Mail*, 18 February 1984: 13; 'Opposition sees red as Liberals present list on job-creation plan,' ibid., 22 February 1984: 8

33 Budget Papers, 'Supplementary Information and Notices of Ways and Means Motions on the Budget.' Tabled in House of Commons, 19 April 1983: 3

34 Interview, Tom Axworthy (principal secretary to the PM, 1981–4), Montreal, 20 April 1988

35 Treasury Board issued circular No. 1983-23, 787926, to all deputy heads of departments and heads of agencies concerning the 'Treasury Board directives, guidelines and procedures that have been amended or set aside in the interests of facilitating the implementation of Special Recovery Capital Projects Programs.' Cited and quoted in James Egan, 'The Politics of Priority Management: An Examination of the Special Recovery Capital Projects Program,' MA thesis, University of Manitoba 1987: 63. The following account of SRCPP draws extensively on this excellent thesis.

36 Egan, 'The Politics of Priority Management,' 6

37 Reported by official present at the meeting, quoted in ibid., 22

38 Quoted in ibid., 21

39 Details on the origins and preliminary development of the program can be found in ibid., 16–22.

40 Quoted in ibid., 29

41 Most of the following is based on ibid., 33 and interview with senior official then working in the SRCPP secretariat, 1 April 1986 (interviewee No. 50).

42 Egan, 'The Politics of Priority Management,' 13–15. Of the $2.4 billion, $700 million was considered new money obtained from sales tax increases also announced in the budget, while the remaining $1.7 billion came ostensibly from departmental A bases. This was in part a sleight-of-hand, however, as the money was drawn not from the current fiscal year but from future years. Again the logic of the SRCPP involved moving forward the timetable of projects scheduled for possible implementation in future years in departmental multi-year plans.

43 Ibid., appendix F.

44 Canada, *Special Recovery Capital Projects Program: The First Year* (Ottawa: Supply and Services 1984), 10

45 Egan, 'The Politics of Priority Management,' 64–7. There were some suspicions that Treasury board, in speeding up turnaround time, was giving SRCPP applications only cursory review. Others, mainly in line departments, felt that the improved turnaround occurred at the expense of regular submissions, which would be knocked out of the queue when SRCPP projects arrived.

46 $18.2 million was allocated directly to Route 11 while another $23.8 million was allocated to reconstruction or upgrading of related highways such as Route 8. Canada, *Special Recovery Capital Projects Program*, 22

47 Pierre De Bané interview, Ottawa, 2 April 1986

48 The authority, assigned to the Quebec government by federal order-in-council in 1922, involved 'administration in all sea fisheries ... as well as jurisdiction over freshwater fish.' The resumption of this authority by the federal government was announced by De Bané in July 1983 and took effect 1 April 1984. A. Paul Pross and Susan McCorquodale, *Economic Resurgence and the Constitutional Agenda: The Case of the East Coast Fisheries* (Kingston: Institute of Intergovernmental Relations 1987), 46, 142

49 Pierre De Bané interview, 2 April 1986

50 Canada, *Special Recovery Capital Projects Program* 28; Canada *Information: The Maurice Lamontagne Institute* (Ottawa: Department of Fisheries and Oceans 1985)

51 As of 1985 it was estimated that the institute's staff would number 265 person-years by 1992 (Canada, *Information: The Maurice Lamontagne Institute*).

52 The move aroused not only controversy among students and Halifax residents but also caused a rift within the Nova Scotia cabinet. 'Outcry growing at move of NSNI,' *Chronicle-Herald*, 21 March 1984; 'Marine school relocation sparks dispute,' *Globe and Mail*, 25 September 1984: 5; 'Culture minister irked by Donahoes,' *Chronicle-Herald*, 10 January 1985

53 Details on this episode are drawn mainly from a written account by Kenzie MacKinnon, Allan MacEachen's executive assistant at the time, and published in the *Port Hawkesbury Reporter*, 14 October 1987 ('Time to set the record straight on "inaccurate load of malarkey" from Billy Joe on Nautical School' [letter to the editor]: 4, 7). MacKinnon's detailed account was an effort to set the record straight after a former Nova Scotia minister, Billy Joe MacLean, made claims to the effect that he had been primarily responsible for the arrival of the Nautical Institute in Port Hawkesbury.

54 Ibid., 7

55 Ibid.

56 See 'Canada–Nova Scotia offshore management agreement,' *Mail-Star*

(Halifax), 5 March 1982: 8, 9. 'Ottawa gets offshore control, most of money goes to N.S.,' *Globe and Mail*, 3 March 1982: 1, 2

57 Interviewee No. 80. The source of the $1.5 million is not clear. One suspects that the money may well have come from the SEI program.

58 'Contract awarded,' *Chronicle-Herald*, 1 May 1985: Canada, *Special Recovery Capital Projects Program*, 29

59 Canada, *Special Recovery Capital Projects Program: The First Year*, 17, 30; Canada, *Information: Special Recovery Capital Projects, Project Master List* (Ottawa: Special Recovery Projects, 17 November 1983), 16

60 Calculated from data in *Special Recovery Capital Projects Program: The First Year*, 19–31. Some of the 160 projects can be broken down further into identifiable projects, the small harbour programs, for example. If the shipbuilding projects are eliminated from the analysis, the percentage of funds going to federal-provincial projects becomes 26.2. As well, the proportion of funds going to wholly federally funded but provincially owned projects (i.e., with no provincial contribution) is likely underestimated. The SRCPP listing designates projects as federal-provincial only when provincial governments make a financial contribution.

61 Egan, 'The Politics of Priority Management,' 81. This additional saving was estimated to be approximately $200 million.

62 The contracts were mainly for Type 1050 and Type 1100 tenders for the supply of navigation aids and ice-breaking and the mid-life modernization of the ice-breaker *Sir Humphrey Gilbert*. The contracts for the modernization of two additional ice-breakers and the construction of a new heavy ice-breaker had not been announced by the time the final report on SRCPP was made.

63 Egan, 'The Politics of Priority Management,' 85

64 'Did DREE drink Canada DRIE? DRIE was supposed to bring regional development into the mainstream of national economic policy-making instead of being marginal to it,' *Atlantic Insight* 6, no. 9 (October 1984): 45

65 See, for example, question in the House by Nelson A. Riis: *Debates*, 14 February 1984: 1374–5: 'Liberal ridings win at handout time,' *Ottawa Citizen*, 30 July, cited in Egan, 'The Politics of Priority Management,' 90.

66 Canada, *Special Recovery Captital Projects Program: The First Year*, 7

67 Egan, 'The Politics of Priority Management,' 88

68 'The cost of job-making,' *Maclean's*, 6 February 1984: 6

69 Egan, 'The Politics of Priority Management,' 93

70 What piqued MacEachen's interests, and concerns, was the threatened closure of the fish plant in the town of Canso, located in MacEachen's riding and in a community which at one point was a focal point of the Antigonish co-operative movement. The plant was heavily dependent on offshore quotas, which it was in danger of losing. Interviewee No. 80

71 De Bané interview, 2 April 1986; Inteviewee No. 80

72 Canada, *Navigating Troubled Waters, A New Policy for the Atlantic Fisheries: Report of the Task Force on Atlantic Fisheries* (Ottawa: Supply and Services 1983)

73 A. Paul Pross, 'The Fishery: Ali versus Frazier' in Barbara Jamieson, ed., *Governing Nova Scotia: Policies, Priorities and the 1984–85 Budget* (Halifax: School of Public Administration 1984), 81–112

74 According to Breau, 'It's no secret that the fishermen in Eastern Canada at least have voted heavily Liberal in the last three elections ... We're concerned about our support there now, because we're not seen to be on the fishermen's side as much as we were.' Quoted in 'Fish subsidy will lure Maritime votes: Breau,' *Globe and Mail*, 4 July 1984: 5

75 Interview, 2 April 1986

76 Ibid.

77 The implementation of what Tom Axworthy called 'the strategic prime ministership' meant, in his words, that 'we cut his [the PM's] meetings and memos on secondary subjects to nil, we spun off patronage and party affairs to the ministers, we pushed as much as possible out and kept as little as possible in.' Quoted in Graham, *One-Eyed Kings*, 64

78 Paul G. Thomas, 'The Role of National Party Caucuses' in Peter Aucoin, ed., *Party Government and Regional Representation in Canada*: Vol. 36, Research Studies of the Royal Commission on the Economic Union and Development Prospects for Canada (Toronto: University of Toronto Press 1985), 104

Chapter Eight

1 'Waiting for Pierre: Lloyd Axworthy thought his time had come,' *Today Magazine* (Saturday insert of the *Globe and Mail*), 19 April 1980: 11; 'Axworthy: Liberals want to know if he looks like a winner,' *Globe and Mail*, 31 March 1980: 1

2 'Prairie Liberal wants to take on Lévesque,' *Gazette* (Montreal), 16 July 1979: 6

3 'Where power is, there's Axworthy,' *Financial Post*, 14 July 1984: 9

4 Canada, *Report of the Task Force on Housing and Urban Development* (Ottawa: Queen's Printer 1969)

5 Lloyd Axworthy, 'The Housing Task Force: A Case Study' in G.B. Doern and Peter Aucoin, eds., *The Structures of Policy-Making in Canada* (Toronto: Macmillan of Canada 1971), 131

6 Ibid., 147, 150

7 Lloyd Axworthy, 'How to Win the West!' *Dialogue* 1 (1975): 10

8 Ibid. 11

9 Lloyd Axworthy, 'Towards a New Phase,' *Canadian Forum*, September 1979: 13, 14. Who Axworthy had in mind in referring to 'senior civil servants' and the 'senior mandarinate' is not clear, especially in light of the organizational changes of the 1960s and 1970s. In the instance of the

rejection of the Housing Task Force report, however, he pointed to the Privy Council Office as the source of opposition. See 'The Housing Task Force,' 152, n. 18.

10 'Axworthy: Liberals want to know if he looks like a winner,' 2. See also, 'Axworthy grooming himself for the top,' *Ottawa Journal*, 30 July 1979: 4.

11 'Winning convention jackpot makes Axworthy a hero,' *Globe and Mail*, 8 December 1979: 8. Scheduled for March 1980, the convention was actually held in July of that year and only as a regular Liberal party convention.

12 'Liberal Plan would make city a centre for research,' *Winnipeg Free Press*, 27 December 1979: 3; 'Grits weighing large role for Petro-Can: Axworthy,' *Winnipeg Free Press*, 9 January 1980: 11

13 'Axworthy: Liberals want to know if he looks like a winner,' 2

14 'The Axatollah rides again,' *Maclean's* 10 March 1980: 19

15 The decline of the party, especially during the Trudeau era, has been well chronicled by David E. Smith, *The Regional Decline of a National Party: Liberals on the Prairies* (Toronto: University of Toronto Press 1981).

16 It should be noted that these problems arise not only in Westminster-type systems, nor are they restricted to the national level. For an analysis of the problem of political control at the local level in the United States see Judith E. Gruber, *Controlling Bureaucracies: Dilemmas in Democratic Governance* (Berkeley: University of California Press 1987).

17 Richard H.S. Crossman, *The Diaries of a Cabinet Minister*, 3 vols. (London: Hamilton and Cape 1975–7)

18 Hugh Heclo and Aaron Wildavsky, *The Private Government of Public Money* (Berkeley: University of California Press 1974), 130

19 J.L. Granatstein, *The Ottawa Men: The Civil Service Mandarins 1935–1957* (Toronto: Oxford University Press 1982), 266–7

20 Walter Stewart, *Paper Juggernaut: Big Government Gone Mad* (Toronto: McClelland and Stewart 1979)

21 Flora MacDonald, 'The Minister and the Mandarins: How a New Minister Copes with the Entrapment Devices of Bureaucracy,' *Policy Options* 1 (September–October 1980): 30

22 The 'political-administration' model has its origins in the work of Robert D. Putnam in *The Beliefs of Politicians* (New Haven: Yale University Press 1973) and the 'The Political Attitudes of Senior Civil Servants in Western Europe,' *British Journal of Political Science* 3 (1973): 257–90 and is fully developed in Joel B. Aberbach, Robert A. Putnam, and Bert A. Rockman, *Bureaucrats and Politicians in Western Democracies* (Cambridge, Mass: Harvard University Press 1981). Assessment of Canada in terms of the model is found in Michael M. Atkinson and William Coleman, 'Bureaucrats and Politicians in Canada: An Examination of the Political Administration Model,' *Comparative Political Studies* 18 (1985): 58–80.

23 See the excellent piece by Colin Campbell, 'Review Article: The Political Roles of Senior Government Officials in Advanced Democracies,' *British Journal of Political Science* 18 (1988): 243–72, which develops further the

typology of different kinds of political-bureaucratic interaction introduced by Aberbach et al. in *Bureaucrats and Politicians in Western Democracies*. It is important to note that the 'political' role of bureaucrats can include efforts, often made under the guise of neutrality, to thwart the desires of their political masters, as well as explicitly 'pro-active' behaviour intended to help their political superiors.

24 Atkinson and Coleman, 'Bureaucrats and Politicians in Canada'

25 Interviewee No. 36 (senior member of Axworthy's personal staff), Ottawa, 25 November 1985

26 Interviewee No. 80, Halifax, 29 February 1988

27 Andrew F. Johnson, 'A Minister as an Agent of Policy Change: The Case of Unemployment Insurance in the Seventies,' *Canadian Public Administration* 24 (Winter 1981): 612–33

28 Ibid., 624. According to Johnson, these 'Old Guard' civil servants 'were simply by-passed in the policy-making process and placed in positions from which they never regained their former authority.'

29 Ibid., 624–8

30 Sandford F. Borins, 'Organization without Environment: A Review of Walter Stewart's *Paper Juggernaut*,' *Canadian Public Policy* 6 (1980): 115–23

31 What made the case of the Pickering airport so interesting was the fact that both the federal Liberal and provincial Conservative governments were in a minority situation when some of the more crucial decisions had to be made; ibid., 122.

32 See Canada, *Labour Market Developments in the 1980s* (Ottawa: Employment and Immigration Canada 1981). Commonly referred to as the 'Dodge Report,' it had considerable influence on structuring the debate over the kind of support Ottawa should be providing to the provinces in areas like post-secondary education.

33 'Axworthy Ottawa's unknown quantity,' *Winnipeg Free Press*, 31 July 1980: 7

34 Canada, Office of the Minister of Employment and Immigration, *The Refugee Status Determination Process: A Report of the Task Force on Immigration Practices and Procedures* (Ottawa: Supply and Services 1981)

35 For example, 'Illegal Immigrants Issues Paper' prepared by W.G. Robinson, special adviser to the Minister of Employment and Immigration (Hull, Quebec, 15 February 1983), 1

36 See also *Illegal Migrants in Canada: A Report to the Honourable Lloyd Axworthy Minister of Employment and Immigration from W.G. Robinson, Special Advisor* (Ottawa: Supply and Services 1983); and *A New Refugee Status Determination Process for Canada: A Report to the Honourable John Roberts Minister of Employment and Immigration from Ed Ratushny, Special Advisor* (Ottawa: Supply and Services, 1984). The report had been requested by Axworthy while still minister.

37 'Political friends ran Axworthy empire: Outsiders hired to steer policy process,' *Globe and Mail*, 5 December 1984: 1, 4

38 The exact number of staff is difficult to ascertain, and estimates vary. James Rusk, for example, estimates at least seventy-five. See 'Transport Ministry staff ballooned under Liberals,' *Globe and Mail*, 4 December 1984: 4. Others who were actually on Axworthy's staff note that at times the number easily exceeded one hundred. (Interviewee No. 36, 25 November 1985). The variation can be blamed in part on the myriad of ways that staff were hired, and often the labels attched to positions were rather misleading. For example, Ingeborg Boyens, a key member of Axworthy's team and working directly out of his office during the fourteen month period at Transport, was never officially a member of the minister's staff but a paid consultant working on a contract basis.

39 J.R. Mallory, 'The Minister's Office Staff: An Unreformed Part of the Public Service,' *Canadian Public Administration* 10 (Spring 1967): 29. Further details on the role and recruitment of exempt staff can be found in Blair Williams, 'The Para-political Bureaucracy in Ottawa' in H.C. Clark, C. Campbell, F.Q. Quo, and A. Goddard, eds., *Parliament, Policy and Representation* (Toronto: Methuen 1980), 215–30.

40 Interviewee No. 53 (senior member, Axworthy's ministerial staff in Winnipeg), Winnipeg, 10 June 1986

41 Interviewee No. 34, 25 November 1985; Interviewee No. 68, 5 June 1987 (senior officials in the air and surface administrations respectively, Department of Transport), Ottawa

42 Interviewee No. 68. Gordon F. Osbaldeston, former deputy and clerk of the PCO, also notes that these sorts of contacts are among the worst threats to the integrity of the reporting relationships between senior officials and middle-level staff. *Keeping Deputy Ministers Accountable* (London, Ont.: National Centre for Management Research and Development 1988), 40–1

43 Interviewee No. 68

44 'Axworthy perseveres, downplays slips,' *Financial Post*, 8 August 1981: 9. 'The exit of an iron will,' *Maclean's*, 2 February 1981; 28–9. Up to that point Axworthy had been assiduously depicting himself as a promoter of women's rights. For example, 'Women's status deteriorating, Axworthy says,' *Winnipeg Free Press*, 16 July 1980: 17. Shortly after the débâcle with the National Advisory Council on Women's Issues Axworthy lost the responsibility for women's issues to Judy Erola.

45 Ronald C. Drews, 'Electoral Manipulation and the Influence of Polling on Politicians: A Study of Political Organization in the Liberal Party of Canada up to the 1984 Election Campaign,' MA thesis, McGill University 1988: 128–9, 224

46 Interviewee No. 66, former senior CEIC official, Ottawa, 5 June 1987

47 Ibid.

48 Love actually arrived in CEIC very late in 1979, having been appointed by Prime Minister Clark, and left in early 1982.

49 Peter Aucoin and Herman Bakvis, *The Centralization-Decentralization*

Conundrum: Organization and Management in the Canadian Government
(Halifax: Institute for Research on Public Policy 1988), 75
50 'Axworthy orders probe into memo,' *Winnipeg Free Press*, 13 May 1982: 1;
'Axworthy disowns memo,' *Winnipeg Free Press*, 15 May 1982: 12
51 Interviewee No. 52 (former member of Axworthy's senior staff),
Winnipeg, 4 June 1986
52 On the organizational problems within Transport see Aucoin and Bakvis,
The Centralization-Decentralization Conundrum, 78–80. See also Ramsay M.
Withers, 'Turning the Organization Around,' a paper prepared for the
Institute of Public Administration of Canada, 19th national seminar, 11–13
June 1986. Withers had previously been deputy at the Department of
National Defence, where he had obtained experience in dealing with
three separate branches and had come to value a high level of
integration between them. For details on the air administration branch
and its recent history see Garth Stevenson, *The Politics of Canada's Airlines:
From Diefenbaker to Mulroney* (Toronto: University of Toronto Press 1987),
esp. ch. 2.
53 John W. Langford, *Transport in Transition: The Reorganization of the Federal
Transportation Portfolio* (Montreal: McGill-Queen's University Press 1976)
54 Quoted in 'The Axworthy empire: Bureaucracy remade to fit minister's
needs,' *Globe and Mail*, 4 December 1984: 4
55 Ibid.
56 'Where power is, there's Axworthy,' 9
57 'The Axworthy empire,' 4
58 The enmity that this generated was greater than in cric. This came to
light after Axworthy left office when at least five Transport Canada
employees who had worked in Axworthy's office were told they were no
longer needed and told not to report to work, though they remained on
salary. 'Partisan tag is not fair, workers say,' *Globe and Mail*, 4 October
1984: 1; 'As dust settles from pc sweep, packing begins,' *Globe and Mail*, 8
October 1984: 1
59 Canada, *Air Accessibility Standards for Disabled and Elderly Persons: A Report
to the Honourable Lloyd Axworthy, Minister of Transport, from Ed Ratushny,
Special Adviser* (Ottawa: Transport Canada 1984)
60 'Political friends ran Axworthy empire,' 1
61 'Axworthy widening deregulation drive,' *Globe and Mail*, 28 May 1984: B5
62 For details on how he dealt with the deregulation process see Lloyd
Axworthy, 'Control of Policy: Changes in the Policy Process Are Needed
to Prevent Departments and Agencies Frustrating Cabinet Intentions,'
Policy Options, April 1985: 17–20
63 '"No free rides," Axworthy tells transport staff,' *Ottawa Citizen*, 9
September 1983: 1, 12
64 Axworthy, 'Control of Policy,' 18
65 Ibid., 19
66 See Stevenson, *The Politics of Canada's Airlines*, 189–93.

67 For example, see Don Mazankowski and his reference to Professor Ratushny's 'excellent recommendations' when announcing their implementation in the House. House of Commons, *Debates*, 24 April 1985: 4060

68 See 'The dream Lloyd prays comes true: His plan to revamp jobless insurance must succeed if he wants his career to keep on track,' *Toronto Star*, 13 June 1981: B4

Chapter Nine

1 Colin Campbell, 'Review Article: The Political Roles of Senior Government Officials in Advanced Democracies,' *British Journal of Political Science* 18 (1988): 268

2 A.J.P. Taylor, quoted in Mallory, 'The Minister's Office Staff: An Unreformed Part of the Public Service,' *Canadian Public Administration* 10 (Spring 1967): 32, n. 14. For details on the 'Garden Suburb,' which existed 1916–18, see John Turner, *Lloyd George's Secretariat* (Cambridge: Cambridge University Press 1980).

3 Interviewee No. 66, senior CEIC official, Ottawa, 5 June 1987

4 'Industrial strategy for West is Axworthy's objective,' *Calgary Herald*, 19 March 1980: A3; 'Axworthy to allocate development funds,' *Winnipeg Free Press*, 29 October 1980: 8; 'Specific proposals emerging for West development fund,' *Star-Phoenix* (Saskatoon), 15 January 1981: 1

5 'Specific propsals emerging for West development fund,' 1

6 See 'That Elusive Western Fund,' *Western Producer*, 23 October 1981.

7 'Gutted development fund bad for Axworthy,' *Calgary Herald*, 13 November 1981: B17

8 For details on the Crow legislation see Grace Skogstad, *The Politics of Agricultural Policy-Making in Canada* (Toronto: University of Toronto Press 1987), ch. 6.

9 For example, 'Axworthy extols Crow rate change economic benefits,' *Winnipeg Free Press*, 13 March 1982: 10

10 'Axworthy says Crow offer is opportunity of lifetime,' *Winnipeg Free Press*, 8 April 1983: 30

11 Barry Wilson, 'Killing the Crow Rate: Government Salesmen, Media Messengers,' paper submitted to the Canadian Studies Program, Carleton University, November 1984: 2, 9

12 Ibid., 15

13 'Bill passes to replace the Crow,' *Globe and Mail*, 15 November 1983: 15

14 See John Loxley, 'The "Great Northern" Plan,' *Studies in Political Economy* 6 (Autumn 1981): 151–82.

15 'Ottawa plans major changes in cost-sharing,' *Globe and Mail*, 13 August 1981: 1, 2

16 Quoted in '$186 million Northlands pact signed,' *Winnipeg Free Press*, 30 November 1982: 4

17 Interviewee No. 36 (senior member of Axworthy's personal staff), Ottawa, 25 November 1985
18 For an overview of the political geography of Manitoba see Rand Dyck, *Provincial Politics in Canada* (Scarborough: Prentice-Hall 1987), 339-87. On the NDP specifically see Nelson Wiseman, *Social Democracy in Manitoba: A History of the CCF-NDP* (Winnipeg: University of Manitoba Press 1983).
19 Interviewee No. 53 (senior official, Manitoba government, 9 June 1986); also interviewee No. 57 (senior official, Manitoba government, 10 June 1986) noted that it was a deliberate strategic decision on the part of the Manitoba government to move as quickly as possible.
20 Ibid.
21 Quotation as recollected by interviewee No. 53
22 J.S. Dupré, 'The Workability of Executive Federalism in Canada' in H. Bakvis and W.M. Chandler, eds., *Federalism and the Role of the State* (Toronto: University of Toronto Press 1987), 236-58
23 Lloyd Axworthy interview, Ottawa, 5 May 1986
24 Canada–Manitoba Subsidiary Agreement on Churchill, Schedule A, 'Background,' 4 April 1984: 13-14
25 Ibid.
26 Interviewee No. 36, Ottawa, 7 May 1986
27 'Axworthy vows to quit if CN moves,' *Winnipeg Free Press*, 30 September 1982: 3. See also 'City, province "kiss and make up" with Axworthy over CNR,' *Winnipeg Free Press*, 1 October 1982: 3.
28 Canada–Manitoba 'Subsidiary Agreement on Churchill,' 4 April 1984
29 Ibid., 'Schedule A,' 19
30 Department of Regional Industrial Expansion, 'Economic and Regional Development Agreements: Agreements and Memoranda of Understanding as of 30 August 1985' (Ottawa, mimeographed). Additional agreements involving Saskatchewan and Manitoba were signed after the Conservatives took office, specifically tourism agreements worth $30 million in each province with the federal government contributing half the funds.
31 The period 1977-82 does not encompass all GDA (and PEI comprehensive plan) expenditures since the GDA period began in 1974 and ended in 1984. The five-year 1977-82 period was chosen by MSERD in 1983 as the most representative period to use as an initial base for allocating the ERDA regional fund.
32 See Alan F.J. Artibise, *Winnipeg: A Social History of Urban Growth, 1874-1914* (Montreal: McGill-Queen's University Press 1975); Alan F.J. Artibise, *Winnipeg: An Illustrated History* (Toronto: Lorimer 1977).
33 On the origins and implementation of the 'unicity concept' see Meyer Brownstone and T.J. Plunkett, *Metropolitan Winnipeg: Politics and Reform of Local Government* (Berkeley: University of California Press 1983).
34 David C. Walker, *The Great Winnipeg Dream* (Oakville: Mosaic 1979)

35 Quoted in 'Axworthy stresses role of business in core area,' *Winnipeg Free Press*, 26 June 1980: 10

36 'Program to upgrade core area ratified,' ibid., 23 September 1980: 3

37 '$32-million core proposal backed,' ibid., 27 September 1980: 3; 'City agrees to share core area project cost,' ibid., 2 October 1980: 3; 'Hail to the Honourable Lloyd,' ibid., 30 October 1980: 6

38 Relocation of the rail yards, something that Axworthy initially promised to support, has been a feature of redevelopment in cities like Calgary. However, given the abundance of relatively inexpensive land in downtown Winnipeg there really was little commercial need for the land that would have been made available. Hence the idea was quickly dropped and attention focused instead on a new overpass to improve connections between the downtown and the northwestern sections of the city.

39 'Core plans threatened by loss of federal aid,' *Winnipeg Free Press*, 14 November 1980: 1, 4

40 'Federal government to back loan for complex' ibid., 15 November 1980: 3; 'New Crown corporation to invest in renewable energy,' *Globe and Mail*, 31 October 1980: B6; 'Energy research centre to be located in city core,' *Winnipeg Free Press*, 31 October 1980: 1

41 For details on the administrative and financial arrangements for this unique tri-level agency see Matthew Kiernan, 'Coordination for the City Core,' *Policy Options* 6 (September 1985): 23–5.

42 'Program slammed, lauded in wide-ranging reactions,' *Winnipeg Free Press*, 4 June 1981: 8

43 Ibid.

44 'Core funding dispute causes bitter feelings,' ibid., 25 November 1980: 7

45 Winnipeg Core Area Initiative, *Status Report of Program Activities to September 30/85* (Winnipeg 1985), i

46 CAI Policy Committee (Axworthy, Mercier, and Norrie), 'Proposed Winnipeg Core Area Initiative,' 16. This item was placed not directly in the downtown area but in Osborne village.

47 'Osborne centre grants top $1.5 million,' *Winnipeg Free Press*, 19 March 1983: 1, 4; 'City to get $41 million research lab,' ibid., 13 May 1983: 1, 4

48 'Osborne centre grants top $1.5 million'

49 For example, 'Scraping the pork barrel,' ibid., 6 September 1984: 6

50 See 'Core doubts gnaw at city confidence,' ibid., 29 November 1982: 1, 4; 'Airline computer site: land speculation denied,' ibid., 26 March 1982: 50; 'Councillors put off Logan park vote,' ibid., 2 December 1982: 1, 4; 'Core plan creates few new jobs,' ibid., 20 June 1983: 1, 4

51 See 'Councillors riled at Kostyra letter,' ibid., 29 October 1982: 1, 4; 'Policy makers agree job creation essential,' ibid., 27 November 1982: 46.

52 'Councillor pegs redevelopment at $100 million,' ibid., 23 April 1983: 1, 4

53 'City continues to ponder project despite warning,' ibid., 5 May 1983: 3

54 'Civic funding refusal clouds core area plan,' ibid., 7 May 1983: 1, 4; 'City endorses development concept, talks,' ibid., 11 May 1983: 1, 4

55 '$300 million facelift urged for downtown,' ibid., 12 August 1983: 1, 4; 'City warned of Portage plan pullout,' ibid., 8 December 1983: 1

56 For example, 'More whip-cracking' (editorial), ibid., 9 December 1983: 6

57 'Spoils of victory the key to battle in Winnipeg riding,' Globe and Mail, 31 August 1984: A3; 'Core initiative chief quits city to join development firm,' Winnipeg Free Press, 2 June 1984: 3; 'Norrie accused of delaying appointment,' ibid., 31 August 1984: 1, 4; 'Norrie alleges 'patronage' bid for job,' ibid., 4 September 1984: 1, 4

58 'Core plan gets last minute $64 million,' ibid., 7 September 1984: 1, 4; 'Norrie calls core deal "blatant politicking",' ibid., 8 September 1984: 1, 4

59 'Research centre may get tenant at last,' Globe and Mail, 27 December 1986: A4

60 See 'Axworthy delivers,' Macleans, 16 January 1984: 16; 'Lloyd Iassos federal loot,' The Citizen (Ottawa), 4 February 1984: 23; 'The Axworthy way,' Globe and Mail, 6 March 1984: 6; 'Strongman Axworthy's future linked to seats he can deliver,' The Gazette (Montreal), 9 July 1984: A7. In an eight-page single-spaced document circulated by Axworthy's office in Winnipeg, Axworthy claimed expenditures of approximately one billion dollars on a total of seventy-one projects.

61 Press release, quoted in 'Lloyd Iassos federal loot,' 23; 'University institute awarded $1 million,' Winnipeg Free Press, 8 June 1984: 5; 'Axworthy announces Prairie link in computer job bank,' ibid., 1 December 1981: 9

62 'Axworthy delivers,' 16; 'Pawley to pen payroll-tax defence for Axworthy,' Winnipeg Free Press, 18 May 1982: 10

63 Quoted in 'The Core Area Initiative has great potential,' Winnipeg Free Press, 13 June 1981: 6

64 Representatives from all three governments would typically meet with their political masters before meetings of the management committee.

65 Called 'The October Partnership,' the Winnipeg-based firm was formed in 1985.

66 Axworthy interview, 5 May 1986

67 'Canada–Manitoba Subsidiary Agreement On Transportation Development: Fact Sheet, Program C: 2

68 Axworthy did not defeat this scheme on his own. Finance Minister Marc Lalonde effectively vetoed De Bané's proposal. What gave the scheme a certain amount of momentum, however, was that part of Air Canada's management was favourably disposed towards it. Interviewee No. 36, 16 June 1989

69 Axworthy interview; corroborated by De Bané (interview 2 April 1986) and LeBlanc (interview 25 March 1986)

70 One such scheme involved the creation by DRIE of a Winnipeg Crown corporation, to be run by natives with good Liberal credentials, who

would be responsible for handing out $345 million in economic development money to native people in specially targeted areas. The proposal was never implemented. See 'Winnipeg pivotal in plan, memo notes,' *Winnipeg Free Press*, 7 May 1983: 1, 4

71 'The Fort Garry tango,' *Globe and Mail*, 4 May 1984: 6

72 Bockstael at one point had hopes of becoming minister of Transport. See 'Bockstael covets transport posting,' *Winnipeg Free Press*, 30 July 1981: 10; also 'Robert Bockstael: le grand oublié,' *Le Droit* (Ottawa), 5 March 1980: 1. On federal allocations, Bockstael did have some grounds for complaint. While his riding did fare better than most in Manitoba, in part by virtue of having a corner of it encompassed by the CAI, the benefits dimmed in comparison to those funnelled into Axworthy's riding. Thus in the case of SFI funds, of the $10.5 million spent in Manitoba, approximately $4.9 million was spent in Axworthy's riding compared to $2.4 spent in Bockstael's. 'The Axworthy way,' 6

73 Interview with J.-L. Pépin, 28 November 1985, Ottawa. Apparently this was the only cabinet committee the meetings of which political aides were allowed to attend.

74 In making this point Axworthy drew an analogy between his team and the New York Knicks basketball team of the early 1970s. 'They weren't the quickest or the strongest [team in their league] but the smartest.' Axworthy interview, 5 May 1986

75 Ronald C. Drews, 'Electoral Manipulation and the Influence of Polling on Politicians: A Study of Political Organization in the Liberal Party of Canada up to the 1984 Election Campaign', MA thesis, McGill University 1988; 153–7, 186, 222–3. With departmental-sponsored polling, a so-called tack-on system was used whereby a second set of partisan items were added to the basic list. There would be two sets of printouts: one on the basic questions that was sent to the department; the other, including the politically sensitive items, would be sent to PMO. Apparently the party paid the difference in the marginal cost in having the additional items included.

76 Peter Smith, quoted in ibid., 235

77 Quoted in ibid., 225–6

78 Interviewee No. 54 (senior member of Axworthy's ministerial staff in Winnipeg), Winnipeg, 10 June 1986

79 On the old-style political machines still found in many American states and cities see Raymond Wolfinger, 'Why Political Machines Have Not Withered Away and Other Revisionist Thoughts,' *Journal of Politics* 34 (1972): 365–98.

80 The agencies were Canadian Public Affairs in Vancouver and Stringham and Grant Tandy in Winnipeg. Normally sizeable advertising contracts, those over $300,000, are allocated by the Cabinet Committee on Communications (CCC), essentially on a patronage basis. Axworthy, however, not trusting his cabinet colleagues, had his own office issue

instructions to the ccc directing that a number of contracts, including one for $1.5 million, be let to the Winnipeg firm, which was contrary to usual practice whereby the civil service simply asks the ccc to appoint an agency for advertising contracts without specifying which one. See 'Axworthy mounted $1.5 million blitz to sell Crow bill,' *Globe and Mail*, 5 December 1984: 4; also interviewee No. 36, 25 November 1985.

81 'Axworthy mounted $1.5 million blitz'
82 See Daniel J. Elazar, *American Federalism: A View from the States*, 3rd ed. (New York: Harper and Row 1984), 180.
83 Peter McCormick, Ernest C. Manning, and Gordon Gibson, 'Regional Representation in Canada' in J. Paul Johnston and Harvey E. Pasis, eds., *Representation and Electoral Systems: Canadian Perspectives* (Scarborough: Prentice-Hall 1990), 101
84 Roger Gibbins, *Regionalism: Territorial Politics in Canada and the United States* (Toronto: Butterworths 1982), 66
85 'Aerospace training centre scrapped,' *Ottawa Citizen* 16 September 1982: 14; see also 'Manitoba loses plant to Quebec,' *Winnipeg Free Press*, 22 July 1982: 1, 4. This involved the decision by cabinet to join the European Airbus Industrie consortium, which would likely run counter to the interests of the Manitoba aerospace industry given its much closer ties with American firms. Unnamed 'sources' outlined Axworthy's opposition to the scheme within cabinet.
86 For a succinct review of this literature see Doreen Barrie and Roger Gibbins, 'Parliamentary Careers in the Canadian Federal State,' *Canadian Journal of Political Science* 22 (March 1989): 137-45.

Chapter Ten

1 'Trimming the barrel,' *Globe and Mail*, 10 February 1988: A6
2 The appointments were made by the soon-to-be deputy prime minister, Erik Nielsen, on 13 July 1984. See 'Nielsen was architect of patronage system, 1984 letter indicates,' *Globe and Mail* 23 August 1989: A5.
3 Donald J. Savoie, *Regional Economic Development: Canada's Search for Solutions* (Toronto: University of Toronto Press 1986), 88-9; Michael M. Atkinson and Richard A. Powers, 'Inside the Industrial Policy Garbage Can: Selective Subsidies to Business in Canada,' *Canadian Public Policy* 13 (June 1987): 208-17
4 Quoted in David Zussman, 'Walking the Tightrope: The Mulroney Government and the Public Service' in M.J. Prince, ed., *How Ottawa Spends, 1986-87* (Toronto: Methuen 1986), 258-9
5 The antipathy many Ottawa-based civil servants displayed towards the former Department of Regional Economic Expansion (DREE) and regional programs generally has been well documented in Donald J. Savoie, 'The Toppling of DREE and the Prospects for Regional Economic Development,' *Canadian Public Policy* 10 (September 1984): 328-37.
6 Canada, Task Force on Program Review, *An Introduction to the Process of Program Review* (Ottawa: Supply and Services 1986)

7 Richard Simeon, 'National Reconciliation: The Mulroney Government and Federalism' in Andrew B. Gollner and Daniel Salée, eds., *Canada under Mulroney: An End-of-Term Report* (Montreal: Véhicule Press 1988), 25–47

8 Quoted in 'Industrial bleeding in Montreal's east end,' *Toronto Star*, 11 January 1986: B6

9 Savoie, *Regional Economic Development*, 91; Department of Regional Industrial Expansion, 'Press Release: Adjustments to Industrial and Regional Development Program' (Ottawa: 9 November 1985)

10 Canada, *A New Direction for Canada: An Agenda for Economic Renewal* (Ottawa: Supply and Services 1984); see also 'Regions wary of development plans,' *Globe and Mail*, 28 December 1984: B1–2.

11 Canada, *Freedom to Move: A Framework for Transportation Reform* (Ottawa: Supply and Services 1985), 1, iii

12 St John's, Newfoundland, 'Communique on Regional Economic Development' (21 August 1985)

13 Quoted in 'The federal eclipse of Atlantic Canada,' *Atlantic Insight* 8, no. 3, (March 1986): 26

14 This was evident in the early 1980s when Jean-Luc Pépin was minister. At that time Transport proposed reducing, and eventually eliminating, statutory freight rate subsidies for maritime shippers. This proposal was shelved after successful lobbying by maritime business interests. See A. Paul Pross, 'Mobilizing Regional Concern: Freight Rates and Political Learning in the Canadian Maritimes' in William Coleman and Henry Jacek, eds., *Regionalism, Business Interests and Public Policy* (London: Sage 1989), 173–200.

15 Memorandum, 18 September 1984, quoted in 'As dust settles from PC sweep, packing begins,' *Globe and Mail*, 8 October 1984: 8

16 'Axworthy's empire shocked incoming Tories,' *Globe and Mail*, 4 December 1984: 4

17 'MacKay denies cabinet split,' *Mail-Star* (Halifax), 3 November 1984: 3

18 Quoted in 'CN will continue to buy rail from both Algoma and Sysco,' *Globe and Mail*, 1 November 1984: B1

19 'CN rail contract rescues Sysco,' *Mail-Star*, 14 February 1987: 1; 'Federal grant is approved for Sysco's mill modernization,' *Globe and Mail*, 5 June 1987: B6

20 'Ontario signs pact,' *Globe and Mail*, 3 November 1984: B16

21 The amount for the ERDA was $1.2 billion cost-shared on a 50–50 basis. The federal government also agreed to carry over $370 million from the previous General Development Agreement. Department of Regional Industrial Expansion (DRIE), 'Economic and Regional Development Agreements: Subsidiary Agreements and Memoranda of Understanding as of May 14, 1986; (Ottawa); 'We'll have what they had,' *Globe and Mail*, 12 March 1985: 6

22 'We'll have what they had,' 6

23 'Ottawa to consider aid to Domtar mill,' *Globe and Mail*, 28 February 1985:

5; 'Under Tories, Ottawa continues to be economic cornucopia,' *Globe and Mail*, 6 January 1986: A2

24 Agar Adamson, 'Atlantic Canada: The Tories Help Those Who Help Themselves,' in Gollner and Salée, eds., *Canada under Mulroney*, 75

25 Ibid.

26 First minister of the environment and then junior minister of state for transport, Blais-Grenier was forced to resign after irregularities in her travel claims came to light.

27 This cabinet committee in turn commissioned a consultative committee composed primarily of Montral area businessmen to report on the development potential of the city and environs. This committee recommended special tax incentives and government contracts to specific firms. See Canada, Comité ministériel sur le développement de la région de Montréal, *Rapport du comité consultative* (Ottawa: Approvisionnements et Services 1986)

28 Brian Mulroney, quoted in 'Politics key theme as inner Cabinet wraps up meeting,' *Globe and Mail*, 5 July 1986; A3

29 Ibid. The other ministers (and their provinces) so designated in 1986 were: Pat Carney (British Columbia), Donald Mazankowski (Alberta), William McKnight (Saskatchewan), Jake Epp (Manitoba), Gerald Merrithew (New Brunswick), Elmer MacKay (Nova Scotia), Thomas McMillan (PEI), and John Crosbie (Newfoundland).

30 'Jet repair contract stirs bitterness,' *Globe and Mail*, 1 November 1986; A1

31 'Ottawa didn't heed own experts advice on CF-18 contract,' *Globe and Mail*, 6 January 1988: A1. It has been suggested, though never fully confirmed, that the CF-18 maintenance contract had been promised to Canadair several months earlier as part of the package that saw Bombardier purchase the money-losing Canadair facility from the federal government. As with all affairs of this size and complexity, there are a number of complications and ironies. There were two rounds of bidding. In the first, Canadair came out slightly ahead. However, at the behest of Stewart McInnes, minister of supply and services and holding the Halifax seat in which the IMP group was headquartered, the bidding was reopened. In the second round it was Bristol that came out ahead. As Jeffrey Simpson points out, dragging out the bidding and raising the stakes allowed the whole affair to become even more politicized. 'A contract lost,' *Globe and Mail*, 5 November 1986: A6

32 Michael M. Atkinson and Kim Richard Nossal, 'Bureaucratic Politics and the New Fighter Aircraft Decisions,' *Canadian Public Administration* 24 (Winter 1981): 549

33 'Divergent speeches infuriate Manitoba,' *Globe and Mail*, 2 February 1987: A5

34 Quoted in 'Winnipeg to get national health lab.' ibid., 9 October 1987: A4

35 'Transfer of rail jobs to B.C. rekindles Manitoba's anger,' ibid., 6 July 1987: A3

36 The exact arrangements for each of the three agencies differ. Fed-Nor, for example, although a separate agency, still operates under the aegis of IST, while ACOA has an independent status with no links to other departments. See Peter Aucoin, 'Organization by Place, Regional Development and National Policy: The Case of the Atlantic Canada Opportunities Agency,' presented to the annual meeting of the Canadian Political Science Association, University of Windsor, June 1988.

37 'Trimming the barrel,' A6

38 Federal financial support for court facilities – the administration of justice is a provincial responsibility – is extremely rare. See 'Ottawa finds $1 million for a court in PC riding,' Globe and Mail, 26 February 1987: A1, A 2. The rail-car works were threatened with closure by the owners, Hawker Siddeley. The rescue package permitted Montreal-based Lavalin Industries Limited to purchase the plant, guaranteeing that at least 450 jobs would be preserved. 'Lavalin buys Hawker Siddeley Trenton plant,' Globe and Mail, 9 March 1988: B7. On the Westray mine see 'Westray to build coalmine in Nova Scotia,' Globe and Mail, 2 September 1988: B1; 'Ottawa offers financial help to develop Westray mine,' Mail-Star, 17 May 1990: C16. Westray also received an $8.75 million interest buydown from the federal government in addition to a $12 million loan from the provincial government.

39 'Westray coal welcomed by Buchanan, MacKay,' Mail-Star, 23 September 1988: 25

40 Quoted in 'Grant for N.S. oil, gas projects serving a spectrum of causes,' Globe and Mail, 30 August 1986: A6. See also 'Oil funds go for highway in Tory riding,' ibid., 28 August 1986: 1.

41 For details on these projects see Report of the Auditor General of Canada to the House of Commons: Fiscal Year ended 31 March 1988 (Ottawa: Supply and Services 1988), paras 10.4 to 10.33 and Exhibit 10.1.

42 Kenzie MacKinnon, 'Time to set the record straight on "inaccurate load of malarkey" from Billy Joe on Nautical School' (letter to the editor) Port Hawkesbury Reporter, 14 October 1987: 7

43 'Tory activists, friends fill new board,' Globe and Mail, 21 November 1987: A1

44 'Ottawa to set up North Ontario development program,' ibid., 10 July 1987: A4

45 Ontario, 'Federal Initiatives in Regional Development: An Analysis' (Toronto: Federal-Provincial Relations Branch, Ministry of Intergovernmental Affairs 1988), 10, 22

46 'Bill McKnight will be the diversification key,' Alberta Report 17 (August 1987): 12

47 'Western premiers slam sluggish federal program,' Mail-Star, 20 May 1988: 4

48 Donald J. Savoie, Establishing the Atlantic Canada Opportunities Agency (Ottawa: Office of the Prime Minister 1987), 36

49 Ibid., 72
50 Ibid.
51 'New Atlantic Agency: development panacea or political pork barrel,' *Globe and Mail*, 27 June 1987: A3
52 'Ottawa plans to retain control of Atlantic agency programs,' ibid., 2 March 1988: A5
53 Canada, House of Commons, Minutes of Proceedings and Evidence of the legislative Committee on Bill C-103, 10 March 1988, 5: 78
54 'Ottawa criticized over funds,' *Globe and Mail*, 28 August 1987: A8; 'Atlantic opportunities agencies too slow – Buchanan,' *Mail-Star*, 28 November 1987: 3. The Nova Scotia government, in the hope of improving its claim for funding from ACOA, created its own Department of Small Business Development in November 1987.
55 'ACOA's McPhail exudes ability,' *Mail-Star*, 10 June 1987: 7
56 See advertisement, 'Made by Atlantic Canadians, for Atlantic Canadians. Atlantic Canada Opportunities Agency Action Program,' ibid., 18 February 1988: 13.
57 'Clean-up funds still likely,' *Mail-Star*, 6 November 1987: 1, 2; 'Premier raps Ottawa, federal programs' ibid., 28 November 1987: 1, 2
58 Adamson, 'Atlantic Canada,' 80
59 Quoted in 'Atlantic agency out to build reputation,' *Globe and Mail* 24 December 1987: A8
60 Nine of the eleven ratios were in the 25 to 33 per cent range; Elmer MacKay's riding of Central Nova had a success rate of 27.5 per cent. Dollar figures were not available. *Nova Scotia Business Journal* (June 1988): 1, 10
61 'News on grants from ACOA,' ibid., (October 1988): 3; 'Opponents critical of Crosbie's ACOA gifts,' *Mail-Star*, 11 November 1988: 42
62 'News on grants from ACOA' 3
63 As quoted by interviewee No. 128 (senior ACOA official), Halifax, 29 March 1990
64 'ACOA gave out year's budget during election,' *Globe and Mail*, 21 June 1989: A3
65 'Opponents critical of Crosbie's ACOA gifts,' 42
66 'ACOA gave out year's budget during election,' A3
67 'Crosbie announces fishery centre for Newfoundland,' *Mail-Star*, 27 October 1988: 10
68 'Atlantic Regional Development after the Budget: Whither, or Should that Be Wither, ACOA?' *Atlantic Report* (Atlantic Provinces Economic Council) 24 (June 1989): 4
69 Ibid. Under the IRDP and AFP programs the approval rate was only 41 per cent.
70 'Turner promises $1.5 billion for regions,' *Globe and Mail*, 12 October 1988: A10
71 'Western fund wins credibility,' ibid., 31 October 1988: B1

72 'Manitoba lags in money from fund,' ibid., 23 May 1988: A3
73 The provincial breakdown of the $383.3 million commitment up to 14
     October 1988 is not completely clear in that it includes $149 million for
     'systemic projects' – that is, those spanning more than province.
     'Western fund wins credibility,' B1
74 Ontario, 'Federal Initiatives in Regional Development,' 8
75 Quoted in 'Quebec bristles at development plan: Province vows to fight
     for role in expansion,' *Globe and Mail* 20 February 1988: A3
76 Quoted in ibid.
77 Ibid.
78 Ibid.
79 'Mulroney makes quick trip to Quebec to sign joint pact worth $970
     million,' ibid., 10 June 1988: A1
80 Government of Canada and Government of Quebec, *News Release: $970
     Million Dollars for Economic Development of the Regions of Quebec* (Quebec
     City, 9 June 1988), 5
81 'Hasty Promises to Lac Saint-Jean blatant vote-buying, MPs charge,' *Globe
     and Mail*, 17 June 1988: A3; 'Quebec anxious to keep Mulroney road pledge
     alive,' ibid., 4 July 1988: A5

Chapter Eleven

1 'Taxpayers miss boat in reversed decision over contract for tug' *Globe and
    Mail*, 13 February 1986: A13; 'National Scene,' ibid., 24 October 1987: A5;
    'Crosbie a good soldier – even when fighting for lost causes,' ibid., 13 July
    1987: A2
2 'Political ground shifting under old boys of PMO,' ibid., 2 September 1986:
    A4; 'Mulroney's office gets the "White House look",' ibid., 1 November
    1986: D2
3 'Mulroney's office gets the 'White House look'
4 '"Maz": PMs man creates his own cabinet network,' *Ottawa Citizen*, 4
    February 1989: B1, B7
5 'PC offshore deal would give more clout to Newfoundland,' *Globe and
    Mail*, 15 June 1984; 5; '"The Shadow Pact" deal,' ibid., 20 June 1984: 6
6 Interviewee No. 40 (official, Intergovernmental Affairs Secretariat,
    Government of Newfoundland), 27 February 1986. Re-interviewed 24
    June 1989
7 Ibid., 24 June 1989
8 'Tories barrage of spending pledges will bring pain,' *Globe and Mail*, 24
    September 1988: A3
9 The federal minister of energy, Marcel Masse, in 1987 struck a special
    Task Force on Energy Options headed by Thomas Kierans. In its report,
    delivered in August 1988, it recommended against supporting any of the
    proposed mega-projects. See 'Report on energy comes out just in time,'

Montreal Gazette, 6 August 1988: c4; 'Energy policy aside,' *Globe and Mail*, 16 August 1988: A6.

10 'Government, industry officials meeting to discuss financing for Husky upgrader,' *Globe and Mail*, 19 March 1988: B5; 'What is tomorrow's price for black gold?' ibid., 21 October 1988: B3; 'Ottawa's role in B.C. gas pipeline hinges on pulp mills along route,' ibid., 24 September 1988: B3; '1.3 billion upgrader finally gets go-ahead,' ibid., 3 September 1988: B1, B6; 'PC majority could hinge on 3 provinces: Standings may explain energy grants,' ibid., 13 September 1988: A4

11 'Negotiations held to push $5b Hibernia oil project,' *Mail-Star* (Halifax), 14 June 1988: 8 'Ottawa's concessions helped Hibernia deal,' *Globe and Mail*, 19 July 1988: B1, B4; 'Crosbie defends Hibernia deal,' *Mail-Star*, 20 July 1988: 3

12 'CN considers closing Newfoundland unit,' *Globe and Mail*, 25 February 1988: B1

13 'Mulroney's friends causing him grief,' *Ottawa Citizen*, 11 February 1987; A 2; 'Door is left open for more fish talks,' *Globe and Mail*, 7 February 1987: A3

14 'Door is left open for more fish talks,' A3

15 'Peckford receives minister's apology over fishing pact,' ibid., 30 January 1987: A3

16 Peter Aucoin, 'Organizational Change in the Machinery of Canadian Government: From Rational Management to Brokerage Politics,' *Canadian Journal of Political Science* 19 (March 1986): 3-27

17 Colin Campbell, 'Mulroney's Broker Politics: The Ultimate in Politicized Incompetence' in Andrew B. Gollner and Daniel Salée, eds., *Canada under Mulroney: An End-of-Term Report* (Montreal Véhicule Press, 1988), 309-34; Michel Gratton, *'So What Are the Boys Saying': An Inside Look at Brian Mulroney in Power* (Scarborough: McGraw-Hill Ryerson 1987)

18 'Operations unlimited,' *Globe and Mail*, 19 May 1988: A6

19 Donald J. Savoie, *The Politics of Public Spending* (Toronto: University of Toronto Press 1990), 84

20 'Operations unlimited'

21 Peter Aucoin, 'The Mulroney Government, 1984-1988: Priorities, Positional Policy and Power' in Gollner and Salée, eds., *Canada Under Mulroney*, 347

22 Office of the Prime Minister,' Release,' 30 January 1989; Office of the Prime Minister, 'Background Paper on the New Cabinet Decision-Making System,' 30 January 1989

23 Gordon F. Osbaldeston, *Keeping Deputy Ministers Accountable* (London, Ont.: National Centre for Management Research and Development 1988), 43

24 The extent of this delegation of authority varied from department to department, subject to specific agreements between Treasury Board and the department in question. See Peter Aucoin and Herman Bakvis, *The*

Centralization-Decentralization Conundrum: Organization and Management in the Canadian Government (Halifax: Institute for Research on Public Policy 1988), esp. 52-4, 123-6

25 '"Maz": PM's man creates his own cabinet network,' B7
26 According to Duguay, who wanted the facility for his own riding, 'I'm standing up for the interests of my community ... If standing up for your area is a crime, then I'm guilty.' 'Proposed federal lab sparks Winnipeg row,' *Globe and Mail*, 5 September 1988: A5
27 'Tories in Quebec rebuke languages commissioner,' ibid., 3 March 1988: A 1
28 'Bouchard hopes of shoo-in wilt under Liberal onslaught,' *ibid.*, 18 June 1988: A1, A2; see also 'Separatist past: Bouchard announces he will bring new Quebec image to Ottawa,' ibid., 1 April 1988; A1, A4.
29 Ibid., A2
30 'Lucien Bouchard s'engage à exiger que l'agence spatiale soit crée à Montréal,' *Le Devoir*, 8 juin 1988: 1, 10
31 'Opting out of Montreal's boom,' *Globe and Mail*, 13 May 1989: D2
32 'Bouchard clears Quebec hurdle to adoption of languages act,' ibid., 18 August 1988: A9
33 'PM appears to contradict Bouchard over sign law,' ibid., 21 December 1988: A1, A8
34 Quoted in 'Meech rejection called provocation,' ibid., 7 April 1990: A1
35 'Quebec MPs emerge as surprise powerhouse,' ibid., 24 May 1989: A8
36 Ibid., A8
37 'PEI lacks voice, Tory says,' ibid., 8 December 1988: A2
38 'Federal grant is approved for Sysco's mill modernization,' B6
39 Quoted in 'Steel ban news to Buchanan,' *Mail-Star* (Halifax), 6 February 1989: 3
40 'Few cuts follow Ottawa's 3-month quest for savings,' *Financial Post*, 1 May 1989: 8
41 'MacKay should keep a lower "reprofile",' *Mail-Star*, 18 May 1989: 7; 'Atlantic Regional Development after the Budget: Whither, or Should That Be Wither, ACOA?' *Atlantic Report* (Atlantic Provinces Council), 24 (June 1989): 3-7
42 'ACOA shuffle possible,' *Mail-Star*, 1 July 1989: 1, 2; 'Petty bureaucrats pull shabby coup,' *Sunday Star* (Toronto), 30 July 1989: B3
43 'Atlantic Regional Development after the Budget,' 5
44 'Atlantic Canada hit by demise of tourism pacts,' *Globe and Mail*, 21 June 1989: B5
45 See 'Government not getting message across,' *Mail-Star*, 19 May 1989: 7; 'Representing N.S. in Ottawa,' ibid., 1 April 1989: 1-WJ.
46 Ibid.
47 Interviewee No. 123 (official, Department of Industry, Science, and Technology), 8 June 1989
48 Ontario, 'Federal Initiatives in Regional Development: An Analysis'

(Toronto: Federal-Provincial Relations Branch, Ministry of
Intergovernmental Affairs 1988), 9

49 'Who's the real kingfish on Parliament Hill?' *Mail-Star*, 12 June 1989: 6
50 'Ottawa accused of sellout for giving bigger fish quotas to France,' *Globe
and Mail*, 5 April 1989: A5. As international trade minister, Crosbie
displayed little hesitation in carrying a big stick, at least verbally, in
defending east coast interests. Thus, in September 1988 Crosbie, in
addressing a 'welcome-to-Canada' dinner for representatives of the
European Community, discarded a speech that had been prepared by
departmental officials and instead launched a stinging attack on alleged
European overfishing practices. The European delegation stormed out in
protest. 'Europeans shun speech by Crosbie,' ibid., 15 September 1988: A5
51 Quoted in 'Cod quota cuts hit big fish firms,' ibid., 9 February 1989: B1
52 'Crosbie "annoyed" by region's attitude,' *Mail-Star* 24 June 1989: 4
53 'Cabinet shuffle upgrades 2 junior ministers,' *Globe and Mail*, 16
September 1988: A1, A9
54 'New minister represents shaky riding,' ibid., 16 September 1988: A9; 'Days
as bridesmaid over for dependable McDermid,' ibid., 16 September 1988:
A9
55 Quoted in 'Cabinet shuffle upgrades 2 junior ministers,' A1
56 'He's setting a bad example,' *Globe and Mail*, 18 January 1989: A7
57 'Democrats take solace as the party defies history and adds to majority:
Incumbents in the House enjoy remarkable success,' *New York Times*, 10
November 1988: B7
58 Canada, *Canada: The 33rd Parliament* (Ottawa: Geographical Services
Division, Surveys and Mapping Branch, Energy Mines and Resources
1986), and *Results of the 34th Federal Election, November 21, 1988* (Ottawa:
Geographical Services Division, Canada Centre for Mapping, Energy,
Mines and Resources 1988). Calculations of incumbency and party
continuity for Canada are based on only 264 seats. Redistribution and the
addition of thirteen seats, resulting in the amalgamation or
disappearance of some older ridings and the creation of new ones, made
it impossible to make note of incumbency or turnover in thirty-one of
the 295 ridings in 1988. For discussion of incumbency and the increasing
stress by politicians on the personal vote in several national legislatures,
see Bruce Cain, John Ferejohn, and Morris Fiorina, *The Personal Vote:
Constituency Service and Electoral Independence* (Cambridge, Mass.: Harvard
University Press 1987).
59 'The federal eclipse of Atlantic Canada,' *Atlantic Insight* 8, no. 3 (March
1986): 26
60 'McInnes: Citadel cutback wrong,' *Mail-Star* 20 October 1988: 39
61 Quoted in 'Quebec anxious to keep Mulroney road pledge alive,' *Globe
and Mail*, 4 July 1989: A5
62 Ibid.
63 Lawrence LeDuc has argued that the level of partisanship over the long

term has generally been lower than that in the United States and the United Kingdom ('Partisan Change and Dealignment in Canada, Great Britain, and the United States,' *Comparative Politics* 17 [1985]: 379–98). See also Herman Bakvis, 'The Canadian Paradox: Party System Stability in the Face of a Weakly Aligned Electorate' in S.B. Wolinetz, ed., *Parties and Party Systems in Liberal Democracies* (London: Routledge 1988), 245–68.

64 Donald E. Blake, '1896 and All That: Critical Elections in Canada,' *Canadian Journal of Political Science* 12 (1979): 259–79

65 'Parties take nothing for granted in fight for Quebec votes,' *Globe and Mail*, 6 September 1988: A4

66 Alan C. Cairns, for example, argues that block voting in Quebec does not really exist but is in fact an artifact of the electoral system ('The Electoral System and the Party System in Canada, 1921–1965,' *Canadian Journal of Political Science* 1 [March 1968]: 67, 73–4). It is worth noting, however, that the mean support among Quebec voters for the party forming the government over the time period examined by Cairns was higher than among voters in Ontario – 52 per cent of Quebec voters versus 44 per cent for those in Ontario. See H. Thorburn, ed., *Party Politics in Canada*, 4th ed. (Scarborough: Prentice-Hall 1980), appendix 308–9. The issue of block voting certainly warrants more detailed examination.

67 The prime minister also indicated that Senator Lowell Murray would be assisting MacKay in his new duties on behalf of Prince Edward Island. Murray, however, who considered himself as no longer having any Atlantic responsibilities after his stint as ACOA minister, responded 'No ... no ... no ... definitely not,' when tackled on the issue. 'I certainly have no responsibilities as regard to PEI whatsoever.' Quoted in 'Who's going to look out for Prince Edward Island?' *Mail-Star*, 6 February 1989: 6

68 Office of the Deputy Prime Minister, 'Release: Funding for Coal Research Projects: Agreement in Principle Reached' (Ottawa, 31 May 1988)

69 For example, at one point it appeared that MacKay was backtracking on assurances that CN would purchase all its rails from Sysco ('Crosbie, MacKay dash hopes for CN rail orders,' *Mail-Star*, 26 November 1986: 10). Buchanan in turn stated: 'I read the account in the paper ... It certainly doesn't match comments made to me by Elmer MacKay, and I'll have to discuss it with Elmer.' Quoted in 'Premier wants explanation: Words don't match "promise",' *Mail-Star*, 27 November 1986: 3. As a compromise it was later agreed that 80 per cent of CN's orders would go to Sysco.

70 'N.B. big winner on frigate contracts,' *Globe and Mail*, 19 December 1987: A3

Chapter Twelve

1 Alan C. Cairns, *From Interstate to Intrastate Federalism in Canada* (Kingston: Institute of Intergovernmental Relations 1979), 6

2 David E. Smith, 'Cabinet and Commons in the Era of James G. Gardiner' in John C. Courtney, ed., *The Canadian House of Commons: Essays in Honour of Norman Ward* (Calgary: University of Calgary Press 1985) 77 (italics added)

3 Quoted in 'Plymouth mine shut down: MacKay blames bureaucrats,' *Mail-Star* (Halifax), 2 August 1989: 3. While coal in the Pictou region is of the low-sulphur variety, mining it has proved difficult. Previous mines – the last was shut in 1951, entombing the remains of twelve men – were prone to high levels of methane gas. The coal itself is very abrasive with a high quartz content, increasing the danger of explosions from sparking. Undoubtedly difficulties related to safety led to the demand by Westray Coal Inc. that the federal government cover more than half the start-up costs of the mine. Neither Westray, nor its chief executive officer (Clifford Frame, former president of Denison Mines, which opened up the troubled Quintette Coal Mine in northeastern British Columbia), had ever constructed or run an underground coal-mine. See the articles by Stewart Lewis, 'Proposed Westray coal mine deal under fire,' *Mail-Star*, 17 August 1989: 10; 'Caution urged in working Westray,' ibid., 18 August 1989: 8.

4 See Raymond Breton, Jeffrey G. Reitz, and Victor Valentine, *Cultural Boundaries and the Cohesion of Canada* (Montreal: Institute for Research on Public Policy 1980), 180.

5 Cairns, *From Interstate to Intrastate Federalism in Canada*, 6–7

6 Paul G. Thomas, 'The Role of National Pary Caucuses' in P. Aucoin, ed., *Party Government and Regional Representation in Canada*: Vol. 36, Research Studies of the Royal Commission on the Economic Union and Development Prospects for Canada (Toronto: University of Toronto Press 1985), 69–136

7 'Operations unlimited,' *Globe and Mail*, 19 May 1988: A6

8 Peter Aucoin, 'Organizational Change in the Machinery of Canadian Government: From Rational Management to Brokerage Politics,' *Canadian Journal of Political Science* 19 (1986): 185–201

9 Keith G. Banting, *The Welfare State and Canadian Federalism*, 2nd ed., (Kingston and Montreal: McGill-Queen's University Press 1987), 83

10 Michael H. Wilson, *The Fiscal Plan: Controlling the Public Debt* (Ottawa: Department of Finance 27 April 1989), Table 4.4, 42

11 Ibid., Table 3.4, 26

12 Ibid., Table 4.4, 42

13 Banting, *The Welfare State and Canadian Federalism*, 2

14 Ibid., 88

15 'Crosbie says group wanted too much money for rail cars,' *Globe and Mail*, 20 May 1988: B6

16 Canada, *Report: Royal Commission on the Economic Union and Development Prospects for Canada*, vol. 3 (Ottawa: Supply and Services 1985), 93

17 Parliament of Canada, *Report on the Organization of the Public Service of Canada*, Sessional Paper No. 57a (Ottawa: C.H. Parmelee 1912), 7
18 Axworthy interview, Ottawa, 5 May 1986
19 Pépin interview, Ottawa, 28 November 1985
20 Donald J. Savoie, *The Politics of Public Spending* (Toronto: University of Toronto Press 1990), 196–7
21 Ibid., 193–4
22 Ibid., 195
23 A. Paul Pross, 'Space, Function, and Interest: The Problem of Legitimacy in the Canadian State' in O.P. Dwivedi, ed., *The Administrative State in Canada* (Toronto: University of Toronto Press 1982), 107–29
24 See column by Dalton Camp, 'Petty bureaucrats pull shabby coup,' *Sunday Star* (Toronto) 30 July 1989: B3
25 Interviewee No. 124 (official, Department of Transport), Ottawa, 8 June 1989
26 Cairns, *From Interstate to Intrastate Federalism in Canada*, 11–12
27 Ibid., 11
28 LeBlanc interview, Ottawa, 25 March 1986
29 Peter McCormick, Ernest C. Manning, and Gordon Gibson, 'Regional Representation in Canada' in J. Paul Johnston and Harvey E. Pasis, eds., *Representation and Electoral Systems: Canadian Perspectives* (Scarborough: Prentice-Hall 1990), 101
30 Quoted in Savoie, *The Politics of Public Spending*, 291. The minister is not named.
31 Walter C. Soderlund et al., 'Regional and Linguistic Agenda-Setting in Canada: A Study of Newspaper Coverage of Issues Affecting Political Integration in 1976,' *Canadian Journal of Political Science* 13 (June 1980): 347–56; Carol Charlebois, 'The Structure of Federal-Provincial News,' paper presented to the Canadian Political Science Association annual meeting, Fredericton, June 1977
32 See William D. Coleman, 'Federalism and Interest Group Organization' in H. Bakvis and W.M. Chandler, eds., *Federalism and the Role of the State* (Toronto: University of Toronto Press 1987), 171–87.
33 LeBlanc interview, Ottawa, 25 March 1986
34 John C. Courtney, 'Federalism and Representation: Voter Equality and Electoral Reapportionment in Canada and the United States,' paper presented to the Conference on Comparative Federalism: Changing Theory and Practice in the Adaptive Canadian and American Federal Systems, Dartmouth College, Hanover, New Hampshire, 22–25 June 1989
35 'What money can't buy.' *Globe and Mail*, 3 December 1988: A6; Roger Gibbins, 'Canadian Federalism: The Entanglement of Meech Lake and the Free Trade Agreement,' *Publius* 19 (Summer 1989): 185–98. Gallup Canada has some interesting data germane to this topic, showing that a number of Conservative ministers are either not as well known in their

provinces as or less liked than provincial premiers. Gallup Canada, 'Provincial Premiers Largely Unknown to Canadian Public,' Toronto, 11 January 1990; ibid., 'Tory Ministers Fail to Excite Canadian Public,' 8 February 1990

36 For example, 'Telegram to PQ "speaks for itself," Bouchard says,' *Globe and Mail*, 21 May 1990: A1; 'Federal politicians express astonishment over Bouchard telegram,' ibid., A3

37 'Federal ministers failed to sell pact, Quebec says,' ibid., 25 January 1990: A5; 'Bouchard shouldn't be spokesman for Quebec, Peterson says,' ibid., 10 April 1990: A12

38 'The first ministers' agreement' (final communiqué from the first ministers' meeting on the Meech Lake constitutional accord), *Globe and Mail*, 11 June 1990: A7

39 The Australian senate provides a good example in the change made in the adoption in 1949 of proportional representation–single transferable vote. At first the change appeared to have relatively benign effects, but after 1960 the partisan composition in the Senate began to change relative to that in the lower house, setting the stage for the constitutional crisis of 1975 involving the contradiction between an independent Senate and parliamentary government. See Campbell Sharman, 'Second Chambers' in Bakvis and Chandler, eds., *Federalism and the Role of the State*, esp. 94–6

40 Canada, *Report: Royal Commission on the Economic Union and Development Prospects for Canada*, Vol. 3: 86–92; Alberta, *Report of the Alberta Select Special Committee on Senate Reform* (Edmonton: Plains Publishing 1985)

41 Peter Aucoin, 'Regionalism, Party and National Government' in P. Aucoin ed., *Party Government and Regional Representation in Canada*: Vol. 36, Research Studies of the Royal Commission on the Economic Union and Development Prospects for Canada (Toronto: University of Toronto Press 1985), 153

A Note on Sources

This study relies on a variety of sources: secondary material in the form of published books, journal articles, and unpublished theses; government documents, both published and in mimeographed form; newspaper records; and interviews with federal and provincial civil servants, exempt staff (politically appointed staff), and politicians, primarily former ministers. A total of 128 interviews were conducted between March 1983 and March 1990 in various locations in Canada, but mainly in Ottawa and provincial capitals. Most took place on a one-on-one basis. Some, however, were conducted in a group setting, involving two or more, and in one instance twelve individuals. Seven interviews were conducted by telephone. Although the majority of interviews were conducted by the author alone specifically on the topic of regional ministers, a number of interviews were also conducted with my colleague Peter Aucoin in connection with related research projects on regional development, government organization, and decentralization.

The interviews ranged in length from twenty minutes to seven hours, and twenty-three interviewees were re-interviewed, sometimes three or four times. The date and position held by the interviewee are indicated in the relevant note, and for each individual a number has been assigned, which is used in subsequent citations. Except for publicly known political figures, all interviewees were promised anonymity. For non-public figures, such as civil servants and exempt staff, only their position, government department, and/or level of government are identified. The use of a tape recorder during the interviews was rejected because it was felt that it might make subjects more guarded in their responses or lead to outright refusal on the part of some individuals.

The specific interview schedule and format used varied from individual to individual, depending upon the subject matter. All, however, were asked about their background, in the case of federal civil servants whether they had any experience in administration outside of Ottawa, and about their values concerning the regional dimension in administration and cabinet decision-making. Again, depending upon the topic, they were asked to recount events, to give specific examples, and to provide analyses of developments or possible consequences. Notes were taken by hand during the interview. Immediately afterwards additional time was taken to record as many impressions and details of the interview as possible, in some instances using a portable dictaphone machine. On occasion if there were gaps or points that were ambiguous, the interviewee would be asked for clarification later by phone or in a further interview. In a few instances clarification was sought, and received, through correspondence.

The procedures used meet the ethical guidelines for research involving human subjects. As required for all research projects supported by the Social Sciences and Humanities Research Council of Canada, the procedures were approved by the ethics review committee at Dalhousie University.

Index